Ideology and Politics in Modern India

By the Same Author

Essays on Indian Nationalism
Essays on Contemporary India
Indian National Movement: The Long-Term Dynamics
Communalism in Modern India
The Rise and Growth of Economic Nationalism

Ideology and Politics in Modern India

Bipan Chandra

HAR-ANAND
PUBLICATIONS PVT LTD

Reprint, 2026

Published by Ashok Gosain and Ashish Gosain for:
HAR-ANAND PUBLICATIONS PVT LTD
E-49/3, Okhla Industrial Area, Phase-II, New Delhi-110020
Tel: 41603491
E-mail: info@haranandbooks.com/haranand@rediffmail.com
Shop online at: www.haranandbooks.com

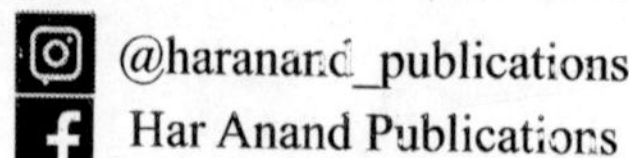

Printed in India at Megha Enterprises

To
Padma and Sushil Kumar Sud

Preface

I have tried in these essays to deal with some aspects of the development of ideology and politics and their inter-relationship in colonial as well as post-colonial India. In particular, the emphasis has been on three major political forces of the period: Jawaharlal Nehru, the left, and communalism.

I

The first essay tries to understand Jawaharlal Nehru as a public person the way he would have liked to be understood—in a broad historical perspective and a sympathetic manner. The effort is to enable the post-independence generation—the Midnight's Children—to understand why so many Indians of the earlier generation, even those who were highly critical of Nehru in his lifetime, look upon the Nehru era with nostalgia. As Nehru himself put it: "we live in an exciting age. I have always considered it a great privilege for the people of this generation to live during this period of India's long history.... I have believed that there is nothing more exciting in the wide world today than to work in India." Nehru was one of the reasons why this was so. He did make a great deal of difference to the lives of the Indian people. The question is what was so exceptional about Nehru. The essay also tries to answer this question.

On my part, this is an exploratory essay which raises a large number of questions which can be fully and adequately answered only on the basis of far more detailed and exhaustive work. The questions that I have tried to answer are, to quote from the essay itself: "What is Nehru's place in India's history? What are the abiding elements of Nehru's contribution to the making of modern India? And what is Nehru's legacy for the India of today and tomorrow? What did he and under his leadership the Indian people achieve, 'what is the evolution he helped India achieve'? What abiding values did he try to inculcate among the people to which we will refer again and again as a guide and as a measure of our actions and achievements? And was Nehru 'equal to his opportunities'?"

In particular, several aspects of Nehru's life and contribution stand out. The first major aspect is his role in the national movement, especially as the one leader who gave it a socialist orientation and helped root the socialist ideas in India. Equally significant was his effort to integrate the struggle for independence with the struggle for socio-economic emancipation. He also clearly grasped that the primary contradiction in India being that between imperialism and the entire Indian people, the national struggle had to be accorded primacy over the social struggle. The two could be integrated through the simultaneous conduct of class struggle and class adjustment so that while status quo was opposed, the Indian people were not divided in their struggle against imperialism.

Nehru also grappled with the question of the form that the struggle for socialism would take during the period of the anti-imperialist struggle. It would take, he said, largely the form of ideological struggle within the national movement so as to transform the entire movement ideologically in a socialist direction.

Nehru also gradually, after 1936, abandoned his own strategic paradigm of a continuous extra-legal mass struggle against imperialism, no negotiations with the colonial authorities, no participation in the colonial constitutional framework and no negotiations for the transfer of power, in favour of the Gandhian strategic framework, which I have discussed at length in another place and described as Struggle-Truce-Struggle (S- T-S).* Many, including I earlier, have criticized this aspect of Nehru's politics and his consequent refusal to split the Congress as a surrender before Gandhiji, Gandhism, and the right wing. In this essay I have tried to understand the reasons for this change in Nehru's politics after 1936 and have come to the conclusion that this was as a whole a highly positive political development.

Over the years, Nehru accepted several aspects of Gandhiji's leadership and broad strategy which other constituents of the left, including the Socialists, the Communists, the Royists and Subhas Bose, continued to oppose. For one, he fully accepted non-violence as a basic policy for the national movement for being "an active, dynamic and

---

**Indian National Movement - The Long Term Dynamics,* New Delhi, 1988.

forceful method of enforcing the mass will". Second, once he accepted the priority of the national movement and its mass character, he also accepted the necessity of its unity around a common goal as also the inevitability of diversity in its ideological and political perspectives.

Nehru had also acquired over time a better understanding and appreciation of the Congress right wing. The latter's right-wingness, he came to understand, lay not in a softer attitude towards imperialism or lack of firmness and militancy in the freedom struggle but in economic conservatism. Furthermore, he no longer saw nationalism as an inherently bourgeois ideology. The Congress was at the time, he believed, under the hegemony of bourgeois ideology, but it was not a structured bourgeois party—as a movement it was capable of being transformed ideologically in a socialist direction.

Above all, Nehru had evolved a positive understanding of Gandhiji. Even while himself committed to Marxism and critical of Gandhiji for not recognizing class division and class struggle in society, he had begun to see Gandhiji as a revolutionary who was playing a radical role in Indian politics and society.

The essay also brings out Nehru's contribution to the process of the making of the Indian nation and the consolidation of India's political independence. Nehru laid the foundations of an independent and self-reliant economy and self-sustaining growth. Being fully committed to democracy and civil liberty, he helped root in the country parliamentary democracy along with its institutional structure. He tried to build the political system on a model in which social change and a democratic and civil libertarian structure would mutually reinforce each other. He also pioneered the historically unprecedented effort to develop economically on the basis of political democracy.

Even though Nehru did not actually build a socialist society, his paradigm of social change contained many innovations of historical significance so much so that I have argued that "the elements of the Gandhi-Nehru strategy are likely to form, in a modified form, some of the necessary building blocks of any alternative (i.e., alternative to the Leninist) strategy of the struggle for socialism." According to Nehru, social change through democratic means would be a prolonged process; social change would be brought about through a series of reforms which would cumulatively amount to a revolution, that is, a qualitative change in the social structure. Social change would also then not be a clear-cut, pre-planned or pre-laid out scheme; it would have to be a vision which would get defined stage by stage as one moved towards its realization.

Nehru also argued that democracy and civil liberty were basic to socialism. The two were inseparably intertwined. The core of the Nehruvian strategy of social transformation was the belief that to be lasting the different steps leading to it could be undertaken only when they had the active or passive backing of the overwhelming majority of the people. Otherwise, the road would be opened to counter-revolution and authoritarianism. Radicalism also, then, lay in the constant effort to change the existing balance of socio-political forces in favour of social change.

In the end, the essay directs attention towards some of Nehru's weaknesses as a political leader, as an agent of social change and as a socialist and nation-builder.

The second essay deals with Nehru and communalism. Here, Nehru's achievement was great indeed. He played a major role in keeping the national movement firmly on the secular course. Under extremely difficult conditions, he helped lay the foundations of a secular state and society in independent India.

During the 1930s, his was a pioneering effort to understand the broader social, economic and political dimensions, character and causation of communalism. Grasping it as a phenomenon that was modern and not a remnant of the past, he tried to analyze the socio-economic and political roots of communalism in modern India. He was also perhaps the first to see communalism of the extremist phase as the Indian form of fascism. In fact, there is a contemporary ring about his analysis of and pronouncements on communalism. The essay also brings out some of the major weaknesses in Nehru's approach to the communal problem. He failed to devise institutions or organizational and administrative means to deal with it. Above all, he became complacent towards communalism in the later 1950s and failed to carry on a sustained mass ideological campaign against it.

II

In the third essay, "Struggle for the Ideological Transformation of the National Congress in the 1930s", I have discussed the failure of the left to ideologically transform the national movement in a socialist direction. In the beginning, I discuss some of the basic ideological elements of the national movement since its inception in the last quarter of the 19th century. An intense ideological struggle between the left wing and the right wing of the movement occurred from the late I 920s. While the movement was increasingly radicalized in the 1930s and the left and the organizations under its influence grew in influence, the left failed to establish its ideological hegemony over the movement. The essay tries to analyze some of the reasons for this failure.

In the main, I have argued that the left fought the right on a wrong terrain. It took up wrong issues, such as office acceptance, collective affiliation, non-violence, and the nature and degree of political militancy, on which to oppose the right. It failed to grasp the Gandhian strategy of political struggle or the necessity for class adjustment between the opposing social classes in colonial India. Above all, it defined the right-wingness of the Congress right wing wrongly or in wrong, non-ideological terms. It accused the right of wanting to compromise with imperialism, thus completely misrepresenting the latter's consistent anti-imperialism. It was at the level of social and economic ideology that the differentiation was to be made. At the same time, the left tended to put Gandhiji and the Gandhians in the rightist camp, rather than seeing them as its allies. It is also to be noted that, after 1936, Nehru was increasingly able to avoid most of these weaknesses and develop a correct understanding of and approach towards the right. He also grasped the role of ideological struggle within the movement as a basic task during the period of the anti-imperialist struggle.

III

In the articles numbered 4 to 7 are discussed various aspects of the communal problem basically in their ideological dimension. First of all, in these essays, an effort has been made to define communalism and it has been argued that communalism is a complex but single ideology with many faces.

I have also suggested that communalism is primarily an ideology with communal violence being one of its conjuctural forms or external symptoms. Moreover, far from being a form of nationalism, that is, nationalism based on religion, it arose and developed in modern India as an alternative to, and in opposition to, nationalism. When understood as an ideology communalism also helps define a communal party. A communal party is a party that is structured around communal ideology; without communal ideology it will cease to exist as a party. A distinction is therefore to be made between a communal party and a weakly secular party which adopts an opportunist approach towards communalism. It is then argued that no compromise should be made with communal forces at least at the ideological plane.

In these essays I also discuss the relationship that communalism bears to communal violence as also to state power.

A major emphasis in these essays is on how the communal challenge is to be faced or on what is the way out of communalism. It is suggested that while communal violence should be dealt with immediately and sternly through the instruments of the state and efforts should be made to set right the social situation which engenders and feeds communalism the main answer lies in carrying on a mass ideological struggle against communalism, for ideas can be opposed only at the level of ideas and not through. the machinery of the state. It is also argued that all communalisms—Hindu, Muslim, Sikh and Christian—have to be opposed simultaneously.

The essay on "Historians of Modern India and Communalism" iscusses the role of the writing and teaching of history in the growth of communalism. In particular, the role of 'vicarious nationalism' and wrong type of 'hero-myths' in promoting a communal view of history and therefore of communalism has been brought out.

IV

The 8th article, "Marxism in India: Need for Total Rectification", is an effort at a critical evaluation of the Indian Marxists. While they had some major achievements to their credit, the Indian Marxists were at no stage able to achieve more than a small part of what was historically possible. My attempt is to highlight their weaknesses and failures in several areas: fearless and objective analysis of the concrete Indian reality, both economic and political; application and development of Marxism in Indian conditions; evolution of viable political practice and strategy and tactics under conditions of political democracy; work among the mass of working masses constituted by agricultural labourers and poor peasants; correction of mistakes in time; and encouragement or rather non-suppression of free discussion and debate. Consequently, the need for total rectification of Marxist theory and practice and. for the creative development of Marxism is stressed. I may also point out that the emphasis is not on personal failure of individuals but on the manner in which Marxism has been applied in India since the early 1920s.

One example of the Indian Marxists' failure to study Indian society and economy is provided in the 9th article on the controversy in the CPI on the changes in the agrarian structure in India after independence. Except for a handful, most of the communist leaders ignored the basic changes in the Indian agrarian structure brought about after 1947 and, instead, went on asserting that it continued to be basically feudal in character and that feudal landlords continued to be an integral and basic constituent of the ruling classes. Consequently, they continued to characterise the Nehru Government as in the Programme of 1951 as "this government of landlords and princes and reactionary big bourgeoisie, collaborating with the British imperialists".

The 10th essay is an address to the Punjab History Congress. It warns against a stereotyped understanding of colonial Punjab's highly differentiated agrarian structure, and discusses some of the problems faced by a student of the peasant movement in Punjab.

V

In Part II, certain themes, parties and persons are introduced through reviews, prefaces and introductions.

In the introduction to Bhagat Singh's pamphlets. *Why I am an Atheist,* and his introduction to *The Dreamland* an effort has been made to bring out the relatively unknown facet of Bhagat Singh as a thinker and ideologue.

The preface to Girja Shankar's pioneering work on the Congress Socialist Party highlights the ideological and political framework of the party. One of the questions sought to be dealt with is as to why did the CSP fail to become a major political force even though it did not suffer from some of the weaknesses of the other contemporary left parties in India.

The third essay in Part II introduces Shantha Sinha's seminal work on the Naxalites (Maoists) in Andhra Pradesh. It becomes clear that the different Naxalite groups were perhaps even more shallow in their understanding of Indian economy and polity than the other Marxist parties and groups. They differed from the latter primarily in their emphasis on immediate armed struggle for bringing about social change. Otherwise, they too ignored the contemporary changes in the agrarian structure as also the growing differentiation in the countryside. They too proved to be incapable of developing Marxism in the context of the concrete Indian and world conditions.

The next preface brings to the attention of the readers the contribution to the freedom struggle of the legendary Oriya tribal leader and martyr Lakshman Naik.

The next essay in Part II is an introduction to Ravi Narayan Reddy's autobiography. Reddy was one of the founders of the Communist Party in Hyderabad and, along with B. Yell a Reddy and D.V. Rao, of the legendary Telengana struggle against the Nizam's autocracy. The effort has been to bring out his innovative character as a Communist leader both in harness and in retirement.

The last three essays in Part II are reviews of books that deal with a few significant historical and contemporary problems.

Since the essays were written over a number of years, they do not necessarily reflect my current understanding of some of the issues and persons involved. But I have let them stand as they were originally published, for the reader may develop his own critical understanding of the issues as also of my approach towards them. For example, I no longer see the entire Indian national leadership as "bourgeois" as I have described it in one of the essays. But who knows? May be I was more right earlier.

VI

As before I am indebted to my colleagues in the Centre for Historical Studies, Jawaharlal Nehru University, and my numerous students for helping me evolve and develop the themes in these essays. Critical interaction with Mohit Sen, Kewal Verma, Mridula Mukherjee, Aditya Mukherjee, V.P. Dutt, D.N. Gupta, Girish Mathur, Bikash Chandra and my wife, Usha, has been crucial to the writing of many of these essays. I am thankful to Anis Syed and A.R. Bedar for providing me the opportunity to develop and express my ideas on Jawaharlal Nehru.

As usual, Usha has shared the burden of editing these essays at all the stages from the hand-written to this final publication in the present volume. I am also very thankful to Ashok Gosain for being very helpful as the publisher of this volume.

Contents

PART I

1

Jawaharlal Nehru in Historical Perspective*

Jawaharlal Nehru was indeed a great but extraordinarily complex personality, and any evaluation of his role in modern history is bound to be equally complex and somewhat controversial. And here, in his appraisal, the approach to history exemplified in Prof. D.D. Kosambi's works serves as a guideline.

Prof. Kosambi has been a great mentor of my generation of historians. A great Marxist, he taught us not only to correlate developments in the realm of the state, institutions and ideas to the material base of the relations and forces of production, and how to look at all human development from the point of view of the people—the masses—but also how to examine critically all the received wisdom even if it came from Karl Marx himself. He saw Marxism above all as a scientific theory and method which, to quote him, "might have to be extended like those, in other fields, of his contemporaries, Gauss, Maxwell, Darwin and Mendeleev."[1] Consequently, the adoption of Marx's theories did not mean, to quote him again, a "blind repetition of all his conclusions (and even less, those of the official, party-line Marxists) at all times."[2] In his own work, Kosambi showed how "What Marx himself has said about India cannot be taken as it stands."[3] Marxism is not what Marx said but how he arrived at his analysis, that is Marxism is really Marx's method and approach. The greatest tribute to Kosambi would be to apply to his writing what he has said about Marx's writing.

---

*D. D. Kosambi Memorial Lecture, delivered at Department of History, Bombay University.

[1]D. D. Kosambi, *An Introduction to the Study of Indian History,* Bombay, 1956, p. 12.

[3]*Ibid.,* p. 10.

[4]*Ibid.*

For example, writing on Nehru, Kosambi tended to see a close, in fact, direct connection between Nehru's politics and actions and achievements and the thought and interests of the Indian bourgeoisie. He saw the transfer of power in 1947 not as the result of the national liberation struggle of the Indian people but as a recognition by the British "of the position of the new bourgeoisie in India.?"[4] The 1942 movement was seen by him, on the one hand, as proof of the fact that "the characteristic thought then current among the Indian bourgeoisie had in fact permeated the Congress leadership"[5], and, on the other hand, as a product of the mass pressure in the direction of revolution exerted by the Indian people. Writing in 1946, he had declared: the Indian bourgeoisie "needs Nehru's leadership, just as India has needed the class itself," though he had also said that "the parting of the ways is clearly visible; what is not clear is the path Nehru himself will choose in that moment of agony".[6] By 1954, Kosambi had no doubts left: through Nehru it was the Indian bourgeoisie which was ruling India. Even Nehru's foreign policy of non-alignment was analyzed by Kosambi as follows: "And there is always the hope that a third world war will lead to even more fantastic profits for a neutral India—as the ruling class dreams of neutrality."[7]

In my view, Kosambi, for various reasons including the fact that he had not made a serious study of Nehru, was quite wrong. In this case he was applying what he had condemned in Dange and others vis-a-vis their approach to ancient Indian society. He was applying an economic deterministic and class reductionist approach. Mine is, today and tomorrow, an effort to apply the Marxist method to the understanding of Jawaharlal Nehru. Prof. Kosambi would probably not have approved of the result. Consequently, in saying that I come before you today with no little trepidation, I am not uttering a mere conventional profession of diffidence. A major problem, which heightens the sense of diffidence, is bow to do justice to a subject so vast and of such importance and magnificence.

For my generation—for those who have lived through one or the other part of the Nehru era—critical evaluation of Nehru is a part of coming to terms with our own past, our very youth. We also owe it to the younger people to explain why so many of us—whatever our political

[4]D. D. Kosambi, *Exasperating Essays*. Bombay, 1957, p. 15.
[5]*Ibid.*, pp 16-7.
[6]*Ibid.*, p. 18.
[7]*Ibid.*, p. 30.

position then—and mine was that of an angry young critic—now look back on the Nehru era with nostalgia? That age was even more filled with misery and poverty than now. Then why did the existence of a Jawaharlal Nehru make so much of a difference?

During most of the Nehru era, despite a multitude of problems and difficulties, which often appeared to overwhelm, there was no feeling of frustration. There was 'the mood of hope' and expectation in the country, a certain faith in its future, a confidence in its future destiny. There was a feeling that new forces were emerging which will change the face of the country. As Nehru himself put it in a message to the Chief Ministers in June 1955: "There is the breath of the dawn, the feeling of the beginning of a new era in the long and chequered history of India", And he rightly added: "I feel so and in this matter at least I think I represent innumerable others in our country".[8] Though dissatisfied with and largely critical of Nehru and his policies, most on the left too shared this feeling, though with an angle different from Nehru's but very much because of what Nehru was doing. Those who have lived through that era often now feel that they were lucky to have lived through those years. Nehru once again expressed this feeling in the middle of his term as the Prime Minister: "There is no lack of drama in this changing world of ours and, even in India, we live in an exciting age. I have always considered it a great privilege for people of this generation to live during this period of India's long history.... I have believed that there is nothing more exciting in the wide world today than to work in India".[9]

Some of this euphoria disappeared as a result of the Indo-China War of 1962. The war brought in greater realism but even so there was no defeatist attitude in Nehru or in the country. Nehru had always believed that "India's greatest need is for a sense of certainty concerning her own success."[10] And this sense of excitement and of the coming success he succeeded in imparting to the millions. Nehru did make a great deal of difference.

The questions that I will try to answer today are-what is Nehru's place in India's history? What are the abiding elements of Nehru's contribution to the making of modern India? And what is Nehru's legacy for the India

---

[8]Jawaharlal Nehru, *Letters to Chief Ministers,* 1947-1964, 5 volumes, New Delhi, 1985—(hereafter referred to as *LCM),* Vol. IV, p. 188. Also pp. 124-5, 133.

[9]*Ibid.,* p. 366.

[10]*Ibid.,* p. 383.

of today and tomorrow? What did he and under his leadership the Indian people achieve, "what is the evolution he helped India achieve?" What abiding values did he try to inculcate among the people to which we will refer again and again as a guide and as a measure of our actions and achievements? And was Nehru "equal to his opportunities"? It is the answers to these questions which will determine his place in history and not what he failed to achieve and what remained to be done.

I must say in the very beginning that I am not going to discuss him asa person, though there was a great deal to admire in him as a person. It is no accident that all those who came into contact with him fell under his spell. The range of his interests and concerns was wide indeed: from basic education to heavy industry, from the gathering of statistics to world peace, from women's position to tribal welfare, and from art to cricket. He was a veritable Renaissance man. He represented a wide and generous outlook on every facet of life and tried to inculcate it among the people as also his co-workers. As he wrote to the Chief Ministers in 1954: "If India is to be really great, as we all want her to be, then she is not to be exclusive either internally or externally. She has to give up everything that is a barrier to growth in mind or spirit or in social life."[11]

Mine is, today and tomorrow, an effort to understand Nehru sympathetically, as a public person, as a maker of modern India, for his life was "essentially the story of the historical process" that India was undergoing.[12] As he himself put it: "We are all something more (than the persons we are). We are all the children of the Indian Revolution. We (still) have something of the fire of revolution in US".[13] I have not had access to his private papers after 1946 or to the official government papers after 1947. Yet this is not such a handicap, for there was hardly any gap between his private conversation and correspondence and his public speeches, statements and articles and books.

In a rich, varied canvass of Nehru's life, several aspects and features stand out.

I

Nehru's place in history would be assured by the leadership role he played in the anti-imperialist struggle. As a national liberator he was second only

[11]*Ibid.,* Vol. III, pp. 380-1.
[12]M. Chalapathi Rau, *Jawaharlal Nehru,* New Delhi,1979 reprint, p. xxii.
[13]Quoted in *ibid.,* p. 173.

to Gandhiji. But, above all, it was Nehru who imparted a socialist vision to the Indian national movement. He turned the face of the movement towards socialism, helped. it acquire a clearer and sharper socio-economic content and gave the Indian National Congress a socialist orientation. He helped bring together or rather relate the struggle for national liberation-with the struggle for economic or class emancipation. There is no doubt that he played a leading role in the rooting of socialist ideas in the Indian soil and in making socialism the accepted creed of the Indian youth during the 1930s and 1940s.Nehru was neither the first Indian to talk of socialism nor the first to commit himself to socialism, nor the first to take up the economic demands of the masses. He was not the first to put 'economic content' into the national movement or make it conscious of economic policy. The Moderate leaders form Dadabhai Naoroji to Gokhale had already taken up the economic demands of the Indian people vis-a-vis colonialism and the colonial state. In fact, they had initiated the movement on the basis of anti-colonial 'economic content' and economic policy. He was also not the first to put 'social content' in the movement or to imbue it with a social conscience. This was not his major contribution.

The movement had been given a pro-poor orientation by Dadabhai Naoroji, Justice Ranade, G.K.Gokhale, B.G. Tilak and above all by Gandhiji. This was, by the way, fully recognized by the mature Jawaharlal. In 1960 he told R.K. Karanjia: Gandhiji "had a deep social conscience, not in the socialist or class-struggle sense, but as reflected in the almost continuous struggle he waged against inequality and for the under-dog, the Harijans and the peasantry, for example.... This is one reason why our freedom struggle was never without its social content—in fact, the latter was its base and this is why the strategy produced such tremendous results. Gandhiji believed in the complete identification of the leadership with the masses."[14] Or even earlier still, in a speech on 31 October 1949: "Mahatma Gandhi taught us to view our national struggle always in terms of the under-privileged and those to whom opportunity had been denied. Therefore, there was always an economic facet to our political struggle for freedom."[15] Similarly, in 1956, he replied to Tibor Mende's question whether Gandhism contained from early 1920s both

---

[14]R. K. Karanjia, *The Mind of Mr. Nehru, an Interview,* London, 1960, pp.21-2.

[15]*Jawaharlal Nehru's Speeches,S* volumes, New Delhi, 1983—(hereafter referred to as *Speeches),* Vol. Two, p. 418.

social strategy and liberation strategy that "Yes, throughout.... Right from the beginning that social aspect was there; removing or fighting against certain vested interests ... ".[16]

But Jawaharlal was the first major Indian leader to raise the pro-poor orientation of the earlier national leadership to a demand for the social emancipation of the peasants and workers "without which there can be no real freedom", to the level of a critique of landlordism and the capitalist system, and to the rejection of capitalist development as also bourgeois civilizational perspective and to try to impart this socialist vision to the entire national movement. As both the British and Gandhiji clearly realised, Nehru stood at the meeting point of nationalism and socialism.

Nehru was the first to proclaim his commitment to socialism from the Congress platform as its President. At the Lahore session of the National Congress in 1929, he proclaimed: "I am a socialist and a republican, and am no believer in kings and princes, or in the order which produces the modem kings of industry, who have greater power over the lives and fortunes of men than even the kings of old, and whose methods are as predatory as those of the old feudal aristocracy", India, he said, would have to adopt socialism if she was "to end her poverty and inequality".[17]

Nehru's commitment to socialism found a clearer and sharper expression during 1933-36. Answering the question 'Whither India' in October 1933, he wrote: "Surely to the great human goal of social and economic equality, to the ending of all exploitation of nation by nation and class by class, to national freedom within the framework of an international co-operative socialist world federation."[18] And in December 1933, he wrote: "The true civic ideal is the socialist ideal, the communist ideal."[19] In 1936, in his Presidential Address to the Lucknow Congress, he put his commitment to socialism in clear, unequivocal, passionate words: "I am convinced that the only key to the solution of the world's problems and of India's problems lies in socialism, and when I use this word I do so not in a vague humanitarian way but in the scientific, economic sense.... I

[16]Tibor Mende, *Conversations with Mr. Nehru,* London, 1956, p. 20.

[17]*Selected Works of Jawaharlal Nehru,* edited by S. Gopal, New Delhi,- I 972—(hereafter referred to as SW), Vol. 4, pp. 192-3.

[18]*Ibid.,* Vol. 6, p. 16.

[19]*Ibid.,* p. 124.

see no way of ending the poverty, the vast unemployment, the degradation, and the subjection of the Indian people except through socialism. That . involves vast and revolutionary changes in our political and social structure.... That means the ending of private property, except in a restricted sense, and the replacement of the present profit system by a higher ideal of co-operative service."[20]

Nehru also accepted the general validity of Marxism as "the scientific interpretation of history and politics and economics" and as representing "scientific socialism" in contrast to "a vague and idealistic socialism".[21] On May 15,1936, he told the Indian Progressive Group of Bombay that "scientific socialism, or Marxism, was the only remedy for the ills of the world."[22] On May 17, he told a meeting of Congress Socialists that history as well as the contemporary state of affairs "could not be explained except by socialism and Marxism."[23] Later in early 1939, writing in the *National Herald,* he said: "Liberty and democracy have no meaning without equality; and equality cannot be established so long as the principal instruments of production are privately owned. Private ownership of these means of production thus comes in the way of real democracy."[24] At the same time, he argued that there would be far greater freedom for the individual under socialism than under capitalism.

But, like all socialists in the colonial situation, Nehru was faced with the problem: How to relate, how to co-ordinate, how to integrate the stream of national struggle for independence and the stream of the struggle for social or class and economic emancipation? How to unite the entire nation, the entire people against imperialism even while carrying on internal class struggles? How to bring the two commitments together, without undermining the anti-imperialist struggle?

Nehru's understanding and answer were clear and were based on his firm grasp over the fact that the primary contradiction in India was between imperialism and the entire Indian people. Consequently, nationalism was here the dominant aspect, the primary issue and the national struggle must have primacy over the social struggle. All issues of social and economic change or reform had to be linked to the national struggle. In fact, the future success of socialism itself would depend on the successful establishment of this linkage.

---

[20]*Ibid.,* Vol. 7, pp. 180-1.

[21]*Ibid.,* Vol. 6, pp. 122 and 22.

[22]Report in *The Times of India,* 18 May, 1936, p.ll.

[23]Report in *The Times of India,* 19 May, 1936, p. 14.

[24]*SW,* Vol. 9, p. 509.

This also meant that, basically, the actual struggle for socialist transformation will come only after the Indian people had overthrown colonialism and gained political power. As he put it in 1936, "Some people believe that socialism is even more important than Swaraj. But I think that independence must precede socialism, because unless we are politically free, we cannot carry out a socialist programme."[25] And referring to Indian politics during 1934-35, he wrote in 1941: "Although there was now much talk of socialism, not even the most ardent socialist thought of it except as something that would follow independence. Socialism was thus not the issue before the Congress and the country."[26] (It also then followed that the National Congress, as the leader of the national movement, could not be transformed into a socialist organisation or party or movement.)

The above formulation raised a host of problems whose solutions were imperative. The CSP and the Communist left had an easy solution. After paying formal homage to the formulation, which had the authority of Lenin and the Comintern behind it, get on with the task of attacking the capitalists and the landlords and what were seen to be their 'political representatives', the National Congress and Gandhiji, and of counterpoising "the struggle of the toilers" to what they saw as the bourgeois national movement; or, at least, of opposing and overthrowing from the leadership of the national movement its 'bourgeois' leaders in order to safeguard class struggle and the future of socialism.

For a short while, under the influence of what may be called mechanical or vulgar Marxism of the 1930s or Stalin-Marxism, Jawaharlal too fell prey to this 'left' sounding notion. He too talked of making the national movement into a mass movement against both foreign and indigenous vested interests and argued that political independence without socialism, without the overthrow of capitalism and landlordism, would have little meaning. Thus, in 1933, he predicted that "political and social emancipation will come together to some at least of the countries of Asia". Freedom of India was necessary, he said, precisely because the masses were having to bear the burden of the vested interests of certain classes in India and abroad: "The achievement of freedom thus becomes a question ... of divesting vested interests". On the other hand, "if an indigenous government took the place of the foreign government and

[25] *Ibid.,* Vol., 7, p. 267.

[26] *Ibid.,* Vol. 11, p. 766.

kept all the vested interests intact, this would not even be the shadow of freedom". Therefore, the immediate objective or goal of the freedom struggle had to be the ending of the exploitation of the Indian people. Politically, this meant independence from foreign rule; socially and economically it had to mean "the ending of all special class privileges and vested interests".[27]

But very soon, he instinctively drew away from this approach and groped for answers which would concretly lead to the implementation of his basic understanding regarding the primacy of the national liberation struggle. Basically, there were two problems. The first related to the status of class struggle in the period of the liberation struggle. Nehru emphasised the role of class analysis and class struggle. Even when united in their interests and in the struggle against imperialism, the Indian people were divided by class—however incoherent the class structure. "Class struggles have always existed and exist today", only "people interested in maintaining the *status quo* try to hide this fact", he wrote in 1933.[28] And, again, in 1939: "Class struggles are inherent in the present system, for the attempt to change it and bring it in line with modern requirements meets with the fierce opposition of the ruling or owning classes."[29] Consequently, class divisions had to be disturbed and class struggle fought; class struggle could not be ignored. To do so was to favour *status quo.* It was therefore not possible for the Congress to hold the balance between capital and labour and landlord and tenant, for the existing balance was "terribly weighted" in favour of the capitalists and landlords. To maintain the *status quo* was "to maintain injustice and exploitation"; to maintain the existing class balance was to keep the exploited at the complete mercy of the exploiters.[30] He therefore criticized the existing dominant tendency in the Congress to totally subordinate the social, class struggle to the political, anti-imperialist struggle or to postpone the social struggle to a later period in the name of national unity and national struggle.[31]

But how was class struggle to be fought under the existing circumstances? Nehru's answer was that the internal class contradictions had to be resolved in a double matrix: in the framework of the primacy and

[27] *Ibid.,* Vol. 6, pp. 12-4.
[28] *Ibid.,* Vol. 5, p. 538.
[29] *Ibid.,* Vol. 9, p. 509.
[30] *Ibid.,* Vol. 4, p. 193.
[31] *Ibid.,* Vol. 6, pp. 3-4.

unity of the anti-imperialist struggle keeping it broad-based, and, at the same time, protecting and promoting the interests of the workers and peasants.

This meant that the national movement, even while recognizing class conflict, must not precipitate it and push it to a point where unity of the Indian people against imperialism was imperilled. And, hence, it must try to adjust class interests. But it must practise class adjustment in the interest of the masses. Class adjustment must be a compromise between two classes with both sides adjusting and yielding. The movement should constantly work for an adjustment that tilted towards the masses. There need be no expropriation of the capitalists or even the landlords at present, but, in any clash between them and the masses, the interests of the rich should be sacrificed—class adjustment should occur in favour of the exploited. While socialism was not immediately on the agenda, the masses must not be asked 'to stand over till Swaraj had been attained'. Consequently, firstly, even here and now the National Congress must 'work for them'. It must take up popular demands and mobilize the people around them. Second, workers and peasants should be organized in their own class organizations—the kisan sabhas and the trade unions. The working people should keep their ideology and class organizations intact, though he felt that there was no need for a separate political organisation for them other than the Congress.

Nehru also argued that it was possible to fight for and achieve radical, pro-poor reformist measures here and now and thus unify the national movement around a radical socio-economic programme which would 'comprehend' the interests of all classes. Class adjustment could moreover constantly move more and more towards working people's interests. This was the significance of the progression from the Karachi Resolution on Fundamental Rights to the Faizpur Congress Resolution and the Election Manifesto of 1936-37, and the ultimate Working Committee Resolution of 1945 in favour of the abolition of all intermediaries between the peasant and the state. It was also within this framework that Nehru structured the national movement's approach to the Princely states. This policy of pro-people class adjustment and radical socio-economic reforms was to be achieved on the basis of the unity of the intelligentsia, peasants, agricultural labourers, workers, petty bourgeoisie and small and even large capitalists and even small landlords. This was another reason why the struggle for establishing socialism would have to be postponed till after independence because it would be based on a different class alliance excluding landlords and capitalists, at least the large ones.

The second question was even more important. If the struggle for the establishment of socialism was to be postponed to the post-independence period, if the national movement was not to be the instrument for the establishment of socialism, if the two struggles were not to come to fruition simlutaneously, then what form would the struggle for socialism take during the period of the anti-imperialist struggle?

Jawaharlal Nehru's answer was profound. While the Congress could not become, could not be and should not be transformed into, a socialist organisation, and could not "adopt a fully socialist programme", it could be made to recognize the need for social change and a new ideological framework, could *be oriented towards socialism,* could be given a socialist bias, could be made to "lean towards socialism," could be made "more and more socialistic,"[32] could be transformed into the instrument for the establishment of socialism after national liberation. Nationalism was no doubt primary but it had to be based on the workers and peasants and the middle classes and had to be given a socialist ideological orientation. Hence the struggle for socialism should take the form of ideological struggle within the national movement. The National Congress was bourgeois because its dominant ideology was bourgeois. The task was to transform it ideologically, to bring the entire movement or its largest segments under the influence of socialist ideas and to commit it to the socialist path after independence, to practise class adjustment within a socialist ideological perspective creating conditions for the turning of the entire movement to the left, to give primacy to the anti-imperialist struggle but within a socialist ideological perspective so that political freedom was followed by the establishment of a socialist society.

As he put it in his *Autobiography,* the task was to "try to spread socialistic ideas among the people, and especially among the more politically conscious Congress workers, so that when the time came for another declaration of policy we might be ready for a notable advance."[33] And, again, that "the immediate task" was "to train and prepare our country", the preparation being "largely an ideological one."[34] In fact, several chapters of the *Autobiography* were an ideological polemic

---

[32]S. Gopal, *Jawaharlal Nehru — A Biography.* 3 volumes, London, 1975—*Vol. One,* p. 181.

[33]Jawaharlal Nehru, *An Autobiography.* New Delhi, 1962 edition, p.403.

[34]*Ibid* . p. 166.

against Gandhiji and the dominant bourgeois ideology of the national-movement. They, as also much in his speeches and writings during 1933-37, constituted an effort to oppose the existing bourgeois ideological hegemony over the movement and to establish, instead, socialist ideological hegemony over it. The task was moreover unprecedented, for unlike China or Cuba or Vietnam or the Portuguese colonies or even Tsarist Russia, the Indian national movement had grown for nearly 50 years under structured bourgeois ideology. Even so, Nehru's success was quite substantial.

Nehru moulded a whole generation of young nationalists and helped them accept a socialist orientation. Often the socialists and the communists reaped the harvest which Nehru had sown. What is more important, the overwhelming majority of nationalist opinion, including Gandhiji, accepted socialism as their long-term objective. Interestingly, this emphasis on ideological struggle and ideological transformation led Nehru to assign a major role to the intelligentsia in the Indian context. In the *Autobiography,* one of his criticisms of the Indian communists was that "they have not realized that in India today the middle-class intellectual is the most revolutionary force"[35]

According to Nehru, along with ideological preparation, the socialist task also was to work for greater worker and peasant participation in the Congress and the national movement. And here, he also revealed a certain grasp of the processes and the manner in which classes establish their ideological hegemony over a movement. This they do by emerging as the representatives of societal interests. In India's case, the workers could do so by being the best fighters against imperialism and by increasing their weight and the level of their participation in the national movement. Being fully aware of the wide presence of the middle classes and small landlords in the Congress and the strong bourgeois ideological influence over it, he urged the workers and peasants tc join the Congress and transform it in line with their interests and desires and ideological framework. In particular, he asked the working class to unite and organize, to acquire and develop "the correct ideology", leading to a socialist programme, and to act politically in the national movement with a view to "orient it in favour of the workers."[36] In December 1933, in a speech delivered at the All-India Trade Union Congress, he told the workers that, if they participated

[35]*Ibid.,* p. 366.

[36]*SW.* Vol. 5, pp. 547, 546.

fully in the national struggle as well as in their own social struggle, they would help bring about not only. "political freedom in India but social freedom also".[37] He also pointed out that the national movement was bound to succeed, and, therefore, those classes which did not join the movement did more harm to themselves than to the Congress or the movement.

During 1935-36, he tried to bring about workers' participation and increase the weight of the workers and peasants in the national movement in a mechanical way by suggesting that their corporate class organizations—the trade unions and kisan sabhas—should be made constituent part of the Congress through what came to be known as "collective affiliation", but, in the end, he accepted that the objective could be perhaps better realized through direct enrolment of the peasants and workers in the Congress and giving greater responsibility and initiative to the lowest, primary committees of the Congress.

II

Even while propagating socialist ideas and trying to establish the hegemony of socialist ideas within the national movement, Nehru abandoned his own strategy of continuous mass struggle, no negotiations with the colonial authorities, no participation in the colonial constitutional framework and no negotiations for transfer of power,[38] and continued to work up to the last within the framework of the Gandhian anti-imperialist political strategy and under the leadership of Gandhiji and in co-operation with the Congress right wing. He also increasingly played down his Marxist commitment and became more critical of the leftwing groups. His language increasingly lost its stringent Marxist tone. Gandhiji loomed larger and larger in his thought and speech. By 1947 he had more or less abandoned his Marxism of the 1930s except perhaps as a mode of historical analysis. Marxism was no longer a guide to his actions.

This is where the pre-1947 Nehru has come under the sharpest criticism. For example, in 1975, writing of the post-1936 Nehru, I described his Lucknow Presidential Address of 1936 as "both the high watermark and the swan song of his radicalism". I argued that from the Marxist revolutionary positions of the years 1929-1936, he "went back to the role

[37]*Ibid.,* Vol. 6, p. 138.

[38]See Bipan Chandra, *Nationalism and Colonialism in Modern India,* New Delhi, 1979, pp. 179-81; S. Gopal, *op. cit.,* Vol. one, pp. 149-50, 182, 186-7; *SW,* Vol. 13, pp. 98, 133.

of a radical nationalist", and gradually abandoned "all the ground gained in the early 1930s".[39] E.M.S. Namboodiripad has in his recent study of Nehru commented that "the radical phrases strewn over his Presidential address to the Lahore Congress of 1929 and all his subsequent pronouncements did not prevent him from acting as the- trusted colleague and comrade of the Mahatma. He has criticised Nehru for continuing, even after Tripuri session and Bose's resignation from the Congress Presidentship, collaboration with the right-wing leadership of the Congress. It was, he says, the "transformation of Nehru from the 'idol of Indian youth' into a reliable ally of the rightist leadership of the Congress" which made him undertake the study of Nehru and come to the conclusion that he was one of the "faces" of the Indian bourgeoisie. Tripuri was, he writes, "the watershed between Nehru and the communists".[40]

Another major ground for ciriticism has been: why did he not make a break with Gandhiji or the Congress during the 1930s when he repeatedly disagreed with the former or with the majority of the Congress Working Committee? Why did he, at Lucknow in 1936, retreat and graciously accept the defeat of his two important proposals regarding collective affiliation of trade unions and kisan sabhas and non-acceptance of ministerial offices under the new scheme of Provincial Autonomy? Even earlier still, why did he accept the Gandhi-Irwin Pact and even agree to move the resolution for its acceptance at Karachi in March 1931? Why did he not revolt when the Nehru Report with its acceptance of Dominion Status was accepted, when the Civil Disobedience Movement was withdrawn in 1934 or when he was humbled in his dispute with the majority of the Congress Working Committee in 1936? Why did he repeatedly "meekly submit" to Gandhiji? And, above all, why did he refuse to support Subhas Bose at Tripuri and, instead, virtually supported the right-wing leaders headed by Sardar Patel? Or even more bluntly, "Why did he not leave the Congress when he found that its class character was a *hindrance in the way of any socialist* programme?" Why did he not join Subhas Bose in "a walk-out from the Congress" when this was likely to "have started the process of polarization in Indian politics"?[41] His contemporary left-wing friends, colleagues and co-workers, as also

[39]Bipan Chandra, *op. cit.*, pp. 196-7.

[40]E.M.S. Namboodiripad, *Nehru: Ideology and Practice,* New Delhi, 1988, pp. 291, 293.

[41]C.P. Bhambri, *Politics in India, 1947-1987,* New Delhi, 1988, pp. 30-1. Bhambri has also provided his answer to this question. PP. 31ff.

colonial authorities, constantly, over the years, expected him to break with Gandhiji, to use his position to split the Congress and to create an alternate revolutionary organization, or, at least, to vigorously attack the right wing, as they themselves were doing, instead of allying with it.[42]

Nehru, of course, himself constantly grappled with this problem in his Marxist phase. In 1934, on reading in jail of the Working Committee resolution condemning the socialists for preaching "the necessity of class war" and "confiscation of private property", he wrote in his diary: "to hell with the Working Committee",[43] and later wrote that the Working Committee was "aggressively anti-socialist and politically it is more backward than it has been for 15 years."[44]

Earlier, in 1933, he wrote in his jail diary: "I want to break from this lot completely".[45] And again: "I am getting more and more certain that there can be no further political cooperation between Bapu and me. At least not of the kind that has existed. We had better go our different ways",[46] for "our objectives are different, our ideals are different, our spiritual outlook is different and our methods are likely to be different".[47] All evidence indicates that by the middle of 1936, under the influence of Marxism, Nehru was setting out to evolve a left political alternative to the Gandhian leadership-an alternative that would challenge the latter in all basic aspects programme and ideology, social character of the movement and of its leadership, and the strategy of its struggle. Even as late as 1943, in jail, he wrote in his diary that he had no place in a Working Committee with leaders like Sardar Patel and Rajendra Prased.[48] *But at no stage did he make the break.* He always drew back form the precipice. *The question is, why?* The answer to this question would provide a basic explanation of the 'paradoxes' of Nehru, as also tell us a great deal about his role in the freedom struggle and his legacy to the Indian people. Critics and biographers have provided many an answer—often with a degree of insight. These are the psychological explanations—weak personality,

---

[42]For these expectations, see S. Gopal, *op. cit*.. Vol. One, pp, 128, 130, 178,180.

[43]*SW*, Vol. 6, p. 259.

[44]*Ibid.*, pp. 271-2.

[45]*Ibid.*, Vol. 5, p. 479.

[46]*Ibid.*, p. 489.

[47]*Ibid.*, Vol. 6, p. 271.

[48]*Ibid.*, Vol. 13, p. 297.

Gandhi's domination, affection for and sentimental attachment and loyalty to Gandhiji, fear of being lonely—or character faults, such as vacillation, or downright opportunism arising out of the fear of losing his leadership position. In my article of 1975, I emphasised the weak grounding in Marxism, attachment and subservience to Gandhiji, absence of an organisational base of his own, weakness of the left, and clever capitalist strategy in 'handling' him.[49]

We get a different answer if we don't accept the basic premise of the question that such a break was desirable, and if we postulate that his never losing sight of the fact that the movement had to remain united and, consequently, his refusal to split the National Congress was, along with the socialist orientation he gave to the movement, his greatest contribution to India's struggle for national liberation. He alone could have split the Congress and the national movement—and he did not. The CSP and the CPI could not and did not try for they could not do it without Nehru. But they would have tried and with success if he had gone with them and headed the split. In this sense, he shares the credit with Gandhiji for preserving the unity of the Congress and the national movement.

The explanation of Nehru's gradual political transformation after 1936 is then to be sought in the following:

Already by 1937, Nehru had accepted several aspects of Gandhi's leadership and strategy, which other left leaders and groups had not, even though he had continued to gently combat Gandhiji ideologically and politically.

First, he had fully accepted non-violence as a basic policy for the national movement. He had also come to believe that it was not a "negative and passive method", flowing out of weakness or the bourgeois character of the movement, but "an active, dynamic and forceful method of enforcing the mass will."[50] Already in 1929, in his Presidential Address, he had gone on to assert that mass movements in which millions participated had to be, by their very nature, non-violent, except in times of organized revolt. He added: "It is not possible to carryon at one and the same time the two movements (violent and non-violent) side by side. We have to choose and strictly to abide by our choice. What the choice of this Congress is likely to be I have no doubt. It can only choose a peaceful mass movement."[51]

---

[49]Bipan Chandra, *op, cit.*, pp. 197-8.
[50]*SW*, Vol. 6, p. 25.
[51]*Ibid.*, Vol. 4, pp. 195-6.

Second, he identified himself fully with the mainstream of nationalism and its leader, the Indian National Congress. Once he accepted the priority of the national movement, he also accepted the imperative of its unity. He repeatedly asserted, as in 1936, that "So far as I am concerned I will try to pull together, even if the decision of the Congress is such as it may be.... We cannot afford to split up, and break up the Congress".[52] And, in 1937: the Congress should "hold together, push together, fight together and win together."[53] By 1939 he was clearer and more categorical: "The Indian nationalist movement has spread and absorbed every advanced element in the country It has big anti-imperialist fights to its credit and it is difficult for a rival anti-imperialist movement to be built up. It is not only difficult but highly dangerous, since it undermines organisation and strength, built up through decades".[54] He also accepted unreservedly that in this movement the leadership of Gandhiji was an invariable factor.

Third, he thoroughly grasped that it is in the basic character of a mass movement which engulfs millions and tries to win the support of the majority of the people that it can have a common goal or vision but not one, single political line. In a mass movement there is bound to be a diversity of political and ideological perspectives and trends. Such a movement can only demand from its participants and its leaders commitment to a common cause, a common goal, and a common form of struggle with trust in each other but not uniformity of political views. Nor could the millions of Indian people be moved into political action around a single rigid political line, however pure in theory.[55] Moreover, Nehru believed that even from the point of view of the left it was wrong to split the Congress along left-right lines; it was better to push the whole of the Congress left or at least its vast centre which was vaguely socialist than to cater to the purist views of a handful.

Fourth, as compared to others on the left, Nehru had a different and more correct perception of wherein lay the rightwingness of the leaders of the Congress right wing. It did not lie in their attitude of compromise towards imperialism or in their weak role in the freedom struggle. They were as firmly anti-imperialist as anybody else and their sacrifices were as

---

[52]*Ibid.,* Vol. 7, pp. 168-9.

[53]Quoted in S. Gopal, *op. cit.,* Vol. one, p. 219.

[54]SW., Vol. 10, p. 18.

[55]See, for example, *SW,* Vol. 7, p. 36, Vol. 9, p. 511, Vol. II, p. 765.

great as anybody else's. Their rightwingness lay in their socio-economic conservatism. And since the main question of the movement was that of anti-imperialism, their social conservatism could not be the basis of separation from them.

Fifth, already, Nehru did not see nationalism as inherently a bourgeois class ideology, though he saw the Indian national movement being dominated at the time by bourgeois ideology. Similarly, he saw the bourgeois character of the National Congress but he did not see the Congress as a structured bourgeois party. He saw it as capable of being transformed in a socialist direction. He felt that it was already gradually shifting leftwards.

Sixth, and above all, Nehru had a positive understanding of Gandhiji and had already developed a complex and critical but non-antagonistic relationship with him. He criticized Gandhiji for refusing to recognize the conflict of the classes, for preaching harmony among the exploiters and the exploited, and for putting forward the theory of trusteeship. At the same time, he fully appreciated the radical role that Gandhiji had played and was playing in Indian society. Gandhiji, he said, was a revolutionary. Defending Gandhiji against his left-wing critics, Jawaharlal contended. in an article written in January 1936 that "Gandhiji has played a revolutionary role in India of the greatest importance because he knew how to make the most of the objective conditions and could reach the heart of the masses; while groups with a more advanced ideology functioned largely in the air". Moreover, Gandhiji's actions and teachings had "inevitably raised mass consciousness tremendously and made social issues vital. And his insistence on the raising of the masses at the cost, wherever necessary, of vested interests has given a strong orientation to the national movement in favour of the masses".[56] Nehru also believed that Gandhiji had the capacity to move forward towards the left because of his basic revolutionary outlook and pro-masses orientation.

After 1936, while Nehru's commitment to socialism and to the radical socio-economic reorganization of society remained as vibrant as before, his election tours of 1936-37, the experience of the Congress Ministries, the struggle against fascism, the happenings in the Soviet Union, and the fear that the practice of sectarian politics and dogmatic Marxism led to ineffectivity and marginalization, increasingly made him re-evaluate the Gandhian strategy of what I have described as Struggle-

[56] *Ibid.*, Vol. 7, pp. 76-7.

Truce-Struggle, The failure of the Bolshevik model in Europe and the successful practice in India of what Antonio Gramsci was to describe as a war of position made Nehru re-evaluate the Gandhian strategy, though he continued to disagree with him on the economic structure of free India. He still remained committed to Marxism but increasingly tried to reconcile this commitment with his understanding of Gandhiji in action.

The crux of the matter was that there was increasing disharmony between Nehru's theory and his political practice. While his practice was that of hegemonic struggle, his theory was that of contemporary Marxism. Basically, after 1936, Nehru instinctively saw the successful working of the Gandhian strategy and the inapplicability of his Marxian paradigm. The Stalin-Marxism of the 1930s, which was basically what his Marxism was, was incapable of grasping or grappling with the nature of Indian politics, the character of the Gandhian strategy, or even the character of the colonial state. No amount of the correct application of the existing Marxism would have enabled him to do so. The answer was very different. What was needed was not the application of the then Marxism to specific Indian conditions but the development of Marxism in the Indian context. But Nehru was no Gramsci. He was incapable of so developing Marxism. He lacked the theoretical mind or capacity or even inclination, In fact, if he could have done so, he would have been more profound than Gramsci, for Gramsci was making a theoretical critique of the failed Bolshevik model in the context of capitalist democracies, and more specifically of the Italian left's failure to successfully oppose fascism. Gramsci's war of position was a theoretical construct—a model—in opposition to the Bolshevik model of war of manoeuvre, of replicating the October Revolution in democratic societies. Nehru had before him the actual, concrete, historical practice of a war of position by the national movement under Gandhi's leadership. The theorization of this practice would have made a major contribution to—as also would have had profound consequences for—the socialist movement in India and the world.

But Nehru could not be a Gramsci. What he could, however, do was to see the inapplicability of the existing Marxism and the futility of the Indian communist practice based on it. And so, increasingly, with the passage of time, he gave up the effort to pose an alternative to the Gandhian strategy and followed, instead, in practice, pragmatically accepting the 'logic of facts' without theorization, the Gandhian strategy. Whenever a clash occurred between his theory and his political practice, the latter won out, though he often, though decreasingly so, went through an agonizing self-questioning. Whenever a choice had to be made between giving up his Gandhian political practice as the Indian left had done and giving up Stalin-Marxism, he gave up the latter. And so a hiatus developed between his theoretical beliefs and his political practice. Increasingly, after 1937, he stopped theorizing-his political practice was without theoretical guidance. Marxist influence over him weakened after 1937 as he was not able to develop Marxism in the Indian context. In fact, he increasingly stopped thinking in terms of Marxism except when interpreting history. And as Marxism lost its dominant position, Gandhiji occupied more of his thoughts-Gandhiji loomed larger on his theoretical horizon and not only in his practice.

Nehru's greateness was that he, on the whole, understood the reality of colonial India and Indian politics and grasped the historical validity of the Gandhian strategy. His practice remained true. Having defined the goal of freedom struggle and its social base in Marxian terms and having made a massive effort to give the freedom struggle and the Indian people a socialist ideological orientation, he ultimately accepted the Gandhian strategy and forms of struggle for achieving independence. His weakness was that he was unable to theorize his practice by developing Marxism. Instead, it was his commitment to Marxism that was gradually eroded. His defence can be that except for Gramsci, and in his case too only in the form of a beginning, nobody else has been able to so develop Marxism so far.

After 1947, Nehru tried to evolve a theoretical framework to understand and explain his past politics and current political practice. He now began to theorize the Gandhian strategy and project it to the building of a socialist society in India. But this theorization did not occur within the framework of Marxism. His thought evolved more and more in terms of Gandhian categories. He now openly questioned the existing Marxism—or the Marxism of his youth—but then instead of developing it, or lacking the capacity to do so, he gradually abandoned Marxism, though he remained loyal to the socialist vision.

This was to make his life and work after 1947 full of contradictions, for, as we shall see, and as he himself recognized, though a committed socialist who commanded Indian politics with power and authority, he became the architect of a capitalist economy and society. But because of his socialist commitment, and because of his pragmatic grasp of politics and social reality, even his political practice and speeches and writings of the post-1947 period provide deep insights into the problems of socialist transformation in the modern world. But before we take up this aspect, let me discuss some of Jawaharlal Nehru's other major objectives and achievements and failures.

III

Jawaharlal Nehru fully kept up his commitment to nationalism, national unity and national independence after 1947. His policies and his thinking after 1947 cannot be understood outside the framework of this commitment. He had to safeguard the political independence won in 1947, but he had also to take independence beyond mere political independence; he had to lay the foundations of a democratic and civil libertarian polity, and he had to push forward the process of the making of the Indian nation.

This was an unchartered path. Marxist theory had at the time little to say; and in any case most Marxists believed that the positive or progressive potential of nationalism was exhausted by the anti-imperialist struggle and therefore either nationalism was now reactionary or it had to be turned against what they believed to be the neo-colonial state, Either way the concept of nation-building under the existing state and social order was a reactionary concept. Similarly, the person who had been Nehru's political guru had left very little direct legacy in this respect. Gandhiji was a philosopher and strategist of the struggle for the overthrow of an unjust political order. He had left few guidelines on how to build a nation. The big advance Gandhiji made in 1948—that is, the idea of Lok Sevak Sangh—related to the, mobilization of the people against a possibly errant regime in the future and to social work. Certainly, this was important for any democratic regime setting out to build a nation and a new socio-economic and political order, but it hardly constituted an overall strategic design or tactical agenda as to how to build a nation. In fact, we may surmise that one of the reasons why Gandhiji had designated Nehru as a successor was because, among his co-workers, Nehru alone had the capacity to chart a path towards and an adequate vision of building an equitable, just and democratic society and of consolidating India into a nation.

A

Nehru's achievements in the task of consolidating independence, nation-building and nation-making were quite considerable. He clearly grasped that independence meant the capacity to resist economic and political domination, In general, independence meant that India must have "full control of her internal and external policy". Translated in economic terms, independence depended upon economic strength. And this battle had just begun. As he wrote in 1949: "In any real sense of the word, this fight for freedom is not over, though we may be politically free. It is not over in the economic sense, and even politically, we have to be continually vigilant".[57]

And so, in the economic field, Nehru set out to build the structure of an independent and self-reliant economy and made an all out effort to break out of colonial underdevelopment and ensure self-sustaining and self-generating growth, both in agriculture and industry.

In his speeches and statements, Nehru constantly emphasised self-reliance and cautioned against dependence. "We must seek to build up our strength relying on ourselves and not by dependence on others. Dependence in one direction leads to dependence in another. Nations, it is said, by themselves are made".[58] And the biggest achievement he claimed for planning and for Congress rule was the creation of "a feeling of self-reliance".[59] Emphasis on rapid industrialization, planning, public sector and development of heavy industry, science and technology and technical modernization, the training of a large technical and scientific cadre, and on atomic energy, were seen by Nehru as necessary parts of the effort at independent economic development. At the same time, independent economy and self-reliance would strengthen the psychological basis of national independence by increasing the self-confidence and self-respect of the people.

Nehru was from the days of independence struggle opposed to large scale intrusion of foreign capital and, after 1947, even though in dire need of capital goods, kept import of foreign capital under strict check and control. A major reason for the emphasis on public sector was to prevent the large-scale use of foreign capital. Interestingly, for technology or

[57] *LCM*, Vol. 1, p. 371.

[58] Quoted in Girish Mishra, *Nehru and the Congress Economic Policies*, New Delhi, 1988, p. 135.

[59] *LCM*, Vol. IV, p. 256.

capital goods, India's public sector did not collaborate with the multinationals. It collaborated mostly with the socialist countries and in other cases with Western governments or smaller firms. Moreover, the terms and conditions on which foreign technology and capital were imported were far better than those on which countries like Brazil did so.

Inevitably, India had to rely to a certain extent on foreign aid. But Nehru was aware that foreign aid led to the weakening of self-reliance and to dependency. And so, foreign aid was always kept within limits, and in no case was planning and development made dependent on foreign aid. The basic approach was laid down by an AICC resolution in 1958, when the Second Five Year Plan was facing a resources crunch: "While external aid would always be welcome for implementing the targets of the Second Five Year Plan, our main emphasis will be on self-reliance."[60] Similarly explaining his approach to Tibor Mende in 1956, Nehru said: "Undoubtedly, help is necessary. But I do think that there is always this danger—both political and economic.... It is better to go a little slower and rely on yourself; it is better than to become dependent", or to encourage the spirit of dependency. And he pointed out that "the extent of help has been relatively little compared to our own effort in India."[61] And this approach he dinned day in and day out among the people and his fellow Congress leaders.

Nehru was fully aware of the fact that the USA was taking over the burden of colonialism from Britain and becoming the chief defender of colonial and neo-colonial regimes the world over; and that too close a political or economic relationship with the United States posed dangers of neo-colonialization. He had also no doubt that a major aim of the US military aid to Pakistan was to put pressure on India to conform to US policies. In his confidential letters to the Chief Ministers, he repeatedly pointed to this aspect. S. Gopal, Nehru's biographer, notes that by 1954 Nehru had "no doubt that the United States was following an imperialist policy, not in the normal sense of conquering a weaker country, but in that she was seeking to force the countries of Asia to conform to her own attitudes. In resisting this, India would have not only to reject offers of military aid and denounce its granting to other nations, but also consider the refusal of economic assistance. Without going out of his way to

[60]Quoted in Girish Mishra, *op. cit.*, p. 154.

[61]Tibor Mende, *op. cit.*, pp. 66,65.

announce that India would not accept such assistance, Nehru ordered budgeting on the basis that it might not be available".[62]

There is hardly any doubt that Nehru was eminently successful in laying the foundations of an independent economy, though a capitalist economy. There were no end of Cassandras who everyday and at every moment of economic difficulties predicted that India was entering a phase of dependency and neo-colonialization, But they were all to prove false prophets. India is one of the few ex-colonial countries which have made the structural transition "from a colonial to an independent economy. And the credit for initiating and laying the foundations of the transition goes largely to Jawaharlal Nehru, who was very conscious of this achievement.

B

Nehru's foreign policy was a many-splendoured phenomenon. Here I am concerned with delineating one of its major aspects. Nehru used foreign policy as an instrument to develop and safeguard India's national interests and to develop the self-reliance, self-confidence and pride of the Indian people, even while serving the cause of peace and anti-colonialism. The policy of non-alignment was formulated in order to assert India's will for national independence and to strengthen its independence. As Nehru put it in 1949 to the Constituent Assembly: "What does independence consist of? It consists fundamentally and basically of foreign relations. That is the test of independence. All else is local autonomy."[63]

Nehru also saw the close connection between foreign policy and economic independence. As early as December 1947, he said: "Ultimately, foreign policy is the outcome of economic policy, and until India has properly evolved its economic policy, her foreign policy will be rather vague, rather inchoate, and will be groping".[64] Nehru's policy of friendship with the two superpowers and of support to the peoples struggling against colonialism can be understood only in the context of the basic design of his foreign policy being the defence of India's independence. Let me quote from a scholar who has studied Nehru's foreign policy in great depth. V.P. Dutt writes: "If India's foreign policy can be regarded in terms of a triangular structure, the base was

---

[62]S. Gopal., *op. cit.,* Vol. Two, p. 188.

[63]Speeches, Vol. One, p. 241.

[64]*Ibid.,* p. 202.

independence, while one pillar was support to other countries of Asia, Africa and Latin America (anti-imperialism), but the other was the maintenance of friendly relations with all big powers—to the extent possible and without damage to India's interests and principles."[65] Nehru was also one of the first statesmen to recognize that military alliances did not strengthen but weaken a country by limiting the receiving country's independence.

The India-China War was a 'body blow' to India's foreign policy. Yet, despite large-scale right-wing clamour, Nehru reaffirmed the basic principles of India's foreign policy specially the policy of nonalignment, and refused to enter military alliances or other pacts with the big powers, especially the United States. As Nehru told R.K. Karanjia in 1963: "We have not abandoned non-alignment. This rand of ours is not so much a postulate of our foreign policy as the projection of our sovereignty, independence, and peaceful values to our international relations".[66]

C

Above all, Nehru succeeded, after 1947, in maintaining the national unity forged during the freedom struggle and made fragile by the manner of transfer of power. More, he succeeded in consolidating the nation and the independent state. This was no simple task, as the dangers we face today indicate. Caste, province, linguistic chauvinism—largely overpowered and transcended during the freedom struggle—were beginning to surface again; the princely states were there; and, of course, there was the monster of communalism.

From the beginning, Nehru recognised the paramount importance of preserving the unity of India. As he repeatedly pointed out to the Chief Ministers, the primary task was the building up of a united India and promoting the process of the psychological integration of the Indian people. All other questions and issues had to be subordinated to this task. "First things must come first", he wrote.[67] And again, "There is no way out for us except to pull together and to realize that India has to advance as a

[65]V.P. Dutt, "India's Foreign Policy in Retrospect and Prospect", unpublished paper, presented at National Seminar on "Economics and Politics of Transformation from Colonial to Independent India," p. 4.

[66]R. K. Karanjia, *The Philosophy of Mr. Nehru,* as revealed in a series of intimate talks with R. K. Karanjia, London, 1966, p. 117.

[67]*LCM,* Vol. I, p. 144.

whole and not In bits and patches". Even the Five Year Plan, he wrote in December 1952, made sense if it was seen that behind it "lies the conception of India's unity". In India's case, unity and freedom were closely related: "We live in a dangerous age where only the strong and the united can survive or retain their freedom."[68]

More positively, Nehru recognized both before and after independence that India was not yet a structured nation but a nation-in- the - making. But he also recognized that this process could not be developed without being aware of the fragile character of the existing level of national unity and without recognizing the diversity of the Indian people and that India was a land of many languages, religions and cultures.

On the first aspect, he repeatedly pointed out: "Our society has for long ages past been very loosely knit with all kinds of inner divisions". India had, of course, he noted, for centuries a cultural unity and continuity of traditions. Synthesis had moreover been a dominant feature in Indian history. The national struggle against foreign colonial rule had broken down many of the inner divisions, united the Indian people in struggle and promoted the process of the nation-in-the-making.[69] But this process was still at an early stage and was constantly open to disruption. "We have still", he repeatedly pointed out, "to aim at and achieve the psychological integration of our country".[70] The emotional thrust towards unity had been promoted before 1947 by the struggle against a common adversary. But, he noted, "When that adversary left the scene, then the urge to unity became somewhat weaker and we began to relapse into our separate groups and our parochial thinking".[71] In fact, an eternal optimist, the only time Nehru would get depressed and had a sense of failure was when he felt that he was unable to check the disruptive forces. As he wrote to the Chief Ministers on 15th August 1957: "I believe we have succeeded in some ways to an extraordinary extent. I believe also that we have failed often enough. The measure of our failure is not so much what we may have done wrongly or what we might not have done which we should have done. The measure (of failure) is the existence in a fairly marked degree today of provincialism, communalism, casteism and also the tendency to violence".[72]

---

[68] *Ibid.,* Vol. III, pp. 77, 204, 368.
[69] *Ibid.,* Vol. II, p. 84.
[70] *Ibid.,* Vol. III. p. 387.
[71] *Ibid.,* Vol. IV, p. 536.
[72] *Ibid.*

So far as the second aspect is concerned, the immense diversity of India did not disturb Nehru. He rather welcomed it; and the effort to impose a single culture repelled him. For example, he wrote in early 1951: "We have to remember always that India is a country with a variety of cultures, habits, customs and ways of living.... It is very necessary, I think, for all of us to remember that this wonderful country of ours has infinite variety and there is absolutely no reason why we should try to regiment it after a single pattern. Indeed that is ultimately impossible, because climate and geography, as well as long cultural traditions, come in the way".[73] At the same time, the hope as well as the answer were there: "But India is far greater, far richer and more varied than any part of it. We have to develop an outlook which embraces all this variety and considers it our very own."[74]

One specific expression of this strategy of unity in diversity was his policy towards the tribal people; for example, towards the Nagas. While firmly opposing the demand for independence of Naga areas and refusing to tolerate any recourse to violence, he was willing to grant the Nagas much greater autonomy than enjoyed by other States in the Indian Union. In particular, he fully favoured the Naga's right to maintain their autonomy in cultural and other matters, even while they were to be encouraged to integrate with the rest of the country "in mind and spirit". His basic approach towards the Nagas has been summarised as follows by S. Gopal: "a friendly rather than a coercive attitude, an acceptance of their social structure, protection from encroachments and advance in such fields as education. They should neither be treated as anthropological specimens nor drowned in the sea of Indian humanity. They could not be isolated from the new political and economic forces sweeping across India; but it was equally undesirable to allow these forces to function freely and upset the traditional life and culture of the Nagas. It was presumptuous to approach them with an air of superiority and try to make of them second-rate copies of people in other parts of India."[75]

Overall, despite the fact that many of the forces of disruption continued, sometimes dormantly, sometimes actively, there is no doubt that Nehru succeeded in pushing forward the process of national intergration—of nation-in-the-making.

---

[73]*Ibid.,* Vol. II, p. 352.

[74]*Ibid.,* p. 598.

[75]S. GopaJ, *op. cit.,* Vol. Two, p. 207.

D

Jawaharlal Nehru was also in a large measure responsible for basing Indian nationalism, both before and after independence, on intense mtemationalism. Of course, the earlier nationalists from the Moderates to Gandhiji had also inculcated the view that the Indian people should be against the colonial system but not against the British people, and had extended full support to other colonial people struggling against imperialism. But Nehru made a big advance in the understanding of colonialism and internationlism by linking colonialism and imperialism to world capitalism. Indian freedom struggle was now seen as a part of the international struggle for human emancipation. Year after year, Nehru argued for the integration of India's struggle for national liberation with the other colonial peoples' struggles against colonialism and with the world struggle against capitalism. India's problem, he asserted at Lucknow in 1936, was "but a part of the world problem of capitalist imperialism".[76] This understanding was symbolically articulated when he wrote in 1937: "The frontiers of our struggle lie not only in our own country but in Spain and China also."[77]

After independence this intense internationlism was to find expression in India's foreign policy of giving all out support to the forces of peace and the struggles against colonialism.

IV

Jawaharlal Nehru was the first Indian to try to understand the broader social, economic and political dimensions, character and causation of communalism. Based on this understanding, he also organized through newspaper articles and speeches a whirlwind ideological and political campaign during 1933-37, leading in 1938 to a ban being placed on members of communal organizations becoming office bearers in the National Congress. His was also one of the first efforts to apply a Marxist approach to the problem.

Nehru was also very perceptive in recognizing that communalism was not a remanent of India's pre-colonial past or a left-over from the medieval period. There was no communalism in the medieval period. It was a product of the colonial period. As he pointed out in 1936; "One must never forget that communalism in India is a latter-day phenomenon which has grown up before our eyes".[78] He, therefore, set out during the early

[76] *SW,* Vol. 7, p. 180. Also pp. 173-4.

[77] *Ibid.,* Vol. 9, p. 235.

[78] *Ibid.,* Vol. 7, p. 69.

1930s to analyse the socio-economic and political roots of communalism and pointed to the social forces, classes and strata whose needs and purposes it served.

Nehru comprehended communalism as a petty bourgeois phenomenon and constantly pointed to the role of the middle classes in its perpetuation. One political lesson, he asserted, was the need to broaden the social base of the national movement and extend it from the middle classes to the masses. At the same time, he pointed out that communalism served the needs of, and was patronised by, the landlords, zamindars, merchants and money-lenders. Communalism was a major weapon of political, social and economic reaction. As early as 1933 he wrote: "It is this political reaction which has stalked the land under cover of communalism".[79]

Nehru was also the first to see communalism as a form of fascism. Before 1947, he saw the close resemblance between the post-1937 Muslim League and fascism both in terms of methods, techniques of hatred and violence, organization and style of leadership and in terms of language and ideology. After 1947, he began to apply this understanding to Hindu and Sikh communalisms, especially to the Rashtriya Swayam Sevak Sangh (RSS). For example, on 7 December 1947, he wrote: "We have a great deal of evidence to show that the RSS (Rashtriya Swayam Sevak Sangh) is an organisation which is in the nature of a private army and which is definitely proceeding on the strictest Nazi lines, even following the technique of organisation".[80] In fact, Nehru was at his intellectual and political best in understanding the character and role of the RSS. On 5th January 1948, he wrote to the Chief Ministers: "It is openly stated by their leaders that the RSS is not a political body but there can be no doubt that their policy and programme are political, intensely communal and based on violent activities. They have to be kept in check and we must not be misled by their pious professions which are completely at variance with their policy".[81] And again on 1 August 1949: "It must always be remembered that the whole mentality of the RSS is a fascist mentality".[82] One last quotation: he wrote in October1951: "Behind these communal bodies are the forces of every kind of social reaction. Some of the old ruling princes, deprived of their powers but having enough money, the

[79]*Ibid.,* Vol. 6, p. 164.
[80]*LCM,* Vol. I, p. 33.
[81]*Ibid"* p. 46.
[82]*Ibid.,* p. 428.

jagirdars, the big *zamindars,* and some of the big capitalists, support these communal bodies and talk loudly of a Hindu State or a Sikh State and of ancient Hindu culture. Behind this garb of ancient culture, they hide the narrowest acquisitiveness and reaction. Essentially, these communal bodies are fascist in ideology and technique".[83]

Nor was Nehru's objection to communalism on ideological grounds alone. It Was politically a dangerous ideology and phenomenon. While communalism before 1947 had divided the Indian people, weakened the national movement and led to the partition of India, it was, Nehru said, no less dangerous after independence. "If allowed free play", he wrote in 1951,communaiism "would break up India".[84] For that reason it had to be seen as "the major evil today", "the most dangerous development today." Moreover, "we can meet and fight an external enemy. But what are we to do when the enemy is within ourselves and in our own minds and hearts?".[85] Communalism, said Nehru, had therefore to be rooted out from Indian life; there could be "no half-way house" in the matter.[86]

Nehru also warned against the use of nationalism and culture by the communalists. He pointed to the irony of people "most of whom had done little in the struggle for India's freedom" now trying to hide "under the cloak of nationalism". But, in fact, behind "high sounding phrases appealing to nationalism and patriotism", communalism was "in its essence, a reactionary and disruptive cry, not a unifying one".[87]

During the colonial period, Nehru had seen the close connection between the growth of communal forces and the British policy of divide and rule. He had, of course, never accepted the simplistic view that the British had created communalism. Communalism had arisen because of certain conditions internal to Indian economy, society and polity. But it also served the needs of colonialism and so the colonial state encouraged and promoted it. For example, he had written in 1934 in a major essay: "Communalism thus becomes another name for political and social reaction and the British Government, being the citadel of this reaction in India, naturally throws its sheltering wings over a useful ally".[88]

Nehru's commitment to secularism and his opposition to communalism were total. From this point of view, the post-independence,

[83] *Ibid.,* Vol. II, pp. 508-9.
[84] *Ibid.,* p. 508.
[85] *Ibid.,* pp. 168,519.
[86] *Ibid.,* Vol. II, pp. 83-4.
[87] *Ibid.,* Vol. I, pp. 59, 513, Vol. II, p. 520, Vol. III, p. 380.
[88] *SW,* Vol. 6, p. 182.

post - partition years from 1947 to 1952 were his, as also Indian nationalism's, finest hour. The bitterness of the partition riots, the forcible exchange of populations between India and Pakistan, the continuous flow of refugees from East Pakistan (East Bengal), the invasion of Kashmir and the continuous anti-India hate campaign in Pakistan were daily vitiating and poisoning the atmosphere. Even sane, secular and decent persons were falling prey to communalism. A rising crescendo of voices was demanding that India do to Muslims in India what Pakistan was doing to Hindus. Rising to his full height as a secular nationalist and humanist, Jawaharlal Nehru stood like a rock in opposition to communal propaganda and in defence of the basic values of India's freedom struggle.

Nehru refused to countenance any excuses of communal violence including that of retaliation against the happenings in Pakistan. He again and again reminded the people of the Congress's commitment to secularism as a value on which there could be no compromise. "It is always a dangerous thing", he wrote in December 1948, "to compromise with something that is definitely evil. The RSS movement is directly aimed at everything that nationalist India has stood for".[89] And again in May 1950: "For all of us in India, and more especially Congressmen and Congresswomen, this issue of communal unity and a secular State must be made perfectly clear. ... (This is) a question having first priority and as something which has been the very basis and foundation of our struggle for freedom. There can be no compromise on this issue, for any compromise can only mean a surrender of our principles and a betrayal of the cause of India's freedom."[90]

Nehru was very clear in his mind that secularism meant giving full protection to the minorities and removing their fears. During the 1930s he, along with Gandhiji, argued that Hindus, as the religious majority, should adopt a generous approach towards the safeguards that the Muslim communalists demanded so that the fear of Hindu domination might be removed from the minds of Muslims. After 1947, he repeatedly asserted that the nation must give every protection to the minorities and produce "the sense of absolute security" in their minds. At the same time, while removing all possible grievances of the minorities, Nehru was opposed to giving any quarter to minority communalism. He branded Muslim and Sikh communalisms also as a variety of fascism which should not be encouraged in any way.

---

[89] *LCM,* Vol. J, pp. 251-2.

[90] *Ibid.,* Vol. II, p. 84.

However, Nehru's approach to the communal problem suffered from a few major weaknesses. He failed to devise institutional means or to use the Congress as a vehicle for taking his understanding of and approach towards communalism to the mass of the Indian people. During 1933-37, he carried on a vast ideological campaign against communalism in his widely distributed articles. But this campaign was increasingly muted after 1937.

After independence too, once the impact of the partition and Gandhiji's assassination faded, Nehru became complacent about the communal problem, especially the spread of communal ideology in quiet and subtle ways. In the euphoria of the Second and Third 5-Year Plans, there developed a tendency to ignore communalism. On the other hand, the Congress increasingly compromised with Musiim communal leaders in order to use Muslims as its vote-bank. The story was repeated with the Sikh communalists in Punjab when more and more Akalis were incorporated in the Congress organization itself.

Nehru was also not able to give adequate organizational backing to his commitment and political vision. As Congress President during 1936-37 and as the tallest nationalist leader after Gandhiji during the 1930s and 1940s, he received regular reports from the rank and file Congressmen that many in the Congress at lower levels were holding communal views and maintaining links with communal or communal-type organizations. In fact, in his *Autobiography* he went so far as to suggest that "many a Congressman was a communalist under his national cloak".[91] Yet, he took hardly any organizational steps to clear the Congress of such elements. After 1947 he took note of the existence of communal-minded persons within the Congress organization. But he, again, did very little about it.

As the executive head of the Indian Government, Nehru felt the need for strong administrative steps against virulent communal propaganda and, in particular, in the case of communal riots. He advised his Chief Ministers to take immediate action against those, including newspapers and their editors, who fostered communal hatred and gave currency to rumours and vague allegations. He was aware that strong administrative steps were needed in case of a riot situation and that a great deal depended on the action or inaction of the District Magistrate or the Superintendent of Police. He therefore advised the Chief Ministers that "it would be a safe policy to put a black mark in the record of every district officer when a communal incident takes place and to inform him of this", "The best of

[91] Jawaharlal Nehru, *An Autobiography*, p. 136.

excuses", he added, should not be accepted in this respect."[92] Moreover, in case of a riot, not only proper compensation should be paid to the victims and the victims fully rehabilitated, but "it is essential also that the guilty should be punished and should be made to feel that it does not pay to create disturbance and to loot and kill".[93]

Yet, hardly any organizer or perpetrator of communal riots was punished during the 1950s and 1960s. The communal minded officials felt no fear that their communalism, especially if it was covert, would stand in the way of their promotion, not to speak of continuation in service. Virulent communal propaganda flourished with impunity.

Above all, Nehru suffered from certain economistic, deterministic and reductionist biases in his treatment of the communal question which led him, in practice, to underplay the role of political-ideological struggle against communalism. Before 1947, he believed that if economic issues were brought to the forefornt, if mass struggles were organised around economic issues, if the anti-imperialist struggle was sharpened, the consciousness of the masses would, on its own, get divested of communalism—communal consciousness would be automatically dissolved as people would come to acquire national and/or class consciousness. Nehru continued this economistic and reductionist approach after independence. He now expected that economic development and spread of education, science and technology would automatically weaken and extinguish communal and casteist thinking. Little attention, for example, was paid to the content of education. After all the spread of education could be a powerful instrument for the spread of communal and communal type ideologies if its content was communal, casteist, chauvinist, or regionalist. Nor was any effort made to take science and scientific approach to the mass of people.

As summing up of this aspect, we may say that Jawaharlal Nehru played a major role in the 1930s and 1940s in keeping the national movement on sturdy secular rails. Even though Indian secularism failed to prevent partition of the land, but its success, under very difficult conditions, in framing a secular Constitution and laying the foundations of a secular state and society, owes a great deal to Nehru. He helped secularism acquire deep roots among Indian people; and he prevented the burgeoning forth of communalism when conditions were favourable to it. But space still remained for communalism.

[92]*LCM.* Vol. II"p. 213.

[93]*Ibid.,* p. 42. 34

V

Jawaharlal Nehru's commitment to democracy and civil liberties was total. He had a profound faith in democracy and democratic processes. To him, democracy and civil liberties were absolute values, ends in themselves-and not merely means for bringing about social change and social development. For example, referring to the question of subordinating democracy to planning, economic development and social justice, Nehru said in 1956: "If the democratic framework is subordinated to something else, it really means that the democratic framework is given up to that extent. I do not see any possibility, nor do I consider it desirable, to give up that democratic framework."[94] In 1963, referring to reverses in the India-China War of 1962, he criticized the role of large-scale criticism in the Press and Parliament in weakening the military effort. But that, he said, "is the price one has to pay for the institutions of parliamentary democracy." The system had its weaknesses but that did not mean that it should be given up or even restricted. "I would not," he declared, "give up the democratic system for anything."[95]

Before 1947, Nehru was a passionate defender of the freedom of thought and expression in general, and the freedom of the Press in particular. He saw democracy as a pillar of the national movement and civil liberty as one of its basic commitments.

This is one field where, judging as a whole, Nehru kept his promise with the freedom struggle. He helped root in the country parliamentary democracy based on adult franchise. Even though enjoying unprecedented popularity and political power, he did not fall prey to populism or plebiscitary democracy. Instead he used his power and popularity to strengthen the democratic process and civil liberties and libertarian tradition. He helped frame a democratic constitution with basic civil liberties enshrined in it. He nurtured the independence of the courts, even when they turned in a very conservative manner against his agrarian legislation. He treated the Parliament with respect and tried to make it a major forum for expression of public opinion as also "an important sector in the public life of the country." He saw to it that the cabinet system functioned effectively. He fought the tendency among many of his colleagues to leave all policy-making to him; but he also insisted that no

[94] Tibor Mende, *op.cit.*, p. 109.

[95] R.K. Karanjia, *The Philosophy of Mr. Nehru*, p. 123.

major policy be framed without reference to him. He gave full play and respect to the opposition. He once defined democracy as follows: "In the ultimate analysis, it is a manner of thinking, a manner of action, a manner of behaviour to your neighbour and to your adversary and opponent."[96]

Under extremely difficult conditions, he tried to protect civil liberties after 1947. In 1948, he did his best to prevent the banning of the Communist. Party in Bengal and Madras till proof of the violent activities not of individual communists but the party as a whole was furnished. He got the communist detenus released and legalized the Communist Party at the first opportunity, as soon as he was assured that the party had turned away form violence to peaceful politics. In 1951, "The Home Ministry shocked Nehru by directing the police to keep a careful watch over schools and colleges, arranging for lectures against communism, and asking guardians to give undertakings that their children would not take part in politics." Nehru immediately protested to C. Rajagopalachari, the Home Minister, and when, in 1951, Rajagopalachari expressed a desire to leave Delhi for Madras, Nehru quietly accepted his resignation.[97] Nehru did introduce preventive detention to deal with those who were spreading communal animosity or advocating and practising violence, but he insisted that "detention should be for short periods, and never longer than necessary".[98] Nehru even found time to chide the Chief Minister of Bombay for arresting a man and a woman for kissing in public.

The one aberration, the one blot on his record, was the dismissal of the Kerala Government in 1959. But the issue was not so simple as is believed to be. Dealing with it at length would take too much time, and I would therefore leave it at that.

Nehru's commitment to democracy was rooted in his deep and unqualified faith and confidence in the Indian people. "That is enough religion for me," he once declared.[99] He was willing to back fully "the free market of ideas" because he believed that in the long-run people could discriminate between ideas, and that their incapacity to read and write was no barrier to political literacy. His own experience of addressing them had convinced him of this. "After all, the average audience in India is an intelligent, sensible, rational audience".[100] It might be necessary for the

[96]Quoted in S. Gopal, *op. cit.,* Vol. Three, p. 65.
[97]*Ibid.,* Vol. Two, p. 157.
[98]*Ibid.,* p. 302.
[99]Quoted in *ibid.,* Vol. Three, p. 170.
[100]R.K. Karanjia, *The Mind of Mr. Nehru,* p. 61.

democratic leadership to educate and train the people to understand their interests and to support and fight for the necessary social and economic changes. But Nehru had no doubt this could be done.

His model of bringing about social change was based on the efficient functioning of democracy. Within the democratic framework one could go far, he believed.[101] People, he believed, would use elections and other forms of democracy to put pressure on the political leadership to take steps towards equality and social justice, leading gradually, over time, to socialism. This is one reason why he placed so much emphasis on elections, community development projects, panchayati raj and co-operatives. Elections were seen by him not only as expressions of popular will and popular control but even more as means of mass democratic education. Decentralization of all kinds of power was, in fact, a basic part of his conception of democracy, for that alone would enable the common people to have an equal share in power. Undoubtedly, he said, planning and modern technology required centralization; but precisely for that reason if was necessary to balance the needed centralization with the dispersal and decentralization of power wherever possible. And he wanted to balance the centralization of power by its dispersal through co-operative institutions in agriculture, industry and trade and through the promotion of village and other small scale industry.

Building people's power was a slow process but Jawaharlal hoped that the process would develop over time-and that this would be building an independent economy, the democratic system, and socialism on a sure basis. Consequently, democracy was also, despite its many weaknesses, seen by Nehru as a source of strength of "permanent and durable strength", to his programme and policies. "It is the only insurance of the continuity of our national policies against reaction," he said in 1960.[102] And again, "once the people are given a proper democratic base or moorings, it should be difficult for the mass of the people to be diverted or reversed."[103]

Democracy was also, in Nehru's conception, linked to the unity of the country. One reason why India must follow a peaceful or non-violent, democratic way of life and politics was because of India's being a fractured and diverse society. India could not be held together by any kind of force, coercion or violence. "In India today, any reversal of democratic

[101]Tibor Menede, *op. cit.,* p. 109.

[102]R.K. Karanjia, *The Mind of Mr. Nehru,* p. 62.

[103]*Ibid.,* p. 67.

methods might lead to disruption and violence," he said in 1960.[104] India could only be held together by a democratic structure with full freedom to the diverse socio-economic, cultural and political trends to express themselves. Just before his death, he said in 1964: "One should not mistake gentleness and civility of character for weakness. They criticize me for my weaknesses, but this is too large a country with too many legitimate diversities to permit any so-called 'strong man' to trample over people and their ideas".[105]

Nehru was aware of the novelty and unprecedented character of his effort to develop economically with democracy. Nobody had done this so far. All other nations and societies had used authoritarian political and administrative structures during the period of their take-off or primitive capital accumulation. Some have argued that this was an 'impossible' task, "an anti-historical effort". And only a leadership with a deep faith in the Indian people and in democracy could have attempted it—and resisted the temptation to first develop and then enjoy the 'luxury' of democracy. In fact, Nehru was standing in frontal opposition to the right-wing and left-wing versions of the notorious semi-racist rice-bowl theory—that the poor need rice more than they need democracy and civil liberties.

Nehru was, of course, aware that democracy enabled him and the Indian state to face the world with a certain political strength, for it indicated that the people of India were behind the state and the government.

Democracy had, of course, its pitfalls. As many economists would agree, it has made capital accumulation difficult. The rich agriculturists cannot be taxed and the tax evaders cannot be properly tackled. It is also not easy to resist various interest groups. But, undoubtedly, apart from its own value, it has helped preserve India's independence and the fear of the people has kept the men and women at the top from inviting foreign capital to move in a big way. Democracy also, as Nehru rightly believed, makes it easier to politically educate and mobilize the people.

In this context, I must also refer to Nehru's contribution to the tradition of intellectual inquiry and free discussion and debate among the intelligentsia. The foundations of the Indian national movement were laid by the Moderates on the basis of hard intellectual effort. It was Nehru who revived this tradition in the 1930s when he insisted on raising and debating

---

[104] *Ibid.*, p. 48.

[105] R.K. Karanjia, *The Philosophy of Mr. Nehru*, p. 139.

the basic issues regarding the social base and social content and the ideological framework of the movement as also the social contours of independent India. Apart from Gandhiji, he is the only major nationalist leader after the Moderates who made a massive intellectual contribution at the level of ideas. He also pointed to the crucial role that intelligentsia had to play in the freedom struggle and development of independent India; and he continued to stress this role after he became the Prime Minister. He involved numerous Indian and foreign economists in the drawing up of the Second and the Third Five Year Plans. In a speech made in the early 1950s at the inauguration of the new building of the Delhi School of Economics, brushing aside speeches in his praise, Nehru said something like this (there is no record and I am basing myself on memory): "Distinguished economists, I don't want you to tell me what great things I have done. I want you to tell me, to explain to me how is it that I am a socialist and am the Prime Minister and am trying to build socialism - but the capitalists are one section of society which is prospering."

We must also remember that all his life he opposed dogma and dogmatic mentality. This was a major objection of his to religion and a major ground for favouring scientific temper and outlook towards life and problems. As he wrote several times, Marxism appealed to him precisely because it was scientific and opposed to all dogma. This explains why he was impatient with certain types of Marxists who treated Marxism itself as a sort of dogma.

While, positively, this rooting of democracy and liberty in India is another of Nehru's achievements, negatively he had, as he put it, "a revulsion against all that smacks of a dictatorship, regimentation and authoritarianism". This sense of revulsion he helped impart to the Indian people and Indian intelligentsia. This is one reason why the Emergency of 1975-77 could not last for very long in India.

VI

Nehru did not devote much time and effort to social reform in the narrower sense of the term. In fact, during the 1930s, as a new convert to Marxism, he had even given way to a certain economistic bias and reductionism and held aloof from, and even disdained, Gandhian anti-untouchability campaign: But he was, all the while, opposed to all social conservatism. And after 1947, he regularly emphasized the necessity of bringing about changes in the social sphere along with economic and political changes. One of his greatest achievements as a Prime Minister was the passage of the Hindu Code Bill introducing monogamy and the right of divorce to women on an equal basis with men, and giving women the equal right of inheritance. Another of his achievements was the care with which he promoted education among girls and public employment of middle class women.

VII

Jawaharlal Nehru's commitment to socialism continued after independence. He kept up the campaign for the spread of the socialist ideas and set up the aim of fundamental transformation of Indian society in a socialist direction. He defined Indian politics in terms of social change. In 1955, at Avadi, the Congress, under his leadership, adopted the goal of the establishment of a "socialistic pattern of society". The goal was redefined as socialism at Nagpur in 1959 and was even more rigorously asserted at Bhubaneshwar in 1964. Throughout, from 1947 to 1964, Nehru shifted leftwards ideologically—and this despite the trauma of the India-China War of 1962.

Even when he could not build socialism, it was Nehru, above all, who carried the socialist vision to millions and thus made socialism a part of the consciousness of the Indian people. If socialism is today still the most respected idea—the hegemonic idea—in the minds of the Indian people (in fact India is the only non-socialist country today about which this can be said) it is largely because of Nehru. This achievement was all the greater because he was virtually left all alone when the CPI and the CSP-his closest ideological comrades during the 1930s and 1940s-had left his side. He was left with the right wing, the centre and the left of the centre of the National Congress. He could have left with the two left-wing parties and practised the politics of futility, become marginalised like them and left the field open to the right. The left wing would have been left with little political space to work in as also perhaps little civil liberty. He preferred to fight for the soul and support of the people, constantly trying to keep down the right, pulling the centre to the left and harnessing whatever left individuals were still there. He could not do the same for the communists since for most of the Nehru period they believed him to be subservient to British and American imperialism.

But what did happen actually? All the time bourgeois or capitalist social and economic order continued to develop and there was intensification of inequality. In the rural sector, power was devolved to the rich peasants, capitalist farmers, landlords and other dominant groups and individuals. In the urban sector, the capitalists, industrialists, and traders became stronger economically and socially as well as politically. Nehru accepted that the existing structure was capitalistic and that the capitalists were growing with the covert aid of the administrative machinery. He only hoped that the socialist process was also being initiated. By the 1970s, nearly 40 percent Indians were still living below the poverty line. Nor were other indicators of progress such as literacy, infant mortality, and supply of drinking water very encouraging. The lineaments of socialism that Nehru was projecting were also not very clear.

In terms of the actual goal of building socialism or laying the foundations of a socialist society, Nehru was a distinct failure. But why did he fail and can we, that is those interested in a socialist India, learn anything from his attempt? I believe that Nehru as a leader of the national liberation struggle was a success even though he was basically acting without theory. (As I have pointed out, he rightly confined his earlier Stalin-Marxism to the realm of pure theory and did not let it influence his political practice in any basic manner; and later he dissociated himself from this theoretical framework.) But his political practice remained sound, despite lack of guidance from theory or a theoretical paradigm, because he had Gandhian leadership and strategic paradigm to rely upon. Therefore, absence of theory did not lead to pragmatism. But, as we have already seen, the situation after 1947 was different. Gandhiji left no practice or paradigm for the construction of a socialist society. Stalin-Marxism had also no adequate model—its only model was the replication of the October or the Chinese Revolution. Nor could Nehru develop a fresh Marxian paradigm for he was already on the way to giving up the Marxism he knew. Initially, he took recourse to pure pragmatism and tried to raise lack of theory itself to a theoretical pedestal. But pure pragmatism was bound to flounder. However, Nehru soon began to grapple with the problems of building socialism in an under-developed country with a democratic polity. He increasingly tried to apply different elements of Gandhian paradigm or strategy to the strategic task of the building of socialism and made many innovations. In the process, he claimed that he was clear that he was not giving up the essentials or basic principles of socialism but compromising only on the inessentials. I may even suggest that while no complete Nehruvian paradigm came into existence, elements of an alternative Gandhi-Nehru strategy or paradigm did evolve over time, and despite the fact that Nehru's overall socialist design did not succeed, these elements of the Gandhi-Nehru strategy are worth detailed analysis, for they may have something to contribute to the struggle for socialist transformation today. More, if the struggle for socialist transformation in India and other democracies is not going to be a revolutionary event, an October Revolution or Chinese armed struggle, that is, a war of manouevre, but is likely to be a war of position in Gramscian terms, then the elements of the Gandhi-Nehru strategy are likely to form, in a modified form, some of the necessary building blocks of any alternative strategy of the struggle for socialism. I may point out that apart form the Gandhian influence, Nehru's ideas of how to build socialism were also profoundly influenced by his personal experience of the national movement and his critical study of the strengths and weaknesses of the Soviet experiment. He was convinced that no people living under a democratic regime would agree to pay the sort of price that the Soviet regime had exacted from its people. A democratic regime trying to follow Soviet policies would soon be defeated.

(i) First of all, in Indian conditions, Nehru saw socialist transformation as a process and not as an event. It was to be seen in terms of continuity. There was to be no sudden break, but gradual change—the pace of change need not be slow, in fact it should be quite rapid; but it also depended on the people themselves. Talking to Tibor Mende in 1956, Nehru said: "I think that the process of change in India can be peaceful and continuous; provided it is not too slow. That is, there is always a kind of conflict. There are two forces at work; the urge to change, and the other, rather conservative, the urge to continuity. Both are always at work in every country. A complete break means break with the past, with your past culture, with everything. Well, essentially a country does not do that. Even after a revolution, it comes back to its past. If, however, the process of change is stopped, if there is too much static continuity, then there is a tendency to break. So, it is the question of balancing the two forces."[106]

(ii) Nehru also seemed to be viewing socialist transformation in terms of a series of reforms, that is within the orbit of existing structures, which will over time, in their totality, amount to a revolution or, as he put it, "surgical operations". Revolution could be a series of "surgical operations" or reforms enacted through the due process of law by a democratic legislature.[107] Referring to the Gandhian strategy of social change, Nehru said in 1960: "Gandhiji always sought to function within

[106]Tibor Mende, *op. cit.*, pp. 49-50.

[107]*Ibid.*, p. 56.

the social fabric in which the masses had been living for centuries and tried to bring about gradual but revolutionary changes, instead of destroying the fabric or uprooting the people from their soil. He insisted on continuity with the past, and he accepted the existing social system as a base for his political and social strategy."[108] Nehru gave the example of Gandhiji's strategy in dealing with the caste system. "He sought the weakest point in the armoury of the caste structure—that is, Untouchability—and by undermining and dynamiting it, he shook the whole fabric without the people realising the earthquake he had unleashed. In this way, Gandhiji introduced new and revolutionary processes in the mass mind and brought about mighty social changes".[109] Socialist transformation might also be seen as a series of compromises in an upward spiralling form provided a compromise was not made on the basic principle and it went "in the right direction."[110]

(iii) Nehru believed that civil liberty and democracy were basic to socialism. In fact the two were inseparable. Democracy was essential for socialism and there could be no real democracy without socialism. This was Nehru's position even before independence. It was more firmly asserted after independence. So close was the integration of the two in his approach that he often described socialism as economic democracy. He quite often talked of following a third way between capitalist development of the West and the socialist development of the past and of reconciling the rival ideologies. But it is important to remember that the two constituents he wanted to incorporate from the two ways were political democracy from the West and economic structure or economic democracy from the East. He defined this third way as "socialism by democratic consent".[111] Just as his objection to capitalist democracies related to the economic structure that led to the supremacy of the profit motive, acquisitive mentality, economic inequality and growth of monopolies and economic concentration, one of the two grounds on which he differed from communism as practised in the Soviet Union was absence of democracy and civil liberty—the second being recourse to and emphasis on violence. Even Marx, he said, put so much emphasis on revolutionary violence because of the absence of a democratic structure of the state in his life time.

[108]R.K. Karanjia, *The Mind of Mr. Nehru,* p. 22.

[109]*Ibid.*

[110]Tibor Mende, *op. cit.,* pp. 104, 30.

[111]R.K. Karanjia, *The Philosophy of Mr. Nehru,* p. 44.

Democracy was not just a question of a formal parliamentary system based on adult franchise; though it was that too. But, basically, it was a question of firmly believing that people must decide, of having faith in the people, and of the need for helping the people understand their real interests and changes in the desired direction. But changes could only be made to the extent the people changed, though one had to have fun faith in their capacity to change. Democracy, asserted Nehru, was not a barrier to social change, only it required recourse to different methods. Once people made up their mind to change society, they could do so according to their wishes. Nehru believed that the people could use the democratic system to generate political pressures to achieve their socialist objectives. Rather, elections and voting rights and the panchayati raj would gradually mobilize the people to exert such pressure from below, compelling the political party in power either to make the necessary changes or get swept away. The vote would build up mass consciousness and force the masses to organize themselves. The poor would use their votes to force the vested interests to accept step by step economic democracy and socialism. "The superior numbers of the poor" would get converted "into a powerful political resource" for the introduction of socialism. The process would take time, that is why socialism as such could not be ushered in here and now. But the process would occur—there could be no doubt about that. Nehru hoped to further push the process by making institutional changes, mainly in the direction of devolving and decentralizing democratic power through panchayats, zilla parishads, etc. These institutions would enable the rural poor to mobilize themselves, and "to organize effective pressure" for social change, to get social justice in the interim, and in general tilt the balance of political and social power in their own favour.[112]

Democracy also, of course, implied building socialism through an electoral majority. There could be no revolution through a determined minority performing "the 'surgical operation' against the inert majority" so far as an adult franchise democracy was concerned.[113] Socialism would come only when the majority wanted it and willed it.

(iv) But the issue went far deeper than the mere majority principle whether among the people or in the legislature. The most important aspect of Nehru's strategy, the core of his strategy, was the belief that virtually the

[112]Francine R. Frankel, *India's Political Economy 1947-1977,* Princeton, 1978, pp. xiii, 25-6.

[113]Tibor Mende, *op. cit.,* p. 57.

entire people should be carried behind them by the socialist forces, that socialist transformation required a societal consensus or the consent of the overwhelming majority of the people. We may describe this as the strategy of socialism by the 95 per cent. Even in the 1930s, Nehru had argued that socialism would be established in India only with the desire and support of the vast majority of the people. After 1947 he emphasized the need to carry all shades of public opinion and the overwhelming majority of the people with him. As he told Tibor Mende in 1956: "One has to carry people with one".[114] And again, making the issue clearer still: "When you talk about legislative changes in a democracy, you necessarily take into consideration the fact that the people have been brought up to the required level".[115] They must be willing to "accept changes".[116] Parliament could, of course, legislate a measure but it was far more important that "a very large section of the people must also accept it—or, at any rate, actively or passively, be ready to accept it.... In other words, the Government and Parliament must have, by and large, the people at their back. The people must have faith in the *bona fides* of the Government".[117] This was also the lesson of the freedom struggle. It was, then, better to push the entire Congress left than to rely on the politics of a handful of pure revolutionaries. Gandhiji had insisted on taking the millions, "the whole mass", with him and not relying upon the conversion of "a small, select group". So also today, said Nehru, Congress "does not concern itself with a few believers but rather with the mass of the people". In fact, Nehru believed, a leader could not afford to divorce himself from the mass of the people. "He may be at some distance, pushing or pulling them. But if he divorces himself, well ... he may be a great man, but he is not a leader".[118] During the freedom struggle, the choice of relying on the millions was made as a strategic choice. In an authoritarian regime a majority might acquiesce in a minority acting on its behalf. In a democracy, the majority knows that it can speak and act for itself. It will not accept a minority acting on its behalf. The majority then becomes open to being mobilized by the counter-revolution.

---

[114] *Ibid.*, p. 37.

[115] *Ibid.*, p. 105.

[116] *Ibid.*, p. 108.

[117] *Ibid.*, p. 105.

[118] *Ibid.*, p. 30.

Nehru was convinced that the existing balance of socio-political forces did not favour rapid introduction of socialist measures. He therefore worked *within* the limits of existing balance in favour of the poor and radical social change. He tried to do so to some extent through legislation or administrative measures, but he relied primarily on educating and changing public opinion. And, as pointed out earlier, he relied a great deal on the processes unleashed by adult franchise, spread of education, and panchayti raj and co-operative institutions to perform the task.

If socialism was to come through the active or passive support of the 95 per cent, then there could be no sharp break. To quote him: Socialist transformation had to be "a long term strategy.... You can't make millions of people suddenly think differently and uproot them from a social fabric to which they have been accustomed for hundreds or thousand of years".[119] The process might also, then, have to be slowed down. But not only because it would take time to cow down the vested interests, but even more because it would take time to win the active or passive consent of the 95 per cent of the people. (It may be pointed out, parenthetically, that this notion was opposite of the belief that the mass of the people are, because of poverty, exploitation, and oppression, ever ready to make revolution). Let me once again quote Nehru: "Gandhiji believed in the complete identification of the leadership with the masses, even if that meant falling behind somewhat and slowing down the pace of progress so as to carry the whole people forward with him."[120]

Nehru also visualized that the strategy of relying upon the whole people would also reduce the hostility of the dominant, propertied classes who would, on the one hand, be faced with the will of the people, and, on the other hand, not be threatened with total destruction. If they were pressed in a gradual manner, Nehru believed, they could be made to consent to social changes which otherwise went against their interests. One of the friendly acts could be payment of compensation for the nationalization of their properties. Princes and zamindars had already accepted the extinction of their position in a peaceful manner. The private sector could also be made to do the same, if similar tactics were followed against them. This notion that vested interests could be made to change, however reluctantly, was an important element in Nehru's strategy for social change.

---

[119] *Ibid.*, p. 29.

[120] R.K. Karanjia, *The Mind of Mr. Nehru,* p. 22.

(v) In a way, Nehru also moved, though rather incoherently, towards the role of hegemonic struggle as against coercion. Earlier he had believed that ultimately coercion would have to be used to dethrone the ruling classes. "Ruling powers and ruling classes", he had written in 1936, "have not been known in history to abdicate willingly".[121] "A measure of coercion" would have to be used to force them to give up their power and class privileges, he had concluded.[122]

And this is the area of major Gandhian influence. Earlier, he had believed in non-violence as a matter of policy, now he believed in it as a matter of principle. He came to believe that a socialist pattern of society could be established through non-violent and peaceful means. Nehru still believed that class struggle existed and had to be resolved. But he no longer believed that it could be resolved only through violence and forcible methods. He now believed that it could be resolved without use of force, peacefully, through democratic methods, since peaceful pressure exercised by the overwhelming majority of the people, and a friendly approach could be effective. The vested interests might not co-operate, they would then have to be removed. But this could be and had to be done in a peaceful and democratic way. He also still favoured trade unions and working class movements and the right of the people to protest and agitate and to go on strike. But all this must follow a peaceful non-violent course.

This is one of the major areas where Nehru came to distinguish the Gandhi-Nehru strategy from the Communist strategy. Let me quote his letter of 15 August 1957 to the Chief Ministers at length: "Contemporaneously with Gandhi's movement came the Soviet Revolution with its Marxist ideology and its stress on class struggle and violence. So far as ideals were concerned, there was perhaps no marked conflict in the ends to be reached between these two methods, although obviously there were many differences. But the basic difference was in the methods to be adopted and the psychology to be created. One was of peace and avoidance of hatred and violence, the other was full of class conflict and hatred and violence. Both ultimately wanted to do away with the domination of one class over another and thus to do away with classes. It was obvious that in the existing social framework class conflict was inherent. But the way to deal with it and ultimately to put an end to it was vastly different".[123] Similarly, in 1964, he told R.K. Karanjia: "Now

[121] Jawaharlal Nehru, A *Bunch of Old Letters,* Bombay, 1958, p. 142.

[122] *SW,* Vol. 6, pp. 24-6.

[123] *LCM,* Vol. IV, p. 535.

between the parties of the Right and the Left, as you differentiate them, I would always prefer a party with some ideology built round social and economic thinking. You mentioned the communists. The communists, with all their faults, function in terms of serious economic solutions. What we repudiate is all the dogma and violence of their approach. If they can divest themselves of this obsession and accept the discipline of our parliamentary democracy in good faith, there is not much difference between their goal of socialism and ours". Inter, estingly, he also added: "The other parties you mention, like the Jan Sangh and Swatantra, seem to be organized around plainly fascist and feudal concepts without any social or economic basis. As such, they are dangerous to the country and our values of democracy and socialism".[124]

(vi) One other major area of congruence between Nehru and Gandhiji was that of relationship between means and ends. Earlier even while admiring Gandhiji for the purity of his means, Nehru had emphasised the social determination of ethical standards and values and had argued that while an individual should act up to the highest moral standards, in general social relations had to be changed so that ethical values could be practised and could prevail. In *The Discovery of India* he had also given expression to the dilemma that a person of action faces in this respect: "Ends and means: Were they tied up inseparably ...? But the right means might well be beyond the capacity of infirm and selfish human nature. What then was one to do? Not to act was a complete confession of failure and a submission to evil; to act meant often enough a compromise with some form of that evil, with all the untoward consequences that such compromises result in".[125] After 1947, and with the passing of years, he adopted a more fundamentalist position on the question. He began to stress that in building a socialist India as much importance should be attached to the means as to the end. Agreeing now more fully with Gandhiji, he said that wrong means would not lead to right results. Already, in 1949, he declared: "I think also that there is always a close and intimate relationship between the end we aim at and the means adopted to attain it. Even if the end is right but the means are wrong, it will vitiate the end or divert us in a wrong direction".[126] This belief in the inseparability of the means and the end was another reason why he gradually condemned

[124]R.K. Karanjia, *The Philosophy of Mr. Nehru,* pp. 159-60.

[125]Jawaharlal Nehru, *The Discovery of India,* Calcutta, 2nd ed., 1946, p. 10.

[126]Jawaharlal Nehru, *Speeches,* Vol. Two, p. 392.

all recourse to violence. And so he wrote to the Chief Ministers in October 1957: "It is more important to adopt the right way, to pursue the right means, than even to have the right objectives, important as that is. No method and no way which is bound up with the creation of hatred and conflict and which bases itself on violence, can ever yield right results, however good the motives, however good the objective".[127]

This was another ground on which he faulted the Indian Communists and the Communist societies. In fact the trials and killings in the Soviet Union during 1937-39 had had a powerful influence in pushing him towards the Gandhian position in this respect.

(vii) Not only would Nehru not define socialism in clear ideological terms, he opposed any effort to do so. There could be "no rigid general principles". To try to do so was to be dogmatic. And so he talked about socialism in general terms: it meant social justice, it meant putting an end to social and economic inequality and disparities created by capitalism, it meant greater equality of opportunity for all, it meant opposing the acquisitive instinct and capitalist competitiveness, and promoting the co-operative tendency, it meant rapid economic development so that all could have access to primary necessities of life, it. meant gradual ending of class distinctions and class domination, it meant complete public ownership or control over the means of production.

But, immediately, socialism meant an economic policy. And what was the economic policy? Here Nehru was less vague and more specific. India was to have a mixed economy as a transitional stage for a long time. Socialism meant first of all planning. Then, it meant that the state was to own and start all basic and strategic industries. The public sector was to grow progressively both in trade and industry till it dominated the economic scene. Within the broad framework of planning, private enterprise was to function for a long time to come. Agriculture and small scale industries would remain in the private sector. It would gradually be squeezed out of big industries, but in the meanwhile big industries would function under increasing government control. Economic concentration and monopoly capitalism would not be permitted, the co-operative principle would be encouraged all along the line. Efforts would be made to promote first service co-operatives and then co-operative farming in agriculture. One form that socialism would take was the organization of small and medium industries through co-operatives. In general, planning,

[127] *LCM*, Vol. IV, p. 585.

public sector, government control of private sector, state trading and co-operatives in agriculture and industry would be used to weaken reliance on the market forces and the profit motive.

(viii) All the elements of Nehru-Gandhi approach to social transformation—social transformation as a process, role of democracy and peaceful, non-violent means, the need to base the effort on the whole people, that is, 95 per cent of the people, hegemonic character of the struggle—had three other aspects, causes and consequences.

A. In the Indian conditions, the entire approach was closely related to the concept of nation-in-the-making and was seen to be necessary to avoid social and political disruption. Nehru was haunted by the ever present forces of disruption which always lay very close to the surface. Any appeal to violence would have unintended consequences and was likely to result not in a revolutionary change but the unleashing of disruptive forces, such as communalism, casteism, and provincialism, leading to national disintegration. Any hastening of change would divide the Indian people when their unity was both essential and fragile. Any clearly defined socialism would divide the socialist forces and further disintegrate the country. To quote him in 1963: "We have set before us certain values which belong to what might be called a national ideology. Within the framework of this ideology there exist, of course, differences—or, rather, *shades of differences.* One might be more passionately dedicated to socialism than another ... but our approach has always been one of *synthesis*. There cannot be any other approach for a government or a party representing a vast country of such diversities as India."[128] In other words, the doctrine of unity in diversity had to apply to the definition of socialism too. At the same time, the opposite was also true: "Our various differences and disruptive tendencies such as communalism, casteism and provincialism can only be countered effectively by this wider approach which leads to a socialist basis of society".[129]

B. Nehru never forgot one lesson of the 1930s: The fascist danger was always present and was not easy to stave off. "An attempt at premature leftism", he had written to Jayaprakash Narayan in 1948, "may well lead to reaction and disruption".[130] The middle strata in India were very large—and it was the middle strata who had formed the backbone of

[128]R. K. Karanjia, *The Philosophy of Mr. Nehru,* p. 138.

[129]*LCM.,* Vol. IV, pp. 101-2.

[130]Quoted in S. Gopal, *op. cit.,* Vol. Two, p. 67.

fascism in Europe. They had to be handled with care and caution. They should not go over to the other side. Any frontal attack on the propertied classes was likely to push the middle strata and the powerful propertied classes into a fascist position. Fascism had to be fought when it became necessary, but it was better not to let the threat mature. Any effort at making a minority revolution or when the overwhelming majority of people had not been won over was more likely to result in counter-revolution and the overthrow of democracy than in the coming of revolution. And I must say that events in Chile and Indonesia confirm this prognosis, just as the successful revolution in Nicaragua supports the strategy of relying on 95 per cent of the people.

C. There was one other major implication of Nehru's approach: once socialist transformation is seen as a process, it is not possible to have a clearly pre-defined pre-laid out socialist schema towards which the transformation process moves. Socialism then has to be a vision and not a clear-cut or neatly defined blueprint. The pattern of socialism would start taking shape only from stage to stage as the movement went along.

Similar was the logic of the idea that the socialist movement must win over the whole people, that is 95 per cent of the people. It is not possible to have such a broad movement with a 'structured' ideology except as a vision which gets defined only for the stage in view, which gets defined only to the extent to which one moves towards the necessary next steps. The movement cannot have an all-time programme waiting to be realized. It can only have "some broad objectives and methods"and within that framework its participants can differ and try to persuade each other of their points of view on specific issues. Any effort to have a more defined scheme would be harmful, for it would become a barrier or a constraint in mobilizing the 95 per cent and would tend to disrupt the unity of the broad movement. The 95 per cent can be mobilized only by uniting a diversity of interests and a multiplicity of views and ideological strands around a common vision or broad framework. In fact, going by the experience of the left-wing parties and movements in democratic countries, one may go further and say that even a bare majority—50 per cent—cannot be mobilized even electorally in any other manner. It is not accidental that no Communist Party, organized along Bolshevik lines, has come anywhere near a majority in a democracy in the last 70 years of the existence of Bolshevism on an international scale. Nor can CPI (M) be faulted for not abolishing the jotedari system (semi-feudal sharecropping system) in West Bengal despite its strong anti-feudal programmatic commitment or not repeating the 1957 Communist thrust in Kerala, for it is doing nothing but following the logic of pursuing a radical social transformational line in a parliamentary framework. (Where the CPI(M) can be faulted is for its refusal to adapt the theory embedded in its programme to suit its practice or to adopt radical and developmental policies suitable to the parliamentary framework and capable of being pursued in this framework out of the fear of losing political power, and .thus for falling prey to 'parliamentarianism' in the Marxist sense of the term, i.e., to parliamentary opportunism).

D. A critical weakness of Nehru's effort at socialist transformation flowed from non-adherence to the Gandhian strategy in one crucial aspect-that is , its emphasis on the mobilization of the masses and on the organization of mass struggles though non-violent in character. Moreover, Gandhiji's was a full war of position, and depended on hegemonising the entire society, including members of the state apparatuses, with the desired ideology and around the basic goal. Nehru had an overwhelming belief in spontaneity, in the poor mobilizing on their own in their own interests. He had this reductionist notion that the exercise of the vote will gradually educate the masses to vote in their own interests. He also had the 19th century liberal notion that his speeches would by themselves arouse and mobilize the people. But, in fact, all this required organization, mobilization, a party, however loosely structured, cadres, however democratically organized, and a minimum of ideology, however broad, non-dogmatic and open ended. Nor did Nehru, unlike Gandhiji, attack vigorously those aspects of the social structure, such as caste system, kinship networks, the economic dependence of the rural poor on the rural rich, and the growing corruption, which were bolstering the existing socio-economic system. Nehru made no attempt to hegemonise the state apparatuses with socialist or even secular and democratic ideology. He also went too far in stressing the role of consent and conversion of the dominant classes. Trusteeship theory had certainly been a weak point of Gandhiji, but it had been evolved in a specific historical context. At the same time Gandhiji had believed in organizing active struggle against the current targets of his politics whether they were the British, or the princes, or the orthodox among the upper castes. A major part of his strategy was to 'convert' them by isolating them from public opinion. Gandhiji, once he had decided that the stage had come to abolish landlordism or limit capitalism, would not have, I am sure, agreed with the manner Nehru implemented the class conciliation or class adjustment strategies.

E. These deficiencies, inherent in Nehru's individualistic style of functioning and the character of the Congress Party after independence, could have been made good by the left parties and groups outside the Congress. Unfortunately, both the Communists and the Socialists failed to grasp the nature of the Nehruvian effort and the different elements of his strategy. Instead of extending critical support to the positive parts of Nehru's efforts and strategy, even while organizing opposition and mass struggles against their negative parts, they adopted a hostile attitude towards Nehru and his policies, making a crude class-political analysis and basing their politics on the belief that Nehru was the political representative of the capitalists and landlords, if not also of the imperialists. Undoubtedly, Nehru shares some of the blame for his estrangement from the Communists, though not from the Socialists with whom he several times tried to unite. Going by the follies and behaviour of the Indian Communist leadership during the freedom struggle and immediately after (1948-55), and by the happenings in the socialist countries, he adopted a contemptuous and derisive attitude towards them. And when they, or at least most of them, began to change during the second half of the 1950s, he failed to extend a fraternal hand to them, perhaps believing that this change was just another political manoeuvre. And then in 1959 came the dismissal of the Kerala Ministry, the beginning of the India-China dispute and the India-China War and the chances of mutual appreciation and cooperation with the Communists became dim. In the process, both the Nehru model and the Communist movement were atrophied. Interestingly, Nehru did not let his aversion to many of the features of the Communist societies come in the way of the appreciation of their positive features or of adopting a genuinely friendly attitude towards them. Unfortunately, he let his personal and political experience of the Indian Communists, with whom he had been on very friendly terms during the 1930s, dictate his policy and attitude towards them even when they were beginning to mature and were one of the few political forces which could enable his model to realize whatever potentialities it had.

VIII

As I have already made it clear, Nehru's place in history is not determined by seeing him as a knight in pure white, a person without personal and political blemishes. His place is there despite these weaknesses, and we must see as also learn from these weaknesses as well.

Nehru had a high degree of administrative capacity as his role as UPCC President, All-India Congress President and AICC General Secretary, Chairman of Allahabad Municipal Committee and as Prime Minister for 18 years indicate. He also had a certain political skill—a good example being the way he dealt with Purushottam Das Tandon. But Nehru was no institution and organization creator or builder. He failed to build institutions and organizational structures to implement his vision or policies or to mobilize the people behind them. He created no social instruments. In general, there was a general weakness in execution of his policies and ideas. This was a major reason for the deficiencies in the implementation of land reforms, the Community Development Projects and in. the management of the public sector. In fact, the failure to evolve institutions and structures to implement his policies impaired his entire political and economic strategy.

Nehru completely neglected party building even after he acquired complete control over the Congress. He was, of course, never a party organizer. Earlier, before 1947, the task of building the pary and rearing the cadres of the movement was performed by Gandhiji, Sardar Patel, Rajendra Prasad, Maulana Abul Kalam Azad and others. On the left of the movement, the CPS, CPI, student and youth associations, etc., undertook the task. And so the deficiency was not felt; and Nehru could frankly acknowledge this weakness of his: "I function individually without any group or second person to support me," he told Subhas Bose in February 1939.[131] In fact, with others there to build and rear the party, this was not a disadvantage but an advantage, since it enabled him to devote his time to that which he did best-agitate among the people and educate and inspire them.

However, this feature became a serious flaw after independence, when Gandhiji and Patel died, Rajendra Prasad and Azad were incapacitated by health and office, and the left was standing in oppostion to him from outside the party. There was no force now to organize secular nationalist and socialist forces to back his policies. schemes and ideas, or even to popularize them. One of Nehru's major failures occurred in the field of the education of the masses as also the Congress members and cadres in the context of his strategic framework or the accepted Congress programme.

---

[131]Jawaharlal Nehru, *A Bunch of Old Letters,* p. 312.

This weakness also gradually led to the Congress Party weakening and losing its role as an instrument for social change or implementation of government policies or even education in the ideology that Nehru and the Congress leadership believed in. Nehru was to confess this in 1962: "We have failed in propagating nation-wide appreciation, of our socialist policies and plans in an effective manner. We have not been able to substitute old ways and superstitions with intelligent and rational comprehension of our new scientific and socialist approaches".[132]

The Congress Party also, in time, came to be dominated by state 'bosses'—e.g., S.K. Patil, C.B. Gupta, Atulya Ghosh, Kamaraj, R.S. Shukla—and its policies began to veer towards machine politics. This tendency was also encouraged by Nehru's democratic, federalist policy of not interfering with the elected State Governments or provincial Congress office-bearers or even, because of parliamentary tradition, with his Cabinet Ministers.

Nehru also frittered away one important heritage of the freedom struggle. As he repeatedly pointed out, Gandhiji's greatest achievement was the arousal of the people to politics and their active participation in the political processes. To put it bluntly, the Nehru period after 1947 witnessed the gradual political demobilization of the people. As we have seen, his own model of development and social change depended on active pressure from below by the deprived, the exploited and the dominated. Such mobilization of the people and their political activity would alone enable parliamentary democracy to serve as an instrument of social change and equity. But Nehru failed to create any institutions or structures or agents through which the people could be mobilized and activized, and politically educated.

Basically, the only form of mobilization was his extensive tours through which he communicated with the people, educated them and created popular support for his policies. Before 1947, the political fall-out of his tours had been harnessed by the local Congress committees and cadres of the left, right and centre. But after 1947, in the absence of any popular, lower level organization to develop the results of his tours, often the organizational benefits were reaped by the party bosses from the local to the state levels; and the educational consequences of his tours were seriously whittled down.

---

[132] R.K. Karanjia, *The Philosophy of Mr. Nehru,* p. 88.

Moreover, there was another flaw in this model of mass contact: it was a one-way street. He talked to the people, but there was no way people or their representatives could talk to him. There was no channel in that direction. To gauge public opinion, he had to rely primarily on his political instinct, which was, no doubt, highly developed in this sense and quite effective in practice. But it was still a retreat from Gandhiji who, despite even a sounder instinctive grasp of popular opinion, retained contact with thousands of lower level political workers through personal contact, correspondence and the columns of the *Young India* and the *Harijan.* After 1947, links between politics from below and the national leadership in power were gradually snapped as were the links between politics and social work. Parenthetically, it may be pointed out that Gandhiji had to a certain extent foreseen all this. He had felt that perhaps it was inevitable that a ruling party would, by its very nature, find it difficult to also act as an agent of mass mobilization and mass struggle. That is why he had suggested that while some Congressmen should run the administration, others should start a Lok Sevak Sangh both for mass mobilization and for carrying on constructive or social work through unofficial, voluntary channels.

A special case of this failure of Jawaharlal Nehru was that of his approach after 1947 to the idealistic youth and cadres of the national movement, most of whom, having joined the movement after 1927, were rather young. Nehru had now little to offer to them, as he had done in 1926-29 and 1936-39 or as Gandhiji had done ever since 1917, in the form of direct Congress work or Gandhian constructive work. These nationalist political workers or youth had no political work before them unless they joined politics of opposition or became the non-ideological cadres of the electoral machinery that the Congress was increasingly becoming. So far as Nehru was concerned, he had primarily one thing to offer them: join the civil service and other branches of administration.

Instead of the party cadres, Nehru increasingly relied on government administration and bureaucracy for nation-building. The youth of our generation were asked to serve the country by joining the bureaucracy. Furthermore, the administrative structure and bureaucracy remained unreformed and unreconstructed. (My objection is not to the continuation of bureaucracy. The type of total breaking up of bureaucracy that Lenin advocated in the *State and Revolution* did not take place even in the Soviet Union after the 1917 Revolution. It could not have occurred at all in a country like India.)

Nehru fully recognized that the administrative procedures inherited from the past were utterly inadequate for the new tasks. As he complained as early as 1951: "We rely more and more on official agencies which are generally fairly good, but which are completely different in outlook and execution from anything that draws popular enthusiasm to it".[133] Nehru was convinced that these administrative procedures and routines "should be changed radically". The administrative machinery could be overhauled in two ways, he said: "One, by educating the whole machine. Secondly, by putting a new type of person where it is needed."[134] He did neither of the two things. Rather, the new IAS was very much formed in the old ICS mould, starting with his or her recruitment and training in the IAS Academy. Those few who joined the Community Development Projects out of idealism and social commitment were soon frustrated to discover that they were being dominated, looked down upon, and treated as low-paid underlings by the traditional, higher bureaucrats.

As a political leader and nation-builder, Nehru suffered from another major weakness. He could set goals and objectives, he could formulate people's desires, he could inspire people with a vision, he was also an efficient political manager; but he lacked the capacity to design a strategic framework and devise tactical measures to achieve the goals set and the formed vision. While strongly opposed to political opportunism and manipulation, he could replace these only with *ad hoc* political and administrative measures. This often left the field to the manipulators. This weakness was heightened by the fact that Nehru was a poor judge of men and women.

Moreover, not only did forces of capitalism develop in industry, trade and agriculture and forces of landlordism survive in large areas, but their social and political weights grew and they gained larger and larger influence in the party and over the Government itself. To his credit. Nehru could see the process, but could do little to counter it. And so, acting as his own leader of opposition, Nehru observed and denounced the corruption, careerism and many other emerging ills of a developing ex-colonial society, but was unable, apart from exhortations, to take, or point to, the necessary concrete steps to combat them.

We may point to several large areas of neglect, among others, which have now assumed monstrous proportions.

---

[133]Quoted in S. Gopal, *op. cit.,* Vol. Two, pp. 158-9.

[134]Tibor Mende, *op. cit.,* pp. 54-5.

(i) Nehru was fully aware of the need for better and wider education as an instrument of both economic development and social change. But, not only illiteracy continued on a wide scale and not even 40 per cent of the eligible children went to school, the entire educational system was left untouched and unreformed and the quality of education that was imparted continued to deteriorate first in schools and then in colleges and universities. The ideological content of education continued to be the same as in the colonial period. For example, it continued to be an instrument for the spread of communalism. In addition, it now increasingly became an instrument for the spread of regional parochialism and chauvinism. Nor did commitment to socialism find any reflection in the economics curricula in schools, colleges and universities.

(ii) As seen earlier, no worthwhile political and ideological struggle was waged against communalism as an ideology.

(iii) The anti-zamindari land reforms were implemented in a manner so that, while the agrarian structure was transformed, the rural poor were left high and dry, leaving behind a legacy of economic inequality, social oppression and violence in rural India. The second stage of land reforms represented by land ceiling legislation was not implemented on the ground for years and was then given up. Two other weaknesses in the agrarian sector were the failure to prevent large scale ejection of tenants-at-will in both zarnindari and ryotwari areas, and the absence of any ameliorative, not to speak of radical, measures so far as the agricultural labourers, who constituted nearly 40 per cent of the rural population, were concerned. Near the end of his life, Nehru, of course, fully acknowledged this failure on the agrarian front. He traced the failure to achieve self-sufficiency in food production to "our failure to carry out land reforms, initiated earlier with the abolition of landlordism, to their logical conclusion... ". "This left our land reform programme well begun, but only half-finished ... today we are paying the price of our default", Nehru added. The remedy lay in implementing the Nagpur Congress Resolution of 1959 calling for "land ceilings, service co-operatives, joint cultivation and State trading in food grains, involving the removal of the middlemen between the State and the cultivator, among other things."[135]

(iv) The battle for socialism and equitable distribution was also getting lost by 1964; and Nehru again frankly accepted this. He told R.K. Karanjia in March 1964: "While industrial and agricultural production

[135] R.K. Karanjia, *The Philosophy of Mr. Nehru,* pp. 155-7.

has increased considerably, though not to the extent we had planned, the tendency has been towards the accumulation of the national wealth with people at the top-that is, the big businessman and the big farmer—and not towards its equitable distribution among the masses of the people. Thus the rich have grown richer. The poor have also gained, but proportionately less, much less, than the wealthier classes. In result, the gap between the 'haves' and the 'have-nots' has widened. To make things more difficult for the poor classes, there is the accumulation of an enormous amount of black money—that is, unaccounted wealth-in private hands by all means of corrupt practices. This creates an intolerable situation, both economically and from the moral point of view."[136]

(v) Corruption was all pervasive in certain departments of the colonial administration. But economic development and developmental functions of the Government opened up many more areas of administration and economy to corruption. Political patronage too was a relatively new field, especially in areas where before 1947 the Congress had been a predominant political force. There were major signals in the Nehru era that political and administrative corruption was beginning its march with hundred-league boots on; but Nehru ignored these signals and failed to squash this evil when it was still possible to do so with a certain ease. At the time, its tentacles were not so far reaching and major barriers to it existed in the form of a political leadership and cadres with their roots in the freedom struggle and Gandhian ethos, a basically honest bureaucracy, especially in its middle and higher reaches, and a judiciary with high integrity.

(vi) A major weakness lay in the realm of ideology and culture. Nearly 200 years of colonialism had also led to the colonialization of the ideology and culture of the Indian people, especially the middle and upper classes and the intelligentsia. For over 100 years, colonial ideology had been opposed in the economic, political and to a certain extent in the social and cultural fields. Still, in large areas of life, especially in the academia, and journalism, India was at the moment of freedom still an intellectual province of the imperialist metropolis. Moreover, the left suffered as much from it as the right. This intellectual compradorism, combined with the continued prevalence of 'feudal' ideology and culture in the realms of family, gender relations, and caste and other social relations, was a major road-block in the path of social transformation. Yet. even when some steps

[136] *Ibid.*, pp. 153-4.

were taken towards cultural and ideological liberation from 'feudalism', intellectual compradorism continued to prevail as before. True, bringing about ideological and cultural revolution or transformation is a long-term project; nor is the political leadership the main instrument for the purpose. But, then, Jawaharlal Nehru was, like Gandhiji, more than a political leader. And while he did oppose imperialism both in his economic and political practice as also in the realm of political and economic ideas, he did not discourage subtler forms of colonial ideological and cultural domination. Two examples readily come to mind, which would be perhaps minor in character in other cases, but for the fact of their being practised by a giant like Nehru whose smallest action or behaviour had wide impact. One was the perpetuation of much of the cultural practices and paraphernalia associated with the colonial political-administrative practices and rituals. The other was his habit of constantly citing foreign comments and commendations of his policies, pronouncements and practices.

IX

As we have seen, by any historical standards, Nehru's achievements were of gigantic proportions. Above all, he rooted certain basic values, approaches, objectives, outlook and goals in the country. He made them a part of the ethos of the Indian people. He consolidated the Indian nation, laid the foundations of a parliamentary democratic and civil libertarian political system, made secularism the basis of our national political system, adopted a foreign policy based on independence, nonalignment, world peace, and anti-colonialism, introduced planning, laid the foundation of a public sector which would occupy the commanding heights of the economy, set India on the road of self-reliant independent economy, and promoted a scientific outlook. He imparted a socialist vision to the people though he failed to prevent the growth of capitalism in industry, trade and agriculture. He initiated radical socio-economic transformation, though he failed to take the process very far. In the legal abolition of untouchability and the Hindu Code Bill he passed two historic measures.

No doubt there were also large areas of failure. Mass poverty, glaring inequality, persistence of the domination of the rural poor by the rich peasants, capitalist farmers and landlords, strengthening of capitalism along with the growth of big capital, the growth of corruption, the gradual erosion of traditional values and their replacement by the degenerate values of acquisitive capitalism. The poor peasants and agricultural labourers and the urban poor, though awakened, were still deprived of effective, day-to-day social, economic and political power. Their political self-activity was still dormant, they were still not a part of the coalition of capitalists, rich peasants and middle classes that ruled the country.

Nehru, of course, failed to build socialism, but there is no doubt that he evolved certain important elements of a socialist paradigm which any socialist movement would have to incorporate if it is to succeed in capturing power and then building socialism-socialism that has been dreamt of since the days of French Revolution, Robert Owen, Karl Marx and the great October Revolution.

It is moreover in the context of the reality of the backwardness of Indian society and Indian people that Nehru's life-work has to be evaluated. What Nehru wrote to Krishna Menon in 1936 is most relevant in this respect: "Try to imagine what the human material is in India—how they think, how they act, what moves them, what does not affect them. It is easy enough to take up a theoretically correct attitude which has little effect on anybody. We have to do something much more important and difficult and that is to move large numbers of people to make them act.[137]

Now that Nehru and the Nehru period are very fast receding into historical memory—only people who are. above forty would remember him as a person—we can take a more objective view of Nehru. People like me were harsh critics of Nehru when he was alive and active, partially because we wanted him to go farther and faster on his own road. But with hindsight and with the experience of nearly 25 years since he passed away, we can say that Nehru's life and work, his legacy, his social vision and his achievements are a source of great strength to us, the Indian people, in our endeavour to build a happier and healthier society and an independent, united, secular, democratic and socialist India, where caste, class and gender oppression will cease to exist.

[137] *SW,* Vol. 7, p. 471.

2

Nehru and Communalism

Jawaharlal Nehru was perhaps the first Indian to try to understand the broader social, economic and political dimensions and character and causation of communalism. This he did mainly during the 1930s. His was also one of the first efforts to apply a Marxist approach to the problem. He was, of course, throughout, especially after 1947, deeply influenced by the humanist and moral approach of Gandhiji.

From the outset of his political career in the early 1920s, Nehru was, like other nationalists, totally opposed to communalism. But this opposition did not go beyond a critique of communal riots and religious intolerance and bigotry, and of colonial authorities for trying to create communal division and conflict among Hindus and Muslims. His remedy for the communal problem also remained confined to the traditional nationalist 'Hindu-Muslim *bhai-bhai*' approach and appeals for Hindu-Muslim unity for the winning of Swaraj.[1] Criticism of communalism as ideology was missing at this stage. Thus, he dealt with communalism and communal riots the way Gandhiji did. In his political tours during 1928 and in his addresses to the youth and student conferences, he made communalism a major target. The rules of the Independence of India League, founded by Jawaharlal and others, barred a communalist or a member of a communal organization from becoming a member of the League.[2] However, from 1929 to 1933, Nehru was relatively quiet on the question mainly because of pre-occupation with the anti-Simon Commission Campaign and the Civil Disobedience Movement, and the peasant movement in U.P.

From 1928, once he started coming under Marxist influence, Jawaharlal Nehru began to realize that the communal problem was more

[1]Jawaharlal Nehru, *Selected Works* (hereafter *SW),* Vol. I, pp. 184-6, 356; *ibid.,* Vol. II, pp. 184-5, 267.

[2]*Ibid.,* Vol. III, pp. 67, 69,183.

complex than the nationalist approach indicated. He was gradually disillusioned with this approach and increasingly convinced of the futility of trying to bring about communal unity through conferences, negotiations and settlement at the top.[3] Consequently, he set out to analyze the broader social, economic and political roots of communalism. He now pointed to the socio-political forces and classes and strata whose needs communalism served. He also equated Hindu communalism and Muslim communalism, seeing them as facets of the same political phenomenon.[4] His analysis contained deep insights even though it failed to meet fully the challenge of analysing communalism in all its complexity and opacity, its ideology, its sources and roots, and reasons for its growth and stubbornness in the face of the secular nationalist attack.

Based on this new understanding, he organized, during 1933-37, a whirlwind personal political-ideological campaign against communalism and communal parties through newspapers, articles, and speeches. Time had come, he repeatedly declared, "to attack communalism root and branch" and to fight it "on all fronts", giving it "no quarter".[5]

I

Jawaharlal Nehru tried to define communalism and secularism in his writings and speeches. In 1937, he wrote that communalism meant that in politics and social and economic matters, Muslims or Hindus "must function separately as a group and deal with other (religious) groups as one nation deals with another. So also in trade unions, peasant unions, business, chambers of commerce and like organizations and activities."[6] Later, in 1944, he wrote in the *Discovery of India* that communalism was "a narrow group mentality basing itself on religious community but in reality concerned with political power and patronage for the group concerned."[7] And in 1955, after having seen the full face of extreme communalism, he wrote that communalism was "politics under some religious garb, one religious group being incited to hate another religious group."[8]

---

[3]*Autobiography,* p. 460; *SW,* Vol. VI, pp. 170, 172.

[4]See, for example, *SW,* Vol. VI, p. 158.

[5]Letter to S. A. Brelvi, 3 Dec. 1933, *ibid.,* p. 172, and "Reality and Myth", statement to the press, 5 Jan. 1934, *ibid.,* p. 182.

[6]*SW,* Vol. VIII, p. 119. Also, ibid., p. 130; *Autobiography,* p, 333.

[7]P. 333.

[8]*Speeches,* Vol. III, p. 37.

Nehru's definition of secularism was four pronged. Secularism meant, first, separation of religion from political, economic, social and cultural aspects of life, religion being treated as a purely personal matter;[9] second, dissociation of the state from religion;[10] third, full freedom to all religions and tolerance of all religions;[11] and, four, equal opportunities for followers of all religions, and no discrimination and partiality on grounds of religion.[12] And, of course, in the Indian context, secularism meant, above all, firm opposition to communalism. Interestingly, over time, Nehru began to see secularism not only as a gift of the freedom struggle but also as a heritage of India's ancient and medieval past.

Basic to Nehru's understanding of communalism was the belief that it did not represent India's social reality or the real problems that affected the country and the people. In other words, communalism was 'false' or, rather, represented a false consciousness of the reality because there was no social truth in the communal definition of the interests of the followers of different religions. Hindus or Muslims or Sikhs did not, because of following a common religion, share common social, economic or political interests. As Nehru put it in 1937, "on political and economic matters to treat the Muslims or the Hindus as homogeneous groups is absurd."[13] Or, again: "In what way are the interests of the Muslim peasant different from those of the Hindu peasant? Or those of a Muslim labourer or artisan or merchant or landlord or manufacturer different from those of his Hindu proto-type?" And he added: "The ties that bind people are common economic interests, and, in the case of a subject country especially, a common national interest."[14] The communalist did not, therefore, represent the interests of Hindus or Muslims on a communal basis because no such communal interests existed. On the other hand, if attention was turned towards "the vital problems facing the country, the problem of independence and of the removal of poverty and unemployment, there is no difference between the Muslim masses and the Hindu or Sikh or

---

[9]*SW*, Vol. III, pp. 181,227,233; *ibid.*, Vol. V, p. 284; *ibid*, Vol. VIII, pp. *120,127; ibid.*, Vol. XII, p. 315; N.L. Gupta, *Nehru on Communalism*, p.238.

[10]*SW*, Vol. XIV, p. 102; N.L. Gupta, *op. cit.*, p. 213.

[11]*SW*, Vol. II, p. 185; *ibid.*, Vol. VIII, p. 126; *ibid.*, Vol. XIV, p. 102; *Speeches*, Vol. V, p. 59; N.L. Gupta, *op. cit.*, p. 213.

[12]*SW*, Vol. VIII, p. 126; *Letters io Chief Ministers* (hereafter LCM), Vol. IV, p. 21.

[13]*SW*, Vol. VIII, p. 181. Also see *ibid.*, p. 221.

[14]*Ibid.*, p. 120. Also *ibid.*, pp. 123,203,767; *Autobiography*, p. 469.

Christian masses in the country."[15] Nor did, said Nehru, any ethnic differences or differences of culture or language divide Hindus from Muslims. In fact, quite often the activities of the communalists were detrimental to the interests of the very people—Hindus or Muslims—whom they claimed to represent.[16]

Nehru was, in our view, quite right in this prognosis. What was perhaps wrong was the conclusion that false consciousness, because it was false, could not be very strong or effective in real life. He again and again said that communalism was "a bogus question", "a myth", "not real", "a ghostly thing of no substance", "an impossible attempt", or that it "has no deep roots", "cannot happen", "can have no real importance in the larger scheme of things", would "vanish at the touch of reality", "does not exist" as a problem.[17] Nehru often confused the notion that communalism was false as it did not represent any real interests of the masses with the notion that, because of this falsity, communalism could not acquire a social base among them and could not therefore become a social or political force. Quite often, he meant the first when he stated the second. When he said that communalism was unreal, etc., he did not mean that it did not exist but that it was politically and socially 'false'.

Similarly, when he said that communalism was of "no real importance" or "an impossible attempt", he did not mean that it was not a major problem but that, unlike imperialism, nationalism and class consciousness, it represented a false consciousness of the reality. This is also what he meant when he wrote in 1937 that, "in the final analysis, there are only two forces in India today—British imperialism and the Congress representing Indian nationalism,"[18] for, virtually in the same breath, he also said: "I have given more thought to this (communal) problem in India than to any other. I know that it is a difficult problem just as every real

[15]*SW,* Vol. VIII, p. 123.

[16]*Autobiography,* pp. 469-72; *SW,* Vol. XII, p. 521; *ibid.,* Vol. XIV, p. 162. From this point of view, Nehru wrote in July 1942, "the problem of Indian minorities is entirely different from nationalities with entirely different racial, cultural and linguistic backgrounds." *SW,* Vol. XII, p.521.

[17]*SW,* Vol. V, p. 283; *ibid.,* Vol. VI, pp. 103,132,185; *ibid.,* Vol. VII, pp. *69,190; ibid.,* Vol. VIII, pp. 120,121, 130,186; ibid., Vol. IX, p. 240; *ibid.,* Vol. XII, pp. 521-2; *Autobiography,* p. 469.

[18]*SW,* Vol. VIII, p. 121. Also, *ibid.,* p. 126.

problem in life is difficult."[19] He also wrote, very correctly, that though the communal problem was not fundamentally due to economic causes, it had "an economic background."[20] It was the colonial economy which created a situation of unemployment and deprivation for the middle classes who then sought to alleviate their condition through the political instrumentality of communalism.[21]

II

Basically, according to Jawaharlal Nehru, communalism represented a major weapon of political, social and economic reaction. "It is this political reaction which has stalked the land under cover of communalsim", he wrote in 1933 in his major essay, "Hindu and Muslim Communalism".[22] And he wrote in his *Autobiography:* "Muslim communal organizations are notoriously reactionary from every point of view—political, economic, social. The Hindu Mahasabha rivals them."[23]

Both the Hindu and the Muslim communalists—individuals, parties and groups—, said Nehru, adopted basically pro-British, loyalist positions and developed a relationship of cooperation with and dependence on the colonial authorities. They sought the favours of the colonial Government, often supported and cooperated with it, and, in any case, avoided conflict with it. "One of the best tests of its (communalism's) true nature," Nehru wrote, "is what relation it bears to the national struggle." And by this criterion it was "wholly anti-national". For years, the communalists had opposed the freedom movement; and even when later they had given up open opposition, they had placed "obstruction in the way of freedom". In any case, the communalists avoided any conflict with colonial authorities, depended on their support and played into their hands. The communalist could think only in terms of the continuation of foreign domination, "to make the best of it for his own particular group." On the other hand, while opposing the nationalists, they had not hesitated to cooperate with each other.[24]

---

[19]*Ibid.,* p. 143.

[20]*Ibid.,* Vol. VII, p. 96.

[21]*Ibid.,* p. 108.

[22]*Ibid.,* Vol. VI, p. 164.

[23]*Autobiograhy* p.382. Also see, *ibid.,* pp. 135, 140.294,460; *SW,* Vol. VI, pp. 57,107,157,163-8,172,182; *ibid.,* Vol. VII, p. 190.

[24]See, for example, *SW,* Vol. VI, pp. *107,* 157, 159, 165-7,182; ibid., Vol. VII,

Internally, said Nehru, communalism represented the vested interests and served the needs of, and was patronised by, the upper middle classes, princes, landlords, and zamindars, and merchants and moneylenders, who were opposed to changes in the existing political and economic structure and were interested, instead, in "the preservation and augmentation of these vested interests." "Groups of upper class people," wrote Nehru in 1934, "try to cover up their own class interests by making it appear that they stand for the communal demands of religious minorities or majorities." They were afraid that any effort to solve the problems facing the people "would upset the present social structure and divest the vested interests." Communalism was, therefore, an effort to prevent the real problems of the masses from being tackled. And since the colonial regime too was interested in preserving the existing political and economic structure, it "throws its sheltering wing over a useful ally"; communalism enabled it to "playoff one group against another."[25]

After independence too, Nehru argued that communal organizations represented the forces of every kind of political, economic and social reaction and were backed by socially reactionary classes such as the old ruling princes, the jagirdars, the big zamindars and some of the big capitalists who hoped thereby to protect their vested interests and fight the progressive economic policies of the Government.[26]

According to Jawaharlal Nehru, communalism also masked the struggle within the middle classes for individual positions and posts. In fact, the middle classes constituted the main social base-the mass base—of communalism. Nehru saw communalism as primarily a petty bourgeois phenomenon and repeatedly pointed to the role of the middle classes in its perpetuation. Because middle class individuals suffered from widespread unemployment and had few avenues open to them, they looked for employment to the colonial state; and, as state jobs were

---

p. 190; *Autobiography,* pp. 136, 382, 467,469; *SW,* Vol. XI, p. 266; *ibid.,* Vol. XII, p. 512; *ibid.,* Vol., XIV, pp. 264,.273-4, 277, 289, *322; Discovery of India,* pp. 342-3.

[25]*SW,* Vol. VI, pp. 181-2. Also see, *ibid.,* pp. 156-7, 170, 176,453; *ibid.,* Vol. VII, p. 96; *ibid.,* Vol. VIII, pp. 143, 178-9,767,769; *ibid.,* Vol. IX, pp. 49,459; *ibid.,* Vo.1. X, pp. 301, 318; *ibid.,* Vol. XI, pp. 133, 172,266; *ibid.,* Vol. XII, p. 511; *ibid.,* Vol. XIV, pp. 183, 245, 249, 259, 263, 273-4, 277; *Autobiography,* pp. 140,465-8,606; *Discovery of India,* pp. 332, 343.

[26]N.L. Gupta, *op. cit.,* pp. 224-5, 230, 232, 237, 239; *LCM,* Vol. II, pp. 508-9.

limited, they constantly fought each other for these jobs, using communalism as a weapon. The communalist was, thus, basically "out for a job."[27]

On the basis of his experience in negotiating with the communal leaders during 1927-29, Nehru also came to believe that the upper and middle classes were also using communalism to garner seats in the legislatures. and for "a share in the spoils of office".[28] On the other hand, there was nothing in communalism for the masses.[29] He also pointed out that though communalism did enable some middle class individuals to get jobs, basically it could not solve the main economic problems of even the middle classes, especially the lower middle classes.[30]

Going into the political implications of his understanding of the role of the middle classes in communalism, Nehru suggested that communalism was an inherent weakness of a national movement based on the middle classes. As he put it in his Presidential address to the Lucknow Congress in 1936: "We have to admit that, under present circumstances, and so long as our policies are dominated by middle class elements, we cannot do away with communalism altogether."[31] Hence, one answer to communalism was to shift the centre of gravity of the national movement from the middle classes to the masses. There was, then, also the need to define nationalism in more radical terms.[32]

Nehru could also see that the communal problem was an economic problem in another sense. At the popular plane, communalism was often a distorted reflection of social tensions and class conflict between the haves and the have-nots, the exploiters and the exploited. In some provinces, such as Bengal, the tenants were largely Muslim and the landlords Hindu. In some parts of U.P., it was the other way around. In Punjab and Sind, the indebted peasants were largely Muslim and the

---

[27]*SW,* Vol. VI, pp. 57,453; *ibid.,* Vol. VII, pp. 69, 82, 97,108, 267; *ibid.,* Vol. VIII, p. 33; *ibid.,* Vol. X, pp. 284, 318, 389; *ibid.,* Vol. XII, p. 521; *Autobiography,* pp. 159,466; *Discovery of India,* p. 343.

[28]*SW,* Vol. V, p. 283; *ibid.,* Vol. VI, p.453; *ibid.,* Vol. VII, pp. 69, 82; *Autobiography,* p. 466.

[29]*SW,* Vol. V, pp. 283-4; *ibid.,* Vol. VI, pp. 176, 178, 181-2, 184; *ibid.,* Vol. VII, pp. 69, 97,190,463; *ibid.,* Vol. VIII, p. 767; *ibid.,* Vol. XIV, p. 264; *Autobiography,* p. 460.

[30]*SW,* Vol. VI, pp. 181-2; *ibid.,* Vol. VII, pp. 190,463; *ibid.,* Vol. VIII, p. 767.

[31]*SW,* Vol. VII, p. 189.

[32]For example, *SW,* Vol. IV, p. 503. 68

moneylenders Hindu. But what was really involved in such cases was class conflict, for there existed "the same conflict between the Hindu landlord and the Hindu tenant." The communalist, however, "in order to hide the main conflict", gave it "the colour of communalism and religion."[33] This aspect also explained why Muslim communal leaders had some popular support among the masses while Hindu communal leaders did not.[34]

Jawaharlal Nehru was also perhaps the first to see communalism as a form of fascism. Before 1947, he saw the close resemblance of Muslim and Hindu communalisms as they were developing after 1937 to contemporary fascism both in terms of methods, organization, techniques of hatred, violence and use of lies, style of leadership and the manner of negotiation with the opponents, and in terms of language and ideas. Thus, in 1939: "Definitely fascist ideas are spreading not only in the Muslim League but in the Hindu Mahasabha also", and "both the Muslim League and the Hindu Mahasabha talk definitely in totalitarian language." In 1940: "There has been a strange similarity in the recent development of the communalist technique in India to Nazi methods." Referring to the Muslim League and Jinnah, he wrote in October 1940: "There was no constructive suggestion, no attempt even to meet half-way, no answer to questions as to what exactly they wanted. It was a negative programme of hatred and violence, reminiscent of Nazi methods." He wrote in 1943: "Was Hitler's analysis correct—that the masses are just fools who can be made to do anything if your lie is big enough? Certainly Jinnah has been an apt pupil of Hitler's." He said in 1946: "There is no doubt that the League is at present the most powerful organization among them (Muslims) but the way this has been built up is strikingly similar to the Nazi technique. It has no constructive approach or objectives and its leaders have openly said that they base their appeal on hatred. There has been and is plenty of hooliganism and violence against political opponents." In 1945, he told Wavell, the Viceroy, that "Congress could make no

[33]*SW,* Vol. IX, pp. 49-50; *ibid.,* Vol. VII, p. 97; *Autobiography,* pp. 140, 466-7. Nehru added that if the class conflict was to develop further and become important, even though in a communal form, the Hindu and Muslim communalists were likely to join hands against the masses. *Autobiography,* p. 140.

[34]*Autobiography,* p. 140.

terms whatever with the Muslim League under its present leadership..., it (Muslim League) was Hitlerian in its leadership and policy."[35]

While before 1947, Nehru had primarily relied on the Muslim League as an example of the fascist character of communalism, after August 1947, he applied this understanding to the growing Hindu and Sikh communalisms. In general, Nehru also came to believe that communalism was "the Indian version of fascism".[36] For example, he wrote to Sardar Patel on 30 September 1947: "We have had to face a very definite and well-organized attempt of certain Sikh and Hindu fascist elements to overturn the Government, or at least to break up its present character."[37] On 2 October 1947, he told the Delhi Pradesh Congress Committee : "The demand for a Hindu state is not only stupid and medieval but also fascist in nature. Those who put forth such ideas will meet the same fate as Hitler and Mussolini."[38] And again on 3 October: "The wave of fascism which is gripping India now is the direct outcome of hatred for the non-Muslims which the Muslim League preached among its followers for years. The League accepted the ideology of fascism from the Nazis of Germany.... The ideas and methods of fascist organizations are now gaining popularity among the Hindus also and the demand for the establishment of a Hindu State is its clear manifestation."[39] In December 1947, he wrote to the Chief Ministers : "We have a great deal of evidence to show that the RSS (Rashtriya Swayam Sevak Sangh) is an organization which is in the nature of a private army and which is definitely proceeding on the strictest Nazi lines, even following the technique of organization."[40]

In fact, Nehru was at his intellectual and political best in understanding the fascist character and role of the RSS. Thus he told Lord Ismay in October 1947: "The RSS was composed largely of the lower

---

[35]*SW*, Vol. IX, pp. 551, 639-40; *ibid.*, Vol. XI, pp. 112, 171; *ibid.*, Vol. XIII, pp. 154-5; *ibid.*, Vol. XIV, pp. 116, 140. Also see *Discovery of India*, p. *338;LCM*, Vol. I, pp. 6-7; *Selected Works of Jawaharlal Nehru, Second Series* (hereafter *SW* (SS)), Vol. IV, pp. 118, 244, 268, 494; *Nehru, the First Sixty Years*, edited by Dorothy Norman, Vol. II, pp. 344-5.

[36]N.L. Gupta, *op. cit.*, p. 231. Also *ibid.*, pp. 225, 228; *LCM*, Vol. I, p. 11, Vol. II, pp. 12,509.

[37]*SW* (SS), Vol. IV, p. 114.

[38]*Ibid.*, p. 118, Also see, *ibid.*, pp. 244, 268, 494.

[39]*Ibid.*, p. 118.

[40]*LCM*, Vol. I, p. 33.

middle class not unlike the Nazi movement. Their aim was an exclusively Hindu state; and they were fascist in outlook."[41]

On January 5, 1948, he wrote to the Chief Ministers: "It is openly stated by their leaders that the RSS is not a political body but there can be no doubt that their policy and programme are political, intensely communal and based on violent activities. They have to be kept in check and we must not be misled by their pious professions which are completely at variance with their policy."[42] In December 1948, he made another longish comment on the RSS: "The RSS has been essentially a secret organization with a public facade, having no rules of membership, no registers, no accounts, although large sums are collected. They do not believe in peaceful methods or in satyagraha. What they say in public is entirely opposed to what they do in private.... The RSS is typical in this respect of the type of organization that grew up in various parts of Europe in support of fascism. It attracts people, essentially from the lower middle classes, many of them frustrated, many of them with vague ideas and little thought behind them."[43] And again on August 1, 1949, to the Chief Ministers: "It must always be remembered that the whole mentality of the RSS is a fascist mentality. Therefore, their activities have to be very closely watched."[44] Nehru propagated this understanding of communalism as "the Indian version of fascism" throughout the 1950s.[45] And in March 1964, just two months before his death, Nehru told R.K. Karanjia: "Now between the parties of the Right and the Left, as you differentiate them, I would always prefer a party with some ideology built round serious social and economic thinking.... The communists, with all their faults, function in terms of serious economic solutions. What we repudiate is all the dogma and violence of their approach. If they can divest themselves of this obsession and accept the discipline of our parliamentary democracy in good faith, there is not much difference between their goal of socialism and ours. The other parties you mention, like the Jan Sangh and Swatantra, seem to be organized around plainly fascist and feudal concepts without any social or economic basis. As such, they are dangerous to this country and our values of democracy and socialism."[46] Nehru also referred to Sikh communalism, especially the

---

[41]*SW (SS),* Vol. IV, p. 244.

[42]*LCM,* Vol. I, p. 46. Also see, *ibid.,* pp. 56 and 179.

[43]*Ibid.,* p. 243.

[44]*Ibid.,* p. 428. Also *ibid.,* Vol. II, pp. 12,509.

[45]*Ibid.,* Vol. IV, p. 380 ; N.L. Gupta, *op. cit.,* pp. 225, 228, 231.

[46]R.K. Karanjia, *The Philosophy of Mr. Nehru,* pp. 159-60. Also see, S. Gopal, *Jawaharlal Nehru-A Biography,* Vol. Three, p. 183.

politics of Master Tara Singh, as fascist.[47]

Nehru's attitude towards religion changed over time, though remaining basically within a sceptical frame. But on one question he was clear: religion did not lie at the roots of communalism, and though India had many religions, religious differences were not the cause of communalism. "The communal problem," he wrote in 1936, "is not a religious problem, it has almost nothing to do with religion."[48] Communal conflict, he wrote in the *Discovery of India,* had "nothing to do with religion, though religion often masked the issue".[49] Religion, he said, was used as a "smokescreen" by the communalists to mobilize the masses to serve interests which had little to do with religion.[50]

From 1938 to 1946 Nehru made a strong critique of the Muslim League and M.A. Jinnah for appealing to religious fanaticism and raising the cry of "Islam in danger". After 1947, he condemned the communal parties for trying" to exploit the sentiments of the people behind a smokescreen of religion and rouse their religious sentiments."[51]

On the positive side, Nehru was willing to offer every guarantee for the protection of religious freedom. He also agreed that organization of co-religionists as a group to deal with religious questions was legitimate. But he was clear on one point: the sphere of influence of religion should be narrowed down. And so he wrote in 1937: "Religion is both a personal matter and a bond of faith, but to stress religion in matters political and economic is obscurantism and leads to the avoidance of real issues." He was, of course, fully aware of the tension and conflict around religious issues such as music before mosque or cow-killing; and so he added: "Religious questions may arise and religious conflicts may take place, and they should be faced and settled. But the right way to deal with them is to limit their sphere of action and influence, and to prevent them from encroaching on politics and economics."[52]

At the same time, Nehru felt that there was too much of religiosity in

---

[47]*LCM,* Vol. III, p. 475.

[48]*SW,* VoL VII, p. 82.

[49]*Discovery of India,* p. 343.

[50]*SW,* Vol. VI, p. 183; *ibid.,* Vol. VII, pp. 82, 96, 107-8; *ibid.,* Vol. VIII, pp. 39,248,639; *ibid.,* Vol. IX, pp. 48-9, 459; *ibid.,* Vol. XI, p. 172; *Discovery of India,* p. 333.

[51]N. L. Gupta, *op. cit.,* p. 228. Also see, *ibid.,* p. 237.

[52]*SW,* Vol. VIII, p. 120. Also *ibid.,* p. 127; *ibid.,* Vol. XII, p. 315 ; *ibid.,* Vol. III, p. 180.

India, too much of religion in Indian people's lives. This excess of religiosity was responsible for "the ease with which communal feelings could be roused."[53] One reason for the greater success of communalism among Muslims and the Arya Samajists, said Nehru, lay in religiosity being stronger among them.[54]

Before 1947, Nehru pointed out that Hindu communal organizations, though as aggressively communal as the Muslim League, often disguised their communalism "under cover of seeming nationalism."[55] In fact, he pointed out, "the communalism of a majority community must of necessity bear a closer resemblance to nationalism than the communalism of a minority group." "The test", he added, "comes in the provinces where there is a Muslim majority and in that testtheHindu Mahasabha has failed."[56] After 1947, he warned against the use of nationalism by the Hindu and Sikh communalists. It was ironic, he said, that these communalists, "most of whom had done little in the struggle for freedom," were now trying to speak in the name of nationalism and hiding their communalism "under the cloak of nationalism."[57]

But, in fact, he pointed out, behind "high-sounding phrases appealing to nationalism and patriotism," communalism was, "in its essence, a reactionary and disruptive cry, not a unifying one, however much it may be called so."[58]

Nor had communalism anything to do with culture which it claimed to be defending, nor was it based on cultural differences. Replying to Iqbal, the poet, Nehru wrote in 1933: "There are racial and cultural differences in India but these differences have nothing to do with religious divisions; they cut athwart the lines of religious cleavage. If a person is converted to another religion he does not change his biological make-up or his racial characteristics or to any extent his cultural background. Cultural types are national, not religious." Questioning the concept of Muslim culture, Nehru asked: "What is Muslim culture? Is it the Semitic Arabian culture or the Aryan Persian or is it a mixture of the two?" And he asserted: "Today in India there is absolutely no cultural or racial difference between the Muslim and Hindu masses. Even the handful of

---

[53] *Autobiography,* p. 295. Also *SW,* Vol. III, p. 1.
[54] *Autobiography,* p. 118.
[55] *SW,* Vol. VI, p. 157.
[56] *Ibid.,* pp. 165 and 168.
[57] *LCM,* Vol. I, p. 59; *ibid.,* Vol. II, p. 520; *ibid.,* Vol. III, p. 380.
[58] *Ibid.,* Vol. I, p. 513.

upper class Muslims in north India, who perhaps think themselves apart from the rest of the country, bear the impress of India on them all over the place and are only superficially Persianised." "Would any of them", he asked, "be more at home or more in harmony with their surroundings in Persia or Turkey or any other Islamic country?" Consequently, he told Iqbal, the communal problem was entirely a political creation of upper class groups and had "no relation to racial or cultural matters."[59]

After 1947, Nehru made a similar critique of the Hindu communalists' claim to speak in the name of ancient Hindu culture. But, he wrote in October 1951, "behind this garb of ancient culture, they hide. the narrowest acquisitiveness and reaction."[60] And again (in 1951): "These supporters of Hindu Rashtra slogan are themselves incapable of understanding the real greatness of Hindu religion, past traditions of India, and the vital need of always keeping a broad open mind."[61] Hence, it was wrong to say that the communalists were protecting culture and religion.[62] In fact, when the communalists talked of having one culture for India, they were setting into operation "a process of disruption" which was "bad for us politically, culturally and in the domain of the spirit."[63]

Nehru was able to see the close connection between the growth of the communal forces and the British policy of divide and rule. He did not, of course, accept the simplistic view that communalism had been basically created by British policy. As we have seen, he believed that communalism had arisen because of certain conditions internal to Indian society. But, argued Nehru, because communalism also served the needs of colonial domination, the colonial authorities had encouraged and promoted it in diverse ways.[64] One of these ways was the easy acceptance of the communal demands.[65] Moreover, the colonial state could always outbid any concessions that the nationalists might make to the communalists. Consequently, there could be no solution of the communal problem "so

---

[59]*SW,* Vol. VI, pp. 175-6. Also see, *ibid.,* p. 183.

[60]*LCM,* Vol. II, p. 509.

[61]N.L. Gupta, *op. cit.,* p. 226.

[62]*Ibid.,* p. 237.

[63]*Ibid.,* p. 232.

[64]*SW,* Vol. VI, pp. 56, 182; *ibid.,* Vol. VII, pp. 69-70. 96; *ibid.,* Vol. IX, p. *177; ibid.,* Vol. X, pp. 204, 318; *ibid.,* Vol. XIII, p. 244; *ibid.,* Vol. XIV, pp. 139-40; *Autobiography,* pp. 136, 460, 464.

[65]*SW,* Vol. VI, pp. 164-5; *ibid.,* Vol. XIV, pp. 139-40; *Autobiography,* pp. 336,576-7,606.

long as the third party is not eliminated."[66] Then there was the introduction of the separate electorates, "the seed of the poisonous tree that has grown now to poison all our national life."[67]

III

Nehru was very clear in his mind that it was very necessary to give full protection to the minorities and to remove their fears. While denying any validity to communalism, he accepted that minorities, whether religious or linguistic, tended to mistrust the majority and were full of fears that, because of their weaker numerical position, they might suffer social, economic, cultural or religious oppression and suppression at the hands of the majority. These fears were further aggravated by the superior position of Hindus in education, services, professions, and trade and industry.[68] This was the psychological aspect of the communal problem. This was what Nehru meant in the much quoted lines from his essay, 'Hindu and Muslim communalism': "It is the fear complex that we have to deal with in these communal problems. Honest communalism is fear; false communalism is political reaction.[69]

Nehru realized that such fears were without a basis in reality. He repeatedly argued that it was not possible for such a large minority as Muslims to be dominated and oppressed by Hindus. As he put it, "only a lunatic can think that the Muslims can be dominated and coerced by any religious majority in India." And again: "Is it conceivable by the wildest stretch of imagination that Islam can be suppressed by the Hindus in India or vice versa?"[70] But even so, he asserted, the feeling of fear had to be removed and the Muslim masses made to realize that "they can have any protection that they really desire."[71] And so, along with Gandhiji, he argued that the Congress as a whole and Hindus as a religious majority, in particular; should adopt a generous approach towards the safeguards that the communalists demanded on behalf of Muslims so that the fear and suspicion of Hindu domination might be removed from the minds of

[66] *SW*, Vol. XII, p. 511. Also *ibid.*, pp. 174, 326, 407, 511; *ibid.*, Vol. X, pp. 280-1 ; *Autobiography*, pp. 136-7; *Discovery of India*, p. 333.

[67] *SW*, Vol. XIV, p. 139.

[68] *SW*, Vol. IV, p. 186; *ibid.*, Vol. VI, p. 164; *ibid.*, Vol. IX, p. 240; *Discovery of India*, pp. 332-4.

[69] *SW*, Vol. VI, p. 164.

[70] *Ibid.*, Vol. VIII, pp. 127, 194; *ibid.*, Vol. X, p. 317; *Discovery of India*, p.334.

[71] *SW*, Vol. VI, p. 181.

Muslims.[72] At the same time, he also pointed out that the Congress had already at its Karachi session in 1931 and subsequently provided the necessary safeguards to minority rights. It had guaranteed full religious and cultural freedom to every one and every group and declared that all citizens, whatever their religion or caste or sex, would be equal before the law and in regard to public employment, office, profession or trade. Elections would moreover be on the basis of universal adult franchise.[73] The Congress had given a similar assurance regarding the personal law of Muslims,[74] and their share in educational opportunities and government services.[75] The Congress, said Nehru, was also willing to accept separate electorates till it was given up by Muslims themselves.[76] Same applied to the Communal Award. Even though the Congress regarded it as harmful, it would seek no change in it except with the consent of those concerned.[77] Moreover, these assurances would be incorporated in the chapter on fundamental rights in the constitution. Furthermore, in a confidential note on Congress policy, Nehru said that "even before the constituent assembly meets, the fundamental laws protecting the minorities and citizens generally should be agreed to, and the constituent assembly should not touch them."[78]

During the 1940s, Jawaharlal Nehru and the Congress offered three other major measures to assuage minority fears. First, apart from the guarantees already offered, any further question directly affecting minority interests would be settled by agreement and not by the greater voting power of the majority; and when an agreement on any particular point was not possible, it would be referred to the League of Nations or the International Court at Hague or any other impartial body mutually agreed upon.[79] Second, India would be a federation with maximum autonomy for

---

[72] *SW,* Vol. IV, pp. 186-7; *ibid.,* Vol. VI, pp. 168-9, 177-8, 181; *ibid.,* Vol. VII, p. 190; *ibid.,* Vol. VIII, p. 769; *Autobiography,* p. 136.

[73] *SW,* Vol. VIII, pp. 126,131,194,208,226,234-7, 765; *ibid.,* Vol. X, pp. 287, 294 ; *ibid.,* Vol. XII, p. 521.

[74] *Ibid.,* Vol. VIII, pp. 208, 235.

[75] *Ibid.,* p. 2~5 ; *ibid.,* Vol. XII, p. 512.

[76] *Ibid.,* Vol. VI, pp. 178.9, 181 ; *ibid.,* Vol. X, p. 280; *ibid.,* Vol. XI, pp. 20, 111 ; *ibid.,* Vol. XII, p. 315.

[77] *Ibid.,* Vol. VII, pp. 37, 108-9,211,402-3, 462-3; *ibid.,* Vol. VIII, pp. 208, 234.

[78] *Ibid.,* Vol. X, p. 306.

[79] *SW,* Vol. X, pp. 280, 294, 3Q6, 317; *ibid.,* Vol. XI, pp. 11, 20; *ibid.,* Vol. XII, p. 315 ; *Discovery of India,* p. 334.

the federating units and with residuary powers vesting with the federating units. The centre would have a minimum of compulsory subjects such as defence, foreign affairs. communications and currency.[80] In addition, there might even be smaller autonomous cultural areas within a province.[81] Nehru was willing to offer this concession even though it went against his ideas of nation-building. As he wrote to Abdul Latif on 6 August 1942:[82]

> Personally I must confess to you that I am not enamoured of this as I think the modem tendency is against it and rightly so. It is essential today to have a planned economy for the nation, and for this as well as for defence, etc., a strong government is necessary. Nevertheless we have agreed to this to meet the wishes of many of our friends who consider it important.

Third, Nehru and the Congress also accepted the principle of self-determination for the federating units. The Congress Working Committee declared in April 1942 that even though it was wedded to Indian unity and regarded any division of India as injurious to all concerned, it could not "think in terms of compelling the people in any territorial unit to remain in an Indian Union against their declared and established will."[83] In July 1945, Nehru made his stand explicit in the context of Pakistan: "If those areas which have predominant Muslim majorities are utterly bent on separation no power on earth can stop them."[84] And even more explicitly in August 1945: "If the Muslims insist on it (Pakistan) they will have it".[85] There was only one, rather prophetic, caveat: this right of self-determination would have to be extended to any other group or area within the separating unit which "cannot take other areas away with it against their will."[86] In the context of Pakfstan, Nehru repeatedly made it clear from July 1945 onwards that, in the event of its creation, Punjab and Bengal would also have to be divided.[87]

---

[80] *SW,* Vol. XII, pp. 521, 527,190; *ibid.,* Vol. XIV, pp. 143-4.

[81] *Ibid.,* Vol. XII, p. 521.

[82] *Ibid.,* p. 527.

[83] *Ibid.,* Vol. XII; p, 190. Also see, *ibid.,* pp, 322, 517, 521, 527; *ibid.,* Vol. XIV, pp. 50-I, 65, 72, 143-5, 162, 187, 191-2.

[84] *Ibid.,* Vol. XIV, p. 50.

[85] *Ibid.,* p. 165.

[86] *Ibid.,* p. 143. Also *ibid.,* pp. 65, 72, 144, 191.

[87] *Ibid.,* pp. 142, 158, 165, 187, 300, 313, 385, 478.

Nehru also argued that communalism did not benefit the religious community whose interests it claimed to defend and promote. For example, writing to Khaliquzzman in July 1937: he exclaimed: "Do you not see that this communal policy which the Muslim League here has fathered is a policy more .injurious to the Muslims of India than anything that a majority could do would be. It is a doomed policy both from the point of view of the community and the larger world."[88] Similarly, in an address at Lahore he advised Sikhs that they would "only be harming their own interests, if they let themselves go into communal channels."[89] Referring to the demand for Pakistan, and even while virtually conceding it, Nehru repeatedly argued that it would be injurious to "the best interests of the Muslims themselves."[90] He wrote in his diary on 21 September 1943: "What a lot Jinnah and his Muslim League have to answer for! They have lowered the whole tone of our public life, embittered it, increased mutual dislikes and hatreds, and made us contemptible before the outside world. I cannot help thinking that ultimately the Muslims in India will suffer most."[91]

IV

Nehru's commitment to secularism and his opposition to communalism were total. From this point of view, the post-independence, post-partition years from 1947 to 1952 were his, as also Indian nationalism's, finest hour.

The bitterness of the partition riots on both sides of the border, the forcible exchange of population between India and Pakistan, the continuous flow of refugees from East Bengal, and the invasion of Kashmir were daily poisoning the atmosphere. Even sane, secular and decent persons were falling prey to communal bitterness. A rising crescendo of voices was demanding that India should do to Muslims in India what Pakistan was doing to Hindus in Pakistan. For example, even stalwarts of the freedom struggle like Sardar Patel and B.C. Roy suggested in 1948 that the Pakistan Government should be warned that if Hindus continued to migrate from East Bengal, India would expel an equal number of Muslims from West Bengal.[92] In September 1949, Nehru

[88] *Ibid.,* Vol. VIII, p. 143.
[89] *Ibid.,* Vol. XIV, p. 177.
[90] *Ibid.,* pp. 50, 65, 73, 133, 164.
[91] *Ibid.,* Vol. XIII, p. 244.
[92] S. GopaJ, *op. cit.,* Vol. Two, p. 76.

admonished Mohanlal Saxena, Union Minister of Rehabilitation, who had ordered the sealing of Muslim shops in Delhi and U.P.: "All of us seem to be getting infected with the refugee mentality or, worse still, the RSS mentality. That is a curious finale to our careers."[93] Nehru was throughout receiving abusive letters and even threats of assassination, and he bemoaned in a letter to Aruna Asaf Ali on 12 March 1950: "An evil fate seems to pursue us, reducing many of us to the level of brutes."[94]

During those troubled years, rising to his full height as a nationalist and a humanist, Jawaharlal stood like a rock in opposition to the communal mentality and the barbarity of communal killings and in defence of the basic values of India's freedom struggle, and waged an incessant campaign against communalism. What he wrote about Gandhiji in Decenber 1947 was equally, if not more, applicable to himself:

> How many of you realize what it has meant to India to have the presence of Mahatma Gandhi during these months? We all know of his magnificent services to India and to freedom during the past half century and more. But no service could have been greater than what he has performed during the past four months when, in a dissolving world, he has been like a rock of purpose and a lighthouse of truth, and his firm low voice has risen above the clamours of the multitude, pointing out the path of rightful endeavour.[95]

Nehru carried on a massive private and public campaign against communalism through public speeches, radio broadcasts, parliamentary speeches, private letters and epistles to the Chief Ministers. Giving expression to his basic political stance regarding "the cancer of communal feelings", he declared in December 1947: "The battle of our political freedom is fought and won. But another battle, no less important than what we have won, still faces us. It is a battle with no outside enemy .... it is a battle with our own selves."[96] Condemning violence on both sides of the border, he refused to countenance any excuse for communal violence including that of retaliation against the happenings in Pakistan. The Government of India, he said, would not try to rival Pakistan in the matter.[97] He rejected outright Sardar Patel's and

[93] *Ibid.*, p. 77.

[94] *Ibid.*, p. 85.

[95] *SW (S5)*, Vol. IV, p. 206.

[96] *Ibid.*, pp. 208-9.

[97] *LCM*, Vol. I, pp. 479, 487; *ibid.*, Vol. II, pp. 27, 113,472 ; N.L. Gupta,

B.C. Roy's proposal referred to earlier. In October 1949, he wrote to the Chief Ministers regarding the disposal of evacuee property: "I know that Pakistan is pursuing a policy of utter callousness in this matter. We cannot copy the methods or the ideals of Pakistan. They have declared themselves openly to be an Islamic State believing in the two-nation theory. We reject that theory and call ourselves a secular State giving full protection to all religions. We have to live up to our ideals and declarations."[98] And he wrote to Sardar Patel in March 1950: "The belief that retaliation is a suitable method to deal with Pakistan ... is growing. That is the surest way to ruin in India and Pakistan."[99] In those years, he branded communalism as primitive, brutal, barbaric and uncivilized, and repeatedly declared: "No State can be civilized except a secular State."[100]

During 1946-47, Nehru took recourse to decisive administrative action against communal violence in Bihar and elsewhere. During August-September 1947, he broke the back of communal violence in Delhi by constant personal intervention, bringing the army on the streets and ordering the police to shout Hindu communal mobs indulging in looting and killing. In West Bengal, in 1950, he kept ready an ordinance imposing martial law if attacks on Muslims did not stop.[101]

Nehru again and again reminded the Indian people of the Congress's and the national movement's commitment to secularism as a value on which there could be no compromise. The country should be willing "to stand or fall by it."[102] "It is always a dangerous thing," he wrote to the Chief Ministers in December 1948, "to compromise with something that is definitely evil. The RSS movement is directly aimed at everything that nationalist India has stood for."[103] And again inMay 1950: "For all of us in India, and more especially for Congressmen and Congresswomen, this issue of communal unity and a secular State must be made perfectly c l ear.... (This is) a question having first priority and as something which has been the very basis and foundation of our struggle for freedom. There can be no compromise on this issue, for any compromise can only mean a surrender of

---

op. cit., pp. 218, 243; S. Gopal, *op. cit.*, Vol. Two, pp. 15, 86.

[98] *LCM*, Vol. I, p. 479. Also *ibid.*, p. 487; *ibid.*, Vol. II, pp. 27, 113, 472.

[99] S. Gopal, *op. cit.*, Vol. Two, p. 86.

[100] N.L. Gupta, *op. cit.*, p. 217. Also see *ibid.*, p. 216; *LCM*, Vol. III, p. 90.

[101] M. Brecher, *Nehru-A Political Biography*, pp. 364ff.

[102] N.L. Gupta, *op. cit.*, p. 216.

[103] *LCM*, Vol. I, pp. 251-2. Also see *ibid.*, Vol. III, p. 243; ibid., Vol. IV, p. 103.

our principles and a betrayal of the cause of India's freedom."[104]

Earlier, replying to a debate on the Bengal situation in Parliament on 9 August 1950, Nehru said that the communal approach—"this brutal and barbarous approach"—would be "completely at variance with all that the Congress has stood for." Referring to the demand for the expulsion of Muslims from West Bengal in retaliation for the exodus of Hindus from East Bengal, he declared: "This is a proposition which, if it is followed, will mean the ruin of India and the annihilation of all that we stand for and have stood for. I repeat that we will resist such a proposition with all our strength, we will fight it in houses, in fields and in market places. It will be fought in the council chambers and the streets, for we shall not let India be slaughtered at the altar of bigotry."[105]

Nor was Nehru's objection to communalism on ideological grounds alone. For India, it was also a politically disruptive phenomenon. While communalism before 1947 had divided the Indian people, weakened the national movement and led to the partition of India, it was, Nehru said, no less dangerous after independence. Indian unity .could be maintained only on the basis of secularism. "We can only maintain our integrity on a secular basis", he said in 1963, lifter the India-China War.[106] On the other hand, "if allowed free play", he had warned in 1951, communalism "would break up India", "The activities of the communalists here amounted to their thrusting a dagger in the body politic of India", he said on another occasion in 1951.[107] And in 1955: the communalist trend "is a separatist trend. It is a disruptive trend. It is a trend full of hatred.... If we maintain this kind of communalism, whether it is Hindu or Muslim or Christian or Sikh or any other, India will cease to be what it is. It will go to pieces."[108] And a month before his death, he wrote that communalism was putting "our freedom and independence ... in danger."[109] Communalism would, moreover, put an end to all economic and other progress; it would "bring disaster in its train."[110]

---

[104]*Ibid.*, Vol. II, p. 84. Also N.L. Gupta, *op. cit.*, pp. 232, 240, 253.

[105]*Speeches*, Vol. Two, p. 175. Also S. Gopal, *op. cit.*, Vol. Two, p. 155.

[106]R. K. Karanjia, *The Philosophy of Mr. Nehru*, p. 129.

[107]*LCM*, Vol. II, p. 508 and N.L. Gupta, *op. cit.*, p. 219, respectively.

[108]Speeches, Vol. Three, p. 135.

[109]S. Gopal, *op. cit.*, Vol. Three, p. 264.

[110]N.L. Gupta, *op. cit.*, pp. 230-31.

Consequently, Nehru regarded communalism as the most dangerous tendency of the times which had "to be combated on all fronts."[111] It was moreover a difficult and invidious enemy to fight. As he put it in a letter to the Chief Ministers in August 1950: "We have repeatedly declared that we are opposed to communalism. And yet in our thinking and action we are often influenced by the communal outlook. That way danger lies. I have been more troubled by this than any other matter in India. We can meet and fight an external enemy. But what are we to do when the enemy is within ourselves and in our own minds and hearts?"[112]

Communalism, said Nehru, had therefore to be rooted out from Indian life. There could be "no half-way house" in the matter.[113] No quarter could be given to communalism. "Let us be clear about it without a shadow of doubt in any Congressman's mind," he told the AICC in July 1951; "we stand till death for a secular State."[114]

Nehru repeatedly declared that so long as he was the Prime Minister of India, he would fight communalism with all his strength and would not permit the communal forces "to lift their heads".[115] Seeing the creeping growth of communalism in the country he wrote to Mehr Chand Khanna in June 1949 in a despondent but defiant mood: "So far as I am concerned, my own mind is perfectly clear in these matters and I have viewed with dismay and sorrow the narrow and communal outlook that has progressively grown in this country and which shows itself in a variety of ways. I shall cease to be Prime Minister the moment I realize that this outlook has come to stay and that I cannot do my duty as I conceive it."[116] Appealing regularly to the Chief Ministers to counter the rising communal tide, he was no less explicit. For Example, he wrote to them in April 1950: "We must work according to our own lights and try to convince the people of the rightness of our action. If they are not so convinced, they will have to choose others to control their destinies for the time being."[117]

---

[111]*LCM,* Vol. III, p. 376.

[112]*Ibid.,* Vol. II, p. 168.

[113]*Ibid.,* p. 83. Also *ibid.,* Vol. I, pp. 93, 179,202,225,513 ; *ibid.,* Vol. III, pp. 233,276; N.L. Gupta, *op. cit.,* pp. 225, 232, 240; *Speeches,* Vol. Two, p. 175.

[114]N.L. Gupta, *op. cit.,* p. 216.

[115]*Ibid.,* p. 234. Also p. 239.

[116]S. Gopal, *op. cit.,* Vol. Two, p. 82. Also p. 155.

[117]*LCM,* Vol. II, p. 61.

In his speeches, Nehru made communalism the central campaign question during the elections to the first Lok Sabha in 1952. The basic struggle in this election, he said, was between the secular and the communal forces. He urged the Congress leadership to choose Congress candidates with particular care so that only sturdy non-communal persons were chosen. Since in the past certain communal elements had succeeded in penetrating the Congress, persons who had been previously connected with communal organizations should be suspect. Nor should the Congress enter into any alliance, cooperation or understanding, explicit or implicit, with any communal organization, whatever its designation might be, and even when it meant an electoral setback.[118] "So far as I am concerned", he was to say later in 1954, "I am prepared to lose every election in India but to give no quarter to communalism or casteism."[119]

V

After 1947, over the years, Nehru took full note of the sense of insecurity and deprivation from which Muslims were suffering.[120] He insisted that they must be given full protection and a sense of absolute security produced in their minds.[121] It was also necessary to remove "all sense of difference from the political point of view between the so-called majorities and minorities", and to "increase the morale of the minorities."[122] The real test in this respect, he pointed out, "is not what we feel about it but what those concerned feel."[123]

Nehru was, in particular, worried about the low and failing ratio of Muslims in defence, police, and other all-India and State services right down to the village level.[124] He urged his cabinet colleagues and the Chief Ministers to make special efforts to provide adequate representation to the minorities in the armed forces and civil services as also in the private sector.[125] It was also because he did not want that Muslims, already feeling

[118]N.L. Gupta, *op. cit.,* pp. 224 and 241.

[119]*Speeches,* Vol. Three, p. 455.

[120]*LCM,* Vol. I, p. 12; *ibid.,* Vol. II, pp. 39, 58; *ibid.,* Vol. III, pp. 462, 536; S. Gopal, *op. cit.,* Vol. Three, p. 172.

[121]*LCM,* Vol. I, pp. 213,478; *ibid.,* Vol. II, pp. 41-2,130,472; *ibid.,* Vol. III, pp. 378-9, 570.

[122]*Ibid.,* Vol. II, pp. 42 and 130.

[123]*Ibid.,* Vol. III, p. 378. Also S. Gopal, *op. cit.,* Vol. Three, p. 27.

[124]*LCM,* Vol. III, pp. 375-6, 439, 451,535,570.

[125]*Ibid.,* Vol. III, pp.376, 451-2,535-6; S. Gopal, *op. cit.,* Vol. Two, p. 206, Vol. Three, pp. 27, 181.

insecure and living in an atmosphere of suspicion and hostility, should feel alarmed that the majority was interfering with their personal law, that Nehru took the reactionary step of excluding Muslims from the ambit of laws against bigamy and ex-tending to women the rights of inheritance to property and of divorce on an equal basis with men. Changes in case of the legal position of Muslim women would be made only when Muslims wanted them, he said.[126]

Nehru also, once again, asserted that it was the duty of the religious majority to rid itself of communalism, to accept responsibility for the maintenance of communal peace, to create an atmosphere in which the minorities felt secure, and to win the goodwill and confidence of the minority groups by fair and even generous treatment.[127]

A major aspect of Nehru's anti-communal stance after 1947 was that he consistently attacked not only Hindu but also Muslim, Sikh and Christian communalisms and wanted all of them to be put down.[128] While he pleaded and worked for removing all possible grievances of the minorities, he would not ignore minority communalisms and was opposed to giving any quarter to them, for, he said, they were equally dangerous to Indian unity. As early as 1948, when he got reports of the revival of pro-Muslim League feeling in some parts of the country, he asked the Chief Ministers to take note of it and discourage it.[129] In 1953, he condemned the "vicious" effort to start a Muslim communal organization on the lines of the old Muslim League.[130] When in 1956 demonstrations and riots occurred during the agitation against the book, *Living Biographies of Religious Leaders,* he condemned the Islami Jamait for being an aggressive communal organization which issued "speeches and writings of a venomous kind". Moreover, he was pained by and angry at some of the slogans raised during the agitation which were "not only anti-national but also treasonable."[131]

---

[126]Tibor Mende, *Conversations with Mr. Nehru,* p. 57; S. Gopal, *op. cit.,* Vol. Two, p. 313, Vol. Three, pp. 172,281.

[127]*LCM,* Vol. I, p. 212; *ibid.,* Vol. II, pp. 114,536; *ibid.,* Vol. III, pp. 440, 570; S. Gopal, *op. cit.,* Vol. Two, p. 206; N.L. Gupta, *op. cit.,* pp. 216-7.

[128]N.L. Gupta, *op. cit.,* pp. 230,237,241,251,253; *LCM,* Vol. I, pp.60, 244,513.

[129]*LCM,* Vol. I, p. 180.

[130]*Ibid.,* Vol. III, p. 440.

[131]*Ibid.,* Vol. IV, pp. 436-7. 84

Similarly, in 1949, referring to the Akali agitation in Punjab and Delhi, he condemned "the most irresponsible and incendiary speeches ... delivered by some Akali leaders" and declared that "we cannot tolerate communalism or accept any demand which is so totally opposed to our general policy." Referring to the ban on public meetings, he wrote: "but there may be a gathering in a local *gurdwara.* We have no desire to prevent any gathering in *gurdwaras,* provided they are for a religious object and do not get converted into a political meeting."[132] Later, in 1954, he likened the activities of the Akali Dal and its leaders to those of pre-1947 Muslim League.[133]

Nehru reiterated the view that communalism harmed not only the country as a whole, and the majority, but the minority itself. I may quote at length from a speech he delivered in the Constituent Assembly on 3 April 1948 on a resolution, which was passed by the House, laying down that, in order to eliminate communalism from Indian life, "no communal organization ... should be permitted to engage in any activities other than those essential for the *bona fide* religious and cultural needs of the community." Nehru said: "The combination of politics and religion ... is harmful to the country as a whole; it is harmful to the majority, but probably it is most harmful to any minority that seeks to have some advantage from it ... a minority in an independent State which seeks to isolate and separate itself does some injury to the cause of the country, and most of all it injures its own interests, because inevitably it puts a barrier between itself and the others, a barrier not on the religious plane but on the political plane—sometimes even to some extent on the economic plane; and it can never really exercise the influence which it legitimately ought to aspire to exercise, if it functions in that way."[134] He was particularly severe on the Sikh communalists in this respect. Master Tara Singh, he wrote in January 1953, "had done enough injury to the Sikh cause by his methods during the last fifteen years or more."[135] And in December 1954, referring to the intense communalism of the Akali Dal, he wrote: "If these

[132]*Ibid.,* Vol. I, p. 294. Also *ibid.,* p. 299 ; *ibid.,* Vol. II, p. 90 ; *ibid.,* Vol. III, pp. 216-7.

[133]*Ibid.,* Vol. IV, p. 103.

[134]*Speeches,* Vol. One, pp. 734. Also *LCM,* Vol. II, p. 150.

[135]*LCM,* Vol. III, p. 216.

ideas spread, India will no doubt suffer, but the Sikhs will obviously suffer most of all."[136] Similarly referring to the efforts of Muslim communal organizations to "create trouble in the way of provocative speeches and slogans", he wrote in 1956: "It is obvious that the ultimate sufferers are bound to be Muslims or other minorities if communal passions are roused." And he referred in this context to the injury suffered by Muslims in the agitation organized by Muslim communalists about the book, *The Living Biographies of Religious Leaders*.[137]

However, while criticizing and condemning minority communalisms, Nehru was clear in his mind that after independence the main threat to national unity was posed by Hindu communalism.[138] Referring to the communal propaganda that Muslims could not be trusted and were likely to prove disloyal, Nehru wrote in August 1951: "There may be Muslims who cannot be trusted. But I am quite sure that in the case of a conflict with Pakistan, the dangerous element will be the communal Hindu element which will then try to act up to its declared policies against the minonties."[139] In October 1951, he wrote that Hindu and Sikh communalisms were "the major evil today."[140] In June 1954: It was Hindu communalism that was "dangerous for us because Hindus are the dominant element in India."[141] This was particularly so as in a democracy majority communalism could acquire power far beyond that of any minority communalism.[142] Let me quote from a letter Nehru wrote to K.N. Katju, Union Minister for Home Affairs, in November 1953: "The fate of India is largely tied up with the Hindu outlook. If the present Hindu outlook does not change radically, I am quite sure that India is doomed. The Muslim outlook may be and, I think, is often worse. But it does not make very much difference to the future of India."[143]

VI

Dsspite its glow and splendour, Jawaharlal Nehru's approach to the communal problem suffered from a few major weaknesses. For one, he

[136] *Ibid.,* Vol. IV, p. 102.
[137] *Ibid.,* p. 448.
[138] *Ibid.,* Vol. I, pp. 46, 202.
[139] *Ibid.,* V91. II, pp. 464-5. Also *ibid.,* pp. 471-2.
[140] *Ibid.,* p. 509.
[141] *Ibid.,* Vol. III, p. 569. Also *ibid*. Vol. IV, pp. 39-40.
[142] S. GopaJ, *op. cit.,* Vol. Three, p. 171.
[143] *Ibid.,* Vol. Two, p. 206.

failed both before and after 1947 to devise institutional means, or to use the Congress as a vehicle, for taking his own brilliant understanding of and approach towards communalism to the mass of the Indian people. There was the relative absence of amass ideological campaign on the communal question both before and after independence. Of course, as we have seen, in his own speeches and writings he analyzed and vigorously attacked both Hindu and Muslim communalisms. During 1933-38, he also carried on a vast ideological campaign on the question in his widely distributed articles. But the Congress as an organization did not take up his ideas and remained confined within the *bhai-bhai* approach. And even his own personal campaign was increasingly muted after 1937, precisely when it was needed most and when communalism was acquiring a mass base. Curiously, he seemed to have lost interest in such a campaign after 1945 till the riots of the 1947 shook him up. Certainly, no mass political-ideological campaign of the sort carried out against colonialism was organized. Even when the Muslim League launched a vicious and patently false campaign against the Congress Ministries for allegedly discriminating against and oppressing Muslims, the Congress did not counter it with a mass explanatory campaign. Nor did Nehru and the Congress educate the people about the feeders of communalism, namely, religiosity, caste, social distance between Hindus and Muslims, the Hindu tinge in much of nationalist thought and propaganda, the communal interpretation of history, and obscurantism. In fact, the Congress leaders were not able to protect their own ranks from penetration by elements of communal ideology, as became apparent during the partition riots. The main, or even the only, critique of communalism in Nehru's own speeches during the 1946 election campaign was that the communalists were not fighting, and could not fight, for independence and that a vote for the Congress was a vote for freedom. Despite Nehru's own personals views, the Congress failed before independence to bring into public view the real problems and anxieties of the minorities or to deal with their causes or to combat the communalist efforts to misdirect the anxieties and fears of the minorities. After 1947, Muslims suffered from a multiplicity of disabilities arid deprivations. Undoubtedly, Nehru and the Congress party and governments made efforts to extend protection to Muslims, but they failed to take adequate concrete steps to alleviate their condition and to remove their disabilities or backwardness.

VII

One of the most positive features of Nehru's approach towards communalism was his opposition to the predominant nationalist strategy of solving the communal problem through negotiations and settlement with communal parties and their leaders. Even though he also had till 1928 placed his hopes on all-parties conferences but the failure of these conferences convinced him that pacts and negotiations and compromises—"artificially arranged marriages of convenience" —with the communal leaders would not get rid of the communal problem. He often expressed this view during and after 1931;[144] and in January 1935 he confided to his diary; "I have felt put out by an item of news in the paper. Secret confabulations going on between the Congress and Jinnah representing the Moslem League. Will people never learn?"[145] In March 1937 he publicly declared at the All India Convention of Congress Legislators: "We have too long thought in terms of pacts and compromises between communal leaders and neglected the people behind them. That is a discredited policy and I trust that we shall not revert to it. And yet some people still talk of the Muslims as a group dealing with Hindus or others as a group."[146] A few months later he even advised Gandhiji not to meet Jinnah as such a meeting "at this stage would not only serve little purpose but might be actually harmful."[147] And in February 1942 he wrote to Syed Mahmud: "You are entirely wrong if you think that I do not attach importance to the Hindu-Muslim problem. Whatever my other failings might be, I am not stupid and I know the vital importance of this question. But my ways of dealing with it are different. I am tired of this pottering about and trying to please reactionaries and fools or those who belong to the upper strata."[148]

The real answer, the real way of facing the communal challenge, said Nehru, was to go to the Muslim masses and defeat communalism politically in the way it had been defeated among Hindus. As he said in February 1937 when discussing the failure of the Congress to win many Muslim seats: "We failed because we had long neglected working among

---

[144] *SW,* Vol. IV, p. 503; *ibid.,* Vol. VI, p.172; *ibid.,* Vol. VII, p. 189; Ibid., Vol. VIII, pp. 62, 77,122,125,128,240; *ibid.,* Vol. XII, pp. 509, 515.

[145] *Ibid.,* Vol. VI, p. 311.

[146] *Ibid.,* Vol. VIII, p. 62.

[147] *Ibid.,* p. 182.

[148] *Ibid.,* Vol. XII, p. 515. Also *ibid.,* p. 509.

the Muslim masses and we could not reach them in time. But where we reached, especially in the rural areas, we found almost the same response, the same anti-imperialist spirit, as in others.... We failed also among the Muslims because of their much smaller electorate which could be easily manipulated and coerced by authority and vested interests. But I am convinced that, even so, we would have had a much larger measure of success if we had paid more attention to the Muslim masses."[149] In this context, wrote Nehru in March 1937, another negative feature of any kind of pact between the Congress and the Muslim League became apparent: "It will mean that we almost lose our right to ask the Muslims to join us directly."[150] It would also mean the Congress giving up its ideals and principles.[151] Nehru also repeatedly asserted that real Hindu-Muslim unity would come from below, when the Hindu and Muslim masses united.[152] It was in pursuance of this understanding that Nehru initiated in 1937 the Muslim Mass Contact Programme, which was unfortunately hastily conceived, ill-planned and ill-organized and was permitted to gradually peter out, without Nehru making any strenuous efforts to keep it alive.[153]

For a short while, ignoring his own understanding, Nehru entered into correspondence with Jinnah during 1937-38 and then carried on negotiations with him in November 1939 with a view to sort out the communal problem. But the correspondence led nowhere and the negotiations proved ineffectual; and Nehru soon declared that to carry on negotiations with Jinnah was "an utter impossibility".[154] He could not meet the very first demand of Jinnah that the League should be recognized as the sole organization representing Muslims to the exclusion of all other bodies, including the Congress, for this would have meant destroying the secular character of the Congress. Nehru's reaction to the Pakistan resolution was also that the possibility of any *negotiations with the* Muslim League was now foreclosed. "There is no question of settlement or negotiations now", said Nehru in April 1940: "The knot that is before us is incapable of being untied by settlement; it

[149] *Ibid.*, Vol. VIII, p. 62. Also *ibid.*, pp. 123, 128,218.

[150] *Ibid.*, p. 78.

[151] *Ibid.*, pp. 178 and 143.

[152] *Ibid.*, Vol. VI, p. 170.

[153] See Mushirul Hasan, "The Muslim Mass Contact Campaign", *Economic and Political Weekly*, 27 December 1986.

[154] *SW*, Vol. X, p. 403.

needs cutting open.... It has become the clear duty of the Congress to fight out the League and its scheme of denationalizing India".[155]

Nehru came back to this stance during late 1945. The Congress, he said, should "keep as far away from the Muslim League as possible". It could have "no truck" with the League; it was "not prepared to have any discussions or negotiations with the League". The Congress would take "the Muslim masses into our confidence"; it would redress their "every legitimate grievance". "But as for going to the Muslim League, never", declared Nehru. Instead, "we shall face the Muslim League and fight it."[156]

But despite all this fire and brimstone, and in between such angry phases, Nehru too many a time fell prey to the strategy of trying to solve the communal problem through top level negotiations with the Muslim communal leaders. This he did during 1938-39, 1941-42 and 1946-47. And by doing so, he, the tallest and the most secular of Indian leaders besides Gandhiji, accorded Jinnah and other communal leaders the much needed respectability and the status they desired of being the spokespersons of Muslims. It also tacitly weakened the right of the Congress to carryon a political-ideological struggle against the Muslim League or even to ask Muslims to join it. Constant negotiations with the League also weakened the position of the secular Muslim leaders. Moreover, the repeated but inevitable failures of negotiations tended to create communal distrust and bitterness and a feeling of despair and helplessness regarding the solution of the communal problem. In general, these negotiations bolstered up Muslim communalism, indirectly aroused and encouraged Hindu communalism and hampered and weakened the struggle against both. Perhaps, one of the reasons why Hindu communalism was successfully contained before and after 1947 was the Congress's and Nehru's refusal tp negotiate with its leaders. On the other hand, as Nehru rightly recognized, the need was to direct the debate with the communalists into hard, rational, analytical channels so that they were forced to fight on the terrain of reason and science and not of emotion and bias, and take this debate with the communal leaders and ideologues to the mases, the youth and the intelligentsia.

After independence too, once the impact of the partition riots and Gandhiji's assassination faded, and in the euphoria of the 1950s, induced

[155]*Ibid.,* Vol. XI, p. 17.

[156]*Ibid.,* Vol. XIV, pp. 91-2.

by the Five Year Plans and the rout of the communal parties and groups in the 1952 elections, Nehru became complacent about the communal problem, especially about the spread of communal ideology in quiet and subtle ways. The communal and language riots of the late 1950s led him to form the all-parties National Integration Council in 1961; but the resurgence of national feeling during the India-China conflict during 1960-62 led Nehru to dissolve it.

On the other hand, the Congress increasingly compromised with Muslim communal leaders in order to use Muslims as its vote-bank. In the bargain, the nationalists among Muslims, who had during the 1940s stood unwaveringly against the overwhelming tide of communalism, facing social ostracism, physical attacks and worse, were increasingly marginalized; and their place in the Congress organization, especially at the district and taluka levels, was taken by the erstwhile Muslim Leaguers. The story was repeated with the Sikh communalists in Punjab where repeated negotiations were held with them, compromises made, and many of them incorporated in the Congress Party. And, as a sort of compensation, concessions were made to the Hindu communalists among Punjab Congressmen, and offices in the Government and the Congress Party conferrred on them. Culmination of this compromising trend came when, after having frowned upon an alliance with the Muslim League in Keralain 1957, Nehru agreed to such an alliance in 1962. The Congress Party in Kerala had even before that made its peace with Christian communalism and Nair casteism.

VIII

Intellectually clear-headed and politically totally committed to secularism and the building of a secular nation-state, Nehru was not able to give adequate party-organizational backing to his secular commitment and vision. As the Congress President during 1936-37 and as the tallest nationalist leader after Gandhiji during the 1930s and 1940s, Nehru received regular reports from the rank and file Congressmen that many in the Congress at lower levels were holding communal views and maintaining organizational links with communal or communal-type organizations.[157] In 1933, he complained that many individual Congressmen were infected with communalism; and in 1934 that "many a Congressman has almost unconsciously partly succumbed to it (communalism) and tried to reconcile his nationalism with this narrow

[157] N .L. Gupta, *op. cit.*, p. 132.

and reactionary creed." Many others "have flirted with Hindu or Muslim or Sikh or any other communalism."[158] In his *Autobiography* he went so far as to suggest that "many a Congressman was a communalist under his national cloak."[159] Yet he took hardly any organizational steps to cleanse the Congress of such elements, though he did succeed at a formal level in 1938 when the Congress barred members of the communal organizations from holding office in the Congress organization.

After 1947 too, he took note of the existence of communal-minded persons within the Congress organization. During 1947-48, he expressed his unhappiness at many Congressmen having "given way to this national turmoil and cofusion". He was pained that elements of communal outlook prevailed even among the higher levels of the Congress leadership and this outlook inspired the decisions of some of his colleagues at the Centre and the States.[160] Some Congressmen had even gone so far as to be "attracted to this development of fascist and Nazi modes of thought and pracitice".[161] In 1949, he complained that "all of us seem to be getting infected with the refugee mentality or worse still, the RSS mentality."[162] And, in 1950: "Communalism has invaded the minds and hearts of those who were pillars of the Congress in the past."[163] These comments were a tribute to Nehru's sturdy secularism and his sense of realism. But they did not lead him to undertake strong political or organizational measures to rid the Congress Party of these communal elements. His anger was more or less confined to verbal admonition in his speeches or the sending of long appeals and epistles to individual Congress leaders, his cabinet colleagues and the Chief Ministers. Similarly, he took up cudgels on behalf of Urdu, but failed to persuade the state governments of the north to change their policy of the neglect of Urdu. To sum up this aspect of Nehru's failure, in the words of S.Gopal, "the gulf between resolution and implementation yawned as wide as ever."[164]

---

[158]*SW,* Vol. VI, p. 183.
[159]P. 136.
[160]S. Gopal, *op. cit.,* Vol. Two. p. 76.
[161]*LCM,* Vol. I, p. 34.
[162]S. Gopal, *op. cit.,* Vol. Two, p. 77.
[163]*Ibid.,* p. 92. Also *LCM,* Vol. II, p. 97.
[164]*S.Gopal., op. cit.,* Vol. Three, p. 28.

IX

As the executive head of the Government, Nehru realized the need for strong administrative steps against virulent communal propaganda and in case of communal tension and rioting. As noted earlier, he took strong steps during 1947-48 in northern India and in 1950 in West Bengal. In 1951, he warned those who were carrying on anti-Muslim propaganda and asking Muslims to go to Pakistan: "If any person raises his hand against another person on basis of religion, all the resources at the command of the Government will be used to put him down with an iron hand."[165] Throughout the years he went on urging the Chief Ministers to deal promptly and firmly with the communal trouble-makers, and, whenever necessary, to take pre-emptive action in case of communal tension and not wait for some incident to occur.[166]

Nehru was fully aware of the role that the communal press played in fanning the communal fire, leading to communal violence.[167] He advised the Chief Ministers to take immediate action against those, including newspapers and their editors, who fostered communal hatred, incited people and gave currency to rumours and vague allegations.[168] In June 1951, the Constitution was amended to enable "reasonable restrictions" to be placed on the right of free speech and expression in order to curb communal writing and speeches.[169] This legislation, being very mild, proved inadequate and Nehru argued for further amendment of the existing law.[170] At the same time, he urged the State Governments not to be overcautious in the matter and to take immediate action under the existing law, including the Preventive Detention Act, even if the chances of successful prosecution were mearge. One result would be to convince the public that the Government would "stand no nonsense in regard to communal troubles."[171]

Nehru was aware that in case of a situation of communal tension and rioting a great deal depended on the action or inaction of the District Magistrate or the Superintendent of Police. "If they are competent and

[165]N.L. Gupta, *op. cit.*, p. 227.

[166]*LCM,* Vol. II, p. 61 ; *ibid.,* Vol. IV, pp. 41, 446; S. Gopal, *op. cit.,* Vol. Three, p. 17J.

[167]*LCM,* Vol. I, p. 60; *ibid.,* pp. 437, 446.

[168]*Ibid.,* Vol. II, pp. 34-8, 150; S. Gopal, *op. cit.,* Vol. Three, pp. 172-3.

[169]*LCM,* Vol. II, pp. 403ff.

[170]*Ibid.,* Vol. III, pp. 109, 129.

[171]*Ibid.,* Vol. IV, pp. 447-8. Also see. N.L. Gupta, *op. cit.,* p. 249.

right-minded", he wrote in October 1950, "nothing wrong is likely to happen. But if they are not competent, or if they temporize with communal or anti-social elements, then trouble is bound to come some time or other."[172] Asking the Chief Ministers to control the deteriorating communal situation in the early 1950s, Nehru urged them to make the Government policy clear to officials of all grades. "I say so", he wrote, "because I find that many of our officials are themselves not clear in their minds and are sometimes biased. Even our police force is not always impartial." "In a crisis of this kind", he added, "half-hearted measures and half-hearted officials are of no use and they should be told so.... If any of them are not prepared to follow this policy honestly and effectively, then it is open to them to leave the service."[173]

Whenever communal disturbances occurred, Nehru assumed that there had been the failure of district authorities. Consequently, he recommended that such erring officials should be duly warned and disciplinary action taken against them. "Every District Magistrate should be made to realize that his reputation depends upon the avoidance of such incidents," he advised the Chief Ministers in a long letter in 1950; and added: "I think it would be a safe policy to put a black mark in the record of every district officer when a communal incident takes place and to inform him of this." "The best of excuses", he concluded, "are not good enough, just as all the reasons in the world which a defeated General may advance for his defeat are not good enough."[174]

Nehru also urged that in case of a communal riot not only proper compensation should be paid to the victims and the victims fully rehabilitated but it was also essential that "the guilty should be punished and should be made to feel that it does not pay to create disturbance and to loot and kill."[175] He further argued that it should be made clear that "the community that takes to aggression will suffer." The thing to do was to impose a collective fine on the offending community as a whole, while compensating the suffering party.[176]

Unfortunately, once again a hiatus occurred between Nehru's ideas and their implementation. The situation was, of course, far better than it is

[172]*LCM,* Vol. II, p. 213.

[173]*Ibid.,* pp. 61-2.

[174]*Ibid.,* p. 213. Also S. GopaJ, *op. cit.,* Vol. Three, p. 172.

[175]*LCM,* VoL II, p. 42.

[176]*Ibid.,* Vol. IV, p. 41.

today. Even so, hardly any instigator, organizer or perpetrator of communal violence was punished during the 1950s and 1960s. Most of the Chief Ministers and his Cabinet colleagues paid little heed to his passionate advice. Communal-minded officials felt no fear that their communalism, especially if it was not overt, would stand in the way of their promotion, not to speak of their continuation in service. Violent communal propaganda through the Press and public platform and word of mouth flourished with impunity. Civil liberties continued to provide an umbrella to all kinds of communal activity. And the last years of Nehru's stewardship of the nation witnessed large-scale communal violence.

X

Above all, in his treatment of the communal question, Nehru suffered from a certain economistic, deterministic and reductionist bias. This led him to underplay, if not ignore, the role of communalism as ideology and of ideological-political struggle against it. It was also responsible for the gross misunderstanding of actual communal parties and politics by him as also by other nationalists, whether belonging to the left or the right, and for their failure to evolve an effective strategy to combat communalism and the communal forces.

Before 1947, especially between 1928 and 1939, Nehru, under the impact of mechanical Marxism, believed that if economic issues were brought to the forefront, if mass struggles were organized around economic issues and if the anti-imperialist struggle was sharpened and based on the masses, the consciousness of the masses would *on its own* get divested of communalism; communal consciousness would be *automatically* dissolved as people would come to acquire national or class consciousness. Economic issues or class struggle between the haves and have-nots would *automatically* liquidate communalism or at least push it into the background. Once the masses were brought into politics, the communal leaders, belonging to the upper and middle classes, would either get isolated or be transformed. The communal problem would fade away once the third party, the British, departed and India became free. Because the communal problem was false, not based on a correct perception or representation of reality, it would disappear at the touch of reality.[177] Let me give a few quotations from Nehru. He wrote in 1931:

[177] *SW,* Vol. III, pp. 226, 261 ; *ibid.,* Vol. IV, p. 573; ibid., Vol. V, p. 203; *ibid.,* Vol. VI, pp. 156, 170, 177-8; *ibid.,* Vol. VII, pp. 69, 82, 108, 112, 127, 190, 238, 270, 277, 363; *ibid.,* Vol. VIII, pp. 62, 129; ibid., Vol. IX, p. 240; *ibid.,* Vol. XII, pp. 407-8,410,511,522; *ibid.,* Vol. XIV, pp. 11,42; *Autobiography,* p. 469.

"The real thing to my mind is the economic factor. If we lay stress on this and divert public attention to it we shall find *automatically* that religious differences recede into the background and a common bond unites different groups. The economic bond is stronger than even the national one. Working among the kisans, among peasants, I have found very little difference when they have this economic bond."[178] And in 1936: "If the masses are fully represented, inevitably economic issues affecting them will come to the forefront and superficial problems, like the communal one, will lose importance."[179] Again in 1936: "The obvious way to deal with the communal problem is to allow the fundamental economic issues to come forward, so that attention can be diverted from the communal issue. The latter will have to be faced and will *inevitably be solved* as the economic issues are allowed to come Up."[180] As President of the Congress, he told the Lucknow Congress in 1936 : "I am afraid I cannot get excited over this communal issue.... It is after all a side issue, and it can have no real importance in the larger scheme of things."[181] And again: The communal issue "is overrated and over-emphasized.... With the coming of social issues to the forefront it is bound to recede into the background."[182] In his *Autobiography* he wrote: "This idea of a Muslim nation is the figment of a few imaginations only ... it would still vanish at the touch of reality."[183]

During these years, Nehru's basic assumption, as has been brought out above, was that communalism was reactionary because the communal parties and their leaders did not favour or demand independence, did not put forward a radical programme around the economic needs of the masses, and remained confined to the middle and upper classes and did not try to go to the masses or organize them. More, he tended to suggest that the communalists were incapable of doing so· and if they did incorporate these three features they would cease to be reactionary. It is quite clear that he was failing to fully understand the role of

[178]*SW,* Vol. V, p. 203.

[179]*Ibid.,* Vol. VII, p. 127.

[180]*Ibid.,* p. 112.

[181]*Ibid.,* p. 190.

[182]*Ibid.,* p. 69.

[183]P. 469.

communalism as ideology. A good student of fascism and Nazism, he was not applying this understanding to communalism even when seeing its fascist character, for fascist ideology and politics become dangerous precisely when the fascists adopt a nationalist and economically radical programme and succeed in acquiring a mass base. Instead, he said that it was possible to cooperate with the communalists or let them join the national movement if they accepted the objective of national freedom.[184] and he welcomed the change in the Muslim League's programme in 1937 in favour of the demand for independence.[185] (Parenthetically, it may. be pointed out that the Hindu communalists and a large segment of the Muslim and Sikh communalists had always done so.) He regularly taunted the communalists to approach the masses with an economic programme.[186] If the communalists disagreed with the Congress, said Nehru, let them go to the masses—"But it is to the masses that the appeal must be made."[187] He also welcomed the change in the Muslim League's economic outlook which had brought it nearer to the Congress.[188] During 1937 and after, he repeatedly said that he would welcome Muslim League's efforts to enrol members through any kind of mass contact. For example, he said in September 1937: "We welcome every attempt at its (Muslim League's) democratisation and that of providing a mass basis."[189] He was convinced that the wider social base would bring the communal leadership into conflict with the Muslim mass demands. In fact, it would be a good idea to insist that "the membership of the Muslim League should be confined only to exploited Muslim masses."[190] Or, as he wrote in the *Discovery of India* regarding the years 1937-39: "For the first time in its history the Moslem League got a mass backing and began to develop into a mass organization. Much as I regretted what was happening, I welcomed this development in a way as I thought that this might lead ultimately to a change in the feudal leadership and more progressive

---

[184]*SW,* Vol. VI, p. 164 ; *ibid.,* Vol. VII, p. 365; *ibid.,* Vol. VIII, pp. 122, 208:

[185]*Ibid.,* Vol. VIII, pp. 201, 209, 223, 758, 767; *ibid.,* Vol. X, p. 214.

[186]*Ibid.,* Vol. VI, pp. 184-5.

[187]*Ibid.,* Vol. VIII, p. 127.

[188]*Ibid.,* p. 223.

[189]*Ibid.,* p. 179. Also *ibid.,* p. 150.

[190]*Ibid.,* p. 179. Also *ibid.,* Vol. X, p. 214.

elements would come forward."[191]

In fact, the Muslim League had no difficulty in adopting a radical economic programme, becoming a mass organization, accepting independence as its goal, and acquiring a 'progressive' or left wing of its own. Only it combined all these with a two-nation theory, the demand for Pakistan, and a militant and extreme communal ideology. It was now that it became a real danger to Indian unity as also to the Indian people.

It is not that Nehru completely ignored the ideological character of communalism. He clearly saw it when he defined communalism as the mixing up of religion with politics, or when the Congress Working Committee defined the Hindu Mahasabha and the Muslim League as communal and closed the doors of the Congress offices to their members. But this aspect of communalism as ideology was ignored when a critique of communalism as reactionary was evolved or the strategy to oppose it was framed. In fact, communal ideology was reactionary in itself and, once initiated, would develop on its own steam unless actively opposed. Unless a conscious effort was made to transform cultural, political and ideological consciousness, even active participants in class struggles and the anti-imperialist movement remained open to communal ideology and could fall prey to communal passions during communal riots.

Nehru continued the economistic and reductionist approach after independence. Though he now recognized explicitly or implicitly the ideological character of communalism[192]—for in an adult-franchise democracy communalism had to have a nationalist and popular economic programme and a mass base—, he still neglected political-ideological struggle against communalism. He expected that planning and economic development and the spread of education, science and technology would automatically weaken and extinguish communal and casteist thinking and politics.[193] Little attention, for example, was paid to the content of

---

[191]P. 339. Even this search for progressive elements in a communal organization is reminiscent of the effort to find progressive Nazis in Germany during 1930-1933.

[192]See, for example, *LCM,* Vol. I, pp. 46,114,179; *ibid.,* Vol. II, pp. 37, 40, 65, 464, 521 ; *ibid.,* Vol. IV, pp. 381, 537. This recognition was also inherent in the characterization of communalism and communal organizations, especially the RSS and Jan Sangh, as fascist.

[193]See, for example, *LCM,* Vol. III, pp. 205,346; S. Gopal, *op. cit.,* Vol. Three, p. 172.

education. After all, the spread of education could be a powerful instrument for the spread of communal and communal type ideologies, if its content was communal, chauvinist or regionalist. Nor was much of an effort made to take science and scientific approach to the mass of people. It was only after the recrudescence of communal and linguistic riots in late 1950s and 1960-61 that Nehru realized that it was not enough to rely on social and economic progress, even though in the long run such progress would have a positive impact by diverting "people's minds to the broader issues."[194] And it was the National Integration Council, convened in 1961, that decided to reorient education and to get textbooks prepared emphasizing secularism and national unity.

X

To sum up: Jawaharlal Nehru played a major role in the 1930s and 1940s in keeping the national movement on sturdy secular lines. His speeches, writings and correspondence on communalism 'had a certain freshness of approach and contained deep insights.' His commitment to secularism was total and unprecedented and all-pervasive. Communalism he hated with all his being; and he fought it heroically and with vigour. If, after independence, under most unfavourable circumstances, India framed a secular constitution and laid the foundations of a secular state and society, it was, above all, because of Jawaharlal Nehru. He helped secularism acquire deep roots among the Indian people; and he prevented the burgeoning forth of communalism when conditions were favourable for it.

But space still remained for communalism. It was not completely uprooted. As Nehru mournfully acknowledged in 1961: "The devil which had been pushed away into some comer of our minds, displays itself again and it becomes evident that we are still far from having developed a broadminded, tolerant and all-India nationalism."[195] Communalism continues to pose a serious threat to Indian society and polity. It can leap forward any time. Nehru's economistic and reductionist understanding of communalism and the lack of political-ideological struggle against it and administrative flabbiness in dealing with communal propaganda and communal violence during the Nehru era, as also in the post-Nehru years, had also something to do with this aspect of the Indian reality.

---

[194] *LCM,* Vol. V, p. 430.

[195] *Ibid.*

Select Bibliography and Abbrevations

Akbar, M.J., *Nehru: The Making of India,* London, 1988.

Brecher, Michael, *Nehru - A Political Biography,* London, 1959.

Chandra, Bipan, *Communalism in Modern India,* New Delhi, 1984.

Gopal, S., *Jawaharlal Nehru - A Biography,* 3 volumes, London, 1975, 1979, 1984.

Hasan, Mushirul, "The Muslim Mass Contact Campaign", *Economic and Political Weekly,* Bombay, 27 December 1986.

Karanjia, R.K., (i) *The Mind of Mr. Nehru,* London, 1960. (ii) *The Philosophy of Mr. Nehru,* London, 1966.

Mende, Tibor, *Conversations with Mr. Nehru,* London, 1956.

Misra, Salil, "Nehru and Communalism", M.Phjl. Dissertation, Centre for Historical Studies, Jawaharlal Nehru University, New Delhi, 1983.

Nehru, Jawaharlal, (i) *An Autobiography,* New Delhi, 1962 reprint.

(ii) *The Discovery of India,* Calcutta, Second Edition, 1946.

(iii) *Selected Works of Jawaharlal Nehru,* 15 volumes, edited by S. Gopal, New Delhi, 1972 -. *(SW).*

(iv) *Selected Works of Jawaharlal Nehru,* Second Series, vols. 1-7, edited by S. Gopal New Delhi, 1984—. [SW (SS)].

(v) *Letters to Chief Ministers,* 1947-1964, vols. 1-5, edited by G. Parthasarthi, New Delhi, 1985—. *(LCM).*

(vi) *Jawaharlal Nehru's Speeches,* 5 volumes, edited in Publications Division, New Delhi, 4th Edition, 1983, 5th Edition, 1983, 1970 reprint, Second Edition, 1983, Second Edition, 1983, respectively.

(vii) *Nehru on Communalism,* edited by N.L. Gupta, New Delhi, 1965.

Rau, M. Chalapathi, *Jawahatlal Nehru,* New Delhi, 1979 reprint.

Singh, Anita I., "Nehru and the Communal Problem 1936-1939", M. Phil. Dissertation, Centre for Historical Studies, Jawaharlal Nehru University, New Delhi, 1976.

3

Struggle for the Ideological Transformation of the National Congress in the 1930s

I

The Indian national movement was one of the most radical of the anti-imperialist movements outside China. Its ideological development occurred between the 1880s and the 1940s based on firm anti-imperialism and a programme of social and economic reform. From the beginning, the nationalist leadership displayed a certain anti-colonial strength. It gradually generated, formed and crystallised a clear-cut anti-colonial ideology. It evolved a clear, scientific and firm understanding and analysis of colonialism and spread it widely among the Indian people. Already by the end of the 19th century, the founding fathers of the Indian national movement had worked out a clear understanding of the three modes of colonial surplus extraction: (a) directly through taxation, plunder and large-scale employment of Englishmen; (b) unequal trade by making India a hinterland for the production and sale of raw materials and purchase of metropolitan manufactures; (c) investment of foreign capital. They had further grasped that the essence of colonialism lay in the subordination of the Indian economy and society as a whole to the needs of the British economy and society, and that India's colonial relationship was not an accident of history or a result of political policy but rather sprang from the very nature and character of British society. This understanding of the complex economic mechanism of modern imperialism was further advanced after 1918 under the impact of the anti-imperialist mass movements and the spread of Marxist ideas. Thus the national movement arrived at, and based itself on, a correct grasp of the central or primary contradiction of colonial India, the contradiction between colonialism and the development and interests of the Indian people. Moreover, at each stage of its development, the national leadership linked its political analysis to the analysis of colonialism. The national movement was thus placed on a firm, anti-colonial ideological basis.

From the beginning, the national leadership emphasised the objective of independent economic development including independence from foreign capital, the creation of an independent capital goods sector based on the latest technology and the foundation of independent science and technology. In the 1930s, the objective of economic planning was widely and universally accepted.

The multi-faceted diversity of the Indian people was fully recognised. The political objective of unifying the Indian people into a nation was to be realised by taking full account of regional, religious, caste, ethnic and linguistic differences. Secularism was made a basic constituent of the nationalist ideology. Similarly, the cultural aspirations of the different linguistic groups were given official recognition. The nationalist movement opposed caste oppression and after 1920 made abolition of untouchability a basic constituent of its programme and political work.

The nationalist movement was fully committed to parliamentary democracy and civil liberties. From the foundation of the Indian National Congress, the nationalist and other mass organisations were organised along democratic lines. From the beginning the nationalists fought for the freedom of the Press, speech and association and other civil liberties. It was the national movement which undertook as well as accomplished the task of making parliamentary democracy and civil liberties indigenous.

On the socio-economic plane, the national movement from the beginning adopted a pro-poor orientation and accepted and propagated a programme of reforms that was quite radical by contemporary standards and was basically oriented towards the people. Compulsory primary education, lowering of taxation on the poor and lower middle classes, reduction of salt tax, land revenue and rent, debt relief and provision of cheap credit to the agriculturists, protection of tenant-rights, defence of trade union rights and of the worker's right to a living wage and a shorter working day, higher wages for, low-paid employees including the policemen, protection and promotion of village industries, improvement in the social position of women, including their right to work and education and to equal political rights, and reform of the machinery of law and order including the jails, were some of the major reformist demands taken up by the national movement.

Over the years, the nationalists, evolved a policy of opposition to imperialism on a world scale, and of expressing and establishing solidarity with the anti-imperialist movements in other parts of the world. On the one hand, from the 1870s, they made an effort to establish solidarity with, and get the support of, the anti-imperialist sections of the British public life and firmly established the notion that the Indians hated imperialism but not the British people; on the other hand, from 1878 onwards they gave support to the anti-imperialist struggles of the Burmese people, the Afghans, the tribal people of the North West Frontier, the Chinese. people at the time of the Sino-Japanese War of 1895 and the I-Ho- Tuan (Boxer) Uprising, the Tibetan people, the people of Egypt and Sudan and the people of other parts of Africa. The nationalists welcomed the Russian Revolutions of 1905 and 1917. From 1927, the Indian National Congress opposed imperialism in all parts of the world. It also took a clear-cut anti-fascist stand and gave active support to the anti-fascist struggles of the people of Ethiopia and Spain and the national liberation struggle of the Chinese people against Japanese aggression.

The national movement gradually involved the large-scale politicisation of the people and their active participation in the movement. The task of activising and mobilising the masses was propagated from the beginning but was undertaken after 1918. The Gandhian era politics derived their entire force from the militancy and self-sacrificing spirit of the masses. In particular, the national movement, starting out as the activity of the patriotic intelligentsia, succeeded in mobilising the youth, the urban petty bourgeoisie, the urban poor, rural and urban artisans, and large sections of the peasantry.

II

Indian nationalism from the 1880's onwards was firmly rooted in a correct critique of the character of colonial economy, but this critique was at the same time confined within the perspective of the capitalist character of modern economic development. Thus the national movement was under bourgeois ideological hegemony from the beginning. Though this hegemony penetrated deep and acquired great strength because it held ground for a long time during which it was unchallenged, it was not very consciously structured on a class basis. It was adopted from the 1880s to 1917 because of the absence or non-availability of any 'Other path of development. Consequently, the socialist path did not meet strong intellectual resistance from the nationalists once it emerged as an alternative after the October Revolution.

After 1919, when the national movement became a mass movement, Gandhiji evolved and propagated a different, non-capitalist out-look but his socio-economic programme was not capable of challenging the basic hegemony of bourgeois ideology; nor did any contemporary see it in that light despite Gandhiji's denunciation of modern industrial capitalist civilisation.

III

The impact of the Russian Revolution was felt widely and immediately and a left current developed from early 1920s within the ranks of the national movement and soon became a part of its ideological spectrum. Beginning with late 1920s, bourgeois ideological hegemony over the national movement was challenged in a serious manner by early Communist groups, Jawaharlal Nehru, Subhas Chandra Bose, and other socialist-minded individuals. The ideological struggle was intensified in the 1930s when these were joined by the Congress Socialist Party and the Royists. Nehru's speeches and writings during 1933-36 played a vanguardist role. The Great Depression in the capitalist world, success of the Soviet Five Year Plans, the anti-fascist wave the world over, and the turn to Marxism among many British intellectuals were major positive influences. Leaders of the youth movement of late 1920s and of the volunteers of the Civil Disobedience Movement (CDM) turned to socialism under these influences as also because of their disenchantment with the Gandhian leadership of the CDM and the substitute for it after 1934 in the form of the constructive programme and parliamentary activity. Most of the young intellectuals brought up during the 1930s turned towards socialism of one type or another. The rising peasant movements and trade unions, too, increasingly moved left. The Congress Socialists and the Communists after 1935 became active members of the Congress. Nehru stomped the country propagating socialism. The Congress was increasingly radicalised. This radicalisation found expression in the Karachi Resolution in 1931, Nehru's Presidential Address to the Lucknow Congress in early 1936, the radical agrarian programme adopted by the Faizpur session of the Congress in late 1936, the adoption of a radical election manifesto for the 1937 elections to provincial assemblies, the formation of the National Planning Committee, the strident stand against war and fascism, and pro-peasant agrarian legislation by the Congress Ministries from 1937 to 1939. During this period several nationalist leaders and a large number of revolutionary terrorist leaders made the turn to Marxism, and the Communist Party and the Congress Socialist Party were able to acquire strong or even dominant influence over the Congress organisation in several parts of the country such as Kerala, Andhra Pradesh, U.P., and Orissa. The period was so favourable to socialist idea's that it appeared as if the left was on the verge of ideologically transforming the Congress and the national movement in a socialist direction. But the opportunity was missed, the possibility was aborted. While the left grew in numbers—Nehru and Subhas became presidents of the Congress during 1936-39, the CPI, the CSP and the Royists grew in numbers in geometric proportions—and it was able to develop peasants' and workers' organisations, the student movement, the Progressive Writers' Association and other similar cultural organisations and women's organizations, publish left-wing journals and newspapers, popularise Marxism on a large scale, and develop sympathy and support for the Soviet Union, it failed to establish ideological hegemony over the national movement, that is, to effect a basic transformation of the Congress ideology in a socialist direction.

IV

Before the left could make a breakthrough in this respect, it had to be clear on the points on which it demarcated itself from the right and relate these to the issue of ideological hegemony. In other words, on which terrain was the struggle for ideological hegemony to be carried on?

It is our hypothesis here that lacking understanding in theory or in practice or both of the role of the central or primary contradiction of colonial India, the nature of the popular mass movement led by Gandhiji and involving millions upon millions of people—often pitting a single demonstration or strike by 50,000 or 100,000 workers in a single city against a massive all-India movement—the strategy of the dominant national leadership, the rules and contours of hegemonic political struggle, an understanding of the different ideological currents in the national movement from the far left to the far right, the left, including the CPI and the CSP and to a large extent Subhas Bose and pre-1937 Nehru, chose to fight the battle for socialist hegemony on a *wrong terrain and on wrong issues* and thus gradually frittered away the ground that attraction of socialism and Marxism had created. Consequently, the left groups and parties grew in numbers but lost the battle for ideological hegemony over the movement for national liberation.[1] Furthermore, the left—the CPI and the CSP—failed to acquire political ground from which they could move towards becoming a hegemonic force in society and in the national movement. The left remained, and was to remain for decades after, a vent or a channel for popular grievances, the organiser of organized social protest, the hope of the oppressed; but its political character was to remain that of a pressure group and not that of a leader of the masses contending for socio-political hegemony over society.

V

The starting point of the left was the view that the nationalist leadership consisted of two wings, one right-wing or reactionary and the other left or revolutionary. Thus the starting point itself was faulty, for a popular, open mass movement is never like that; it is always much more open-ended and a many splendoured thing. Right and left are not two nodal points but part of a wide ideological spectrum.

In any case, the left defined the right in wrong, non-ideological terms, often seeing tactical questions in ideological terms and equating strategic perspectives with ideological positions. Instead of grasping the complex real world in an equally complex manner, the left first conceived political India in terms of its criticism and critical model and then successfully criticised it. Quite often those who did not accept its understanding of the current political situation, who did not share its political perceptions or its current strategic and technical models were branded as right wing. Let us in this light examine some of the major issues on which the left fought its battles against the right.

(A) Office Acceptance: The decision to resume parliamentary activity during 1934-35 was seen by the left as a retreat from radical politics and a surrender of ideals and as going back to the non-mass movement phase of pre-1919 years.[2] But the real large scale demarcation was made on the question of office acceptance. Office acceptance was seen as falling prey to the imperialist strategy of co-option, cooperating "in some measure with the repressive apparatus of imperialism" and

---

[1]The entire, wrong approach of the left over the years is codified in R. Palme Dutt's work, *India Today,* 1948 edition, Bombay.

[2]The left saw the earlier Swarajist phase of 1924-29 as of cooperation with imperialism and the result of vacillations of the bourgeoisie.

becoming "partners in this repression and in the exploitation of our people". It would mean a surrender before imperialism.[3] Others were even less charitable. They saw it as a hall-mark of the rightist mentality, as the right's repudiation of, and alternative to, mass struggle, and as a symbol of the right's desire to cooperate with imperialism. It represented the class essence of the bourgeois-landlord classes. The proletariat, on the other hand, it was said, never stopped fighting or accepted constitutional phases.

It was not difficult for the other side to show that the left was wrong on the question, especially regarding the motive behind office acceptance, and that what was involved were questions of perception and strategy and not ideology. Those who favoured office acceptance denied that they were constitutionalists and said that they were equally committed to combating the 1935 Act. They argued for office acceptance as a short-term tactical step which the national movement had to take in view of its incapacity at the moment to resume the extra-legal mass movement; but they argued that "real work lies outside the legislatures" and that for achievement of freedom a mass struggle was needed. The case for office acceptance was put forward by several leaders with a degree of clarity. J.B. Kriplani, for example, said: "Even in a revolutionary movement, there may be times of comparative depression and inactivity. At such times, whatever programmes are devised have necessarily an appearance of reformatory activity but they are all a necessary part of all revolutionary strategy".[4] Nor was the issue of socialism involved in the debate. As T. Vishwanathan of Andhra put it: "To my socialist comrades, I would say, capture or rejection of offices is not a matter of socialism, I would ask them to realize that it is a matter of strategy."[5]

The pro-office acceptance leaders agreed that there were pitfalls involved and the Congressmen in office could give way to wrong tendencies from corruption to co-option into the imperialist administrative and constitutional structure. But the answer, they said, was to fight these wrong tendencies and not abandon offices themselves.

---

[3]Jawaharlal Nehru, *Selected Works,* edited by S. Gopal, New Delhi, Vol. 7, pp.185-6.

[4]J.B. Kriplani, speech at Lucknow Congress, in A.M. and S.G. Zaidi, editors, *The Encyclopaedia of the Indian National Congress,* Vol.1.10, p.48.

[5]*Ibid.,* p.42.

Moreover, the colonial government was determined to hold elections and implement the provincial autonomy part of the 1935 Act. Even if the Congress rejected office there were other groups and parties, mostly pro-Government, who were willing to assume office. If the Congress left the field clear to them, they would use the ministries to weaken nationalism and encourage reactionary and communal policies and politics. The basic question that the ministerialists posed was whether office acceptance invariably led to co-option by the colonial state or could ministries be used to defeat the colonial strategy. The answer, in the words of Vishwanathan, was: "Do not look upon ministries as offices but as centres and fortresses from where British imperialism is radiated"[6] In other words, the real question was the manner in which the provincial autonomy was to be worked and not whether it was to be worked or not.[7] It is also interesting that the left entirely ignored the fact that Gandhiji was basically an extra-constitutionalist, was till 1937 personally opposed to council entry and office acceptance, and put forward the constructive programme as a non-constitutional alternative to parliamentarianism. For example, he wrote in 1934, even when permitting those who wanted to participate in elections to do so: "I hope that the majority will always remain untouched by the glamour of council work. In its own place, it will be useful. But the Congress will commit suicide if its attention is solely devoted to the legislative work. Swaraj will never come that way. Swaraj can only come through an all-round consciousness of the masses."[8]

(B) Collective Affiliation: A second issue picked up by the left for struggle and polemic against the right wing, especially during 1935-36, was that of collective affiliation. Nehru proposed the widening of the mass base of the Congress and its identification with the interests of the masses

---

[6]*Ibid.*, p. 142.

[7]The decision of 1934 to withdraw a movement which had declined and to go in for elections closely resembled the 1951 decision of the CPI to withdraw the call for the overthrow of the Government and to go in for elections. Similarly, the decision to accept office in 1937 was similar to the Communist decision to form ministries in Kerala in 1957, 1967, 1969 and 1977 and in West Bengal in 1967, 1969 and 1977 and in Tripura in 1977. But it is surprising that despite this latter practice, almost all left-wing historians continue to describe the advocacy of council-entry in 1934 and office acceptance in 1937 as right-wing policies or decisions.

[8]*The Collected Works of Mahatma Gandhi,* New Delhi, Vol. 58, p. II.

by the collective affiliation to it of the workers' and peasants' organizations. While the objective was sound, the method was surely spurious and manipulative. The notion that the masses could be brought into the Congress and its base could be radicalized only via affiliation of their class organisations was based on three assumptions: (a) that the Congress was a bourgeois organization and should have united front with workers' and peasants' organizations; (b) that the Congress was not a popular mass organization or movement but a united front of separately organized parties and classes which contended with each other for control over it; or (c) that the masses could not be brought into the Congress through direct membership of the organization. The question was whether the Congress as a popular organization-movement could be better radicalized through collective affiliation or through ideological-political work among the masses in the Congress and by bringing the radicalised masses into the Congress. In fact, could a popular mass organization exist by permitting such collective affiliation? It seems that the left did not realise at the time that the Congress was not a conclave of parties and class organizations, a sort of body coordinating existing like-minded organisations, such as the Popular Front of France or the Communist-Kuomintang alliance of China, but a historically developed mass organization leading the freedom struggle.

The right had little difficulty in showing that perhaps collective affiliation was put forward as an instrument for changing the balance of political and ideological forces inside the Congress in an artificial manner, as a sort of *coup d'etat,* by the left because it did not have the political support in the movement to do it any other way. In any case there was nothing right-wing about opposition to this demand. Its rejection did not debar the left in any way from organizing workers and peasants in their own class organizations or enrolling the workers and peasants into the Congress or carry on socialist propaganda and education within the Congress or for fighting for greater, and wherever possible majority, representation in the leadership bodies of the Congress. In fact, the left was able to do so without hinderance and even successfully in Kerala and to a certain extent in Bengal, Orissa, V.P. and Andhra. On the other hand, in a situation where kisan sabhas and trade unions were poorly organized in terms of properly enrolled membership, etc., even while acting as fighting organs of class struggle at the economic plane, any collective affiliation would surely have opened the floodgates of bogus membership and organizational manipulation."[8a]

(C) *Constituent Assembly:* From 1935 onwards, the left rightly regarded the slogan of a Constituent Assembly, elected on the basis of adult franchise, to frame the constitution of free India as a revolutionary slogan. But the right dominated Congress had already put forth the slogan at Patna in June 1934 simultaneously with the decision to enter the legislative councils. The slogan was vigorously campaigned for later by the entire Congress.

(D) Non-violence: A fourth major issue that was constantly posed by the left was that of violence vs. non-violence. Instead of posing the question of non-violence in terms of its usefulness as a form of struggle and political mobilisation in the specific conditions of colonial India, it was projected in terms of class essence and abstract criteria on the assumption that methods of struggle have class essences. Non-violent struggle was seen to be a form of struggle which was in essence 'bourgeois-landlord'.[9] The Communists and Socialists regularly demanded revolutionary action which was defined, in the ultimate, as violence in general and armed insurrection in particular. The Communists in particular made methods of struggle basic constituents of a strategic perspective, and as revolutionary or non-revolutionary in themselves. They often defined a strategy of struggle in terms of methods of struggle.

Non-violence was one issue on which Nehru and gradually elements of the CSP came to terms with Gandhiji. The Communists, on the other hand, not only made non-violence, one of the points of demarcation from

[8a]Even when direct membership was involved, the Congress failed to avoid these two evils, especially after 1937. Trade unions till this day suffer from this aspect and no mechanism has been evolved so far to avoid it when it comes to measuring the relative strength of various trade union centres. Consequently, we have the spectacle of the AITUC and the CITU being relegated to a position far below that of the INTUC and the BMS.

[9]Just as in recent years all talk of peaceful coexistence or settlement of struggle between the socialist bloc and the imperialist bloc has been portrayed as a revisionist concession to bourgeois outlook. Same is the case with the political line of parliamentary road to power adopted by Italy, Great Britain, etc. The point of course is that these may be wrong politically, but they are not manifestations of a right-wing or bourgeois-landlord essence.

Gandhiji's leadership and the existing national movement but made it one of the grounds for total opposition to Gandhiji.

(E) Militancy: The left also had a tendency to demaracte itself from the right on the basis of political militancy, especially verbal militancy. It was mostly on this basis that the election battle for the Congress presidentship in 1939 and the consequent split at Tripuri were defined as struggles between left and right. Thus a question of strategy and of perception of people's readiness to struggle and the manner in which the struggle should be started and fought was wrongly posed as an issue of left vs. right. Similarly, during 1939-41 and 1945-47, militancy was taken to define left-rightness, while in reality, as 1942 showed, this was a wrong point of demarcation.

(F) The Question of Strategy: There was a crucial difference between the strategy adopted by Gandhiji from 1919 to 1947 and the strategy advocated virtually unanimously by the left during 1933-37. Under the Gandhian strategy, which may be described as Struggle-Truce-Struggle (S-T-S), phases of a vigorous extra-legal mass movement and open confrontation with colonial authority alternate with phases during which direct confrontation is withdrawn, political concessions or reforms, if any, wrested from the colonial regime, are willy-nilly worked and silent political work carried on among the masses within the existing legal framework, which, in turn, provides scope for such work. Both phases of the movement are to be utilised, each in its own way, to undermine the twin ideological notions on which the colonial regime rested—that British rule benefits Indians and that it is too powerful to be challenged and overthrown—and to recruit and train cadre and to build up the people's capacity to struggle. The entire political process of S-T-S was an upward spiralling one, which also assumed that the freedom struggle would pass through several stages, ending with the transfer of power by the colonial regime itself.

The alternative left strategy was never put forward as such except as a carping critique of the Gandhian leadership; nor unlike the Gandhian leadership did the left ever put its strategy into practice, the ground offered being the relative weakness of the left. For a short period, from 1933 to 1937, Nehru gave adherence to the left strategy and also gave it a certain cogency and coherence.

The left believed that the national movement should have a permanent mass and extra-legal confrontation and conflict with imperialism till it was overthrown. The movement might suffer setbacks and phases of upswing and downswing but these should not lead to a passive phase where open confrontation is withdrawn, some of the colonial institutions worked, and energy diverted to the non-political and non-class constructive programme. In the words of Nehru, the Congress must maintain "an aggressive direct action policy". The nationalist mass struggle must become perpetual and could go forward only through unconstitutional and illegal means. Once the masses enter and take over a movement, no halfway house is left. The left strategy may be characterised as Struggle-Victory (S-V). While the Gandhian strategy was based on the assumption that a mass movement could not be carried on for a prolonged period,—that the broad masses, especially the land-owning peasants, could not sustain a mass movement for very long—and periods of rest and consolidation must intervene, the left assumed that masses once aroused never tire and were ready to continue fighting continuously, advancing from lower to higher forms of struggle ending with armed insurrection, till victory was won.

The left did not, however, at any stage believe that the Gandhian movement had a strategy. Consequently, it neither made an effort to understand this strategy nor did it subject it to a serious critique from the perspective of an alternative strategy. No responsible leadership anywhere would permit a movement it leads to operate outside the parameters of its broad strategy. Hence an effective critique of Gandhian leadership and its tactics at any specific period of time or its stand on particular issues could be made only if the critique extended to the Gandhian strategy. Then alone could its strong and weak points have been understood and its historical effectivity seriously challenged or accepted.

Denying or failing to see any strategic perspective or conception to the dominant leadership of the Congress, the left critique of the leadership was based on the assigning of bourgeois class essence to it and the movement and organization it led. This then led the left to criticise this leadership, especially Gandhiji, in terms of not wanting mass struggle, getting frightened of mass upsurge especially when it became or tended to become "revolutionary", that is, violent, putting breaks on the activity of the masses, curbing mass struggle, etc. Since the assumption was that the masses were always ready for struggle, that the leadership had limitless human resources at its command, and that therefore all that was needed was for the leadership, which was trusted by the people, to summon them for struggle, any withdrawal or slackening of the movement or failure to raise it to 'higher forms' of struggle, or effort to confine it within non-violent limits was portrayed by the left, especially the Communists, as a betrayal under the pressure of the bourgeoisie and landlords, who felt threatened, or because of its class essence.

The fact was that the left had hardly any conception of hegemonic struggle, or of what Gramsci described as a war of position, or, even more important, of a struggle which combined a war of movement (Satyagraha phase) with a war of position (non-Satyagraha or passive phase) when the hegemony of the ruling classes is eroded inch by inch and in every area of life.[10] So far as the left was concerned there existed only two political choices in the situation. In the words of R. Palme Dutt : "It is evident that two opposing conceptions of the campaign were possible, according to the conception of the aim. Either it was to be a decisive struggle of all the forces of the Indian people for the ending of British rule and the establishment of complete independence ('A Fight to the Finish' in the terms of the official Congress History's chapter-heading for the struggle), or it was intended to be a limited and regulated demonstration of mass pressure with a view to securing better terms and concessions from British rule."[11]

Failing to understand the strategy of S-T-S, the left never raised the questions whether it was suited to the Indian political reality, including the semi-hegemonic, semi-suppressive character of the colonial state, whether a mass movement which involves millions of people in a continent-size country could follow any other strategy, or, more generally, were Gandhiji' s technique and forms of struggle, for example, non-violence, law-breaking Satyagraha, constructive work, emphasis on

---

[10]This lack of understanding is clearly revealed in R. Palme Dutt's writing. On the one hand, he says "that nothing whatever had been gained" as a result of the Gandhi-Irwin Pact, and, in fact, "all the aims of complete independence and no compromise with imperialism, so loudly proclaimed at Lahore, had gone up in smoke"; and similarly that the 1932-34 struggle ended with a fiasco. On the other hand, he writes: "The unhappy final ending of the great wave of struggle of 1930-34 should not blind us for a moment to its epic achievement.... Within two years, after all those heavy blows, the national movement was advancing again, stronger than ever. The struggle had not been in vain. The furnace of those years of struggle helped to forge and awaken a new and greater national unity, self-confidence, pride and determination". Dutt is utterly unaware that the 'epic achievement' was related to the strategy of the struggle; the strategy was precisely designed to achieve this result. This is what hegemonic struggle is all about. R. Pal me Dutt, *op.cit.*, pp. 348, 353-5.

[11]*Ibid*.. p. 339.

political morality and open-functioning, mere matters of principle and/or tactics or were they geared to a wider strategy designed for change in state power under semi-democratic and semi-civilized rule. And were the passive phases periods of bargaining with imperialism and periods of political weakness or were they essential to the strategy of the anti-imperialist struggle in terms of rest, consolidation, and preparation for another phase of mass struggle ? Did withdrawal of an active civil disobedience movement mean betrayal of the struggle or was Gandhiji's claim right that "suspension of civil disobedience does not mean suspension of war"[12] and that it meant carrying on the war by other means?

Because of the failure to understand the S- T -S strategy and the role of the periods of truce or passive phases, the left also failed to understand and therefore meaningfully critcise the role of consturctive work. It was branded in a rather simple manner as "reactionary" simply because it did not explicitly take up the political and economic demands of the masses.[13]

(G) *Class Adjustment* A very important ground for the strong left attack on the right was because of the left's failure to fully and properly understand the role of class struggle within Indian society in the context of colonialism or the role of inner contradictions within Indian society vis-a-vis the primary contradiction between colonialism and the Indian people as a whole.

The left rightly emphasized the organization of the workers and peasants in their class organizations such as trade union. and kisan sabhas and the necessity of fighting for their class demands and the organization of popular struggles around them. It also recognized in theory or in its programmatic- documents the primacy of the primary contradiction. But it did not in practice, in its policies, and even in its programmatic pronouncements know how to correlate the two, how to combine class· struggles with the primary contradiction, that is, how to wage class struggles within the camp of the people in a non-antagonistic manner.

[12]*Collected Works,* Vol. 67, p.226.

[13]The post-independence history of India, as also nearly 100 years of West European and U.S. history, show that one of the most difficult but necessary political tasks is to provide political activity to the cadre as also the people during the inevitable intervals between mass movements. In fact, failure to provide meaningful activity during these intervals has led to these intervals being so prolonged that mass struggles appear to be short intervals between long periods of passive phases!

By any reckoning, the inner class contradictions within colonial society had to be fully recognized and not ignored and overlooked as the right often did. At the same time, they had to be seen as secondary to, and therefore subordinated to, the primary contradiction. While the right had to be opposed when it propagated that internal contradictions should be overlooked and all class struggle suspended for the duration of the national liberation struggle, the left had to see the internal contradictions as contradictions within the camp of the colonial people; and class struggles based on them had to be fought in a non-antagonistic fashion. Treating the inner contradictions as secondary or in a non-antagonistic manner as being within the camp of the people would mean not pushing class struggles within Indian society to their limits. *It would mean making class adjustments among the mutually hostile Indian social classes.* The objective of class struggles had to be to create a new balance of class forces and class gains at the point of production and not the overthrow or expropriation of the Indian exploitative classes. The attempt was to be to gain an improved socio-economic environment for the working people and not their liberation from class exploitation. In other words, the right was to be criticised and opposed when it objected to organization of the exploited classes or class struggles or mass movements around their class demands but not when it proposed class adjustment and confining of class struggles within the parameters of broad unity within all sections of the Indian people. The left tended to do the very opposite.

Interestingly, the right agreed at Karachi in 1931 and after to the organization of the Indian masses into their various class organizations such as trade unions and kisan sabhas—it even organized them in its own way especially when facing the colonial state as an employer, as in the railways or foreign enterprises. It also did not object to struggles around the class demands of the workers and peasants even when internal exploiters were involved.[14] But it pecisely said that class struggles should be adjusted and fought for in a non-antagonistic manner and therefore without physical violence against the internal exploiters or without being pushed to the extreme of demanding their liquidation as classes. Consequently, it agreed, though often under pressure of the left, to the

[14]For example, in Gujarat, Sardar Patel and others supported *Halpatis*—bonded labourers—to fight against bondage. In 1931, Sardar Patel as president of the Congress and Gandhiji sanctioned the no-rent campaign in U.P.

embodiment of radical, though adjusted, class demands—on this side of the total liquidation of class exploitation and exploiters—within the Congress programme at Karachi and Faizpur and in the Election Manifesto of 1937. It also agreed to have supporters of class struggles as presidents of the Congress from 1936 to 1938 and as members of the Working Committee.[15]

In this regard, one cannot help but notice the complete contrast between the politics of the left in India and in China. In India the left gave the slogan of fighting inside the Congress against the policy of 'class-collaboration' (thus making the multi-class organization an instrument of class struggle!) and class adjustment. The All India Kisan Sabha, for example, passed a resolution in March 1938 strongly condemning "the theory of class collaboration, i.e., the principle that the interests of the exploited classes can be adjusted and reconciled within the framework of the present society." The resolution further stated: "This Sabha is convinced that such collaboration even on the excuse that the anti-imperialist struggle demands such a policy for the sake of the so-called national unity, can result only in perpetuation of economic enslavement and checking the growth of the struggle of Swaraj for the masses.... This Sabha deems it its duty to carryon a relentless fight against the advocacy and propagation of such a theory...." Instead of seeing class adjustment as a necessary weapon in the anti-imperialist struggle, the Sabha saw it as a policy that would end "ultimately in a settlement between the traditional exploiters of the masses and imperialism for a more stable and intensive exploitation of the masses."[16]

The task of integrating the anti-imperialist struggle with class demands or class struggles was accomplished in a very different manner by the Chinese and the Vietnamese Communist parties in the1930s. In the face of the imperialist enemy, or a situation in which the entire society, irrespective of class divisions, faced a common colonial or colonising enemy, class struggle was to be adjusted, with all mutually hostile classes within the colonial or semi-colonial society making concessions to one another. The classical Marxist position in this respect, though initiated by

[15]These steps have often been seen as right manoeuvres or the right's efforts to co-opt or bamboozle the left. A better explanation is that the right recognized the need to build up a wider popular movement based on class adjustment, etc. *C.f.* Francine Frankel, *India's Political Economy* 1947-77, Princeton, 1978, pp. 35 ff.

[16]N.G. Ranga, *Kisan Handbook,* p.71.

Marx and Engels[17], was fully developed by Mao Ze Dong during the anti-Japanese struggle of the Chinese people.[18]

> To subordinate the class struggle to the present national struggle to resist Japan-that is the fundamental principle of the united front....In a nation which is struggling against a foreign foe, the class struggle assumes the form of national struggle, a form indicating the consistency of the two. On the one hand, the economic and political demands of the classes during the historical period of national struggle should be based on the condition of not disrupting the cooperation of these classes; on the other, all the demands of class struggle should start from the requirements of the national struggle.

And again:[19]

> It is a settled principle that in the anti-Japanese War every thing must be subordinated to the interests of resistance to Japan. Therefore the interests of the class struggle must not conflict with, but be subordinated to, the interests of the War of Resistance. But the classes and class struggle do exist.... *We do not deny the class struggle, but adjust it....* In order to unite against Japan we should carry out a suitable policy that can adjust the class relations.

Mao also explained what he meant by class adjustment:[20]

> The workers should demand that the factory owners improve their material conditions, but at the same time they should work hard in order to facilitate resistance to Japan; the landlords should reduce rent and interest, but at the same time the peasants should pay rent and interest to the landlords and unite with them against foreign aggression.

The Vietnamese Communists too practised and wrote about class adjustment in the same fashion.[20a] Interestingly enough, the Communist Party of India too practised class adjustment during the period of the People's War once it located the primary contradiction in the anti-fascist struggle on a world scale.[20b] Moreover, unlike Mao and the Chinese

---

[17] *Ireland and the Irish Question,* Moscow, 1971.

[18] Mao Ze Dong, *Selected Works,* Vol. Two, London, 1954, p. 264.

[19] *Ibid.,* p. 250. Emphasis added.

[20] *Ibid.,* p. 263.

[20a] For details of their stand as also Mao Ze Dong's, see Bhagwan Josh, "Ministries and the Left", Mimeo.

[20b] This is what P.C. Joshi, then General Secretary of the CPI, wrote to Gandhiji in 1945 regarding the party's class struggle policy during the War: "We gave up our strike

Communist Party, the CPI adjusted the class struggle in an empiricist fashion without theorising it in terms of the relation between primary and secondary contradictions or antagonistic and non-antagonistic contradictions. We may also note that Sahajanand Saraswati, who would not give an iota of concession to or make accommodation with the Congress Ministry during 1937-39, was openly asking the peasants not to struggle against the zamindars during 1942-44.

Thus the point of contention had to be not class adjustment but the terms on which it was to be made and the manner in which class struggle was provided for within the parameters of colonial society and the anti-imperialist struggle.

Then, there was the specific demand for the abolition of landlordism without compensation. The right wing was, again wrongly, defined as consisting of all those who opposed this demand. In semi-colonial countries, where state power is shared or even largely wielded by domestic classes, mainly landlords and compradors, the political objectives of the struggle alternate. Sometimes the struggle against. feudalism and for liquidation of landlordism becofnes primary because, while remaining an enemy, colonialism *is not* and *cannot* become the target of the immediate and main political movement for arousal of the people and struggle for state power. Examples are Chinese struggle from 1922 to 1934, whose direct targets were the warlords with their social base among the landlords, and the Civil War, 1946-49, whose task was the overthrow of Chiang Kai-Shek's power. In both cases agrarian revolution took the centre of the stage. On the other hand, when colonialism directly threatens or rules, the colonial state or colonial state-to-be becomes the immediate target of mass mobilization and the struggle for abolition of landlordism is either not taken up or abandoned. This was the case in China in 1918-19 and 1937-1945 and in Vietnam after 1939.

In India colonialism ruled directly; none of the Indian social classes shared in state power. Therefore the slogan of complete liquidation of landlordism or agrarian revolution was invalid throughout. The radical

---

policy because we considered it anti-national in the conditions of today.... That we successfully prevented the Indian working class from resorting to strikes even in a period of their worsening material conditions is the measure not only of our influence over it but its capacity to *understand* national interests as its own." *Correspondence Between Mahatma Gandhi and P.C. Joshi*, p. 12.

demands could only be for the mitigation of its harsh aspects. The bourgeois democratic stage of revolution was directed against feudalism in Europe; in India it had to be directed against colonialism. The mixing up of anti-colonial and the agrarian revolution here was a mixing up of recipes, not good for the health of the national movement or the left. Furthermore, class adjustment was not to be a fixed position. It would be a moving point on a wide spectrum. As the national movement advanced and class organization and class and anti-colonial consciousness of the working people advanced, and as the national movement shifted leftwards, the level of class adjustment would also shift 'leftwards' towards positions more favourable to the working people. This is what happened in concrete practice. For example, the left-led kisan sabhas did not anywhere, in British India, wage an actual mass struggle for the abolition of landlordism. In Kerala, for example, the peasant struggle started with demands for abolition of *begar* and social oppression, moved on to the demand for abolition of illegal cesses, and advanced to the fight for permanent tenancy and no ejection. Similarly, the most advanced peasant struggle of pre-independence British India, the *Tebhaga,* was for reduction of rent and not its abolition. The slogan of land to the tiller remained an annual resolution of kisan sabha conferences and did not become, at any stage, a concrete slogan for peasant mobilization. It is also interesting that, as we have pointed out earlier, over the years, starting with 1931, the right agreed to go quite far vis-a-vis lanlordism (and usury), short of its liquidation. And in 1945, the Congress Working Committee accepted, at the level of a resolution, the policy of the abolition of all intermediaries between the state and the actual cultivators.

(*H*) *Compromise with Imperialism*: Above all, all the wrong aspects on which the left demarcated itself from the right combined and culminated in the view that the right wanted "compromise with" and "surrender to" imperialism. This was the most serious error of them all, for the right-wingness of the right was not to be and could not be located in its approach towards imperialism. Instead of seeing all the issues discussed above or the different positions taken up by sections of national leadership on them as aspects of differing anti-imperialist strategies, or of tactics based on differing perceptions of the political situation, balance of political forces, nature and position of the enemy, the state and level of people's politicisation and preparedness to struggle, and the role of different political groups and social classes, the left regarded them as barometers of the degree of anti-imperialism of different political trends within the national movement. The right's positions on these issues were seen as aspects of the proclivity of the bourgeoisie and therefore the dominant Congress leadership (Congress leadership being always equal to the bourgeoisie) to bargain, collaborate and compromise with and surrender to imperialism. Any suppleness in negotiations, any change in tactics of frontal confrontation, etc., in the extremely complex struggle against a semi-hegemonic and politically subtle enemy with great deal of political resources at its command was seen as betrayal of the movement.

Consequently, the consistent anti-imperialism of the national movement and its dominant leadership was missed, and the left waged a fight with the right on an issue and a premise which guaranteed its isolation from the mass of the people. After all, who, except those intoxicated with their own words, would believe that Gandhiji or Sardar Patel or Maulana Azad were soft towards imperialism, not to speak of being betrayers of nationalism. The right, on the other hand, once again scored. It did not question the patriotism of the left and insisted on unity of all patriotic trends, left or right. The CSP and the CPI both were guilty of this blunder during the 1930s. Nehru escaped isolation from the people because, despite his sharing of many of the left positions on other issues, he did not, except for a brief period, question the total anti-imperialist commitment of Gandhiji and the right wing of the Congress. The CSP and the Communists too survived and grew after 1935 because in most parts of the country, especially in Andhra, Kerala and Tamil Nadu, where they were led by P. Sundarayya, they came before the people as Congressmen and as builders of the Congress.

The most vulgar form in which the theory of the right's tendency to compromise with imperialism was put was by Subhas Bose during and after his election to the presidentship of the Congress. During the campaign, Bose accused the rightist majority of the Working Committee of working for a compromise with the Government on the question of federation, having even drawn up a list of prospective central ministers, and therefore of not wanting a leftist—himself—as the president of the Congress. The best comment on this style of distinguishing the right from the left was made by Jawaharlal Nehru in a letter to Subhas Bose, dated 4 February 1939.[21]

[21] Jawaharlal Nehru, *A Bunch of Old Letters*, Bombay, 1958, p. 309.

> I do not know who you consider a Leftist and who a Rightist. The way these words were used by you in your statements during the presidential contest seemed to imply that Gandhiji and those who are considered as his group in the W.C. are the Rightist leaders. Their opponents, whoever they might be, are the Leftists. That seems to me an entirely wrong description. It seems to me that many of the so-called Leftists are more Right than the so-called Rightists. Strong language and a capacity to criticise and attack the old Congress leadership is not a test of Leftism in politics.... I think the use of the words Left and Right has been generally wholly wrong and confusing. If instead of these words we talked about policies it would be far better. What *policy* do you stand for? Anti-Federation, well and good. I think that the great majority of the members of the W.C. stand for that and it is not fair to hint at their weakness in this respect.

Even the CSP and the Communist Party shied away from supporting Subhas Bose at Tripuri in March 1939. Explaining its position, the CPI declared that the interests of the anti-imperialist struggle "demanded not the *exclusive* leadership of one wing but a *united* leadership under the guidance of Gandhi".[22] But this was pragmatism. No theoretical or political lessons were drawn from the episode. The CPI continued to criticise the Congress Ministries not on grounds of ideology or policy weaknesses or even class bias but because the Congress leadership, representing the upper classes, and out of the fear of the advancing working class and peasant movements, was increasingly compromising, cooperating and collaborating with imperialism and working the 1935 Act in accord with British plans and policies and as organs of imperialist administration.

This line of critique by the left had full play during 1939-41 and culminated in 1947-48 when the achievement of freedom was portrayed as false freedom *(Yeh Azadi Jhooti Hai)* and as capitulation of the national leadership before imperialism because of its fear of the revolutionary movement of the post-war years.

VI

If the Congress right was nationalist first and right wing later, where was its right-wing character to be located. In our view, it was to be located in its ideology or in its social vision of a free India. The Congress right

[22] *National Front,* 19 March 1939.

continued to accept the confines of a bourgeois perspective of social development. Apart from the ideological realm, its differences with the left lay in the social, class content of the Congress programme, in the nature of the socio-economic structure of free India, and on the question of class struggle. Interestingly, on the question of the social content of the movement most of the right-wing leaders were willing to go quite far in accommodating the left so long as the changes were within the parameters of class adjustment and peaceful change. The reason why most of them could cooperate first with Nehru and then with the Congress Socialists and adopt a non-hostile attitude to the Communists was because they were not reactionary in the way the left defined them but were more akin to the radical democrats of 19th century Europe or contemporary China and other countries of Asia. In other words, they were bourgeois in their outlook but reformistically or radically so.

This understanding of the right would once again indicate that the main edge of the left's struggle vis-a-vis the right had to be at the levels of ideology, a visibly greater capacity to suffer, sacrifice and work in the national movement, and the organization of the workers and peasants, the youth, the petty bourgeoisie and the intelligentsia without pitting their organizations against the Congress. In fact, the rapid growth of the left in the 1930s was due more than any other factor to the ideological attraction of socialism and Marxism. Another major factor was the reputation that the leftists acquired as the most hard working, devoted and sacrificing of the anti-imperialist fighters.

The primacy of ideological struggle under colonial conditions so far as the left was concerned had another aspect. Since no anti-colonial movement could take up the task of the abolition of private property, the socialist project could not be given a programmatic shape except in the ideological realm. So long as colonial rule persisted, there could be no struggle for socialism, only struggle for organization of the working people and for the amelioration of their social condition. which meant not only economic amelioration but also social amelioration around women's question, caste and secularism, and for socialist ideology and the ideological transformation of the national liberation struggle. The heart of the right wing was. for example, the ideology at the back of class adjustment and the terms of class adjustment and not the notion of adjustment itself. But waging ideological struggle was an extremely difficult and complex task requiring a deep understanding of the Indian social reality and culture, on the one hand, and of Marxism, on the other. The task was made even more difficult because the struggle had to be waged in a non-antagonistic fashion, that is, from within the camp of the people. The left also found the task difficult because of its shallow, easily acquired Marxism-most of its leaders had not themselves gone through the prolonged process of the acquisition of the new ideology—especially when it was faced with the extremely complex, contradictory, and socially radical ideologies embodied in Gandhism and radical democracy. Precisely because the right readily accommodated left demands, policies and programmes, the left found it difficult to contend with the right and with Gandhism in ideological terms. It therefore took recourse to the easier, though politically costly, course of defining the right as soft towards imperialism. Similarly, unable to grasp the Gandhian strategy and the consequent capacity of Gandhiji to politically arouse and mobilise the people, the left misrepresented the struggle over strategies in terms of their own uncompromising anti-imperialism and compromising, half-hearted anti-imperialism of Gandhiji and the right wing.

A popular mass movement, especially in colonial conditions, had to be open-ended, without definite hegemony or class character. It had to be a multi-class movement rather than a mere alliance of classes. It could not be, nor it was, a movement of the bourgeoisie, national or otherwise. Nationalism, or anti-imperialism, in a colony did not represent only the ideology of the bourgeoisie or express only the bourgeoisie's contradiction with imperialism. It represented the entire colonial society's contradiction with imperialism. The question here was, would one be a nationalist from the bourgeois perspective of social development or from the socialist point of view. Another way of looking at the reality was to grasp that the task in India was not that of the working class or the left groups and parties supporting bourgeois nationalism because of its historically progressive character, but that of waging the nationalist struggle because it was the struggle of the Indian people, including that of the working class.

The Indian national movement had from the beginning, even when it accepted the bourgeois pattern of social development as its objective, two very important positive features. One was its basic orientation towards the people and acceptance of the notion that politics must. be based on the masses who must be politicised, activised and brought into politics. The other was its ideological open-endedness; it was open to competition and contention by different ideological currents. Even in the Gandhian era only two conditions were laid down for becoming a part of the Congress-anti-imperialism and non-violence as a tactic or policy (not necessarily as a principle). Even those ideological currents were permitted to continue in it which were committed to capturing or transforming the Congress or which openly stood out as alternatives to it. The top leadership of the movement did not at any stage, from 1870 onwards, give way to its contemporary right-wing ideologies. The Revolution of 1917 was given warm welcome. The Soviet Union was admired and supported throughout. The left cultural currents of Europe, Asia and Americas had an immediate impact. For example, Gorky's *Mother* was translated in Indian languages by Congressmen in the late 1920s and early 1930s and was one of the most widely read books of the time. The Congress supported anti-imperialist movements irrespective of the political colour of their leadership. Marxism found a ready welcome and no strong anti-Marxist intellectual current developed in the nationalist ranks till 1947. Left leaders and groups and parties were not subjected to isolation. Interestingly, at no stage did a break in the Congress occur over ideology. In other words, the Indian national movement and Indian National Congress, the organization which led it, were quite open to transformation towards a socialist perspective.

VII

Even in terms of ideological struggle and transformation there existed scope for wrong understanding and approach. Even in its ideological practice, the left made a major error because it failed to understand the specific historical context and character of the Indian national movement. While correctly noting the bourgeois social developmental perspective and ideology of a large part of its leadership, it failed to see the significance of the increasingly radical socio-economic-political programme and policies of the movement and the intermediate, popular ideological positions of Gandhiji and many other segments of the nationalist leadership. As pointed out earlier, the left did not systematically analyse or explain or even ask as to what were the components of the ideology of what they described as the right.[23]

[23] As pointed out earlier, the Congress right did not share any of the attributes of the European, or Arab, or Latin American, or Chinese or Japanese right wing of the 1920s and 1930s. Nor did it have much in common with what was known as the right in Europe in the 19th century (Guizot, Thiers, Bismarck, British Tories or even Liberals, and so on).

Above all, Gandhiji was not only put in the right-wing camp, especially by the Communists, but was even seen as the ideological fountain-head of the right. But Gandhiji could be put in the right wing only if the assumption was that anyone who did not accept Marxism was a rightist, or that if an ideology was not socialist it had to be bourgeois, or that if a movement was not under socialist ideological hegemony it must be under bourgeois or bourgeois-landlord hegemony. Thus, it is correct that Gandhiji did not accept class analysis of society, class struggle and socialism as Marxists would define it. He was not a socialist in the scientific sense of the term. But he was committed to basic changes in the existing social order and judging from his overall ideological framework and his stand on economic, social and political issues during the 1930s, he was not bourgeois or feudal either. He was certainly not committed to the preservation of private property.[24] His stand favouring nationalization of large-scale industries, on exploitation inherent in capitalism and landlordism, on land to the tiller, against untouchability, on civil liberties, and on many other issues created constant openings for any pro-poor programme, policies and *ideology* and therefore for cooperation between Gandhiji and Gandhians and the left. Nehru and later, after 1944, the Congress Socialists did take note of this aspect of Gandhism. But the Communists did not raise the important question: To what extent was Gandhiji's overall social ideology with its orientation towards the lowly, the exploited and the down-trodden open to transformation in a socialist direction though not by him but by socialists? In other words, were the Marxists to oppose him and expose him or was it possible for them to interact with Gandhiji, his thought and the Gandhian cadre and, through ideological struggle, though in a non-antagonistic manner, to shape the national movement in a socialist direction? The Communists and the CSP of the 1930s did not raise this question; they did not even make a serious study of what Gandhiji and Gandhians were by analysing their writings or their social practices. Instead, they decided to see in Gandhiji a total rival rather than an ally. They opted for the line of regarding him as the *main hurdle* to the growth of socialist ideas and movement and therefore of isolating him from the radical-minded youth, a task in which they were

---

[24]Gandhiji's theory of trusteeship, opposite of Marxism, was not used by Gandhiji to justify the existing pattern of property relationships and was constantly developed by Gandhiji and Gandhians in a more radical direction.

quite successful but at the cost of losing all chances of hegemonising the national movement as a whole. They showed intense hostility to Gandhiji, non-violence, constructive programme, his tactical withdrawal of the movements, etc., and concentrated on 'exposing' them. The tactical line adopted was to unite all the left-wing forces in a concerted attack on Gandhiji and the right.[25] And anybody on the left who put forward a different view, for example Nehru, was not spared, especially during 1940-41.

Similarly, the overwhelming majority of the Congress cadre were not socialists or Marxists but were not ideologically right-wing either. In fact, throughout the 1920s and 1930s the area of popular politics based on wide popular demands and issues was growing and the majority of the nationalist cadre were getting attracted to socialism and socialist ideas. But because of the left's treatment of Gandhiji and the Gandhians as hostile elements and as the agents of the upper classes, and by making leftism coterminus with anti-Gandhism, the vast mass of these radically-oriented cadre were pushed away. They remained apathetic to Marxism and continued to remain under bourgeois ideological hegemony. A vast number of potential allies and supporters of socialism were lost.

[25]There were a few contrary voices. See, for example, S.G. Sardesai in *National Front,* 30 April 1939 . The hostility to Gandhiji was codified in R. Pal me Dutt's *India Today* and has, on the whole, held sway since then. See, for example: Gandhi "was the most subtle and experienced politician of the older group". He was "the ascetic defender of property in the name of the most religious and idealist principles of humility and love of poverty." He was "the prophet who by his personal saintliness and selflessness could unlock the door to the heart of the masses where the moderate bourgeois leaders could not hope for a hearing—and the best guarantee of the shipwreck of any mass movement which had the blessing of his association. This Jonah of revolution, this general of unbroken disasters was the mascot of the bourgeoisie in each wave of the developing Indian struggle". Regarding the period 1928-29, Dutt wrote: "All the hopes of the bourgeoisie (the hostile might say, the hopes of imperailism) were fixed on Gandhi as the man to ride the waves, to unleash just enough of the mass movement in order to drive a successful bargain, and at the same time to save India from revolution". *India Today,* p. 334.

VIII

In the end, we may suggest that in the context of a popular anti-colonial movement, the socialist alternative had to be posed not in terms of its leadership by the working class or by a working class party but in ideological terms, that is, as a moral and intellectual and social developmental alternative and not as a class alternative. A major task of the left was to give Indian nationalism a new socialist ideological orientation and not struggle to create alternatives to the existing national movement or to Gandhiji's leadership. Nehru, in a way, had an instinctive grasp of the correct approach in this respect. Throughout the 1930s, he pointed to the inadequacy of the existing nationalist ideology and the hegemony of the propertied classes over it, and stressed the need to inculcate a new socialist or Marxist ideology, which would enable the people to study their social condition scientifically, to give the Congress a new orientation, and to win over the others in the Congress to the new ways of thought. Several chapters of his *Autobiography,* written during 1934-35, were an ideological polemic against Gandhiji but couched in a mild, friendly, even reverential tone. At the same time, he defended the Congress from hostile criticism from the left, stressing and analyzing the possibilities of its transformation in a socialist direction.

4

Historians of Modern India and Communalism

At the outset, it may be pointed out that this paper does not deal in the main with the question: why communalism arose and grew in modern India? It essentially tries to trace the connection between the writing and teaching of history and the growth of communalism in India. It also tries to shed some light on the question: why were some Indian historians so prone to taking up a communal position? It is widely accepted today that the teaching of Indian history has a great deal to do with the spread of communalism in the last 100 years. In fact, it would be no exaggeration to suggest that a communal historical approach has been, and is, the main ideology of communalism in India. Take away that and hardly anything is left of the communal ideology.

I

We may note in the beginning that both nationalism and communalism are the products of the same modern process-the gr owing economic, political, and administrative unity of the country. This process made it imperative to have wider links and loyalties and to base political life and loyalties on new, uniting principles. Both are, therefore, essentially modern, post-18th century phenomena. Nationalists as well as communalists may try to appeal to the past and try to establish links with the ideologies, movements and, in fact, history of the past. But that does not mean that either of the two existed in the past. In fact,Romila Thapar and Harbans Mukhia have shown in their papers that communal identity did not exist in the ancient and medieval periods of Indian history.[1]

Similarly, nationalism was an entirely new organising principle and ideology. This was clearly recognised by the early nationalist leaders such

[1] See *Communalism and the Writing of Indian History,* by Romila Thapar, Harbans Mukhia and Bipan Chandra, New Delhi, 1969.

as Surendranath Banerjea and Lokamanya Tilak, who referred to India as a nation-in-the-making. Nationalism as an ideology acquired its validity from the fact that it was a correct reflection of an objective reality: the developing identity of the common interests of the Indian people, in particular against the common enemy, foreign imperialism. On the other hand, communalism developed in certain areas and sections of society due to their failure to develop the new national consciousness. In other words, communalism was generated by the lack of deeper penetration of nationalist outlook and ideology.

In a situation where wider unity and links among people were becoming essential, appeal to the pre-existing principles of compartment-alisation and organisation of social and cultural life, even for the newly-emerging political life, was inevitable in so far as the new principle of organisation, i.e., nationalism, did not penetrate. In other words, where need for identity was obvious and the new national identity was not available, the search for identity led to the older, more familiar identities, however unsuitable they might be in the new situation. Identity around religion was of course not the only one available. Caste, language, tribe and region also could, and did, serve the purpose. For example, in Maharashra where at one time Hindu communalism was quite strong—and of course it persists as a force till this day—the tables were turned on its leaders by the anti-Brahmin mpvement. Something similar happended in Madras. Similarly in South Punjab (now Haryana) casteism organised around Jat-feeling cut the ground from under both Hindu communalists and nationalists.

It would, therefore, be incorrect to treat communalism as a remanent of the past or the revival of traditional ideology. Communalism was, and is, the false consciousness of the historical process of the last 100 years. Later, as we shall see, under the impact of contemporary communal politics, it also became, in the hands of historians, a false representation of the past.

II

In both spheres, i.e., in contemporary politics as well as in modern Indian historiography, the communal view meant accepting the notion that there existed in India religious communities having common social, economic and political interests and possessing the tendency to act as a unity or entity in these fields. The historians usually wrote of Hindus and Muslims 'thinking' or 'speaking' as distinct entities. Sometimes they even wrote of 'Hindu' leaders, 'Muslim' leaders and so on. Thus they applied the two nation theory (others were to extend it to Sikhs, etc.) to medieval and modem Indian history and created the communal view of Indian politics and society. .

While holding the view that Hindus and Muslims together were not integrated into cohesive units at village, local, regional or any other level, the historians with a communal bent of mind rejected the view that Hindus or Muslims were not forming such cohesive units on a religious and communal basis either. They would not accept that Hindus and Muslims were also each separately lacking cohesion, i.e., if Hindus and Muslims together did not form a nation in premodern India, Hindus and Muslims separately did not form homogeneous communities either.

Interestingly enough, the British historians and administrators, who had initiated and developed the entire 'Hindu-Muslim' approach to Indian history, had also talked of caste and race (Bengali race, Punjabi race, Maratha race, etc.) as organising principles for Indian society and politics. They had written of the Brahmin domination of the Maratha Empire in the 18th century in the same manner as they had written of the Muslim domination of the Delhi Sultanate or the Mughal Empire. Just as they had talked of Muslim rule, Muslim action and Muslim view, they had talked of Brahmin rule, Brahmin action and Brahmin view. But the Indian historians rejected this latter approach. This shows what role contemporary communal assumptions could play in the writing of Indian history. For example, a.s. Sardesai remarks: "It is said that during Madhav Rao's and Narayan Rao's regime, the Deshasthas and Konkanasthas (Brahmins) were at loggerheads, but this does not stand a critical examination. I can show members of both the castes ranging themselves strongly on each ofthe opposite sides."[2] At the same time Sardesai would not accept the same criterion for rejecting the view that Hindus and Muslims were at loggerheads. In other words, while Indian society is seen as nonhomogeneous or even disintegrated, especially along religious lines, Hindu society is seen as one whole. In fact, this view does not reflect the historical reality; it really reflects Sardesai's and other similar historians' own level of national integration.

The communalist writers, of course, ignored all other principles of organisation but religion. But it was inherent in this approach that others would follow them but replace religion by caste, etc. In fact, many western

---

[2]G.S. Sardesai, *Main Currents of Maratha History,* Bombay, 1949 edition, p. 178.

writers today are reviving the emphasis on caste and language. For example, they insist on seeing the rise of the national movement in India as a reflection not of nationalist, anti-imperialist urges, or of communal-religious consolidation, but of pressures of caste and linguistic loyalty and cohesion. And, of course, many Indian propagators of casteism and linguism, as also of other communalisms, such as Sikh communalism, are following suit.

III

Communal ideology might not have penetrated so deep into modern Indian consciousness but for several factors working in the realm of ideology. But before we discuss some of these factors, I would like to stress the point that a full understanding of these factors is not possible unless we fully grasp the extent of this penetration. A student of mine once exclaimed after a discussion of communalism that every time he leaves after discussion with me he thinks he has cleansed his mind of communalism but that during the next discussion it emerges that his thinking is still permeated with large traces of it. The fact of the matter is that many of us who believe ourselves to be *pucca* nationalists and even those among us who have undertaken to actively propagate the cause of national integration have been deeply though subtly penetrated by the communal approach. This is mainly the result of the communal view of history and society and culture on which nearly all of us are brought up from our childhood.

As pointed out earlier, the lack of deeper penetration of nationalist ideology has in itself been a factor in the prevalence of communal ideology. In the absence of the wide prevalence of a scientific nationalist outlook, nationalist appeals against communalism, etc., do not make any impact on the people. Nationalism in this case cannot make an appeal to an existing consciousness, while communalism does seem relevant in view of the religious element with which people are familiar in their daily life. This point was firmly grasped by early nationalist leaders and they not only appealed to nationalism but also set out to generate and spread national consciousness. On the other hand, many of the nationalist leaders during the 1920s and 1930s made the mistake of assuming that national consciousness had already permeated society, as in the western countries, and that their task was merely that of arousing it to a fighting pitch. Thus, their struggle against communalism mainly took the form of telling the people that communalism was antinational. This made no impact on those people who were not already nationalist. This mistake was perpetuated after 1947. Our educational institutions, mass media, including the newspapers and the All India Radio, and the political parties have made no effort to disseminate among the people a modern, scientific understanding and awareness of nationalism. They have failed to spread a nationalist outlook. Consequently, their formal appeal to nationalism against communalism leaves a large number of people cold. On the contrary, often while trying to appeal to nationalism, they strengthen the communal outlook by being themselves confused in their nationalism.

IV

Finding the task of inculcating the spirit of modern nationalism—a new spirit—among the people a strenuous one, especially as this meant revealing to the common people the link between their lives and concerns and the anti-imperialist struggle, some of the nationalist leaders took an easy way out. They decided to appeal to the old consciousness, the consciousness of religion. It is true that they did so for an entirely modern and laudable purpose. But by doing so they not only weakened popular understanding of nationalism, but also made their own thinking and writing hostages to communalism.

The British use of Indian history to denigrate Indian national character and to 'prove' India's unfitness for independence and democracy produced another distortion in Indian historiography and politics. The Indians countered this unscientific' and unhistorical approach with an unhistorical approach of their own. They began to glorify the past. This is not the place to deal with the historical validity of this approach. Obviously, its mainspring was the need for national identity and pride. What was unfortunate form the national point of view, however, was that the only past chosen for glorification was the ancient past. This was partially because of the fact that the period of Mughal rule was still fresh in the memory of the people and could not, therefore, be easily glamourised. On the other hand, the ancient past was remote and known only through official or near official texts. In fact what applied to Mughal rule also applied to the Maratha Empire and Ranjit Singh's administration, which therefore had to wait for full grown communalism to develop to be glorified. Thus gradually developed several myths, each one of which weakened healthy, secular nationalism and gave an opening to, if not strengthened, communalism. And, of course, each one of these myths gained its strength, as well as the infinite capacity to do harm, from the fact that it was believed in and propagated by many staunch nationalists and secular minded persons.

The first of these myths is the belief that Indian society and culture—Indian civilisation—had reached a high water mark, the Golden Age, in ancient India, from which high watermark it gradually slided downwards during the medieval period-branded the period of decay and of 'foreign rule'—and continued to slide down till the revivalist movements made partial recovery but that the real task of reviving the past glory and civilisation still remains. To repeat, I wonder how many educated Hindus are there who do not subscribe to this view in its essentials. The next step, of blaming this decay on 'Islam' or 'Muslim' rule, and the alien west, was easily taken. And, of course, the educated Muslims reacted by harking back to the Golden Age of Arab achievements, for how could they accept that their religion has been the causative factor in the 'decay' of Indian civilisation. Needless to say, if communal ideology is to be uprooted, our educational system, the political parties and the mass media should stop propagating this illogical and unhistorical view and stress the historical development of Indian culture through various ages and through various streams. I may also once again point out that the widely prevailing model is bound to lead to further mischief. Already the DMK movement in Madras has refused to accept it. Whenever the lower castes become vocal and self-conscious they will rebel against any model of the Golden Age which is based upon caste hierarchy and domination. Nor will the tribal people relish it.

The second myth arose out of the necessity to prove that India of the ancient past—the Golden Age—had reached the highest achievement in human civilisation. But this was obviously not true in material civilisation, cranks who talk of atom bombs and aeroplanes in ancient India notwithstanding. Therefore the myth that Indian genius lay in 'spiritualism' in which respect it was superior to the 'materialistic' west. Thus it was said by Aurobindo Ghose that while the west had developed reason, science and capacity to produce goods, "India developed the spiritual mind working upon the other powers of man and exceeding them, the intuitive reason, the philosophical harmony of the dharma informed by the religious spirit, the sense of the eternal and the infinite". Even Indian caste system was superior to western class because the latter was based on material considerations while the former rested on a spiritual and moral basis. Interestingly, the Chinese Confucian mandarins had evolved a similar slogan at almost the same time, for they too believed that

Confucian China had reached a higher stage of achievement in civilisation than modem western Europe. And so they had talked of "Chinese learning for the fundamental principles, western learning for practical application". This view was encouraged both in India and China by western writers and authorities for they wanted the people of these countries to leave the 'material' tasks of administration and management of the economy to the imperialist powers of the west while they revelled in their 'spiritual' tasks and functions.

The third was the Aryan myth, which was a copy of the Teutonic and Anglo-Saxon myths, and was the Indian response to the white racialist doctrines. This was the myth that the Indian people were 'Aryans' and that the 'pure' Indian culture and society were those of the Aryan, Vedic period.

All the three myths encouraged a backward-looking mental outlook and discouraged that faith in progress, that faith in the future, which lies at the heart of healthy nationalism. For example, they did not encourage the people to boldly accept the historical weaknesses of their society and to work for their removal through development in the present and the future. They encouraged them to glory in the fact that they had once been great.

These myths fostered, as well as reflected, the belief that the Indian historical process was an exceptional one and was not, therefore, a part and parcel of universal history.

These myths were also, by their nature, unacceptable to the vast majority of the Indian people, as I have pointed out earlier. Interestingly, all three of them were borrowed from the west in spite of their claims of 'real' Indianness. The notion of the Golden Age and the use of the past to arouse and inspire the people were borrowed consciously from the European national movements. The idea of Indian spiritualism was originally propagated by the British to prove the unfitness of Indians to manage mundane affairs on their own. The Aryan myth's ancestry is no secret. But such myths had not done as much damage in Italy or Greece or Poland because their societies were not as full of diverse religions and cultural elements or castes as India. Here, their positive value in arousing nationalist feeling and a sense of sacrifice for the nation were soon exhausted—often in the lifetime of the second generation of nationalist leadership—while the long-term price is being paid to this day. Any genuine effort at correcting the misuse of history for communal purposes must also come to grips with these myths.

V

A major point I would like to make in this paper is that communalism among a section of the Indian people, especially among the historians, spread mainly because of its ability to serve as 'vicarious' or 'backdoor' nationalism. Communalism enabled them to feel nationalistic without opposing imperialism or the foreign power that was then ruling and oppressing the Indian people. It enabled them to combine personal safety with nationalist sentiments. Let me explain this point at length.

Most of the modem Indian historians before independence in 1947 showed little overt, direct, frank concern with nationalism. They did not take up questions that overt concern with nationalism would indicate or lead to. The pressing problems with which people of India were faced did not find reflection in their research either at the level of choice of topics or their treatment. They did not look upon the militant national struggle then going on as the central or the crucial problem of the day, not only from the national but also from the historian's angle. In fact, I suspect that if most of them saw any crucial question at all, it was not that of the nationalist struggle but that of official constitutional change and of Britain's 'trustee-role' transforming British rule gradually, step by step, from 'benevolent despotism' to 'benevolent democracy'.

The Indian historian was in this respect on the horns of a dilemma. A fundamental political struggle was going on in India since the 1870s and in particular since 1905 between the rulers and the ruled, between foreign imperialism and the rising national movement. But living in this period of intense and living antagonism, most of the Indian historians found themselves, mostly because of their being 'employed in government-run or government-controlled institutions, unable to actively side with the ruled; yet, except for the most sycophantic among them, they could not side with the rulers either, at least not emotionally. Moreover, they were part of the nationalist era; their own nationalism desired expression.

The chief way out ofthe dilemma was 'vicarious' or 'backdoor' or 'false' nationalism, which took the form of regionalism and communalism which could satisfy their nationalist urge and yet not be looked askance at by the authorities, who encouraged any and all approaches which would create divisions in Indian society. Thus the strange tendency of the failure to be real-life nationalists and anti-imperialists and of an all out effort to be 'illusory' nationalists, as we may call them. Thus the phenomenon that those who coveted British titles even in the heyday of nationalism, and even earned them, became fiery nationalists in their treatment of Rajput or Sikh or Maratha chieftains. I may also point out, in parenthesis, that this is also true of communal parties and individuals before 1947. Active communalists were seldom active nationalists, especially in the era of struggle after 1919.

In the case of 'vicarious' nationalists among the Indian historians, nationalism found expression not in criticism of British rule but in praise of Indian rulers of the 18th and 19th centuries as well as of the earlier centuries. Their nationalism did not take the direct form of anti-imperialism, i.e., exposure through historical studies of the nature of British rule, its motivations, exploitative policies, etc. Rather, their nationalism, because it was vicarious, took the indirect form of glorification of ancient and medieval Indian empires and rulers as also the rulers of 18th and 19th century Indian states, of discovering nationalism in the Punjab, Rajputana or Mysore or even among the Jats, and, most of all, full blown nationalism among the Marathas, and of popular base of and benevolent character of many of the Indian rulers. Here we come across such sonorous phrases as 'liberation of motherland' or 'homeland', 'children of the soil', 'national welfare', 'popular leaders', etc. But even here, seldom were those who actually fought against British rule, for example leaders in the Revolt of 1857 or Tipu Sultan, glorified. It may also be noted in this context that no academic historian wrote on any aspect of the Indian national movement. On the other hand 'vicarious' nationalism led to distortions which have greatly damaged Indian historiography as well as Indian politics.

VI

Many of the modern Indian historians projected the contemporary communal politics into the past, leading to the tendency to look upon 18th-century politics as a struggle between Hindus and Muslims which continued into the 19th and 20th centuries. For the 18th century, many historians tend to look upon this so-called struggle as the dominant problem of the period. This communal view also finds expression: as noted earlier, in the effort to see Hindus, Sikhs and Muslims as distinct, separate socio-political entities. In its extreme form, even 'Islam' is made an active entity—almost given a personality: 'Islam' conquers, 'Islam' thinks, 'Islam' decides, 'Islam' benefits. There is also the tendency to treat the Mughals and other medieval Muslim rulers as 'foreigners'. Some historians even talk of Hindu and Muslim principles of land revenue and administration, and so on. The Maratha empire and states, Rajput states and chiefs, Jat chiefs, etc., are all lumped together as Hindu states, while the southern and northern states headed by Muslim rulers are described as Muslim states. We have, thanks to these and British historians of India, got so used to such characterisations that we tend to forget that perhaps nowehere else in the world do such characterisations prevail. Interestingly, none of them describe the Britishrule as Christian rule even though the higher bureaucracy was Christian to a far greater extent than the higher nobility of the Mughals was Muslim.

In fact, the communal historians turned every fact or evidence topsy-turvy to prove the 'Hindu' character of the Maratha states, the Rajput states and chiefs, etc., and even that of the Punjab under Ranjit Singh. First this picture or hypothesis is accepted as the starting point, then all other 'facts' are fitted in. Inconvenient facts or incidents are usually explained away by treating those chiefs and rulers, who do not conform to this picture, and who in fact often constitute the majority of their own sample, as 'bad' men, 'bad' Hindus, 'traitors' to the 'community' or 'nation', and 'selfish' creatures. Inconvenient actions of even a 'good' Hindu ruler are explained away as aberrations. Similarly, if it becomes evident that the Hindu cheifs did not act in concert or even according to a set pattern in defence of Hinduism, or that they did not combine on a religious basis even for political ends, this is not taken to prove that no such communal digits prevailed at the time. Rather it proves to the communal historian that Hindus have had a natural tendency to get divided or to act selfishly.

VII

Communal approach in history-writing is thus an aspect of 'vicarious' nationalism as well as a reflection of contemporary communalism, i.e., Hindu communalism and Muslim communalism projected backwards.

But it is also the carrying on of the European bias. To some extent the Indian students of European history tended to project the Catholic-Protestant struggle into India as Hindu-Muslim struggle. Moreover, nearly all the basic generalisations regarding the Hindu and Muslim character of the Indian states, of Hindu-Muslim struggle in the 18th century and before, of Hindu-Muslim antagonism in the 19th and 20th centuries had been made earlier by British historians and publicists. Indians merely followed in their footsteps. It was easy to do so because the

British officials did not object to a communal interpretation of history or the glorification of the ancient and medieval rulers and 'heroes'. They unfailingly suppressed only the effort to criticise British imperialism itself.

The communal approach of many of the historians is also to some extent the product of their preoccupation with military-diplomatic history where considerations of religion appear important. Many factors are balanced and appealed to in diplomatic and military alliances. Appeals to marriage ties, kinship, language, 'race', caste, as well as religion are made, without any of them being necessarily the main factor leading to the alliances which are invariably based on hard considerations of interest.

The communal view would, however, have been virtually dissolved if history had been studied and written in its wider sense. For example, economic history would have revealed class interests, class solidarity and class antagonisms which cut across religious frontiers. By revealing economic exploitation it would have destroyed the notion of communal equality or solidarity among people following a common religion. Division of society between those who produce economic surplus and those who appropriate it would have formed multireligious groups on both sides of the line. Social and economic history would have revealed that there was no Muslim rule under the sultans or the Mughals. All the Muslims did not form the ruling class. The Muslim masses were as poor and oppressed as the Hindu masses. Moreover, both of them were looked down upon as low creatures by the rulers, nobles, chiefs and zamindars, whether Hindu or Muslim. Social history would show that if the Hindus were divided by caste, among Muslims the Sharif Muslims behaved as a superior caste over the Ajlaf or lower class Muslims. Administrative history, by revealing the employment policy, revenue policy, basis of administration, etc., would have shown the hollowness of the notion of the Muslim or Hindu character of the medieval and 18th century states (e.g. similarity between Maratha, Mughal and even British revenue administrations) and the inoperativeness of the communal approach in actual administration. Even a careful study of political history would have brought out that the politics of Indian states, as politics the world over, were moved by considerations of economic and political interests and not by considerations of religion. Rulers as well as rebels used religious appeals as an outer colouring to disguise the play of material interests and ambitions. Social and cultural history would have brought out the forces of cultural co-operation and integration and the emergence of a composite culture at the top, as well as harmonious Hindu-Muslim relations at the lower, village level. It would have shown that in the 18th century, or in the 20th for that matter, an upper class Muslim had far more in common culturally with an upper class Hindu than he had with a lower class Muslim. Or that a Punjabi Hindu stood closer culturally to a Punjabi Muslim than to a Bengali Hindu and, of course, the same was true of a Bengali Muslim in relation to a Bengali Hindu and a Punjabi Muslim.

Social and cultural history would have also revealed social divisions and diversities other than those based on religion, for example, those based on sect, cast, etc. For example, there was the fierce struggle between the right-hand castes and the left-hand castes in 18th century south India. Would one be justified in describing this conflict in terms of a two-nation theory? Even such a simple demographic fact as that the population of the Rajputs in Rajputana was only 6.4 per cent in 1901 would throw a flood of light on the so-called national or Hindu struggles of the medieval Rajputana states. Most of all, the study of the life of the common people and their role in social, economic and political development would have shown the utter inapplicability of the communal approach to history. It may also be pointed out that if the historians had dealt with imperialism and the national movement, they would have been compelled to take note of the common subjection and common interests of all Indian people in the struggle against imperialism.

The historians of the 1920s and 1930s, who adopted the communal approach, are of course not to be anathematised. Many of them were not fully aware of the weaknesses of their approach. It is only when history has fully worked itself out that the full implications of events and approaches become clear. But we, who have lived through the partition of 1947 and who are daily feeling the necessity of national integration, have to realise that the communal approach had hardly anything to offer and has not only caused immense damage but can cause even more of it in the future. For example, much before the Muslim League created the two-nation theory, Indian historians, as also the British, had created their own earlier version of it-what may be called the one-nation theory-that the Indian nation meant the Hindu nation, that the Indian people meant the Hindus, that Muslim rule was, foreign rule and, therefore, the Muslims were foreigners and outsiders in India, and so on.

VIII

Since the Indian national movement and the 'Indian social and religious reform movements were the products of a historical process, and were created through a process of groping and trial and error in a new and rapidly developing situation, it was inevitable that they would contain mutually contradictory aspects. They were also bound to generate and give expression to both healthy and unhealthy tendencies. At a time when Indians began to grope towards nationalism, it was inevitable that communalism, casteism, etc., would intermingle with the developing nationalism. It is the function of a developing movement, its leadership and later generations to constantly go on separating the gold from the dross, and, if they fail to do so, the blame is much more theirs than that of the pioneers, just as punishment for faulty thinking too is visited upon them.

Unfortunately the tendency to accept uncritically the past, has prevented this healthy process of crystallisation and separation in Indian politics and has done, and is still doing, immense damage. We have adopted an uncritical attitude towards the 19th-century reform movements and the 20th-century political movements. We live in cliches so far as Raja Rammohan Roy, Swami Dayananda, Vivekanand, Aurobindo Ghose, Lokamanya Tilak, Lajpat Rai and others are concerned. It has become a tradition with our mass media, school textbooks, All India Radio, etc., to uncritically praise them. Consequently, the communalists and others can exploit their negative features. We never tell the people, especially the young, that these great men, being human, had imperfect understanding and also imperfect actions.

While excusable at the time, though having some injurious effects even at the time, their imperfections could prove disastrous in another historical context. In fact, the habit of uncritically praising them is a sort of surrender before communalists, casteists, etc. For, we are able to see others like Gokhale, Ranade, Dadabhai Naoroji and B.C. Pal in their historical context. We recognise their great contribution to the growth of nationalism even while criticising their weakness in not firmly struggling against imperialism. It is equally necessary to see and point out that some of the 19th and 20th centuries Indian leaders made great contribution but that at the same time their understanding of the relation between religion and politics, of the role of the caste system, or of the problems of history, or of the making of Indian society in history, or of the religious minorities was at fault. It is particularly important that our textbooks, newspapers, the All India Radio, and the political leadership must stop being all things to all men, thus indirectly even strengthening the forces of national disintegration.

IX

The communal approach to history, the vicarious nationalism, the policy of being a 'nationalist' without antagonising the ruling foreign power before 1947, the deep and subtle imprint of communalism on the minds of even secular nationalist persons, the continuing surrender before communalism and even its propagation by the national mass media and the educational system, and the dangers of a policy of trying to be all things to all men, of a policy of uncritical approach towards the past, including the recent past of the national movement, can be illustrated by taking up a practical example with which all of us are familiar: the creation and propagation of 'national heroes'.

As nationalism emerged in the second half of the 19th century and the task of spreading national consciousness was undertaken by the national leadership, it was felt that the task would be immensely facilitated if 'national heroes' could be held up as examples. The national heroes could also serve as foci for emotional attraction in case of people who could not intellectualise their nationalist commitment. The national heroes were to serve as emotional symbols, a purpose for which they are still used on a wide scale. Secondly, large number of writers, journalists and academics took up the task of creating and propagating the cult of national heroes as an expression of their nationalist urges as well as a part of their day-to-day propagation of nationalism. Thirdly, Indians needed to glorify certain historical characters to counter the British view that the Indian people lacked the capacity or inborn desire for self-government and the needed spirit to fight for it. Lastly, the communal political leaders needed symbols both for the illustration of their historical and political views and to counter the emerging, real-life heroes of the nationalist struggle. And so it came to be that many historical personages, and particularly Rana Pratap, Shivaji and Guru Gobind Singh, emerged on the platform, in newspapers and pamphlets, in stories, poems, and dramas, in schools and on the All India Radio as 'national heroes'.

It should be clearly understood that in this process of hero-creation no historical analysis or judgement was involved. It was entirely a political question, a question of political instrumentality or engineering. The validity, the usefulness, the socio-political justification of the choice of this and not that hero had hardly anything to do with historical evidence, role or analysis. The heroes were meant to serve a purpose, they had a role to play in modern Indian politics. This means that their political utility or validity should be analysed from the latter point of view and not on the basis of interpretation of history.

We may now take note of the fact that heroes as political instruments were not chosen out of the large cast of historical characters who had waged, for one reason or another, determined fight against the British: the rebels of 1857-Bahadur Shah, Rani Jhansi, Nana Saheb, Tantia Tope, Maulana Ahmedulla of Fyzabad, Kunwar Singh-Rani Jindan, Diwan Mulraj, Vasudeo B. Phadke, the Chapekar brothers, the heroes of the Santhal uprising and indigo riots, and later still Khudiram Bose, Kalpana Dutt and the entire range of nationalist leadership.

Similarly, in literature, in northern India for example, that powerful firey, genuine and modern nationalist play, the *Neel Darpan,* dealing with the indigo struggle was neither staged nor sold in print. On the other hand, nationalism was aroused through popular plays around Prithvi Raj and Hakikat Rai. Of course, in time, the Muslim communalists countered by creating their own separate heroes, often going back to the struggle against the crusaders.

Why was this so? Undoubtedly, the most important factor at the time in the creation of hero-myths was the attitude of the British authorities. They frowned upon any expression of genuine natioalism or anti-imperialism. They were particularly allergic to the glorification of persons who had opposed the establishment of their rule. They did not hesitate to take action against anyone who wrote or spoke favourably of the heroes of 1857. The large number of school and college teachers, writers, journalists, etc., dependent usually upon official patronage, were not willing to take the risk of displeasing the officials to any marked degree. On the other hand, the officials even encouraged 'vicarious' nationalism for it fitted in with their policy of divide and rule. Thus the history books, school texts in history and literature, were permitted and even encouraged to play up communal, caste and regional 'heroes' so long as the opponents of the raj were kept out. In fact, it may be pointed out that not only in ideology but also in politics the British, the Hindu and Muslim communalists and the casteists cooperated to the full, particularly in the struggle against the secular national movement.

It is also of interest to note that it was in the 'moderate' phase of Indian nationalism that most of the hero-myths were created. It is Surendra Nath Banerjea, Justice Ranade, Madan Mohan Malaviya, R.C.Dutt and Tilak in his moderate phase, who created Shivaji, Guru Gobind Singh and Rana Pratap as 'national hereos'. That generation of nationalists regarded British rule as a historical step forward and would not therefore glorify those who had opposed its foundation. Moreover, they were not willing to get on the wrong side of the rulers at that stage of history. We may refer here to British action against Tilak in 1897. The authorities did not at all oppose glorification of Shivaji as an anti-Muslim hero. They, however, stepped in when they felt that Tilak was using the Shivaji cult to propagate anti-British sentiments.

I may once again point out here that the early national leaders had some justification for their creation of the hero-myths. They were just charting the course on an unknown sea; the full implications of their actions were not yet visible to them. It was the task of the later nationalists to have corrected their errors while advancing on their massive contribution.

The hero-myths—all of the major heroes, Rana Pratap, Shivaji and Guru Gobind Singh, belonged to medieval India and had fought against Mughal authority—have done as much to undermine secularism and national integration as any other ideological factor. At one stroke, and in a sort of immanent fashion, these hero-myths proved the case for the two-nation theory or the basic communal approach. By what definition are they 'national' heroes and their struggle a 'national' struggle? Because they were fighting against foreigners? How were the Mughals foreigners? Because they were Muslims. What Was the uniting principle in the 'nationalism' of Rana Pratap, Shivaji and Guru Gobind Singh? Their being Hindus or non-Muslims. Thus, the hero-myths spontaneously generated communalism.

A child or an adult, who heard Rana Pratap or Shivaji being hailed as a 'national' leader, spontaneously accepted the view that a Hindu nation existed in medieval India and that it was in a perpetual confrontation against the 'foreign' Muslims. And so till this day, our textbooks, our political leadership, our mass media and in particular the All India Radio, continue to use the medieval hero-myths to arouse nationalism particularly at times of national crisis, but with much less justification than the pioneers, for their injurious effects are by now obvious and historical personages who were genuine fighters in the real life anti-imperialist struggle are available for glorification. The absurdity of the hero-myths is fully brought out when in innumerable plays on the AIR, e.g., those of Seth Govind Das, every petty struggle by a zamindar or a jagirdar is played up as a national struggle so long as the zamindar happens to be a Rajput or Hindu and the ruler a Muslim.

Let me repeat. This has nothing to do with historical objectivity or integrity. For hero-myths are not the creation of genuine historical writing. They are a political creation and therefore must satisfy the criterion of political usefulness. Secondly, by suggesting that the hero-myths were not, and should not be, played up as 'national heroes', I am not in any way trying to denigrate them or deny them their historical role. Certainly, Shivaji, Rana Pratap and Guru Gobind Singh were important men in their own historical context. But that context was not one of national struggle. Otherwise, if we project communalism back- wards and declare them as Hindu nationalists, then others might project their secular, integrated nationalism backwards and declare them to be disruptionists of Indian unity, state and, therefore, nationality. While the absurdity of the latter view would be acknowldeged by all, we should Sf e that the former view is no less absurd. Moreover to say that a historical character was not a nationalist in an era when nationalism did not exist is not to denigrate him. Being a 'national hero' is not the only type of badge of honour. Otherwise, why did not we declare that anybody who does not call Ashoka or Harsha or Guru Nanak or Chaitanya or Akbar national heroes is insulting them? In fact, what I am suggesting is the rescuing of Shivaji, Rana Pratap and Guru Gobind Singh from the misuse to which they have been, and are being, put by the communalists. In fact, Rana Pratap was no more a national hero than Akbar, or Shivaji than Aurangzeb, and so on. Moreover, by giving them a false 'national' character in illusory history, we have been serving an anti-national, disintegrating purpose in modem and contemporary history.

The communal aspect of the hero-myths can be seen in another manner. Surprisingly little effort has been expended by the communalists in installing as 'national leaders' Ashoka or Chandra Gupta or Harsha, etc., even though they lived in the so-called Golden Age. But, then, the communalists know that their names cannot be used to arouse anti-Muslim feeling, their 'nationalism' would not be anti-Muslim "nationalism", i.e., communalism,. It is also interesting that one of the leading communal historians of today has tried to cut "down to size, in the name of historical objectivity, Rani of Jhansi and Nana Saheb, even though they were Hindus and fighting against a real foreign power. But, then, they were not only not fighting a Muslim ruler but were even cooperating with him, going to the extent of acknowledging him as their emperor.

We should also not underestimate the negative impact these heor-myths have on national integration through their impact on minorities and hitherto submerged groups. It is not easy for a Muslim to take part emotionally and feel real enthusiasm for a nationalism whose 'national heroes' win 'national' honour because they fought against the 'foreign' Muslims. As social and political awareness spreads to the lower castes and classes, they may be expected to react in a similar manner against the glorification of zarnindars, chiefs and rulers whose relationship to these castes and classes was that of oppressors and exploiters.

I would also not suggest merely the replacement of these hero-myths with other, more national hero-myths. It is high time our educational system and mass media, including the AIR, as well as the political parties and personalities, started placing before people real people, with their positive and negative contributions. This is abetter way of giving them political education as well as of inspiring them with high social and political ideals. But if, for some reason, hero-myths are found necessary and inevitable, they should be chosen with care for their effectiveness in serving the ends in view and they should have a firm foundation in reality.

5

Communalism—The Way Out

I am not going to provide a history of the communal problem or its sociological or class analysis. I am going to do something very un-historian like and that is to try to suggest what should be done. After all the ultimate goal of all social sciences is to contribute to the building of a better present and a happier future. I ap1 also going to be extremely frank. I believe that if one has something sensible to say one should be able to give the same lecture to audiences of Hindus or Muslims or Sikhs or a combination of all of them.

I am also not going to discuss the communal problem of just Punjab though naturally that is something which is currently occupying the minds of people, specially in this part of the world. In fact communalism is a problem not only for Punjab, it is a problem which is facing the entire country and the entire Indian society, It is a conjunctural aspect that sometimes it may break out here or there in a virulent form. But, in fact, communalism has been pervading, sometimes growing sometimes receding, but still pervading on a large scale in the entire Indian society. So it is not a problem that Punjabis alone are facing, it is a problem that people all over the country are facing.

I

One of the starting points of what I have to say about "communalism: the way out" is that it is going to be a very long haul—the way out. We are in a kind of dark tunnel and the way opt is also going to be a very long one. Historical problems generated over generations do not get solved in a jiffy. There are no short-teeth or instant solutions to this problem. So far as the way out is concerned, it is a problem of initiating and pushing forward the process of the long haul.

In this respect, I must point out that I am aware of this long haul character from personal experience. Educated in an Arya Samaj school, in a predominantly Hindu communal milieu, I know how long the struggle has to be to overcome the communal elements in one's thinking and one's personality. I have been teaching now for over thirtythree years and know how difficult the task is. When students, who come under teachers' secular influence for three, four or five years, go back into society and are once again open to communal currents, how it breaks the heart of the teacher and how one realises then that it is going to be a very, very long haul. It is like the *banvas* of Ram, Sita and Lakshman, which was a fourteen years haul. Yet, in this long haul there are a large number of positive points so far as one's own life is concerned. Let me share one experience with you.

In the early fifties I had a student whose hair were all grey and who was so strongly secular and so strongly anti-communal that he would pick a quarrel with anybody with RSS bias in the college. Once, when he sat down with me I asked him why he was so strongly secular when he was a Punjabi. He said he was not a Punjabi but a refugee and so I said it was even more surprising. He said this was how his hair had turned grey. "It is like a story in the films. I am from Rawalpindi. My mother and father and five of my brothers and sisters were killed before my eyes. I was hiding behind a box and as I was then very small, those who killed members of my family did not see me. I was too frightened to cry, seeing seven members of my family being wiped out. Only one of my brothers survived because he was not in town. That is when my hair turned grey." I said: "How come that you are so secular?" He said: "Sir, very early I realised that my parents had not been killed by Muslims, they had. been killed by communalism." I got a very important lesson regarding communalism from this young boy when he said:" My parents have not been killed by Muslims, they had been killed by communalism." He said: "Whether it is the communalism of the Muslims or of the Hindus I am very strongly opposed to it. I react very strongly psychologically when I come across any communal-minded person because I see the murderers of my family before my eyes." So in this long haulthere is also hope.

II

There is one other very basic point, but since there is not enough time to deal with it I will just state it. It is that communalism is the product of a particular situation of a particular society, economy and polity, which creates problems for its people, problems of which the people are not able to understand the cause. Communalism is often the effort of the people to come to grips with the situation of their personal and social crisis without correctly grasping what the social situation is. In other words, communalism is not a correct diagnosis of the social situation, nor is it the correct solution of the social situation.

There is a social situation lying at its back, which is stoking it, without which communalism could not have survived for long, and unless that particular social situation is righted or effort is made to right that situation, solve that situation in the right way, ideologies like communalism and casteism and other similar ideologies of hate—false ideologies—will go on rising. Therefore, the way out of communalism in a permenant direction lies in righting the social situation.

At the same time, one cannot rest with this social aspect because communalism is an enemy in itself and communalism comes in the way of the righting of the situation. Communalism is the product of a particular social situation but to right that situation communalism has to be opposed; otherwise one cannot right the situation. Of course, the social roots have to be discovered and a social analysis of communalism has to be evolved. Without that there can be no long term strategy or a permanent fight against communalism. But one has to combat communalism even in the existinng situation, precisely in order to transform that situation. Therefore, social analysis of communalism should not be used, as many people do, as an alibi for not fighting against communalism. It is not true that communalism will not end till socialism comes and that believers in socialism should not fight against communalism but should fight only for socialism.

This type of outlook can also become, in the name of social analysis, an alibi for not fighting against communalism, because the type of political ideology communalism is, it is rather difficult to fight against it. When one fights against capitalism one fights against class enemies who are distant. When one fights against communalism one fights one's brothers, sisters and parents, one's friends and colleagues and relations and persons one comes across daily. It is a very difficult task. But the difficulty of the task should not mean that we should give it up in the name of fighting for the ultimate solution. In other words, fighting for the ultimate solution does not take away from the task of fighting against communalism.

III

First of all, in my analysis of the way out in Punjab, the most important aspect or concept is the fact that communalism is basically and above all an ideology. Communalism is not in the main communal riots, it is not in the main communal violence or communal terrorrism. Certainly, communal violence is linked to communal ideology, but basically communalism is an ideology of which these three others are conjunctural consequences. Communal ideology can prevail even without violence, but communal violence cannot exist without communal ideology. It is possible to have communal ideology for decades without communal violence taking place at all. Therefore, communalism is above all a communal ideology and it is at the level of struggle against that ideology that the way out has to be found. Any other way out will prove to be no way out at all. That will be like treating a cancer patient with aspirin because there exists a headache or a stomach-ache. A headache can be caused by many diseases. The real problem is the disease, not the headache or some otherache.

What is communal ideology? I believe that communal ideology consists of three elements, one succeeding the other. First of all, according to communal ideology, people who follow the same religion have common secular interests, that is, people who follow the same religion have not only common religious beliefs or interests but they also have common political, economic, social and cultural interests. This is the first bedrock of communal ideology. From this arises the notion of a religious community functioning as a community for secular purposes. A person who talks about the Hindu community or the Sikh community or the interests of the Sikh community or the Muslim community or the Hindu community is already taking the first step towards communalism whether he knows it or not, and however secular he might be feeling privately or genuinely at heart, unless the concept of community is used for religious purposes only.

The second step is taken when in a multi-religious society it is said that some of the secular interests, that is economic, social, political and cultural interests, of the followers of one religion are different from some of the interests of the followers of another religion. One does not say that the Hindu religion is different from the Muslim religion; that is true by definition. But when one says that the secular interests of Hindus are different from the interests of Muslims or Sikhs, one has taken the second step towards communalism.

The third step is taken when it is said that not only are the interests of the followers of different 'communities' different but are hostile to each other, that is, what is economically, politically, socially orcultu-rally in the interests of Hindus is not so in the interests of Muslims or in the interests of Sikhs, that the two cannot have common economic, social, political interests, that their secular interests are bound to be opposed to each other. This last step brings communalism to the stage of what I would describe as extreme communalism or fascistic commu-nalism.

The first stage is the beginning of communal ideology. The second stage is what may be described as liberal communalism or what some people describe as moderate communalism. The third stage is reached when the secular interests of the followers of one religion are counterpoised to the secular interests of the followers of another in a hostile fashion. Then we get the last stage of communal ideology. It is this communal ideology in all its stages which has to be opposed, and the way out from communalism means decommunalising ideologi-cally the people of this country, of this state, of this area, and our different institutions, etc.

This is very important because if one equates communalism not with communal ideology but only with communal violence, then one will have to say that Punjab was a happy land where there was no communalism after 1947. Because, after the communal riots of 1947 and till 1982, there was no communal violence or communal rioting in Punjab. According to this theory, communalism came in Punjab either only after 1982 when communal killings started by Bhindranwale's followers or in June 1984 when the Indian army marched into the Golden Temple. But in actual fact communalism was growing stronger every day in Punjab since 1947. It was not only growing stronger under the surface after 1947, it became visibly stronger in the last six or seven years before anybody had heard of Bhindranwale. Some of us started warning of the dangers to Punjab of communalism in about 1974 when I spoke in the Punjabi University, Patiala. Others must have done so even earlier. I remember speaking in the Punjabi University in 1974 warning against the danger which Punjab was beginning, and going, to face with the brewing of communalism.

In other words what we find is the slow growth of communalism in Punjab over the years. How deep that communalism has penetrated this province-and in fact more or less the other parts of the country also-especially among the middle classes of the Punjab was revealed by the June events. Large sections of the Hindu middle classes thought that the entry into the Golden Temple was something to be celebrated, to be overjoyed about, something which was good. One can understand if the feeling was that through this action a major danger to Punjab, that is of communal killings, and to India, had ended. But only communal people or people pervaded with communalism could have celebrated this, event. Similarly, the reaction of a large section of the middle class Sikhs and Sikh intelligentsia was also communal when they talked about the army's entry into the Golden Temple as a hurt to the Sikh community. Of course, any Sikh or any Hindu in Punjab would be sad at the entry of the army into the Golden Temple. But I cannot understand this reaction except as an aspect or consequence of the pervasive nature of communal ideology because the normal reaction of any person, Hindu or Sikh, would have been that this hurt was caused by Bhindranwale and his group. This is not Indira Gandhi's propaganda; this would be the normal secular reaction anywhere in the world. How is it that the intelligentsia of Punjab, both Hindu and Sikh, reacted in a different way? This can only be because there was the' all-pervasive character of communalism growing since 1947 underneath and above the ground.

I remember one of my students who studied with me for five years, three years for B.A. and two years for M.A., a middle class Punjabi, a judge's son. He started discussing the communal problem and I started pointing out to him day after day, at every discussion, how he was communal, how his assumptions were communal. After four years he came to me once and said: "Every time I meet you, you say I am communal; I go back and get rid of that particular assumption or concept and I come back and say I am secular; you again show to me that I am still communal; does it mean that when all my flesh disappears and only my bones remain, intellectually speaking, only then will my communalism go?" I said: "No my boy, communalism has entered even the bones of the Punjabi middle classes. Perhaps what many of us can do is to minimise the damage. It may be difficult for your generation and mine to get rid of communalism fully. It is a very pervasive thing."

Similarly, if one was to go by the criterion of violence, one would say that Muslim communalism in India is very weak. After all, Muslims are the victims of communal rioting, they are not the instigators. May be in one case out of a hundred they are the instigators. May be they kill but they kill only more or less when they are forced to defend themselves. Therefore, one would say that in areas like Moradabad, Aligarh, Meerut, Bhiwandi, Bombay, Jabalpur,

Indore, or Bhopal there is no Muslim communalism or it is extremely weak because Muslim communalists are not creating violence; it is the other side which is creating violence. But the fact is that communal ideology is extremely strong among Muslims in India.

Similarly, a large number of Hindus pride themselves over the fact that in their area there is no communal rioting and, therefore, they say they have no communalism. Particularly South Indians used to tell us that you North Indians are communal but we are not. But now, increasingly, they too are discovering that they too have communal elements in their ideology and that is why communal forces are making a breakthrough in the South. In fact, communalism among Hindus has been equally strong whether there was violence or not.

Communalism seen as an ideology alone explains why anti-Hindu and anti-Sikh communalisms could grow in post-1947 Punjab. As I have defined communalism, communalism, especially of the extreme variety, is based on the theory of mutual hatred and clash of mutual interests; and liberal communalism is based on the notion of some of the secular interests of the followers of the two religions being different or separate. But once one sees communalism as looking upon the followers of one religion as constituting a community, as having separate secular interests, and as having opposite interests, then one can clearly see that simply because Punjab was partitioned and Muslims were driven out from Punjab jointly by Hindu and Sikh communalists, it did not mean that communalism came to an end.

In Punjab, Punjabi Hindus and Sikhs have what is called *roti beti lea rishta.* Not only do they eat together but they intermarry. There would not be very many Hindu families in urban Punjab who would not have a Sikh in the family, one way or the other. Why should communalism have then developed among them, unless one sees that if there is a communal ideology which is turned against Muslims-the notion that Hindu interests are separate, Sikh interests are separate, and Muslim interests are separate—once this ideology is not overthrown and constitutional changes do not overthrow such ideologies—once no effort was made to overthrow this ideology and this ideology continued, then it was bound in time to turn Hindu and Sikh communalists against each other, once Muslim communalism disappeared from the scene. Hindu communalism was bound to be anti-Sikh and Sikh communalism was bound to be anti-Hindu. Then the notion that Hindu and Sikh communalists had cooperated together in killing Muslims or in defending themselves against Muslim communalists in West Punjab, and, therefore, should not fight each other would not hold and communalism would develop, this time in its anti-Sikh and anti-Hindu forms.

Here we may take note of a very interesting aspect. Sikh communalism, from the days of Bhai Vir Singh's novels, was based on the theory that Sikhs were the defenders of Hinduism and that Sikhism developed in order to defend Hindus. Hindu communalists too accepted this theory that Sikhs were the sword arm of Hinduism. That is .why their main communal body, the RSS, has three great heroes, Shivaji, Guru Gobind Singh and Rana Pratap. In fact it is very interesting that throughout the Fifties and Sixties and even in the Seventies the two groups of communalists tried to avoid hatred against each other. The Akalis never preached hatred of Hindus because it would go against the entire grain of the development of their communal ideology during the 20th century and against their particular mythology regarding the history and role of the Sikhs in the past. Similarly, the RSS and the Jan Sangh found it an extremely difficult and unpleasant job to rouse hatred against Sikhs; their mythology was that Sikhs were part of Hindus and that in fact they were the toughest, the biggest defenders of Hinduism against Muslim tyranny. And, therefore, the RSS and the Jan Sangh (BJP) could not easily breed hatred towards Sikhs. However, despite the two communal groups making every effort not to spread hatred, hatred did come finally because communal ideology has its own inner logic. Once you propagate communal ideology, the consequences are not in your hands. Once you promote the notion of community and community separateness and separate interests of communities, it is inevitable that one communal group should deny its mother tongue and the other demand Punjabi suba in the name of Sikh majority.

It is interesting that no communal riots accurred in Punjab but at the same time communal killings did occur over the last two years. Perhaps no Sikh was killed or communally murdered in Punjab, but a few were killed in the neighbouring state of Haryana. In other words, the two communal groups could not prevent their own development into the third stage, that is the hatred stage, of communalism.

Consequently, the most important aspect of the way out is an ideological struggle against communalism, if communalism is primarily and basically an ideology, if it is not communal riots, if it is not communal violence, which are only conjunctural manifestations of this ideology. In Aligarh you may have riots for three years running and you may have no riots for the next ten, fifteen, twenty years, and yet communal ideology is pervasive, whether it takes the from of a riot or not. Violence is a conjunctural fact depending on many factors, including, sometimes, which Deputy Commissioner or Superintendent of Police is holding the position in Aligarh district or Aligarh town. If we accept that, then the way out of communalism lies above all in waging an ideological struggle against communalism.

If communalism is basically an ideology, it cannot be suppressed by force. No ideology can be suppressed by force. Ideology has to be fought at the level of ideas. This is what we learn from history.

Secondly, if communalism is basically an ideology and has to be opposed, then there can be no compromise with or concession to communal ideology in any form. I stress this because we find all around—in the past in the pre-1947 period and now in the last few months in Punjab—people are reeling under communal pressure and are beginning to make or advocate compromises with communal ideology in one form or another.

Thirdly, the ideological struggle has to be fought not only among the masses, not only among the communal persons, it has to be fought also among secular persons because what we witness in periods of crisis is that communalism burgeons forth, and it burgeons forth because secular people join it in a burgeoning manner. This happens because there are communal elements also among the secular persons and these elements suddenly grow. It is not true that educated persons can necessarily handle communalism or communal ideology better than others. They are as much victims of communal ideology. In fact, they are the main purveyors of communal ideology. It is they who have revealed the biggest weakness regarding communalism in the Twenties, Thirtees, and Forties and in the years after 1947, as well as in Punjab for the last one year and especially after June 1984.

It is very interesting that when the franchise was extremely narrow and limited and confined mostly to middle classes, business people in the urban areas and landlords and rich peasants in the villages, we find that in 1926 the Swarajist Party got defeated in Bengal, Punjab and the Central Provinces and its majority got extremely narrowed down in Madras, UP and Bihar precisely becuase the middle classes and intelligentsia gave way to communalism. Many of them accused Motilal Nehru of being a beef eater, an Islam lover and what not. Therefore, this struggle against communal ideology has to be waged not only with the help of intellectuals-of course with the help of intellectuals along with the masses-but it also has to be waged first of all among the intellectuals themselves.

In the last six months and very much so in the last two or three months, themes which were basic to communal ideology-to Muslim and Hindu communalism specially since 1922 when Hindu and Muslim communalism started growing on a large scale—are being unconsciously picked up even by many secular persons. That is, themes, notions, ideas, which were the very bedrock of communal ideology among Hindus, Muslims, Sikhs and Christians, are today being expressed by extremely secular minded Hindus, Muslims and Sikhs. For example, in March this year there appeared a statement in the Press and there was something similar again in August or September that one should respect the pride of Sikhs in their history, implying that Sikhs have a separate history of their own.

In fact, many historians were for years fighting against this notion in the syllabi committees and among our colleagues. They were saying, do not talk about anything called Sikh history, there is no such thing called Sikh history any more than there is anything called Hindu history or Muslim history. There is the history of Punjab. History is common to the people of a region or country, to the peasants, to the artisans and so on. For example, Banda Bahadur Singh's history is not the history of Sikhs. In my textbook on modern India, I have also written glorifying Banda Bahadur Singh's struggle, but I have not called it Sikh history. It was a struggle of the oppressed and downtrodden people of Punjab in the first two decades of the 18th century against particular types of oppression. The other day I read a statement by highly secular persons referring to 'the pride of the Sikhs in their theology' or 'pride of the Sikhs in their language'. This notion that Punjabi is the language of Sikhs was the bedrock of Hindu communalism in Punjab in the 1950s. Now we find secular people talking about the pride of the Sikhs in their language. In other words, Punjabi in Gurrnukhi script is seen as the language of the Sikhs; it is not the language of the Punjabis. There can be nothing more communal than this. In fact it is very interesting that all these themes were articulated by Hindu communalism much earlier.

When I was asked to sign the statement in March about the Sikhs' pride in their history, I said to the organisers: "I am not willing to sign any statement unless you are willing to sign the same statement with the word Sikhs replaced by the word Hindus." But what is this Hindus' pride in Hindu history? Secular. historians have been for years fighting against this notion of Hindus' pride in Hindu history. They have been fighting against the notion of Hindi being the language of the Hindus. And how can then one talk about Sikhs' pride in their theology. Because, how would it be for this country if Hindus were also asked to have a pride in their theology? I hear the phrase, "effort is being made to divide Sikhs," as if all Sikhs should be united irrespective of their politics. By the way, these statements are not being made by communal Sikhs only. They are being made by many secular Sikh and Hindu intellectuals. When Bhagat Singh came across this notion being propagated by Lajpat Rai that Hindus must be united, that they must not be divided, he branded Lajpat Rai, his political guru, as a communalist for propagating this notion. This notion that the Hindus must not be divided, they must remain united and anyone who tries to divide them is a dirty dog-if that is communalism, how is it not communalism to talk about Sikhs not being divided? Rather one wishes that Sikhs were divided ideologically, that is, communalists were divided from the secularists, landlords from peasants, an so on.

We sometimes read that 'Sikhs must have an identity'. What is this notion of Sikhs' identity? This is the very notion which created these two communal forces in the Twenties: Hindu *sangathan,* Muslim *tanzeem.* What was Hindu *sangathan?* Hindu *sangathan* was based on the notion that Hindus had no identity; they must acquire an identity. And yet we find highly secular people now writing about Sikh identity.

All this shows how deep and penetrating is communal ideology in our minds. When we suddenly come out with concepts, symbols and ideas which we thought we had long buried; when they come up in our minds though we have been struggling in our minds against them for years as secular persons; when we suddenly issue a statement under the stress of the situation and find these notions coming forth; this shows how important it is to go to the marrow, not only to the bone but the marrow, in order to fight communalism.

What does the struggle against communal ideology mean?

Briefly, it means bringing home to the people that communalism is anti-development, it is anti-national unity, it is anti-class struggle, it is anti-humanist, it is in fact anti-religion in so' far as all religions are based on certain humanist values. Also that secularism is not just an instrumental value. Secularism is a value in itself because it is a humanist value. Secularism is not important only because communalism stands in the way of the struggle for socialism. After all we fight for socialism because we cannot stand oppression of man by man; we cannot stand poverty in the midst of riches; we believe that a human being should not be exploited and should not be starved. The same value is involved also in secularism. That is, nobody should be hated, nobody should be discriminated against, because of his or her religion.

The ideological struggle against communalism above all means bringing home to people, masses, as well as the middle classes and intellectuals, the falsity of commmunal assumptions, of communal logic, of communal answers; of bringing home to people that what the communalists project as problems are not the real problems and what the communalists say is the answer is not the real answer; that the communalist not only gives the wrong answer, he also raises the wrong question. This is the long haul which we have got to undertake, of going to the people and explaining to them with the help of history, with the help of sociology, with the help of everyday life, with the help of our social struggles, class struggles and what not, through all the channels to bring home to the people that the problems that the Hindu and Sikh communalists have raised in Punjab are totally false-from the notion of religion in danger to the notion of identity in danger, to the notion that Sikhs are becoming too big and Hindus are going to be oppressed, to the notion that Hindus are going to oppress and eliminate Sikhs—that all these are not the real problems. The unemployed youth should know what their problem is. Their problem is not Hindu oppression, their problem is unemployment, What are the causes of unemployment? The communal answer is wrong. It is not Hindus and it is not Sikhs who are responsible for it. The communal solution is also wrong. Neither the elimination of Hindus nor the elimination of Sikhs will solve the problems plaguing the society. In other words, the problem is posed wrongly and the answer given is wrong. This looks very simple but in fact this is the basic task that has to be performed.

In this respect let me point to one other aspect. Some people, especially some liberal-minded people, who have been brought up on common sense at their mother's knees, say how can an ideology or a movement spread if there is not some truth in the complaint; communalists must be pointing to some genuine complaint, some genuine cause, because otherwise how would millions of people believe it? The common sense part lies in the saying 'where there is smoke there is fire'. But the fact of the matter is that this is not true. It is a specific aspect of communal type of ideologies that they reflect a social situation of crisis but they do not reflect it-either its cause or its solution—correctly. In other words, the communal type of ideologies can have no basis in reality and yet they flourish.

This is the case not only in Punjab. This problem is raised sometimes in the case of Bhindranwale. There must be some reason why Bhindranwale was so popular. There must be some reason why so many Hindus have become communal in Punjab. There must be some reason why so many Sikhs have become communal in Punjab. If one is soft towards Hindu communalism, one says there is some reason and it ·lies with Sikhs. If one is soft towards Sikh communalism, one says there must be some reason and it must be lying in what Hindus are doing. But the fact of the matter is that the 20th century is rich in ideologies both in our country and abroad which spread without having any genuine basis in reality. On a world scale, the ideology of fascism is a very good example. Were the Jews oppressing Germans? Was there some truth in this assertion? Was there some truth in Nazism because millions of people loved Hitler and followed him to the grave? Twenty million Germans died, from children of eleven onwards, in defending what Hitler stood for. Does it mean that there was some truth in Nazism, that Hitler had something true in him? Or that the Jews must have oppressed Christian Germans; their behaviour must have had something to do with the rise of Nazism.

Similarly, for three hundred years racialism has been rampant in the western world, sometimes in a most vicious form till the Fifties or Sixties of this century in the USA. Was there some truth in the notion that Blacks are inferior? In our own country, Hindus constituted over seventy per cent of the population before 1947 and constitute more than eighty per cent of the population today; and yet millions upon millions of Hindus under communal influence believe that they are in danger, their culture is in danger, their religion is in danger, their very existence is in danger, and not merely in Punjab or Kashmir, it is in danger all over India. Projections are made. In the year 2020 Muslims will be in a majority because they do not practise family planning. The Sikhs also might start not having family planning and in the year 2500 they will become a majority and Hindus will be extinct because they would have practised family planning like the Japanese or Russians or Americans. Yet, many more than those who follow Sikh communalism—millions upon millions—believe that Hinduism is in danger, and they vote for communal parties.

It was on this type of falsehood that Jinnah built up a powerful movement for communalism and then for the partition of the country around the notion that no Muslim can survive in free India, that they will be wiped out—and then left nearly half the Muslims to survive in India at the mercy of people who, he had claimed, would wipe them out. In fact, Muslims, with all their disabilities and with all the discriminatory conditions in this country, are better off than they are in Bangladesh or Pakistan. Therefore, this notion that there must be some truth in communal ideology is really an aspect of the pervasiveness of communal ideology. I came across this notion as a young man in Lahore during 1942-46, and I am shocked when I come across this type of notion today in Punjab and in the rest of India.

Here I would like to make one other point. If there is a real crisis where fire fighting is needed, when your house is on fire, you do not start buying the right type of fire extinguisher, you start extinguishing the fire. I can very well understand that in a moment of real crisis of a communal riot in Moradabad or Aligarh, or in the type of situation which prevailed in Punjab and may prevail again, every effort is to be made to arrive at some compromise at the political level. Not being a political leader, I would not say what sort of compromise should be there on Chandigarh or water-sharing or this or that. But one thing I can say, that there should be no compromise on the ideological plane. Compromise on some problems helps solve them. This is not the case with communalism; a compromise on the communal plane will only make the position worse. I must also say that if a compromise is found absolutely necessary it should be for gaining time. A compromise makes some sense only if time is gained in order to fight better against communal ideology. In fact, compromises have been made several times in Punjab with Sikh communalism as well as Hindu communalism, sometimes by denying Punjabi suba and sometimes by giving it in a particular manner. At both times, after the compromise, it has been assumed that the situation is now safe and one can go home and go to sleep. In fact, if a compromise becomes necessary it makes sense only if it is used to launch a powerful ideological battle against communalism.

In this connection one other lesson has to be learnt from the pre-1947 experience: Under no circumstance should one make communalism and the communalist respectable; one should never stop attacking communalism ideologically. One of the major errors which we committed was that we waged no ideological and political struggle against communalism in the Twenties and Thirties and we made communalism respectable by .negotiating with it and by treating it as a respectable force. We paid the price in 1946 and 1947.

Communalism is an ideology. There is no such thing as Sikh communalism which is different from Hindu communalism or Muslim communalism. Hindu communalism, Muslim communalism, Sikh communalism are communalism first. I would regard them as different varieties of communalism. They are like a rose which is of different colours but a rose is still a rose. The simile is perhaps' not appropriate, it is a bit of an insult to a rose. But you can get my meaning. This is another important reason why one should look upon communalism as a communal ideology. If one sees it as a communal ideology, then one does not fight only against Sikh communalism or Hindu communalism; one fights against communalism as a whole; even when one fights against its particular mainfestations. This means that among Sikhs one fights against Sikh communalism, among Hindus one fights against Hindu cornmunalism, and if one has both of these in an area then one fights against both; in other words, one wages simultaneous struggle against an forms of communalism.

Here the role of education and the Press is crucial. Paradoxically, the spread of literacy can also have negative consequences in this respect. In simple terms, literacy is supposed to be the panacea for all social ills; and spread of literacy is seen as of the highest value. It is of course of the highest value, and literacy is one of the three or four basic developments which all societies must achieve. But in this development there also inheres a great danger. Long time back, one of my American professors warned me against complacency regarding literacy. He said: "Bipan Chandra, when you go back to your country do not be a blind follower of literacy." I asked him "Why". He said: "Remember one thing: the illiterate Russians produced Lenin as their leader; the illiterate Indians have produced Gandhi as their leader; the illiterate Chinese have produced Mao Tse Tung as their leader; and the country with the highest literacy, with the largest number of Ph.Ds, has produced Hitler as their leader; therefore be warned." Thus, literacy makes sense only if it is used to spread the right type of ideas, not if it is used to spread poisonous ideas; and it is this that has happened in our country. Even peasants who were guarded by illiteracy and by their centuries old culture are being affected. But this culture is being eroded as what is spread among them is the most rotten from of education.

Along with literacy came the notion of a Sikh history and inherent in that also is the notion of a Hindu history and a Muslim history and so on. When I was a school boy, when I read the highly provocative and unhistorical play on Hakikat Rai, taught to me in my *dharma sikshaclass* as a true story, what—a powerful impact it had on me. I felt angry with Muslims for putting an eleven year old boy in chains and burying him between two walls. Therefore, there is a special duty on educationists and intellectuals to see that in the name of value-free education the wrong type of education does not spread.

The same is the case with the Press. The Press has played a very important role in sustaining and spreading communalism. This has been done not only by the communal Press, but also by the secular Press in the name of freedom of information. The Press has indulged in sensational reporting and accepted communal leaders at their face value by designating them as Hindu leaders, Muslim leaders or Sikh leaders. I agree with the concept of freedom of information, with the theory that reporting must be fearless and objective. But I ask our Press people only one question: When freedom of the Press is attacked, do they report the event in a 'fair' and 'objective' manner, in a value-free manner? The government imposed censorship on the Press during the Emergency. Was this to be reported as an interesting piece of information only. Or was it also to be condemned In a manner in which the reader would know that something rotten was happening? What about crimes against. women, rapes and so on? Can you report them objectively? Then why is communalism also not seen as as much poisonous, and, in a society like ours, much more so? Then how can one report the communal aspect in the manner of reporting a cricket match?

This is what was happening in Punjab by the way for several years, that the entire reporting of the communal Press was no different from the reporting of a cricket match between the West Indies and the Indian teams, or something like that. At the same time, we should perhaps still be thankful that our Press and our media are not yet as bad as they are in countries which are dominated by the state and ruling groups which are communal. How would it be if in the name of information photographs of people, who have been brought down from a bus and shot down, were put on the front half page in the Tribune, or if the TV was to show them in the evening with all their wounds and with their mothers and daughters and sisters crying over the death of their loved ones? Bad enough that you have to report that a certain number of people have been killed. But how to you report it? As I said we are lucky that we have not had this type of 'fair' reporting as yet. When we reach that stage, the communal problem would perhaps be really beyond our control.

A part of the ideological struggle lies in distinguishing between communalism, semi-communalism and communal elements. This is very important. Let me take up communal elements.

If communalism is an ideology then it- is constituted of several elements. The three basic elements I have already described. It is possible for people to be secular and yet have some communal elements. There is a great danger that if these elements are not opposed, they will grow and develop in a crisis situation and lead to the burgeoning forth of communalism. But there is also the danger that if one starts branding those who have som, communal elements-as communal then one will be throwing a large number of secular persons into the ranks of communalists. Once we see communalism as an ideology, we have to handle the entire problem in an extremely complex manner. We have to deal harshly with those who are communal ideologues. Those who are intellectuals but are giving way to communalism should also be dealt with firmly. They have no business to do so. But those who are victims of communal ideology, even if they are communal, have to be handled as sick people, not as vicious people, not as enemies.

My favourite simile is that we do not kill somebody who is suffering from tuberculosis; we treat him. The vast mass of people believe in communal ideology without knowing the full implications. Among them, deep educative work has to be carried out. That is what I mean by ideological struggle. Those who have communal elements have to be told that they are secular people; that their secular feelings and commitment are a very healthy thing; but that these communal elements do not go with their secular personality and ideology. Therefore, they must get rid of these elements. In this context a deep analysis has to be made of what is communalism and what are communal elements.

Similarly, we should distinguish between liberal communalism (Muslim League before 1937; All-India Muslim League after 1947, Akali DAI, B.J.P.) and extreme or fascist communalism (Muslim League after 1937, Jamaat-i-Islami after 1947, Extremist Akalis in-eluding followers of Bhindranwale, RSS). But this distinction is to be made because the two have to be opposed in different ways. The distinction is not to be made in order to take a softer attitude towards liberal communalism. If the latter is not opposed successfully, it tends to grow into extreme or fascist communalism.

In this respect I must say that not all use of religious language and Symbols in politics is communalism. Though it is not a correct thing to do still it is not communalism. N.T. Rama Rao goes round Andhra in saffron coloured clothes in a Chaitanya Ratham and surrounded by all sorts of religious symbols. I would criticise him very sharply and I would point out how bringing in of religious signs and symbols even at the symbolic level softens up the personality for the intrusion of communalism. But I would not describe it as communalism. By describing it as communalism one would be throwing N.T. Rama Rao and others into the wrong camp.

Similarly, Reagan is today raising the question of religion and politics. Religion, he says, cannot be divorced from politics. This is an extremely reactionary step which can have dire consequences. But one will not say it is communalism. Similarly, the people of this country have the right to, and should, criticise it when the President or the Prime Minister visits holy places and the news is flashed on radio or television. Of course, it is their personal business to visit as many holy places as they may want to. But the reporting of such visits is to be criticised. But it is still not communalism. The point is that one has to make this type of distinction, though after making the distinction one should be able to make a critique.

Similarly, one should differentiate between religion and religiosity. This point cannot be discussed here at length. Ideological struggle against communalism does not at all mean a struggle against religion. Religion is a personal affair. Religion has something which sustains people spiritually and in case of some people the older they become the more they want some sort of religious sustenance. It is an individual's personal business. At the same time, though ideological struggle against communalism does not mean struggle against religion, religiosity, that is religion encompassing large areas of life, is extremely conducive to the intrusion of communal ideology, even though religiosity is not yet communalism. Communal ideology finds a fertile ground if a person is all the time surrounded by religious symbols and by religion. Religiosity is when religion is not something from which you derive morality or spiritual sustenance or faith in the next world or faith in salvation but when one uses it to enngulf many other areas of one's life.

In fact we find that communalists in India have been consciously trying to encourage religiosity, whether you take activities of the Muslim communalists or you take the *yagna* organised by the Hindu communal elements who have been trying to encourage religiosity, or you take the Sikh communal notions that Sikhs are different because for them the *khalsa* is above all and. every thing or that religion cannot be divorced from politics because this is the inner nature of Sikhism. But I believe that all this type of religiosity is still not communalism. A person deeply imbued with religiosity may still be secular but religiosity does lend to soften up people and make them open to communal ideology, and it has, therefore, to be avoided and opposed.

The struggle against communal ideology has to be a mass level struggle. One of the weaknesses of Indian society Which should be overcome, if we want to find a way out. is that there has been no mass ideological de political campaign against communalism in India since 1947. At least I do not remember any. There may have been meetings here and there and statements, but there has been no massive, all-India campaign against communalism. I have been a critic of the fact that our national movement failed to struggle adequately against communalism ideologically; and this was one of the biggest weaknesses of the national movement. But even the type of mass struggle that Gandhiji carried out for Hindu-Muslim unity, though it was inadequate, has not been carried out by us.

One of the basic features of any way out has to be—whether it is done by political parties or intellectuals coming together or non-political groups coming together or by a federation of societies like the one here—the carrying out of a mass level campaign against communalism. For: years some of us have been asking why We cannot follow our national movement and at least have what used to be called in those days 'a week of struggle against communalism'. Why cannot people all over India set apart one week in which they will fight against communalism, they will speak against communalism, they will analyse communalism, all over the country simultaneously? This is particularly important because if you do not carry on a mass campaign simultaneously all over the country there is a danger that the struggle against communalism in one place will strengthen communalism in another manner. If we carry on a struggle against Hindu communalism, Hindu communalists can ask why should only we be struggled against; if you carry out a struggle only against Sikh communalism, Sikh communalists will raise slogans that Sikhs are being discriminated against, why only their communalism should be called bad and not the communalism of others? The same slogan can be raised by RSS, why are Hindus being treated in this discriminatory manner?

Secondly, as pointed out earlier, intellectuals have a special role in this field. First of all, by not giving way to communalism, by analysing their thinking very minutely, by analysing every word that they write and every word they think, ari' by seeing whether this thinking has any communal instrusion; and then, having done that, by acting as teachers of the people. I am not one of those who down-grade intellectuals. Intellectuals have the habit of downgrading themselves and their functions. In the United States businessmen call them eggheads and dismiss them with a flourish of hand. But, in fact, intellectuals, particularly in societies like. ours, have a very important role to play and they must not hesitate to play this role. Here one last warning, they must not give way to communalism or show ideological cowardice when pressure from communal surroundings mounts. To be genuinely secular one should be secular when one is under popular pressure. My respect for Gandhiji has gone up ever since I studied in some depth what he did in 1946 and 1947 in Noakhali, Bihar and Calcutta and other places. Here was a man who, at a moment of crisis was able to stand up. I think this is what .distinguishes a Jawaharlal Nehru from a Sardar Patel, that at a crucial moment Nehru was able to stand firm even though all round him there were pressures to which secular people were partially giving way. I think it is very necessary for intellectuals in India today, when there are riots and communal violence all over the country in one form or another, to show this firmness in commitment to secularism.

IV

My last point in this respect, before I come very briefly to the second theme of what is not the way out, is : what about communal violence? I have no problem in saying that when faced with communal violence-a communal riot, il knifing in the dark or communai terrorism where people are killed because they are riding in a bus pr they are killed, as in Karnal, when they are boarding il train, whether one person is killed or one hundred are killed—immediate and effective counter violence of tile state is needed. This must also be clearly stated because communal ideology has to be fought ideologically but when communal ideology manifests itself conjuncturally in violent situations—and violent situations feed communal ideology, make it grow in geometrical proportions—when society is racked with violence, then the state alone is capable of saving the situation. No other counter-violence is available, When a commuunal riot is taking place, say in Bhiwandi, the criticism against the state should be why it did not take preventive action one day earlier, and when communal riots broke out why did it not use the maximum of state force to crush communal violence in a manner that it would not have lasted one hour or one day instead of lasting six, seven or ten days. Therefore, the type of situation that Punjab is faced with in the last one and a half years, the criticism should not be why the state took recourse to violence in the end but what was it doing for so long. This is a very important point.

However, we may take note of some historical experiences. We have the example of fascism in Italy and Nazism in Germany and Austria, where once fascism took recourse to violence it was impossible to meet it without state action. Initially, violence was sought to be checked by organised defence by working classes of Italy, Germany and Austria. However, this counter-violence by the organised working class movement was not sufficient. Because the state gave way, fascism won. Communalism is today in its extreme form of fascism, and once communalism takes to violence, of which the most common form in India is the communal riot, then it is absolutely necessary that the state must act with complete integrity and with the total use of violence. Otherwise there is no point in having a state.

The second point I would like to make is that if it is true, as the European and the Japanese experience indicates, that fascism grows with the help of the state, then under no circumstance should the state be permitted to be in any way contaminated by or participated in by communal elements. This is very important. Therefore, I do not agree that the solution to the problem of Punjab or the problem of India, of Bombay, of Moradabad, lies in sharing state power with the communalists. It will be a sad day when that happens; it will only mean weakening the struggle of the state against communal violence in one way or another. In fact, in the last two years, communalism has increasingly penetrated the state apparatuses and this is one of the' major reasons why communal violence is breaking out in different. parts of the country.

What is not the way out of communalism? I believe that giving concessions to communalists is not the way out. Concessions do not lead to the recession of communalism; instead, they lead to its aggravation and escalation; they lead to the popularisation and spread of communal ideology; they make communalism more respectable. We again have a history of this. In 1916 the Congress-League Pact was signed on separate electorates and it was declared by no less great men than Tilak and Jinnah, who were the architects of this plan, that the communal problem was solved forever. In fact, it was the beginning of the communal problem in a serious form. Communal negotiations took place in the Ninteen-twenties and, Nineteen-thirties and by 1935 almost every single concession that the Muslim communalists wanted had been given. There was virtually not a single major demand raised by Muslim communalists which was not accepted in 1935.

Did this put an end to communalism? It did the opposite. The , Muslim League found that it had no demands left. Jinnah was repeatedly asked by the Congress leadership, Nehru and Subhas Bose, in 1937 and 1938 to tell them what his demands were. His answer was that he would do so only after they had accepted that the Congress was a Hindu body and that he represented Muslims and they Hindus. In other words, he asked the Congress to commit harakiri or political suicide as a secular body. Thank god, the Congreess did not do so. If it had accepted this demand in 1937, that it was a Hindu body, we would have been by now under Hindu fascist rule. Whatever the negative features of its rule might be now, it is not Hindu fascist rule. When pressures for making public the Muslim League demands got built up, and the League could not go on with vague communal politics for more than two or three years, then the last demand that Jinnah could make was for the partition of the country.

In fact it cannot be believed that a time will come when a communal politician will say that all his demands are satisfied and he will therefore dissolve his communal political organisation—no more Bhartiya Janata Party, no more Akali Dal, no more Muslim League—all his demands having been accepted. I do not think communalists will commit suicide in this fashion. Thus, the logic of communalism leads towards separatism. Precisely at the stage when the communalist has no more demands left and it appears that all the demands of communalism have been accepted, the communalist is pushed towards the most irrational demands, because that is the logic of communalism.

Something similar has happened in Punjab also. It was the simultaneous appeasement of Hindu and Sikh communal isms by the Punjab Congress since 1947 which has gradually pushed Punjab towards the brink, towards the Anandpur Resolution and the slogan of Khalistan. In fact, the history of Punjab is a very good example of the proposition that the policy of conciliation towards communalism does not pay. What has been the policy of the Congress in Punjab since 1948? It has been a policy of conciliating, co-opting, and incorporating communal forces into the Congress itself. The Akali, Assembly Party was twice dissolved in 1948 and in 1956. Simultaneously, the Congress got rid of the threat of Jan Sangh by appeasing Hindu communalism and by incorporating and permitting people like Lala Jagat Narain—I am sorry to speak ill of the dead, but I think that in the case of a political leader one can speak ill of the dead also—to enter or stay in the Congress. Thus communal persons were permitted to be brought in from outside into the Congress or they were permitted to develop from within the Congress in the name of conciliating, co-opting and incorporating communalism.

What were the consequences? Communalism did not weaken in Punjab. It grew. One group of communal leaders would get incorporated and a new group would emerge to take its place—as in a relay race where the baton is passed on by one runner to another. So after one group of communal leaders joined the Congress, another group of communal leaders would emerge, both among Hindus and Sikhs. In fact, one of the best ways of getting ministerial positions was to become a communal group and then ask to be conciliated by the Congress! What was the result? Communalism was not weakend but the Congress Party which was quite a secular party in 1947 became increasingly weak and its integrity as a secular party was increasingly weakend. In fact, the Congress increasingly became three parties in one, consisting of Sikh communalists, Hindu communalists and a handful of people like Darbara Singh, that is sturdy secularists. But the third category was getting smaller and smaller over time, and, above all, because of this communal intrusion, the Congress became incapable of opposing communalism.

Similarly, I would say that the way out does not lie in fatalism or panic either. One should not give up the ghost and say—as I am now hearing many people say in Delhi and Chandigarh—that everything is lost, that the divide between Hindus and Sikhs is too great to be bridged. I said earlier that it is going to be a long haul. The two communal groups have got very strong and they will have to be weakened inch by inch. It might take a decade; it might take more than that. But the hope lies in the fact there are the traditions of our national movement. There are extremely healthy secular forces in India as well as in Punjab, which have reacted in a very secular fashion to the present situation. Therefore, it is not as if one should give way to despair.

A few words about the question of the healing touch. What does the healing touch mean? If the healing touch means gradually, over a long period of time, to show to the mass of Sikhs and Hindus of Punjab that by the Operation Blue Star no hurt was meant to Sikh religion, that the events of June should not be intrepreted in a communal manner or as a threat of extinction to the Sikhs or as a symbol of the fact that the Hindu communalists have come out on top, then the healing touch is of course very necessary. But if the healing touch means to accept the communal charge that there was something communal about what happened in June, that the army's entry into the Golden Temple represented some form of anti-Sikh action, then I am afraid I would not like to call that a healing touch. I would rather call it a big concession to communalism. By giving concessions one cannot have the healing touch because if we provide this type of healing touch to Sikh communalism today, we will have to do so for Hindu communalism tommorrow.

The real danger of fascist rule in this country is not from Sikh communalism but Hindu communalism. Tomorrow the Hindu communalists will demand the healing touch for themselves and the matter would be over for our country. Healing touch should not, in other words, mean a policy of appeasement of communalism in any shape or form. Communalism has to be fought, however tough the fight might be or however prolonged. The healing touch has to be there but it has to be in the context of the struggle against communalism, and not in the context of appeasement. Otherwise the healing touch will itself become a way of strengthening communalism in Punjab, of strengthening both Hindu and Sikh communalisms. I would say that the best healing touch that can be given not only in Punjab, but also in Moradabad, Meerut, Bhiwandi, Jamshedpur, Bombay, Aligarh, Banglore and the fishing villages of Kerala, which are also being rocked by communalism today, is to convince the people by one's words and deeds, and by struggling for policies which will convince the people, that no follower of any religion is in danger, that if there is any danger to the religion of any people then the defence of that religion is not the responsibility of the followers of that religion but of the followers of all religions.

Lastly, therefore, I would like once again to point to another harsh truth, that all communalism has to be fought simultaneously. This has another corollary: that the theory that the Congress Party since Nehru's days and the left wing in India have been following, i.e., that minority communalism is somehow ideologically superior to Hindu communalism or that it is not as rotten, not as dangerous, as anti-humanitarian as the majority Hindu communalism, is not correct. It is true that in this country the main danger of fascism comes from Hindu communalism. It is not possible for Muslims to impose fascism in this country; it is nol possible for Christians or Sikhs to do so. If Sikh communalism becomes extremely virulent and encompasses Sikhs over a long period of time, the worst that can happen is the harm to the people of Punjab. including Sikhs. It is Hindu communalism which may become fascist and which can threaten the entire country and the entire people. Therefore, I do believe that the main struggle in the country as a whole has to be against Hindu communalism. But this does not mean that minority communalism is not equally dangerous or equally anti-humanitarian and is not to be opposed as strongly. This is so for the following reasons:

First, minority communalism is extremely dangerous because it increasingly hands over a religious minority to communal leaders. After all, communalism is the enemy not only of the nation, etc., it is above all the enemy of those sections of the people who believe in it. Who paid the price for Nazism? Not only the Jews; even more so the Germans. If we oppose Hindu communalism it is not only because it is a threat to Sikhs or Muslims, but, above all, because it is a threat to Hindus themselves. Sikh communalism should be opposed by Sikhs not noly because it is anti-national or anti-Hindu but above all because Sikh communalism will mean fascism so far as Sikhs themselves are concerned. In other words, communalism is above all the enemy of those who believe in it and whom it professes to represent.

Second, minority communalism, unless one struggles against it, makes the struggle against majority communalism very difficult. As just pointed out, undoubtedly our major struggle is against majority communalism. But it is impossible to fight successfully against it if one is soft towards minority communalism. In fact, the real danger of the Bhindranwale phenomenon was, and even today the real danger of communalism in Punjab is, not Khalistan. I have no fear of Khalistan coming into being in this country; nobody is going to accept a second partition. This is an objective fact.

So, if there is communalism in Punjab, if Bhindranwale had grown stronger, the real danger would not have been that Bhindranwale would have been successful in creating Khalistan—that would not be permitted by the rest of the country—he real danger would have been of a Hindu fascist regime which would appeal to. the strong sentiment of th Indian people for national unity and integrity and declare that only Hindu fascism could keep this country united and strong. A distinguished editor of a prominent daily has been saying and writing that India is after all a Hindu country, and if it becomes a fully Hindu country that would be an effective way of establishing the unity of the country. So, Hindu fascism can then claim that it is the final guardian of national unity. This is the real danger of any communalism or any communal ideology. Therefore, to avoid Hindu fascism it is very necessary to oppose minority communalisms.

Lastly, the experience of Punjab makes it clear that if we are soft towards minority communalism, we become passive in the fight against communalism as a whole. What has been happening in . Punjab, in fact all over India, in the last many years. is. that parties issue statements against communalism, Intellectuals once in a while speak a few words against communalism in seminars, but no urgency is shown in fighting against communalism on a large scale. This is true not only *vis a vis* minority communalism; we do not see any struggle going on against Hindu communalism either in the country.

Thus the way out lies in understanding communal ideology, in waging a prolonged struggle against it, and in waging an ideological struggle against all types of communalism, because all types of communalism are branches of the same ideology, that is the communal ideology.

6

Communalism and the State: Some Issues in India

I

Communalism is an ideology and to some extent politics organised around that ideology. This might look like a very simple statement of an obvious fact, yet it has some deeper implications. The word ideology is not used here in the sense in which Marx used it, but to mean .a belief system-a belief system based on certain assumptions regarding society, economy and polity.

Communalism is a way of looking at society and politics. If so, certain political and other consequences follow. The elements of communal ideology, which we see all around us, are the result of the existence and spread of communal ideology for the last over hundred years. Therefore, it is not possible to explain it only in terms of the social and political conditions of today; because of its persistence among the people it has become what Marx would call a material force on its own.

The premier task of the communalist is to spread the communal belief system or communal ideology. Other aspects of communalist activity are secondary and follow. One must not confuse communalism with communal violence, rioting, etc. No doubt communal violence acts as a means of spreading communal ideology hot-house fashion; also, communal ideology leads to communal violence. But under no circumstances should one equate the two. Communal violence is a consequence of the spread of communal ideology. But it is not the crux of the communal situation at all. Communal ideology can not only exist, but can grow for decades before it takes the form of violence.

For example, in India, though communal ideology was preached in a minor fashion, primarily through history writing, from the 1830s, and It started emerging as a more structured ideology in the 1870s and 1880s, except for very short spurts of violence in one place or another, say in 1893 in Poona and Calcutta, communal violence became a force in India only in the 1920s. But it was precisely because of the spread of communal ideology in the previous four decades that this happened.

Similarly, communal violence was virtually absent during World War II, from 1939 to 1945, and yet this was precisely the period when communalism was growing very fast in India, both among Muslims and Hindus as well as among Sikhs. A very good example of this proposition is Punjab. It was believed that the partition had solved the communal problem in Punjab, because before 1947 Hindu and Sikh communalists were on one side and were anti-Muslim, and Muslim communalists were on the other side and were anti-Hindu and anti-Sikh. So, it was assumed that with the partition and with the virtual disappearance of Muslims from Punjab, communalism would die out. When people talked about communalism in Punjab, they talked about the anti-Muslim sentiment, which was fed by migration from west Punjab to east Punjab and to Delhi, etc. But, in fact, Hindu and Sikh communalisms were growing very fast from 1947 onwards. Perceptive observers, primarily the communists, were constantly warning against the spread of communalism in Punjab in the 1950s. Jawaharlal Nehru was very conscious of it, although he did not do much about it. Therefore what happened in the 1980s was precisely the consequence of what had been happening since 1947.

The distinction between communal ideology and communal violence has to be made for they have different relations to the State. I shall come to this point later, but here I must point out that communal violence requires immediate political and administrative steps. Perhaps, it-also requires peace marches and peace committees and similar other steps. And I would agree that when communal, violence is taking place ideological struggle has very little meaning. When the house is burning, you do not tell people why the fire and how to prevent it and all that; you extinguish it. But communal ideology requires long-term political struggle.

As mentioned earlier, once commnunal ideology prevails for a long enough period, it becomes a material force and has, therefore, to be consciously combated. No automatic results follow in this field because of other indirect steps. It was believed in the 1930s that the growth of the anti-imperialist struggle would· get rid of communalism or that class struggles would do so. After 1947, many believed that with economic development or spread of education, etc., communal ideology would disappear. But the fact is that once communal ideology has emerged in a crystallised form, it is very necessary to wage a conscious anti-communal ideological struggle against it. It will not go on its own, whatever other steps might be taken.

The State comes in, in one respect, because it can promote either communal ideology or ideological struggle against it, or it can take a weak stand. *vis-a-vis* communal ideology.

Once we are clear on this question of communalism as ideology, we can take a step forward towards defining a communal party. This might seem to be a very simple point, but I remember arguing with many of my friends a few years back at a seminar here, organised by the *Social Scientist,* who were arguing that the Congress was a communal party and Indira Gandhi was a communal leader because she had got subterranean support in Delhi or Jammu. elections from the RSS. Surprisingly, when the RSS openly supports another secular party, the Janata Dal, in the elections, the same people do not brand the Janata Dal as a communal party.

In fact, it would be as wrong to brand the Janata Dal as a communal party as it was to brand the Congress as a communal party earlier or now. I think once we see that communalism is an ideology, our definition of what is a communal party gets better grounded. Communal parties and groups are those which are structured around communal ideology. Take away communal ideology or make them abandon communal ideology, and nothing is left of them; the group or the party disintegrates. It is this which was realised by the Muslim League leadership and Jinnah in 1937 when they were faced with the choice either to put further chips or major elements of communal ideology, religion, militancy, and extremism into their programme and propaganda or to face disintegration of the Muslim League and Muslim communalism. The same dilemma was faced by the Akali leadreship ill 1981, once they lost the elections in Punjab.

In this respect, we should not forget that it was the so-called moderate leadership which gave the slogan that genocide of the Sikhs was taking place in India and that the Sikh religion in Punjab was in danger. It was not Bhindranwale who gave this slogan in 1981 and 1982. We hear and read lot of talk about reforming the BJP, of asking the RSS to give up its. anti-Muslim stance. Some say that the BJP minus communalism would be all right. But, in fact, the BJP minus communalism would not only be all right, it would be a big zero; and the BJP leaders know this very well. Even the effort to disguise their communal ideology behind 'Gandhian socialism' and Din Dayal Upadhayayism was seen by the leaders to have resulted in the disaster of 1984 in electoral terms. In other words, the raison d'etre of a communal party is communalism. And here an additional point may be made. If a communal party uses communalism to capture power, but knowing that it cannot build society on that basis it wants to give up communalism, it will not be able to do so. The belief that it can do so is a chimera, because when the communal ideology prevails for a long enough time, and especially if it enables its leadership to come to power, it acquires a life of its own. If the leadership which has used communal ideology to capture power wants by some miracle to give it up, it cannot do so. We have a very good example of this in Mohammed Ali Jinnah who used the most vicious form of communal ideology from 1938 to 1947, but on 13th August, 1947, declared that Pakistan would be now a secular State, where politics would not be determined by religion, where citizens following different religions would be equal and religion would have no relevance to their status as citizens. But even Jinnah was not able to stem the tide of the ideology that he had unleashed. In Jinnah's personal case, of course, the miracle worked because he had lived most part of his life as a liberal intellectual, which is not the case with most of the present-day communalists, certainly not the ideologues of the RSS, the Sikh separatists, and the Muslim communalists.

Once we see communalism as an ideology, we also realise that no ideology is a single formation. The belief system, as I said, consists of assumptions and conclusions and arguments which follow from those assumptions. Even the assumptions are many. Therefore, the communal ideology consists of many communal elements. The point is that these communal elements-and this is true of any ideology once it has prevailed or penetrated a society for a long time, even when it has not hegemonised it—exist among a large number of us; I would even say among all of us.

Therefore, it would be wrong to think that a single communal element or a few communal elements are equal to communal ideology. What are described as religiosity and fundamentalism are not the same as communalism. Only when particular communal elements are articulated or integrated in a particular manner, do they give birth to a full-fledged communal ideology. One of the functions of communal parties is precisely to play upon these elements among secular persons and to exaggerate them in their personalities and thus to make them accept the other communal elements, which they are trying to popularise. And thejob of the secular ideology is precisely to oppose these pre-existing elements, but also to point out that even if one cannot get rid of those pre-existing elements at least one should not add on to them the elements the communalists are trying to propagate.

In recent years, many middle-class individuals who were secular are becoming open to the Hindu communal appeal. Take, for example, the view promoted since January-February 1978, that a Muslim calls himself a Muslim and he is respectable, a Sikh calls himself a Sikh and he is respectable, but when a Hindu calls himself a Hindu he is branded a communalist. This view plays upon a certain pre-existing notion and is beginning to be widely accepted.

It is necessary to distinguish between communalism and opportunism. This is closely related to the manner in which communalism is growing and beginning to influence the Indian state structure. Because there is a difference—once we see communalism as an ideology, there is a crucial, critical difference—between communal parties which are structured along communal ideologies, and secular, even weakly secular, parties taking an opportunistic stand towards communalism.

It is said that even Nehru used to put up Muslim candidates in Muslim majority areas and Brahmins in Brahmin 'dominated' areas and so on. Therefore, he was also a communalist or a casteist and so are all those who do this sort of . a thing. The fact of the matter is that this is really electoral opportunism; and though opportunism has to be opposed, it is to be opposed as opportunism and not as communalism. Moreover, this particular brand of opportunism is found in all political parties including the left parties. Have we not seen the Communist Party always putting up a Muslim candidate from Bhopal or from Amroha near Bareilly; and it would not easily put up a Muslim from an area where the Muslim population accounts for only three or four per cent of the population. In fact, opportunism is partially a response to the communalisation of society. Opportunism is a wrong way of opposing or facing the communal parties, and it has to be fought but it has to be fought in a different fashion.

Communalism in India is a form of fascism. We will not understand communalism, if we see this just as another inadequate or harmful ideology. The regionalist or linguistic ideologies even when they cross proper bounds are very different in character from communal ideology. It is not accidental that the Shiv Sena, which tried to develop a fascist ideology on the basis of anti-South Indianism, soon found that it was not able to grow beyond a certain point. It, therefore, gave up regionalism and adopted what is the Indian form of fascism-Hindu communal ideology. Communalism is irrational and its basis lies in hatred. Communalism in India today more and more takes a mass form; it glorifies violence. Consequently, we must understand communalism as the Indian form of fascism. This fascist form, in the case of the minorities, because of the way they are structured in Indian society, can only take the form of separatism. Sikh communalism in Punjab cannot take the form of conquest of India. It can only take a separatist form. On the other hand, Hindu communalism cannot take a separatist form; it inevitably takes a fascist form.

If communalism is an ideology, education, formal or informal or through the media, acquires a crucial importance. This aspect has not been given enough attention in this country till this day. After all, it took years and a great deal of effort to have some social science and science textbooks written along scientific lines. But even they have a more or less narrow circulation. They are used only in a few central and private schools.

If communalism is an ideology, another aspect follows which is also very crucially related to the question of State power. This aspect is that there can then be no compromise with communalism. The notion that you can somehow evolve some compromise with it is impractical. Jawaharlal Nehru tried such a compromise with communalism twice, in 1948 and 1956 when the Akali Legislature Party in Punjab was dissolved and merged with the Congress, but the communal ideology was not opposed. The result was that, as the late Darbara Singh was very fond of saying, the Congress Party in Punjab came to consist of one-third Hindu communalists, one-third Sikh communalists and one-third secular persons. He also said that these one-third secularists were getting reduced day by day.

Therefore, while certain political concessions might have te be given here and there, such concessions have not meant and do not mean dealing effectively with the communal problem. Even if concessions are given, they have to be seen as only a first step in the struggle against communalism. For example, if the Akalis were merged with the Congress, if the Jan Sanghis were permitted to join the Congress, if the Muslim Leaguers in 1947-48 were permitted to join the Congress and the nationalist Muslims virtually ignored, then these steps can be justified only if they are seen as the beginning of an anti-communal ideological campaign.

II

This brings me to the question of communalism and state power. The basic proposition is again very simple: do not let communal parties and groups come anywhere near state power. And by state power I do not mean only the Centre. I do not take the view that state power is concentrated in the so-called Centre or in the executive at the Centre only. State power has a diffused character. In the Indian Constitution, the states also have state power, and if the Panchayati Bill comes up and is accepted, then the panchayats would also have state power, though the weight of state power at different levels may be very different.

So, my basic proposition is that we must not let communal parties and groups come anywhere near state power, and this is not only because through state power, as for instance in Madhya Pradesh, they control the police and the bureaucracy. It has been said that the PAC which behaved with such brutality in Meerut and Moradabad was recruited in 1977 by the U.P Government in which the BJP was an important element. But my argument is much wider. If the problem was only this, perhaps some sort of mechanical steps could be taken to contain the harmful results; but state power today means, above all, control of education, it means control of media, it means control of ideological state apparatuses in general.

Communalists in control of state power, in fact, may not encourage violence for some time. They may not promote violence and on the surface it might then appear that where the communalists rule there is much less communal rioting and communal violence; that communal violence takes place only in Congress-ruled or Janata Dal-ruled states, and that, therefore, the Congress is communal and not the BJP. This can happen because violence is not the heart of communalism. The communalists may reduce the level of communal violence and take steps against it, even while spreading communal ideology through various instruments. They may not attack trade unions; they may not attack kisan sabhas; they may not even attack the Communist parties. But they will certainly attack the secular intellectuals.

One reason why the communalists are likely to concentrate on the spread of communal ideology and not take recourse to pogroms and concentration camps is because communalism is not yet the dominant mode of thought of the Indian people. Even where the communalists have come to power, even where during the last forty years the communal parties have won elections, they know that even the people who have voted for them have not yet imbibed communal ideology on a significant scale. The Indian people are still basically secular.

The State can be used to take advantage of the communal elements among us all. For example, even secular persons may, and this is already happening, start muting their secularism. They may no longer be so assertive; they may no longer be so strongly anti-communal. In other words, the communalists may try to change our mode of thought and expression just as they are succeeding among the middle-classes and even among the working classes in Bombay, in Jamshedpur and other places. In this respect, I must make one point. I recently read the memoirs of a German anti-fascist. He was asked the question as to what horrified him most, what made him most miserable in the 1930s in Germany—was it the pogroms or the attack upon Jews or the killing of the communists and socialists or the concentration camps? He said: "The worst thing that happened to me was when my son came back from school spouting fascist ideology and I could not even correct him because I knew that if I corrected him, he would go back to the teacher and tell him that my father said that what was being taught him was wrong and then you can imagine what would have happened to me and my family."

In other words, it is the ideological aspect that the State under communal influence or control is likely to promote and this is a major reason why they must not be permitted anywhere near state power.

In India, there is another reason why communalists should not be permitted to get a share in state power. Faced with loose bourgeois political formations, which are increasingly corrupted and de-ideologised, the communalists in India have the cadre to make use of the state apparatuses for spreading communal ideology. To give an example: when the bourgeois political parties get corrupted and make appointments to university faculties, they appoint their nephews and nieces, friends' children-and even in the most corrupted and right-wing regimes, if the right type of connections are there, even communists get appointed. But when the communal parties take charge of the State they appear to be very honest because they may not probably indulge in this type of corruption. Instead they appoint and promote politically committed, communalized academics. Thus they use their state power in various ideological ways-ways in which the de-ideologised, de-caderised, weakly secular parties cannot act; I would say ways in which even communists do not act because they also have lost the ideological edge in their thinking and working, they also downplay the role of ideology.

Once the society has strongly imbibed certain ideological elements, certain things follow. This is another important reason why it is necessary to see the difference between the weak secularism of the Congress or the Janata Party or the Janata Dal and the commualism of the structured communal parties, because I believe that while weak secular parties may not have taken proper action against communal rioting, may not discipline communal officials, may not be very conscious of certain communal ideological elements within their own ranks, they do not spread communal ideology.

For example, in India, Doordarshan and the Radio have not been used to spread communal ideology. Those who give the example of the *Mahabharata or Ramayana* do not know what the spread of communal ideology could be like if this is done through the media in a conscious, planned manner.

In other words, one should critique the weakly secular parties and groups for not fighting against communal ideology, for even letting certain elements of communalism penetrate society, but I think it is very necessary to see the difference between them and communal parties and groups. This is crucial, especially when communal parties are likely to come to power in certain states and, perhaps, even in the Centre.

If this is the relationship between communalism and the State and if it is an objective fact that communal parties and groups are acquiring positions of power in the states, then what is to be done? Here I may point out that it is not true that, working under a democratic Constitution, it is very difficult to prevent them from coming to power. Of course, we can take certain political steps, which we have not taken. We could have made the defeat of the communalists the first priority, which we did not do. Thus, indirectly, we may have enabled them to acquire positions of state power. But even if we were to avoid these mistakes, these historically wrong actions, even then in an electoral democracy, constitutional democracy, it may be very difficult to bar the communalists from getting into power if the people vote for them. Therefore, it is all the more important that both when they are out of power and when they are in power, we take recourse to that which is the best and the only way of fighting communalism in a democracy, that is, struggle at the ideological level.

In other words, basically it is ideological struggle which is on the agenda, not only where the communalists are out of power and therefore to keep them out of power, but even where they are in power since we cannot constitutionally dislodge them.

This brings me to the question, what is the ideological struggle? I think. the first major aspect of ideological struggle is to make people aware of the assumptions behind the communal belief system. That is, to enable them to see through patient academic and popular analysis that communal assumptions and consequently communal analysis and answers are not true.

Some people are very afraid of the word truth. I am not. I think that there is no way in which you can ideologically fight against communalism unless one goes to the people and points out that the assumptions of the communalists, the questions they raise, the answers they give, do not conform to the reality of social life. In other words, they are not true. Since I am not a philosopher, I feel very hesitant in making such a statement, So, I have fortified myself privately with lot of quotations from Marx, where he uses the word 'Not True'. I may be wrong, but I do not think I am committing some sort of a 'bourgeois error' in talking of truth. For example, one must ask the people, is it true that Hindu religion or religions or Hindu interests are under threat or that Muslim interests are being promoted in India-the entire communal propaganda for the last one-and-a-half years has been that Muslim interests are being promoted and Hindu interests are being downgraded.

There is a letter written by Jawaharlal Nehru which is profound in many ways and goes something like this: I agree that there is Muslim communalism in India and I would also probably agree that Muslim communalism is much worse and stronger than Hindu communalism. But Muslim communalism cannot dominate Indian society and introduce fascism. That only Hinndu communalism can. Therefore, we have got to be very chary and very aware and to struggle against Hindu communalism above all.

Once we take this type of position of attacking and exposing all types of communalisms simultaneously, it is not difficult to go to the people and point out to them that communal assumptions and therefore communal answers are wrong.

It is necessary to show to the people as to who benefits from communalism. The role of the petty bourgeoisie has to be examined and thought out in this respect. This is one class which does benefit from communalism and casteism and which is growing by leaps and bounds in India. Every strata of Indian society, every class of Indian society is contributing to the growth of the petty bourgeoisie. Even the agricultural labourers' children are, through education, acquiring petty bourgeois social positions or at least aspiring to acquire petty bourgeios social positions.

The linkages of communalism with the social structure and the pattern of India's socio-economic development also need emphasis. What is it in the Indian social condition which makes people adopt or accept communal positions? Having found an answer one must then go to the people and explain to them that it is their social condition which is making many of them adopt communal positions, but that this social condition cannot be rectified by communal answers because communalism has a false analysis of the social condition. Therefore, the remedies that they are giving are also wrong. 'The communalist either deceives others or he deceives himself?'

Therefore, if we want to fight communalism, especially when it is now reaching the gates of state power—and we will fight it even if it occupies those positions—then ideological struggle in India must become a mass movement, and the intellectuals must fit into this mass movement. Their work must be geared towards this, which first of all means writing in a language which an average educated person or at least other intellectuals can understand. But in fact what is happening is that while we are reaching at best thousands, the communalists are reaching millions and crores. In other words we also have to build up a mass movement of the order of the *shilapujan.*

We have had several centenaries, those of Acharya Narendra Dev, Acharya Kripalani, Maulana Azad and, above all, of Jawaharlal Nehru, but not a single idea of theirs on any aspect was taken to the people. The RSS had Hedgewar centenary. They had at least one meeting in every taluk headquarters, every district headquarters, every state headquarters and then in Delhi, which was deliberately muted so that intellectuals may not get frightened of the RSS strength. In the district headquarters and state headquarters the communal ideology was taken to millions of people. Then they had the *shilanyas* and *shilapujan* with which they went to almost every *mohalla* and village. What did the secular groups and parties do? We took out marches in a few cities. But did we go to the people, did we go to the *mohallas?* At present, particularly, when the communalists are getting close to state power, when they have already occupied certain seats of power in the states and are sharing it in other states, when they are getting influential even. in the Centre, it is very necessary that ideological struggle is made a mass movement. Unless this is done, we would have lost the battle even before it started.

7

Communalism and Communal Violence in Modern India

The emphasis in this paper will be on ideology and violence based on religious identity. Thus we will be dealing with communalism and communal violence which pit Hindus against Muslims or Sikhs or Jains, Muslims against Sikhs, Christians against Hindus or Muslims and soon.

I

Communal violence in the form of riots, or pogroms, or terrorism draws our attention in a dramatic manner but the underlying and long-term cause of this violence is the spread of communalism. Communalism, in our view, is to be basically studied as well as opposed as an ideology, especially where long-term action against it is desired. Study of communalism as ideology is the crucial area for the containment of communalism as well as communal violence. Communal violence in its different forms, based on extreme communalism and feelings of fear and hatred, is ultimately the ugly and barbaric expression of and the logical extension of the prior spread of communalism as an ideology. While communal riots, for example, give credibility to the basic communal ideological precepts among the ordinary people and enlist further support for communal politicians, it is communal ideology and politics, which the communal politicians and ideologues preach in normal times, which form the real basis on which communal tension and violence occur. In other words, communal ideology and politics are the disease, communal violence only its external symptom.

Political power as well as social and religious issues are involved in communal violence, but communalism is precisely the development of politics without basing them on any social issues.

It may be suggested that relationship of communalism to communal violence is very similar to the relationship of racialism to racial riots, Nazism to Nazi violence, and anti-Semitism to anti-Jewish pogroms.

II

Communalism is to be seen as a modern ideology and not a carry over, a survival, of the pre-colonial past, as something. that had its roots in the medieval period. Communal politics and communal violence were more or less absent in pre-colonial India. Religion was, of course, then an important part of people's lives. People also quarrelled over religion. There was also religious suppression. But politics of the ruling classes were not organized around communal lines of Hindu vs Muslim. Communalism was, as was the case with nationalism, a product of the transformation of India under the impact of colonialism. It was generated as a new way of looking at modern politics—politics of mass participation based on the doctrine of popular sovereignty. It was an effort to use pre-modern identity of religion to organize wide strata of people to participate in the new politics.

Communalism was also not, and is not, a half-way house to nationalism. It arose and continues to function as an alternative to nationalism. Communalism was not nationalism based on religion, as was the case in Indonesia and many of the West Asian and Northern African countries. In India communalism developed in opposition to nationalism and was devoid of anti-imperialist content.

Communalism was also not a reflection of popular consciousness. Throughout the medieval period the common people shared and till this day share large elements of common social life and culture, especially in the villages. Even at the level of popular religions, there were many common beliefs and practices, for popular religions were highly eclectic. This has become evident in recent years with the rise of rabid Hindu and Sikh communalisms in Punjab. Certainly, there was no popular consciousness of mutual antagonism among Hindus and Sikhs vis-a-vis each other. Hindus and Sikhs interdine and intermarry. Hindus and Sikhs worship and revere each other's religious books, scriptures, and gurus and gods.

In fact, popular consciousness has posed a major barrier to the spread of communalism and is responsible for the inability of communal hatred and communal violence to spread to the rural areas and also to large parts of urban India. This also explains why communalism, making a beginning in the last quarter of the 19th century, has still failed to take deep roots in large parts of the country and has taken such a long time to acquire even its present strength.

III

To reiterate: communal riots and other forms of communal violence are only a concrete conjunctural manifestation of the communalization of society and politics. Communal ideology leads to politics and psychological differentiation, distance and competition along religious lines. Sooner or later it leads to mutual fear and hatred and ultimately to violence. Once communalism segments politics along religious lines, violent conflict becomes a matter of time. Behind every riot lies a strong collective communal mentality.

A major advantage of seeing communalism as an ideology emerges in this respect. We then see the 'moderates' and 'extremists' among the communalists, soft practitioners and preachers of communalism and the organizers of hate-campaigns and violence as part of the same species. (We are also enabled to distinguish between different categories of extremism and violence. Without a basic focus on ideology, communal and fascist violence tends to be treated on par with social and economic radicalism and violence based on such radicalism).

Communalization can go on growing for years before it results in violence-and these are the years when real preventive steps against communal violence need to be taken. Recent Indian history is replete with examples. Communal ideology was burgeoning fourth during 1938-1946, but large scale violence occurred only during 1946-47. There was no communal violence in Punjab during 1948-81; but that is when the basis for the violence of the years since 1982 was being laid. South India is being rapidly communalized, though as yet instances of communal violence are rare.

Perhaps, the most recent examples of the horrendous consequences of the spread of communal ideas have been the communal killings of Sikhs in Delhi and other parts of Northern India during early November 1984 and the brutal killings of Hindus in Punjab since 1982. We may point out, parenthetically, that we differ in a basic manner from some other analysts of the November killings. We believe that the Hindus of Northern India and Delhi were being intensively communalized by the killings in Punjab since 1982; and the secular forces did virtually nothing to counter this process. Instead many justified directly or indirectly Sikh communalism in Punjab though not the communal killings there-by emphasising the need for recognition of Sikh identity, 'Sikh' desire for sharing power, negotiations with 'Sikh' leaders, and so on and by blaming the entire Punjab problem on Indira Gandhi. Consequently, the assassination of Indira Gandhi was seen as the work of two Sikhs and not of two communalists or communal terrorists. It was this heightened communal outlook which found reflection in the November attacks on Sikhs and their property and in the end in the killing of hundreds. The very fact that the process occurred all over Northern India and within a day or two of Indira Gandhi's assassination confirms us in our analysis. On the other hand, some others have seen a deep-seated and well-organized conspiracy by the ruling Congress Party to annihilate the Sikhs to achieve electoral gains by arousing Hindu sentiment.

They specifically deny that the November 'riots' were the result of the spread of communal sentiments among Hindus of Northern India and a communal response to the killing of a Prime Minister,[1] who was immensely popular among the urban poor and was seen by them as their guardian and protector.

Here, we may also point out that though communal violence leads to loss of life and property, this is not its main consequence. Nor are physical annihilation and suppression the cheif objectives of its organizers. The main consequence as also objective of communal violence are the hot-house creation and spread of communal ideology. Communal violence threatens all the residents of the area covered by it and inevitably induces them to think in terms of self-defence along communal lines. Even secular persons are forced to think in terms of self-defence along communal lines and to depend upon communal forces to defend their lines and property. If a frenzied mob is going to attack a person's home or place of work because he or she belongs to a particular religion, then that person is forced to support or join communal groups which set out to organize defence against such an attack.

---

[1] *Who are the Guilty?* Report by PUDR and PUCL. Delhi, 1984; and *Truth About Delhi Violence,* by Amiya Rao, A. Ghose and N. D. Pancholi, Delhi, 1984. The latter work explicitly states that "One and all have given us to understand that it was sponsored by the Congress-I members and there was nothing communal about it". (P.ix).

Since causes of communal violence are conjunctural and can often be tackled through immediate administrative or community action, they have to be studied on a very sound micro empirical basis. In India, they have been studied by several official commissions, which have investigated specific communal riots, and by voluntary groups. More recently, the Centre for Research in Rural and Industrial Development, Chandigarh, has carried out several intensive and extensive studies of communal violence in different states of India. (We hope that these studies, carried out on behalf of the Home Ministry, will be published in good time). I do not, however, intend to undertake the task of discussing the conjunctural causes of communal violence here, except to point out that these are often local and specific except in terms of the communalization of the area. This latter aspect I intend to take up because it has long-term and deeper roots. It is communalism that transforms conjunctural causes into viable causes of violence. A great number of riots have occurred over some minor religious issues such as the cutting of a *peeple* tree, playing of music before a mosque, throwing of coloured water on a Muslim during the Holi festival, killing of a cow or desecration of a place of worship, abuse of a religious figure, route of a religious procession, and so on. But such problems can exist for years without leading to communal violence. People either take them in their stride or resolve them through mutual goodwill. It is only when an area has been deeply communalized that they provide the occasions for communal violence. The chief remedy against communal violence, our major concern in this paper, also therefore lies in studying communalism as such and opposing its growth and spread.

Communalism and communal violence are the products of the overall social, economic and political situation of a society. The situation creates problems for the people which they are unable to understand or solve. The people make efforts to come to grips with the resulting personal and social crises but without grasping their real roots or causation. This often leads them to seeing the other 'community' as the cause of their woes. Communalism thus reflects the objective reality but in a distorted way. It neither represents a correct diagnosis of the social situation nor its correct solution. Neither the questions raised nor the answers given are correct. At the same time there is a particular social reality which is generating communalism and which has to be set right if it is to be opposed successfully.

In the colonial period, colonial underdevelopment of India led to a situation of a prolonged social crisis for the people. In the post-colonial period the eapitalist pattern of development has aggravated communalism and communal-type politics and ideologies in two ways. On the one hand, capitalist development has not occurred at a rate where it could solve the basic problems of poverty and unemployment and thus prevent frustration and unhealthy competition for scarce jobs and other economic opportunities. On the, other hand, capitalist development has generated prosperity for certain social strata leading to sharp and visible inequality and new social strains and social anxieties. Those who gain have their expectations rise even higher; they also feel constantly threatened in their newly-gained prosperity. Their relative prosperity arouses the social jealousy of those who fail to develop or who decline in power and prestige. The limited efforts of the Government to uplift the rural poor and the socially deprived through special programmes, such as food for work, loans on concessional rates, the IRDP and reservations in government services, arouse intense resentment among those who feel that any rise in social scale of the poor threatens their social domination. The soil for the growth of communalism and casteism is thus continually prepared.

In this respect, the colonial and post-colonial social conditions affected the middle classes or the petty bourgeoisie with particular force. The petty bourgeoisie has been faced with the constant threat of unemployment and deterioration in its socio-economic condition. Moreover, its growth has constantly outpaced economic development. After independence, the spread of education and the pattern of social change has led millions of peasant and working class youth to look for jobs in the cities and in administration and to join the ranks of the petty bourgeoisie. Communalism (and casteism), moreover, seems to conform to the reality, however superficially. The petty bourgeoisie comprises a group of social strata who can through reservation of jobs, etc., benefit to a certain extent through the practice of communalism. Moreover, the rapid breakdown of traditional social institutions such as the caste system and the joint family threatens the social status, class position and value systems of the petty bourgeoisie with particular force and intensity. Consequently, as I have pointed out in a detailed study of communalism, during the colonial period, "In one of its main aspects, communalism was an expression of and deeply rooted in the interests, aspirations, outlook and attitudes and psychology and point of view of the middle classes in a social situation characterized by economic stagnation and the absence of a vigorous struggle to transform society—the communal question was a petty bourgeois question *par excellence*.... While communalism was able to draw supporters from all classes of people, its main social base was to be found in the middle classes or the petty bourgeoisie."[2] This generalization continues to be valid for the post-1947 period too. This also explains why communalism remained relatively dormant till early 1960s. In the immediate years after independence, tremendous opportunities were opened up for the petty bourgeoisie as a result of Indianization of the army and private firms, immense expansion of administrative apparatuses, the first three 5-year Plans, the rapid development of banking, trading and industrial companies and the vast expansion of education and other social services, and sectors like engineering, medicine, and scientific research. But this initial push was exhausted by middle-1960s and the petty bourgeoisie was back in a situation of job scarcity and competition, though at higher levels of employment.

Communalism, especially in its violent form, makes a ready appeal to the urban poor and urban lumpen elements whose number has grown rapidly as a result of lop-sided economic development and large scale migration into cities. Rootless and impoverished, millions today live on the margins of society in urban conglomerates. Their social anger and frustration often find expression in spontaneous violence and loot and plunder whenever opportunity arises. A communal riot provides an opportunity for both.

Apart from the petty bourgeoisie, it is not easy to assign class roots to communalism today. The social class character and base of communalism have undergone a major change since 1947. During the colonial period the landlords and bureaucratic elements (what K.M. Ashraf describes as the jagirdari elements), and moneylenders and merchants, apart from the petty bourgeoisie, provided the main internal social base and the colonial state the external base for communalism. The colonial state (and colonialism) as a support base of communalism has disappeared; nor do the jagirdari elements serve this purpose on a significant scale any more. In our view, the Indian bourgeoisie did not, as a whole, support communalism before 1947; nor does it do so now, even though sections of the small bourgeoisie may support communal parties and groups out of ideological considerations. In some areas, struggle among the capitalist strata and groups is also beginning to take on a communal form. But this is not

[2]Bipan Chandra, *Communalism in Modern India,* New Delhi, 1984, pp. 40-41.

yet a major phenomenon. In fact, one reason for the failure of communalism to become a major political force in independent India as a whole has been its inability to attract support of any major social class or class fraction apart from sections of the petty bourgeoisie. An emerging factor in this respect is the growing class tension between the rural proletariat and the rich peasants-capitalist farmers in many parts of the country. The rural rich, in order to solidify the support of the middle and poor peasants around their class interests and to maintain their hegemony over them, increasingly promote communalism and casteism. This, we believe, provides a basic explanation of the growth of militant communalism in Punjab and casteism in Gujarat, Bihar, *V.P.* and many other parts of the country.

Class analysis of communalism, is however, fraught with pitfalls, and extreme caution has to be exercised. No simplistic models will do. A major empirical and theoretical effort is needed. At present, all remarks in this regard should be considered highly tentative and taken with a pinch of salt. A positive feature of the Indian situation in this respect is that the Indian intelligentsia continues to be on the whole and basically non-communal.

I do not believe that religion as such is responsible for communalism. Communalism is neither inspired by religion nor is religion an object of communal politics, even though the communalist bases his politics on religious differences, uses religious identity as an organizing principle and in the mass phase of communalism uses religion to mobilize the masses. As I have explained elsewhere, "the religious difference was used to 'mask' non-religious social needs, aspirations and conflicts .... religion served politics arising in spheres other than religion and as a garb or rationalization".[3] However, religiosity, that is, 'too much religion in one's life' or the intrusion of religion into areas other than those of personal belief, tends to create a certain receptivity to communal ideology and politics. Moreover; religious obscurantism, narrow-mindedness and bigotry in the name of going back to fundamentals tends to divide people whom life and history have brought together. In this respect different religions have different elements in their structure, rituals, and ideological practices which relate to communalism in different manners. Their analysis and elimination has to be specific to different religions.

---

[3] *Ibid.,* p. 160. I have dealt with this aspect at length in this work. See chapter 6.

Increasingly, with the widening reach of the media, religious conversion is beginning to playa provocative role. I believe that in a multi-religious society conversion should be increasingly eliminated except on highly personal and ideological basis. But it has to go as a social phenomenon.

As pointed out earlier, a crucial difference in the communal situation has been a basic change in the role of the state. The colonial state encouraged communalism by its acts of omission and commission and gradually came to serve as its major prop.[4] The state of independent India is, on the other hand, secular. Secularism is enshrined as a basic element in the Indian Constitution. Despite many weaknesses, the practice of the Indian state has also been on the whole secular. Moreover, all but one of the major all-India political parties —the exception being the Jan Sangh or its incarnation the Bhartiya Janata Party—have accepted secularism as a part of their political ideology. The existence of strong left-wing parties which are not tinged with communalism is also a very positive factor. There have, however, been two major negative features. One is the penetration of state apparatuses, especially the police, by communal outlook and ideology. The other is the tendency of secular political parties to make opportunistic compromises with communalism and their failure to wage active and persistent political and ideological struggle against it.

V

Policy measures to meet the challenge of communalism and communal violence can be subdivided into two categories: long-term and short-term or immediate. The long-term remedy lies essentially in initiating the process of de-communalising the people at all levels. This means waging a continuous and intense ideological-political struggle against comunalism: to bring out the different elements which constitute communalism, to explain to the people its socio-economic and political roots, to bring home to them that communal assumptions are false. that what the communalists project as the problems are not the real problems and what they say are the answers are not the real answers. This is the basic task, the patient task, the long-term task that has to be undertaken.

[4]See *Ibid*. chapter 8.

In this respect, a distinction has to be drawn between communalization of the state and of civil society. Unfortunately, the Indian intelligentsia tends to concentrate on the former. Certainly, communalization of the state is dangerous for it leads to inaction against communal violence and covert or overt political and ideological support to communalism by the state apparatuses including the media under state control. But it is the communalization of civil society which leads to communal riots and other forms of communal violence. Moreover, if society is communalized it will invariably affect the state, especially where the system of popularly elected governments prevails. The state, even if secular and run by an essentially secular party, will then tend to yield to communal pressures arising from civil society. It is in the realm of civil society that ideological struggle becomes important and, of course, it is here that intellectuals, political parties and voluntary bodies can be most effective.

The role of education and the media inevitably becomes important. Both in the colonial and the post-colonial periods, communal press and communal teachers have played an important role in the spread of communalism. Paradoxically, role of literacy has been quite negative in this respect. Illiteracy, combined with traditional culture, protected the mass of Indian people from philosophies and ideologies of hate. Literacy has opened them to the influence of communalism and casteism and obscurantist and irrational ideas purveyed through newspapers, pamphlets and posters, even children's books. Particularly harmful in the Indian context has been the role of the teaching of history. Communal interpretation of Indian history, particularly of the ancient and medieval periods, forms the bedrock of communal ideology in India. Teaching of history along scientific lines both in schools and colleges and at the popular level has to be a basic element in any ideological struggle against communalism.

It is also necessary to prevent intrusion of religion into secular fields. Increasing privatization of religion and its complete separation from the state have to be promoted.

An economistic and economic reductionist approach both among the ruling elite and the left-wing parties and groups has been in the past responsible for the underplaying of ideological struggle against communalism. The assumption has been that growth of capitalism, economic development and industrialization, spread of science and technology, and the growth of modem classes, especially the working class, would automatically weaken and ultimately eliminate communalism by promoting more modern identities and group formation. The left-wing parties, groups and individuals also believed that popular and class struggles were the best antidotes to communal poison. But, in reality, in the absence of struggle in the realm of ideology and culture, modern economic development generates rather than contains communalism and it is not class struggles which eliminate communalism but communalism which hampers class struggles and even hampers the process of the constitution of all-India classes. Communal violence is precisely most prevalent in Jamshedpur, Ahmedabad, Baroda, Bombay, Bhiwandi, Hyderabad Kanpur and Delhi.

VI

While fighting communalism ideologically and politically is a long-term task and the only effective way of eliminating communal violence, communal violence has to be prevented from breaking out and curbed and stopped once it breaks out. This is an immediate task. This can be done in three ways: Hie Gandhian and liberal methods of creating goodwill and non-violent resistance; self-defence by the aggressed group; and use of the counter-violence of the state.

The traditional secular nationalist approach to a communal riot has been to set up peace committees and organize peace marches through which leaders and individuals belonging to different religious communities work together to spread goodwill and fellow-feeling and to remove feelings of fear and hatred in the riot-affected area. This approach has certain effectivity in diffusing communal tensions; but it has invariably failed to prevent riots from breaking out or continuing. In any case, often physical and psychological damage has already been done before the peace committees, etc., become effective.

During the 1930s, Gandhiji advocated that the affected population should offer non-violent resistance to the aggressors arid asked Congress workers to jump into the fray and oppose rioters of both sides by non-violent methods. The Congress was unable to put non-violent resistance into operation and Gandhiji reccognized its inefficacy by advising the Congress Governments during 1937-39 to use police to suppress communal violence.

For a short while Gandhiji also advocated self-defence by those who were attacked by the communal mobs. In any case, all those affected by communal violence inevitably practise this remedy. But this invariably exasperates communal feelings and aggravates communal tension. If practised on a large scale the consequences would be the creation of Beirut and Belfast.

Immediate and effective state action is, we believe, the only viable way of dealing with communal violence. The state should have no qualms in this respect. India's experience in recent years confirms this generalization. Whenever strong and secular administrators use or threaten the use of strong steps, riots either do not occur or are of short duration. The Communist Party (Marxist) Government in West Bengal has several times scotched communal riots in the state. Strong police and army intervention in Calcutta in early November 1984 prevented a repetition of Delhi events. In fact, chances of communal violence breaking out would be drastically minimised if it was realized by all concerned that the Government was both strong and impartial and would put down communal violence with all the force at its command. The spread of this realization should also be seen as a part of ideological-political struggle.

Effective state intervention against actual or potential communal violence requires the ideological purity of state apparatuses. In particular the people and intelligence machinery and the higher bureacracy have to be rid of communal elements. Communalization of law enforcement agencies is, in fact, becoming a major problem in India today. Experience of riots in Moradabed, Bhiwandi, Gujarat, Bombay, etc., shows that a communalized police force invariably makes the communal. situation worse. Similarly, a major reason for th failure of the Government to curb violence in Punjab was the communalization of the police and the Central Reserve Police; for years the Punjabis looked upon the state police as soft towards Sikh communalism and the CRP as soft towards Hindu communalism, One result is that in Punjab as elsewhere the threatened minorities invariably clamour for intervention by the armed forces which are still believed to be untouched by communalism.

A major weakness of the colonial state as well as the Indian state has been the failure to take strong action against the instigators - and organizers of communal violence. While those who participate in communal riots, etc., as foot-soldiers do many a times face the might of the state, the generals—the ideologues and instigators—inevitably remain outside the fray and escape unscathed. But it is precisely these latter who are the really guilty and deserve the severest punishment.

The role of the media is immensely heightened during the course of communal violence. They can pour oil over troubled waters or stoke the raging fire. Communal violence generates an atmosphere in which rumours flourish and increase -fear and hatred many fold. The Press, radio and T.V. can report the situation and events of violence so as to soothe the frayed nerves of the people or inflame the tempers further. They can promptly contradict the rumours and report the actual events in a sobre and impartial manner or they can take a partisan approach and indirectly, if not directly, put the blame on one side and egg on the other to greater activity in the name of retaliation. The positive role that the media can play was brought out on Ist November 1984 in Delhi when a wild rumour spread that some Sikhs had poisoned Delhi water supply. The rumour was immediately contradicted by the radio and T.V. and next day by the newspapers and thus the further worsening of the situation in large parts of the city was avoided. Often the media do not deny rumours on the assumption that the denial would give greater currency to the rumour. There is a point here. This is particularly true in regard to the figures of persons of different religious communities killed. A careful balance has to be exercised. If the rumour is widespread, its denial would have a salutary effect. Three examples may suffice. Prompt denial of a widespread rumour during early November 1984 that trains coming from Punjab were full of dead Hindus would definitely have had a positive impact. Similarly, the reporting from Punjab giving the religious affiliation of those killed by the terrorists has had a positive result in so far as it has shown to the people that the terrorists were also killing a large number of Sikhs with whom they disagreed. During Hindu-Muslim riots since late 1950s, it is Muslisms who get killed in large numbers. Yet the Hindu communalists talk of aggressive approach of Muslims. The media, while giving the number of people killed or injured, invariably refuses to give the religious affiliation of the victims. If this is done, people would come to know that the vast majority of the victims are Muslims. This would have a dampening effect' 0" Hindu communal propaganda.

Ever since communal violence started occurring on a large scale, an important question posed has been as to how far should a detailed description of communal violence be given through the media or the platform. One view has been that gory details of what was done to the victims should be publicly given in the interest of truth and honest reportage. Usually this point of view was adopted by extreme communal leaders who wanted the freedom to narrate what happened to their 'community' members in order to further arouse communal passions. More recently, after the Delhi killings of November 1984, several scholars, including sociologists, have suggested that such description would have a cathartic effect on the victims.

We do not agree. Such description, apart from a statement of the fact of violence, would only inflame communal passions. Obviously, those who belong to the religion of the victims would be aroused to anger and retaliation. But even those who belong to the religion of the perpetrators of violence do 'not feel ashamed, but are angry that their 'community' is being defamed. We have enough historical experience to back up our views. In 1921, the British-owned newspapers like *Times of India* published details of what Mappilas had done to Hindu women and how Hindus had been forcibly converted. The Government also permitted the screening of films of the Mappila atrocities on Hindus. The result was immense growth of Hindu communalism. Otherwise also, the British-owned and communal newspapers were given free reign to publish details of 'communal' violence including rape, abduction, gory killings, maiming, etc. The nationalists, on the other hand, stoutly condemned this licence given to the communalists and the nationalists Press refrained from discussing details of communal violence even while highlighting and condemning the violence itself. One of the most admirable features of the Indian media was their refusal to give details of the atrocities committed on Hindus migrating from Pakistan in 1947. One wonders what would have been the fate of Indian society and of Muslims in India if these details had been given wide publicity in the name of assuaging the feelings of the victims. We may point out that just as the family of a dead person feels a certain relief by dilating on the disease and pain suffered by the dear departed, the victims of communal violence may also feel a certain psychological relief if the details of their experience are made a "part of public discourse". But it would have a disastrous impact on the rest of society.

In the case of violence in Punjab also, we feel that if the full horror of those who had been massacred in all sorts of ways and in many cases with all sorts of ingenuity in torture had been recounted in the media through pamphlets, and on the platform, the whole of India would have witnessed many a November 1984 by now. In fact, it should be noted that the so-called civil rights groups which have documented the details of Delhi carnage have been quite selective in their work, and that even those who have insisted on recounting the horrors of Delhi carnage in order to enable their victims to reclaim 'the reality of their suffering' have rightly, though illogically, refrained from doing so in case of the victims of the terrorist violence in Punjab. Perhaps, unconsciously, they have realized that it is one thing to play around with Sikh communalism in Punjab and quite another to do so in case of Hindu communalism in whole of India.

We would like to make three other points in this respect. Firstly, studies of the experience of Northern Ireland, Lebanon and Sri Lanka would be useful. Though we cannot discuss this point here we believe that the case here is different from discussion of Nazi atrocities. Secondly, some good could possibly result if the circulation of the details of communal violence could be confined to the co-religionists of the perpetrators of violence. But this is not possible where mass media are concerned. Moreover, violence and communalism are not confined to any community. There is seldom such one-sidedness in real life. Usually, provocation can lead to violence by all and all are open to 'communal passions' and actions based on these passions. Thirdly, detailed studies of communal violence at a scholarly or academic plane and with the full use of scholarly apparatuses would be quite useful in dealing with such violence. What we have found unacceptable is the instant production of such works and their wide propagation among the mass of people.

8

Marxism in India: Need for Total Rectification

Marxism has been an active political and intellectual force in India for over 50 years now. One need not therefore apologise for an attempt to evaluate critically the record of the activities of the Indian Marxists.

I would like to make two points in the very beginning. Firstly, because of the very basic character of Marxism as the philosophy of revolutionary social action, the activities of the Marxists as thinkers and as organisers of political action cannot be separated. This is even more true in India where Marxism and the communist movement have from the beginning had an inseparable existence. Secondly, the record of the Indian Marxists has not been only a negative one. They have many an achievement to their credit which should not be ignored. One need not therefore be carried away by the 'twisted' dictum: nothing fails like failure.

(1) Against heavy odds and facing the full repression of the colonial State and the ideological opposition of both the traditionalists and the modem bourgeois political leadership and intellectuals,[1] the Indian Marxists succeeded in popularising basic Marxist ideas, in laying the foundations of organized peasant and trade union movements, in establishing the idea that social revolution cannot be made without a revolutionary party, and in creating a viable Communist Party, however weak.

---

[1]The theory of Indian exceptionalism and spiritualism, 'foreignness' of Marxism, and intellectual derision by the sophisticated bourgeois intellectuals were often used to denigrate or deny the applicability of Marxism to India till early 1960s.

(2) The Marxists. have been the only consistent propagators of rationalist and humanist ideas in India. Here, they have tried to make up for the absence of a genuine and widespread and committed liberal bourgeois movement of rational and humanistic thought. In addition, they have fought for genuine secular ideals, which rise above the unscientific and syrupy Hindu Muslim *bhai bhai* outlook.

(3) They have contributed most to the wide propagation of that internationalist outlook which has been to a extent characteristic of Indian politics since the 1930s. Even the errors in the application of the notion of People's War from 1942 to 1945 and the resulting heroic facing up to the widespread popular nationalist hostility had this aspect: it revealed the Marxist commitment to internationalism. Increasing weakening of this commitment since the 1950s has of course to be noted.

(4) In the intellectual and cultural realms, the Marxists have given a basic turn to several social sciences. In history, they have succeeded in focussing attention on the role of the social classes, on the mode of production as the basic characteristic of a social system, on the social analysis of religious and philosophical ideas, on the nature of colonial economy and colonial system, on the class character of all nationalist and other popular movements. In economics, the Marxists have had to face the full force of the most advanced bourgeois ideological formation, which has, moreover, its own attractive left-wing variations. Yet, in spite of their thin ranks, they have succeeded in rivetting attention on agrarian relations, the role of foreign capital, and the basic characteristics of Indian industrial and commercial capital. Stray Marxist scholars have also made contributions in political science, sociology, and philosophy, which are in general dominated by bourgeois outlook. Ever since 1937, when the Progressive Writers' Association was founded, the Marxists have been a major force in literature and in literary criticism in almost all the Indian languages. Their contribution in the fields of drama and cinema is also significant.

Having noted all this, it has to be said that their record of failure is rather long, for at no stage during the last 50 years have the Indian Marxists succeeded in achieving more than a small part of what was historically possible. But before this aspect is taken up, I must make a personal explanation. My interest in raking it all up is neither denigration of the large numbers of the finest men of the last three generations of the Indian Marxists, nor that of the vicarious pleasure of a jesting pilate or an armchair academic who likes to mock others from the so-called olympian heights. My interest is that of a Marxist who has been fully involved for the last 25 years and who has, in some way or the other, participated in, and shared with joy or with sorrow, the small successes and the much larger failures of the Marxists, and to whom much of the criticism could be personally applied. If I no longer prefer to remain silent, if I do not mince words, if I even sometimes use harsh words, it is because there has been little genuine and severe heart searching among the Indian Marxists, who have after all much to criticize in their past and present, and because I beleive that Indian Marxism cannot go forward today unless a process of total rectification is initiated.

The extent of the failure of the Indian Marxists is brought out by one simple political fact. For years, their entire thought and activity have been guided by the prospects of a revolution to be made when a deep and all-pervading economic crisis would occur and lead to a similar political crisis. Often, in their rightful anxiety to look for the ripening of the 'objective conditions' for revolution, the Marxists have clutched at straws and mistaken a recession for a deepening political crisis. But now that both economic and political crisis are here, the Marxists are not even in a position to make a bid for power. They stand paralyzed now that the bird of revolution stares them in the face. They suddenly find themselves facing two choices: they can either, ignoring the semi-fascist threat, cheer, usually from the sidelines, the spontaneous or right-wing led petty bourgeois populist movements, or rely on the Congress, the main party of the bourgeoisie, to save the day for democracy, even if it does so by becoming more and more authoritarian.

The failure lies, of course, not in the political impotence and the *immobilisme* of today but in the manner in which Marxism has been applied in India for the last 50 years. It is one of the ironies of history that the leaders who find themselves helpless before history today are the very people who have been applying Marxism in India from its virtual inception! And in this respect, one may make another important point particularly for the benefit of the young Marxists: the failure has never been that of lack of courage or the spirit of sacrifice or devotion or hard work. The personal record of the long line of the founders of Marxist thought and movement in India is unmatched, almost heroic, in this respect. Whatever personal degeneration one sees among a few today is the consequence of the failure to apply Marxism correctly and not its cause.

I

The basic failure of the Indian Marxists lies in their inability to emerge as the standard-bearers of an alternative political leadership, *however small.* For the pre-1947 period, the criticism is *not* that they failed to become the leaders of the national liberation movement (many objective factors would also contribute to such a contingency) but that they failed to *organize an independent anti-imperialist struggle* which would have a necessarily changing relationship with the bourgeois-and the petty bourgeois-led nationalist struggle.[2] Instead, they either became carping critics of Gandhiji or Nehru, or took on the mantle of the most militant fighters in the ranks of the bourgeois-led movement. They either cut themselves off from the nationalist stream or became its 'tail'. Similarly, after 1947, they have tended either to become 'tails' of the Congress or the petty bourgeois radical opposition or to indulge in heroic but sectarian adventurism or to indulge in empty talk. In the intellectual realm, there is the failure to project Marxism as an alternative world view. India is one of the few countries where no strong anti-Marxist movement exists because the Marxists did not make Marxism a major intellectual current. The number of Marxist books, pamphlets and journals or of Marxist intellectuals is pitifully small. This is apart from the extremely poor quality of the Marxism of many Marxists.

In fact there has been a certain regression in this respect during the last decade or two. While earlier the poor might not vote for the communists or join their demonstrations, they tended to see them as the hope of the poor, the submerged, the exploited—they were seen as the coming alternative. Moreover, they were seen in every field as men of a special stamp, of a higher morality. Today they are seen by most as another opposition party, as just another group competing for popular favour and for leadership over trade unions, student unions, teachers' associations, etc. I was shocked to hear from an agricultural labourer in Punjab the other day that the capitalists *(sarmayadars*—a

---

[2]They had Lenin's clear-cut guidance in this respect. See Bipan Chandra, *Nationalism and Colonialism in Modern India,* New Delhi, 1979, pp. 297ff. Instead they wasted their energies on debating sterile questions such as which class should have hegemony in the anti-imperialist struggle, whether the bourgeoisie had gone over to imperialism or not, should the struggle be violent or non-violent, and so on.

category in which he included rural landowners, i.e., the rich and middle peasants) had three parties in his area-the Congress, the Akalis, and the Comrades!

II

In this essay I would like to highlight a few of the basic weaknesses of the Indian Marxists which go beyond weaknesses in the understanding of the Indian situation, or of programmes and their implementation. These relate to the style of application of Marxism in India.

Firstly, there is the failure to make the masses aware of their social condition, to make them politically conscious, to make them aware of their own class identity and objective social role, politically to fully activise them, to make them aware of their own capacity to act politically and of their own active role in making their future, to make them their own leaders. This is the most elementary basic task of a Marxist. On this basis alone does he enable the masses to organize themselves for political action. This is one of the distinguishing marks of Marxist political work from other radical movements under bourgeois or petty bourgeois leadership.

This was the historic task that Gandhiji performed for Indians *as members of a nation:* he gave the Indian people confidence in their capacity to fight and defeat imperialism. True, he did not go further and teach them to become their own leaders and organizers. Their political activity was kept under strict control from the top. The leaders of a bourgeois national movement could possibly not do otherwise without transcending one of the basic limits of a bourgeois national or popular movement. But the fact is that the Indian Marxists have also failed to perform this task for their own classes and for their own politics.

Today, the urban worker, the agricultural labourer, the poor peasant is discontented, is angry, but does not believe that he can be the main actor, the redressor of his own grievances, that the solution of his social condition lies in his own *hands.* He still looks to others whether Congress, or the Jana Sangh, or the Akalis, or any of the three or four communist parties, but *others—to* find the solution. Even when he is pro-communist, he sees the communist leaders and workers as the saviours who will do things for *him.*

The problem here is not merely that of taking politics to the people. Politics, even of the Marxist variety, are beginning to reach them. In two Punjab villages I recently visited, all the three communist parties have done some political work and are widely known. But what politics have they taken to the village poor? Not the politics of self-reliance, but of what the comrades will *do for the poor.*[3]

Equally, there has been the failure, with some admirable exceptions, to work politically among exploited classes, especially in the rural areas. 'This is the very *raison d'etre* of Marxism. True, social-change cannot be brought about by the working and exploited classes without allies, but the allies would remain allies and not become masters only if the Marxist political work is based on urban workers, agricultural labourers, and the poor peasants.

Yet, the Indian Marxists have repeatedly failed to act upon this elementary precept. They have spent a great deal of their energy in debating such questions as (before 1947) whether the Indian bourgeoisie has gone over to imperialism or not, the role of violence in the anti-imperialist struggle, which class should exercise hegemony over the struggle or in the new society, the relative roles of parliamentary and extra-parliamentary work, whether the main struggle in India is against feudalism, or semi-feudalism, or the capitalist landlord, or the kulak, whether the Indian bourgeoisie is national or comprador, whether it is increasingly collaborating with imperialism or building independent capitalism, whether the strategic goal of Indian revolution is national liberation, national democracy, peoples democracy, or socialism.

And, undoubtedly, these controversies are quite meaningful and have to be settled one way or the other. *But unless the Marxists are rooted in their own class, no amount of correct understanding of the objective situation would be of much use.* Lenin could succeed not because in April 1917 the majority of the Russian people were with him; not even the majority of peasants supported the Bolsheviks. But the Bolsheviks were rooted in their own class and so could make useful alliances with other classes and parties.

---

[3]I may point out parenthetically that 'comrades' fail even when it comes to doing something for the people. Bither they refuse to fight adequately, or even at all, for reforms in the name of revolution; or the reforms they fight for benefit not the basic exploited rural classes and the vast mass of the unorganized urban proletariat but the middle and rich peasants and the strata of organized white collar and factory workers. In other words, for the former, the 'comrades' are not even good reformers.

This basic weakness of Indian Marxism was recently brought out dramatically by the events in Gujarat and Bihar. These movements of the petty bourgeoisie against price rise and corruption in administration were hailed by the Marxists without bemoaning the massive fact that the working class of Ahmedabad and Gujarat and Bihar was throughout inactive, as were the rural poor. Even more interestingly, when the Marxists tried to intervene, they did so through a parallel student movement of the left (a united movement of the AISF and SFI in Bihar) and not by organizing the intervention of the working classes. Yet, any Marxist should be able to see that a political crisis during which the working classes of the cities and villages are politically passive can only lead to fascism, or militarism, or authoritarianism of the more traditional bourgeois parliamentary type.[4]

This failure to get rooted in one's own basic classes is in pari the result of two other sins: the reliance on spontaneity and the desire to keep together one's existing voting base. Any radical party which does not do sustained political work among the people and does not arouse their political consciousness is compelled to rely on spontaneity. One form of spontaneity is the over-reliance on economism. A second is the dependence on people's existing political consciousness which is, even in the case of working people, a bourgeois or petty bourgeois consciousness.

Even worse, spontaneity or 'instant' radicalism compels the Marxists to rely for support on those social groups who have already been brought into active politics by the nationalist movement before 1947 and by the spread of education, the modem mass media, and parliamentary politics after 1947. Inevitably, these groups are the petty bourgeoisie (the educated white collar employees in private and public sectors, students, teachers, petty shopkeepers, etc.) in the towns and middle and rich peasants in the villages. (The rural petty bourgeoisie). It is easy to take radical politics to them since they are already in politics and are under conditions of underdeveloped capitalism 'ready-made' radicals for they are aware of the possibilities of the modem world, fully conscious of their 'deprivations' and, consequently, acutely and increasingly frustrated.

On the other hand to politicalise the agricultural labourers and poor peasants, neglected by Gandhiji and Nehru and made passive

---

[4]To celebrate unreservedly the victories of the politics of other classes is, to use one of Tilak's phrases, to enjoy 'decorating another's wife'.

believers in their fate, is a very strenuous and time-consurnig job. The task is made tougher by the fact that any effort to arouse the agricultural labourer would arouse the full fury of the rich peasant who has been hitherto not averse to supporting radical causes and movements, especially if he was their chief beneficiary. This is one reason why the Marxists find it difficult to give up the notion of struggle against feudalism and semi-feudalism, in the countryside and against 'reactionaries', 'authorities', 'elites' and the establishment in the cities, for to do so and shift to concrete class struggles of the proletarian and semi-proletarians would mean giving up their entrenched political base in the urban and rural petty bourgeoisie. And, so, almost everywhere, except partly in Kerala and Bengal, the rural proletariat votes for the Congress.

Secondly, the Marxists acquired voting strength among the rural petty bourgeoisie over the last 30-40 years by espousing its demands for lower rents, land revenue and water rates, land to the tiller, etc. Work among agricultural labourers and semi-proletarian poor peasants may initially weaken their political support among the middle and rich peasants. This may initially reduce their votes and seats in the legislatures and other forms of visible political strength, e.g., mass demonstrations in state capitals, etc. And so the efforts to find an answer in theory and practice that will enable them to keep their existing mass base both in cities and villages while trying to spread downwards.

This reliance on the petty bourgeoisie for radical politics and neglect of the proletarian and semi-proletarian masses also partially explains another interesting phenomenon of Indian Marxism—the failure to produce cadre, leaders, and intellectuals from these social classes during the long period of 40 to 50 years. This failure is, of course, also linked to other aspects some of which will be discussed later in this essay.

III

The Indian Marxists, most of whom came to Marxism from the petty bourgeoisie attracted by Marxist ideas, have grossly neglected theory and ideology as factors in Marxist politics. This is surprising for their own experience should have convinced them that individuals from the bourgeois or petty bourgeois origin cannot be won over to Marxism and Marxian politics except on the basis of ideological struggle and transformation. Radical politics and trade unionism can bring a student, a white-collar employee, a teacher, or a professional into the folds of the Marxist movement, but these cannot sustain him there for long. Even when he is quite radical or even a member of a Marxist party, his class outlook, his ideology quite often remain bourgeois or petty bourgeois. To sustain him in his new politics it is necessary that he undergoes ideological remoulding in which Marxist theory would playa crucial role. Otherwise, the 'movement' goes on because there is enough in life to make people come near it and into it, but the turnover of the personnel is shockingly large.

The point is that unless a petty bourgeois is consciously, ideologically transformed, he remains a petty bourgeois, however radical and 'anti-authority' or even 'anti-system' he might become in day-to-day life and politics. This radicalism can even be put at the service of the capitalist parties. One should not forget in this respect that fascism is distinguished from bourgeois authoritarianism precisely because of its reliance on petty bourgeois radicalism. Fascism is not merely right-wing, it is 'right-wing radicalism'.

In fact, one needs to go further. Even the working classes are 'inherently' permeated with bourgeois or petty bourgeois ideology and consciousness. Unless they consciously acquire working class ideology and consciousness, they too 'normally' remain non-working class in outlook. One of the primary tasks of the Marxists in any country is precisely to carry the working class ideology to the working classes. All Marxism has ever held is that it is easier and natural for the working class to acquire proletarian ideology because it is its own class ideology. But the act of its conscious acquisition is still involved. Nor does mere trade unionism, even in the case of a worker, inculcate proletarian ideology. This, by the way, is elementary Marxism; otherwise the U.S. and British workers with their powerful trade unions would have made the socialist revolution long, long ago.

The overriding necessity for emphasis on ideology in a country like India arises out of another important aspect of Marxist politics. Inevitably, because of the low cultural level of the masses, the Marxist movements and parties rely on petty bourgeois youth to build their ranks and to carry Marxist ideas and politics to the peasants and workers. However, this simultaneously opens the way to the penetration of Marxist thought and parties by the ideologies and the life and work styles of the dominating classes. *This was and is an objective limitation in the situation.* But is was necessary to break out of its boundaries and to transform and transcend the objective necessity. The only way out lay in an intensive programme of ideological education within the rank of those who have politically come over to Marxism. This task has seldom been seriously undertaken in India, with the result that those who propagate the party programme or lead militant economic and political struggles remain deeply imbued with bourgeois or even feudal ideas.

The mistake made here is two-fold: the belief that participation in the political movement and membership in a Marxist political party, and grasp of the party programme would automatically lead to the transformation of a person's ideology. But a party card cannot cleanse an individual of the previously dominant ideology the way Ganga water or a *taviz* are supposed to do.

Secondly, in India ideological education has invariably meant the study of the current political programme, policy resolutions, and agitational literature. The study of Marxian classics and of Marxism as theory and system of ideas as elements in ideological remoulding and in inculcating a new way of thinking itself has always been neglected. Now, the study of party programme, etc., is certainly necessary for political action, but the party programme cannot act as a *Kalma* or a *mantra* whose recitation guarantees a change in ideology, for a change in ideology is not like a change in religion.

It is to be noted that the Indian Marxists have made little effort to find out what forms do bourgeois, petty bourgeois, feudal, and colonial ideologies take in their own ranks. Consequently, such elementary manifestations of these ideologies as bossism, heirarchy, competition, jealousy, lack of comradeship and trust, and careerism within the party and outside, a basic non-democratic personality structure (often betraying feudal outlook), tendency to uncritically ape and adopt things and ideas foreign, prevail unchecked.

It should also be pointed out that the problem is not solved simply by recruiting more cadre from the working class, though this would be a distinct step forward. Ideologically, even the Marxists of working class origin are only a few steps ahead of others. Firstly, their own existing ideology is bourgeois. Secondly, they too are constantly surrounded by a hostile ideological and social atmosphere which daily and hourly affects their consciousness. They too tend to get impregnated with bourgeois ideology and life-style. They too need constant ideological education and struggle.

A recent manifestation of the failure to see the proper role of the petty bourgeois youth and ideology is the widespread belief that the students' main role today is to act as revolutionaries on their own or in their own right and not as carriers of Marxist ideology and as potential cadre of the Marxist movement, which would put emphasis on their own acquisition of Marxism as theory and ideology. Inevitably, what results is only the growth of petty bourgeois radicalism.

Another aspect of the weak theoretical base of the Marxists in India is the repeated failure to raise practical problems and political issues to the level of theory. Instead, theory's main use is found in the *post facto* justification or denunciation of an essentially pragmatic policy. In practice, party programme and resolutions, which are the consequences of the practical application of Marxist theory, are invariably confused with theory, and education in Marxist theory and ideology gets confined to the study of the party programme and resolutions.

Consequently, the rank and file Marxists or even leaders become incapable of critically evaluating the programme and political practice based on it. The leaders change the programme pragmatically when it has 'failed'—that is, it no longer corresponds with life even as a shadow—and the ranks of members and sympathizers either leave the party in bewilderment since they have nothing to hold on to in the absence of faith in the programme, or they stick to it out of loyalty to the movement and the party hoping and praying that the new programme will not meet the fate of the old one. Theory is now brought in to explain why the old programme and policies failed-but *after* they have failed in practice. The fact is that programme-based political education can harness the enthusiasm and activity of the people temporarily and is necessary, especially during periods of intense political activity, i.e., during and before the revolutionary situation, but it fails miserably in sustaining a prolonged revolutionary consciousness and therefore political activity. For that the inculcation of Marxism is needed.[5]

Moreover, the underplaying of the role of theory and ideology leads to the propagation of an entirely mechanical and 'vulgar' understanding of Marxism and to its dogmatic application. In other words, even the theory that is sometimes applied is a flawed one. Even worse, what is sometimes applied is not even bad or dogmatic Marxism, it is not Marxism at all—take away the verbiage and nothing is left.

---

[5]Note should also be taken of the fact that the Bolshevik programme already included in it basic elements of Marxism, such as nature of state power, workers' control, dictatorship of the proletariat, the incapacity to solve the problems of the poor peasants, etc. In India party programmes have been basically non-theoretical.

In the Marxist writing on India one rarely sees-with the exception of Ajoy Ghosh and E.M.S. Narnboodiripad at their best-the subtle and dialectical application of theory in the manner of Marx or Lenin. What we have is the one-sided stolidity of Stalin's dictums. It is one of the profoundest tragedies of Indian Marxism that from its infancy it was brought up on Stalin's writings rather than on those of Marx, Engels, and Lenin.

This neglect of theory and ideology has many facets and consequences, only a few of which can be discussed here. For one, the theoretical and agitational tasks are mixed up, with the result that the theoretical effort is often conducted as agitation, while agitation is carried on in the language of theory so that it often goes above the heads of those who are to be agitated. Similarly, in the absence of correct theoretical foundation, the Indian Marxists constantly swing from one extreme to the other. The later theoreticians describe each swing as a punishment for the earlier swing, but weakness in theory invariably fails to stem the swing from going to the other extreme. What a heavy price is paid for the absence of theory among the rank and file Marxists!

Neglect of ideology by the Marxists has meant that one of the strongest props of the existing social order is virtually left intact. Long ago, in its very infancy, Marxism grasped that force is. only the ultimate-weapon of defence of the dominating social classes, and that it is through control over the ideas of all men—including the exploited and the suppressed—that a social order is stabilised. This is even more so in a modern bourgeois democracy where the social order is legitimised through a subtle and complex network of ideas and institutions. A basic task of those who want to overthrow class domination through mass action and mass organization is to dethrone the ideas of the ruling classes from the minds of men and to imbue them with an alternative consciousness. Not only has this task been neglected but even its importance has not been properly recognised.

Emphasis on spontaneity and economism has inevitably meant radicalization of men's politics without overhauling of their thought processes. Spontaneous consciousness is seldom working class consciousness even in the case of workers and never in the case of the petty bourgeois. Consequently, what is born again and again is bourgeois or petty bourgeois radical consciousness which is sooner or later absorbed by the complex ideological and political structure of the existing social system or is even utilised to strengthen it.

An interesting example is that of the rapidly spreading popular sentiment and struggle against corruption. But the entire struggle and consciousness are developing within the ambit of bourgeois or petty bourgeois ideology; the Marxists merely put the gloss of formal Marxism over it. For example, in the Parliament there is little to distinguish the performance on this question of the anti-communist H.V. Kamath or Raj Narain from that of the Marxist M.P.s. And an excellent opportunity to lay bare before the people the negative character of capitalism and thus to help transform their ideological parameters is missed.

The neglect of ideology has led to an overall failure to initiate a wider cultural revolution that would cover all aspects of people's lives as is done by the socially dominant classes who leave no area of life outside their economic, political, intellectual or cultural influence and control. On the other hand, it is common in India for even Marxists to have the most traditional ideas of religion, of caste, of relationship with women, of careers and aspirations for their children, of popular and Rational culture. There has hardly been any worthwhile struggle by the Marxists against the mental bondage and religious superstition to which the Indian people have been subjected for centuries. The caste system has been a major barrier to political unification of the working people in the countryside. Yet the struggle against it, and a very weak struggle indeed, has been confined to the cities in large parts of the country.

Here was scope enough to expose the utter inadequacy of underdeveloped capitalism to advance society, and for the working class to emerge as the leader of the entire submerged humanity and of social progress in general. Here was opportunity for the Marxists to win the cooperation of the best of bourgeois thinkers and humanists who are not yet able to come over to Marxism but who are able to see the betrayal of their own social and cultural ideals by the capitalist social order and who could be helped to see that the Marxists and the working class alone can maintain and advance all that is best in the achievements of humanity in general and the Indian people in particular.[6] Moreover such struggle would immediately separate the

[6]Unfortunately, the Indian Marxists rarely raise questions relating to values and quality of life, humanism, etc. All social failure or success is reduced to statistics of production. But not many decades back the Mar-xists used to keep such questions in the forefront of their critique of the existing social order.

Marxist radicals from the 'right-wing radicals', for the latter can join in the struggle for higher wages but not in the struggle for the ideological remoulding of the people.

Once theory and ideology were neglected; it was inevitable that the Indian Marxists would find no 'role' for the intellectual as an intellectual. He could be active on the peace or friendship fronts or in his own professional associations and trade unions. He could contribute to the movement financially. But there did not exist any 'task' for him in his own field. And since no theoretical or ideological work was being done by the Marxist parties, he had no role as an ideologue or propagator of Marxism, not to speak of a creative Marxist in his own chosen field. All Marxian wisdom in the different fields of human thought and activity is to be derived from the 'party', which in practice means one or two men in the top leadership or at the most a few top intellectuals to whom this right is delegated by some mysterious and immanent process. That intellectual effort is a collective effort of the many has been completely missed. Instead, using the example of Marx or Lenin or Mao, the notion of the cult of one or a few all knowing Marxist theoreticians has been spread widely.

The questioning intellectual is silenced off, and given a guilty feeling in the bargain, with the assertions (i) that what are needed are not 'pure' researchers but men of political action, and (ii) that, since he is not practising, he cannot see the reality or make an analysis of society. The implication is that intellectual or ideological work is not political practice.

The logic is usually not taken further; for example, that Bakunin, the travelling initiator of revolutions the world over, and the hard-working British trade union and labour leaders were doing political practice but Marx, studying in the British Museum, was not; or that participating in, and hopefully, winning, student union or teachers association elections is politics but scientifically studying one's society or spreading Marxist ideas or fighting against reactionary ideas is not politics. Is it then surprising that Marxist students of bourgeois or petty bourgeois origin have for decades spent more time and effort in fighting for 'student demands' or fighting student union elections than in acquiring Marxism for themselves, imparting it to others, and studying Indian society in its light: Here they have of course been dutifully following in the footsteps of their Marxist teachers.

Let me make two points very clear at this stage. I am not out to exalt the intellectual or the intellectual function which is a basic feature of all class societies. I am only suggesting that they be assigned their due place in the struggle for social revolution. Secondly, social analysis, the development of Marxist theory, and ideological work are not by any means the task only or even in the main of the Marxists making their living as intellectuals. It is the task of all Marxists.

IV

The weakness of the Indian Marxists in Marxist theory has many aspects, so that Marxism has been seldom in practice used as a guide to social analysis and political action. In fact it has been seldom living Marxism or Marxism as a science that has been applied in India.

For instance, quite often a thesis is believed to have been proved if enough examples are brought out in its favour. No search for counter-examples is made, nor is an analysis made of the dominant tendencies. For example, the fact that elements of various social formations *always* coexist in history for long periods[7] is used to prove through selective examples the existence of one's favourite thesis regarding the character of the social system and state power in India. Or that any government follows at any moment a multiplicity of policies, some of which pull in opposite directions, is used to bring out only those instances of policy which prove one's current point of view. The entire Marxian concept of the chief contradiction or of the emerging and the dominating tendency is often missed, except formally.

An even worse form of scientific sloppiness is the habit of verifying a thesis through anecdotes or stray instances, or proving it by just stating or asserting it in a different form, etc. An interesting example of this sloppiness is the mixing up of two separate questions: the extent of the penetration and control of Indian economy by foreign capital and the extent of exploitation by the already invested foreign capital. Both questions are important and are inter-related; but they are also distinctly different with different political and economic aspects and policy implications.

---

[7]"In England, modern society is indisputably developed most highly and classically in its economic structure. Nevertheless the stratification of classes does not appear in its pure form, even there. Middle and transitional stages obliterate even here all definite boundaries..." Karl Marx, *Capital,* Vol. III, Charles H. Kerr & Co., Chicago, 1909, p. 1031.

One also finds a certain lack of scientific precision in the use of Marxian terms. This is a bit surprising, for Indian Marxists have built up quite a tradition of quibbling about minor words. Let me give an example. The term landlord has been used by Marx and Marxists to signify a landowner who extracts from a tenant either feudal rent (feudal or semi-feudal landlord) or capitalist rent (capitalist landlord as in Britain).[8] On the other hand, a farmer who uses hired labour and manages a farm as a miniature factory has been described as a capitalist farmer (an element of 'rent' in his profits remains).

Yet, we have today Indian Marxists who base their agrarian analysis and programme on the definition of a landlord as one who owns more then a certain acreage of land and who and whose family members *do not work with their hands.* Here is a class being defined not with reference to its relation to the means of production and to other men in the process of production but by a virtual moral category.[9] By this definition all capitalists could be described as landlords. We are back to the pre-Marx radicalism and socialism.

It is, moreover, not realised that the vast mass of large rural landowners (10-30 acres of wetland) would be excluded by the definition of 'not working with their hands', and only the purely capitalist farmers would find themselves being declared capitalist landlords. But instead of a frank statement that in India capitalist agriculture should be abolished in favour of petty commodity production, we have recourse to dubious theory and sloppy thinking. Another allied example can be given. The Indian Marxists do not even use the category 'peasant bourgeoisie' what to speak of analysing its social, economic, and political role. The category *kulak* is sometimes used in politics, but we are seldom told as to who constitutes a *kulak.*

---

[8] "The owners of mere labour-power, the owners of capital, and the landlords, whose respective sources of income are wages, profit and ground rent, in other words, wage labourers, capitalists and landlords, form the three great classes of modern society resting upon the capitalist mode of production. *Ibid.*

[9] "Classes arc large groups of people differing from each other by the place they occupy in a historically determined system of social production, by their relation (in most cases fixed and formulated in law) to the means of production, by their role in the social organisation of labour, and, consequently, by the dimensions of the share of social wealth of which they dispose and the mode of acquiring it. Classes are groups of people one of which can appropriate the labour of another owing to the different places they occupy in a definite system of social economy". Lenin, *Collected Works,* Moscow, Vo1.29, p. 421.

There are no Marxian formulations which are not historically specific. Lenin, for example, repeatedly stressed that there are no fixed formulae or general statements apart from their concrete historical context.[10] An important aspect of this historical specificity is the knowledge of a country's peculiarities and historical. development. "Marxist theory absolutely requires", he wrote in 1914, "that every social question be examined within definite historical limits and....,—if it refers to a particular country—that due account be taken of the specific features distinguishing that country from others within the same historical epoch."[11] He further emphasised that it was particularly important "to establish concrete economic facts and to proceed from concrete realities, not from abstract postulates."[12]

Now, it is remarkable that on the whole, and for nearly 50 years, the Indian Marxists have evolved their programmes and policies, strategies and tactics, without making an exact appraisal of 'the specific historical situation and, primarily, of economic conditions', that is, without making a historical and economic study of India.[13] Whatever economic analysis has come—historical development being largely ignored[14]—has in each period followed the programme and has come as its *post facto* justification. The answers have not followed study or establishment of concrete economic facts but preceded it. At a cruder plane, this has sometimes resulted in the wholesale foisting on India, including even the language, of the analysis made specifically in a country that has been more successful in making a revolution.

---

[10]Lenin, *Collected Works,* Vol. 22, Moscow, p.149 f.n.

[11]Lenin, *The National-Liberation Movement in the East,* 2nd impression, Moscow, 1969, p.70. Also pp 70-1,

[12]*Ibid.,* p. 264.

[13]The brilliant work of R. Palme Dutt appeared too late to influence the politics of the pre-1947 era and was immediately drowned in the politics of the post-1947 era. It has been widely read since then, but has not influenced Marxist politics to a significant extent, partially because his post -1950 writings became issues of controversy among the Marxists.

[14]Contemporary history has been ignored except by E.M.S. Namboodiripad whose understanding of the historical development of Kerala has something to do with the grass roots development of Marxism there. His other historical writings also deserved to have had greater influence on the development of Indian Marxism. On the other hand, the fundamental writings of D.D. Kosambi, R.S. Sharma and Irfan Habib have been influential among academics, but have so far failed to have an impact on politics.

This failure to make a deep and serious study and analysis of the Indian social situation has been a major deficiency of the Indian Marxists. This has sometimes been done in the name of the supremacy of practice. Now, it is true that a Marxist studies society primarily with a view to change it, but he studies it all the same. In fact, Marxism is precisely different from other world views not only because it links theory or knowledge to practice but also because it assigns a very high place to social knowledge as an instrument of changing society.

The result has been the frequent inability to grasp the reality as it is changing. The Indian Marxists have quite often used Marxism successfully only when explaining what happened 10 or 15 or 20 years back. And this has, of course, been disastrous when faced with the political leaders of the ruling classes who have learnt many of the lessons of the past and who have developed quite a capacity to grasp the changing political and economic situation even when the constraints of class interests have prevented them from acting positively on that knowledge.

The neglect of Marxism as a system of thought has led to some peculiar confusions of which two or three may be discussed here. For example, the Indian Marxists have consistently failed to distinguish the State from a government. The State is the executive committee of the ruling classes, it looks after their overall and long term interests. It is the expression of the hegemony of a certain social class or classes over society and social development during a certain stage of social development. The government is a changing bloc of classes, parties, and political forces. The bourgeois state of pre-1832 Britain was led by semi-feudal aristocracy; the semi-feudal Tzarist regime promoted the growth of capitalism; the bourgeois state of France acquired in 1851 a petty bourgeois Emperor.

On the one hand, their characterization of the State is often that of a government and therefore leads to an incorrect definition of a stage of social development and therefore of revolution; on the other hand, since the character of the State does not change during a stage of revolution, while that of the government does often, their characterization of the government as State gives their politics a rigidity which prevents all flexibility in tactics. Moreover, it prevents them from understanding the changing contours of governments and government policies, reduces analysis from a theoretical to an agitational plane, takes out all subtlety out of political analysis, and promotes instead a conspiracy theory of history and politics.

If the 'State', i.e. the government in Marxian terms, has a permanent class base and policy, then all shifts in governmental policies, which Marxists would normally see as the consequence of changes in the balance of political forces either within the domain of the dominating classes or class or in their relationship to the dominated classes, are seen as the diabolical effort-the much used word is manoeuvre—of the ruling class or the fixed coalition of the ruling classes to bamboozle the people. Thus in place of individuals conspiring the classes become the conspirators. But it is a conspiracy theory of history all the same.

Let me give an example from recent history. The Congress split in 1969. Almost every serious Marxist or Marxist party had to adopt a concrete political stance, often different to their previous stances. Yet, this was done without making a concrete class and political analysis of the contending groups precipitating the split in the Congress. The reaction was pragmatic and without any theoretical effort to guide it. This was in part the result of the rigidity in describing the government (the 'State') as a fixed bloc of classes.

Linked to this weakness in theory, and even more important, is the failure to make a Marxian analysis of the social classes, political parties, and politics and their linkages and interrelationships. Consequently, a vulgar—in the Marxian sense—understanding of politics prevails. There is the failure to understand the role of political parties in a modern State in general and in a bourgeois democratic political system in particular. At a more complex plane, the relative autonomy, as distinct structures, of political parties, leaderships and elites as political representatives of social classes is ignored. Also missed are the role of the State as the overall guardian of the social system as a whole, of all sections of the ruling classes, of the long term interests of these classes, and the fact that these functions are performed by governments composed of representatives of blocs of classes, strata, and sections, who have their own personal traits and interests as political leaders and parties.

Such a complex understanding of complex social phenomena would normally enable the Marxists to see that governments are capable of going against the narrower individual or group interests of sections of the ruling classes, sometimes of the short-term interests of the entire ruling class, and, when pressed by the masses, even the long-term interests of the subordinate, junior members of the ruling classes. Political parties and leaderships would then be clearly seen as distinct structures though based on and representing the political interests of the social classes, and the two would not be confused and muddled together in economic and political analysis.

Reading Indian Marxist literature, one would not ever) know correctly how a social class, for example, the capitalists, controls a political party. The impression is that this is done by bribing the leaders, by financing the party and its election campaigns, and by such other direct controls. While there is plenty of such influence and control, this certainly does not constitute the heart of the matter. The capitalist class controls, promotes, and brings down political parties and leaderships primarily by controlling the production process, i.e., the economy. It can bring any regime to heel by going 'shy', etc. And so a political leadership is compelled to pay heed to the social interests of the capitalist class. Similarly, it bows before the monopolists not mainly because they have more money or because they are big in size but because their control over the economy is even tighter.[14a]

An interesting example of the failure of Indian Marxists to apply class analysis to politics is found in the virtual abandonment of the use of the words petty bourgeoisie in their political and social analysis. Going through the Marxist writing on India one will not find out as to which parties, or factions, or policies represent the interests of the urban or

---

[14a]Cf. Excerpts from a diary entry made in September 1931 in London with reference to the Second Round Table Conference. "It is necessary to realise that England is also not one. One England is that of the humble and the oppressed, of the common poor people, of the daridra-narayan (poverty personified), which is welcoming Gandhiji, which has no animosity toward India, and which has no voice in Indian affairs. The other England is that of the ruling class (Thakurs), who rule and who have power and authority (Satta). One can say that if ten members of this class decide to give freedom to India, they can. Those who are greeting Gandhiji with hurrahs are powerless even though they are thousands in number. The state power is even now in the hands of this ruling class. In name only does there exist a labour government. When the labour government also tried to make noise and go out of line, the capitalists (Seths) refused to give it loans and Mr. MacDonald came to his senses. Therefore, it is good to have the welcome of the poor, but the intentions of the 'rulers' are not good." The writer? Ghanshyamdas Birla in *Leaves from a Diary,* in Hindi, 5th impression, 1958, pp.26-7. Clearly, the Indian capitalists acquired very early a correct grasp of the nature of State power, of the ruling classes, and of the mechanism through which the bourgeoisie exercises control even in the most advanced bourgeois democracy of the world.

the rural petty bourgeois. Reading them one would never know that the petty bourgeois have been and are an active, perhaps the most active, and influential political strata in Indian politics since the last 50 years or more.

Today, every class, every political force is rightly making the most determined attempt to acquire hegemony o:ver the politics of this 'class', to harness its political influence and energies to its own class interests. In fact, before 1947, the Indian bourgeoisie was successful in both struggling against imperialism and keeping this struggle confined within bourgeois limits because of its hegemony over the politics of the petty bourgeoisie. From restricted land reform to bank nationalisation, from 'unlimited' expansion of university, including technical, education to the salary scales in the government and public sector organizations, from the brutal suppression of peasant protests to the kid glove treatment of the linguistic agitations, student struggles, etc., one witnesses the efforts of the post-1947 bourgeois governments to keep this volatile, politicalised, and politically effective conglomeration of classes and strata on their right side.

It is not of course suggested that the Marxists should ignore the petty bourgeoisie[15] or not exert themselves to the full to win it over to their side. But it is imperative that they specifically analyse this 'class', its interests, its politics, etc., and demarcate their own politics from its politics. They must take up its cause, but do so with their eyes open. And they should in no case follow petty bourgeois policies and describe them as Marxist. Their aim should be to establish the political and ideological hegemony of the proletariat over the petty bourgeoisie and not vice versa.

The theoretical weakness of the Indian Marxists also explains the repeated recrudescence of certain false or non-issues as controversies. Before 1947, the Marxists at regular intervals agreed to differentiate the revolutionary content of their politics from that of Gandhiji's politics on the basis of the use of violent or non-violent methods, while in reality the question always was that of the role of the masses, of their organisation, and of mass action. After 1947, they have repeatedly let themselves be divided over the question of

[15]Unlike some bourgeois intellectuals, the Marxists do not use the word petty in petty bourgeoisie to slight it. To them, to be a bourgeois is much worse than to be a petty bourgeois for the former belongs to the category of class enemies while the latter is part of the camp of the people.

parliamentary versus non-parliamentary work. In both cases, they have ignored the basic writings of Marx, Engels, and Lenin; and specifically Lenin's.

It should also be noted that this is precisely the sort of dichotomy which bourgeois political thinkers and leaders like to utilise for demarcating their politics from Marxist politics. Above all, it is obvious that those who cannot mobilize and activise the masses in militant 'non-violent' politics could hardly do so in 'violent politics', or that persons and leaders who got corrupted by parliamentary work could hardly have survived other forms of corruption for long. Instead of parliamentary work being used to test leaders, it is suggested that the leaders should be 'saved' by not being subjected to parliamentary temptations. This novel method of keeping the purity of the advance guard could perhaps occur only in a country whose people have for centuries tried to protect the 'virtue' of their women by putting them in purdah and the *brahmcharya* of their youth by sending them to the forests.

I may add just two other points. Firstly, this way of posing the question even evades a proper definition of what Marxists call 'parliamentarianism'. Parliamentarianism is not fighting elections and working in parliaments; it is to place an inherent value on winning elections and seats in parliament, it is to want to win them by political opportunism, it is to place higher value on winning elections than on politicalising and organizing the masses, and on parliamentary elections and speeches than on politics as such. So defined, parliamentarianism is wider than parliament. It can cover efforts to win majorities in trade unions, teachers' associations, and student unions; it can cover even the organisation of demonstrations, *hartals,* and *bandhs.* The question always is of the nature of the politics that one is practising.

Secondly, to pose the issue of forms of struggle in the way it has been done is to ignore the historical and sociological fact that no people like to go through greater pain than historically necessary, that people would not follow a road of greater sacrifice till the roads of lesser sacrifice are barred to them, that people have to learn the inadequacy of lower forms of struggle from their own experience. Lenin revealed full understanding of this fact by following extremely complex and all-sided tactics during 1917. Instead of posing the question of power as that of violence or non-violence or of parliamentary *versus* non-parliamentary road to power, he constantly asked: power to whom-to the Provisional Government and the Constituent Assembly or to the Soviets of Workers' and Soldiers' Deputies?

The Communist Party of China, led by Mao Ze Dong, leading the longest armed revolutionary struggle in history, agreed to negotiate a peaceful settlement with Chiang Kai-shek during 1945-1947; in the end the Chinese people could see that the Chinese Communist Party fought for peace, democracy, national unity and end to the civil war while the Kuomintang forced a civil war on the country in order to keep its dictatorship intact. And the Vietnamese people, fighting a historic armed struggle, followed the most flexible of tactics throughout.

The point is that a Marxist *does not* agree to pose the question this way—i.e., violence versus non-violence or parliamentary versus non-parliamentary work—just as he would not stake all on 'non-violent' or parliamentary work or ignore preparations to meet the violence of the ruling classes with all measures including revolutionary violence. To a Marxist the real task is to organize and mobilize the masses. A politically conscious, organized, and mobilized people would certainly use, and would be *capable* of using, all forms of struggle that a historical situation may make imperative. 'Higher' forms of struggle cannot be a *substitute* for the *inadequacy* of the Marxists in applying the 'lower' forms of political struggle.

V

Almost all aspects of the weakness of the Indian Marxists in analysing the social reality, in applying Marxism to India, in evolving correct political practice, and in the failure to correct mistakes in all fields in time,[16] are linked to the virtual absence of free discussion among them. The need for free discussion is seldom denied in theory; it is, however, denied in practice as a result of several well-entrenched thought processes or political formulae.

1. First, at every stage there exists the firm assumption that, whatever might have been the mistakes in the past, finally truth has been reached in the current political understanding embodied usually in a precise programme. Free discussion would, therefore, it is assumed, serve no useful purpose and would, on the other hand, detract from united political action. This is of course not true at any time. At the most this reasoning may become partially valid when the actual

[16] Lenin pointed out long ago that the real harm is caused not because mistakes are made—that is inevitable—but because they are not corrected in time.

process of revolution is going on. But often this reasoning serves as an alibi for the denial of free debate. Instead, it serves, along with other factors, to perpetuate the idea that the current moment is revolutionary or near revolutionary and is, therefore, unsuitable for free debate.

It may be pointed out that some of the most creative thinking was done by Marx and Lenin during 1848 and 1917 respectively, that Lenin developed his ideas and programme and tactics in a free debate with his comrades precisely between March and November 1917, that some of the richest and sharpest polemic in the history of Soviet Marxism occurred during the period of the Civil War and the International Intervention during 1918-1922 when often the very life of the new Soviet regime was in danger, that Mao Ze Dong succeeded in changing his party's line precisely during the Long March and developed new concepts and programme, and even organized a major rectification campaign inside the party, during the life and death struggle against Japanese imperialism.

2. Free debate has also been avoided in India in the name of secrecy and this often when the daily movements of the leaders, their collective gatherings, and party conferences and congresses are held with full fanfare and newspaper publicity and when almost anybody with whatever antecedents can gain easy entrance into the parties and groups. Sometimes, then, in the name of secrecy, what is offered is inner-party discussion within the small cell for members and occasional chit-cliat for sympathisers. *But the basic fact is that free debate can be free only if it is also an open debate,* except on questions relating to the actual implementation of tactics. Lenin and the Bolshevik Party succeeded in observing this principle even under conditions of complete illegality, Tzarist repression, and complete absence of civil liberties. It is much easier, and more imperative, to do so in bourgeois democracies with all their disguised and undisguised repressive mechanisms and instruments.

In the absence of *open debate, free* debate tends to become a mere formality, an empty ritual, for if a person cannot reach out to others, cannot *communicate* his ideas to others, who may be beginning to think in the same direction, or who can by the force of argument be persuaded to do so, then he has got no right to free debate in practice.

3. The Indian Marxist political worker or intellectual has learnt to exercise drastic, and disastrous, self-censorship. This is itself the result of several factors. The cult of the great man or men has greatly eroded the democratic and scientific notion that the acquisition of

knowledge of society is a collective activity. The average Indian Marxist therefore genuinely comes to feel that he is not *fit* to think on or debate matters of theory, ideology, and higher or broader political practice. His thinking and discussion are confined to his own particular area of work and understanding of the current programme and resolutions, and, in rare cases, to asking a higher leader to come and remove his 'doubts' in a question-answer session conducted most reverentially. Those with strong belief in their capacity to think wait for and work for the chance to join the select ranks of leaders who have the 'right' to think for themselves.

Secondly, the Indian Marxist is terribly afraid of being considered or of becoming a heretic or a deviationist. The basic Leninist emphasis on the need for a monolithic revolutionary party gradually created the sentiment that being considered an anti-party element was worse than death. A person, party or non-party, who was once 'outcasted' lost all human contact with other like-minded people. His life, intellectual or political, tended to become a desert. To a certain extent this power to outcaste, to anathematize, was as powerful a weapon in the hands of leaderships in opposition to silence criticism or prevent free debate as were more dire forms of control and suppression in the hands of leaderships wielding State power.

The Marxist intellectual would, therefore, not think or at least not publicize any thoughts even relating to 'an exact appraisal of the specific historical situation and, primarily, of economic conditions', if these thoughts contradicted the current programme. And if he did want to publish such thoughts, where would he do so? The established Marxist organs would not publish what he wrote, and any publication outside these organs only went to prove that he was taking bourgeois help and therefore his thoughts were being rightly anathematized! Gradually, the Indian Marxist was drained of the courage and the will to think critically. It was better to play safe, even if it meant giving up the quality that Marx prized above all and that had originally brought him within the Marxist fold.

Similarly, the rank and file Marxist worker felt safer in feeding back the middle level leader, who in turn fed back the higher leadership, an image of reality that corresponded more to the programme and resolutions than to what he was actually seeing or hearing or thinking. Gradually this tended to become a habit so that he genuinely and in all seriousness did not see or hear anything other than what his particular grasp of the programme, etc., indicated. Any 'heresy' then becomes an act not of will or thought but of failure to understand the programme, etc. Inevitably, the sole test of the soundness of the political and ideological health of a person tended to become not his ideology, his politics, his political commitment and work, but his 'loyalty' to the programme, etc.

Under such conditions, how was it possible to raise basic questions regarding Indian economy, society, classes and class struggle, the State, and Government policies? Marx and Lenin might insist that Marxism must be constantly enriched or that it must always be applied afresh to new conditions and to specific historical societies and situations. But can those Marxists do so over whose heads hangs constantly the sword of 'deviation'?

It may also be pointed out that the very notion of 'deviation' contains the germs of self-censorship, for free thought and free debate mean nothing if they do not include the possibility, and even the inevitability, of committing errors in thought or action. Marxism demands that a person should be willing, and should have the intellectual and political modesty and integrity, to admit his mistakes once other thought and action have proved him wrong. However, he who wants to think freely, creatively, and in a historically specific manner but without making mistakes and 'deviations' had better not even make the attempt. In this respect, even a hurried reading of the correspondence between Fredrick Engels and Paul and Laura Lafargue between 1882 and 1895[17] is quite rewarding. Engels is constantly trying to grasp the changing French political situation, and quite often finds his analysis and predictions proved wrong by the unfolding of events. Yet at all stages he remains a non-deviationist!

Even the top leaders of the Marxist parties become victims of the notion of deviation. If every word that one has written can be later held as proof of deviationist tendencies, it is better to swim in the mainstream so that if proved wrong later, one is in good non-deviationist company.

The lack of freedom to think critically and to follow one's thoughts through has produced another tendency that leads to what may be described as 'the disaster school of thought'. Analysis must' show constant deterioration in every field of life and the constant weakening of the enemy and the constant growing of the people's camp. Anything else would amount to 'praising' the enemy and giving him indirect 'support' and 'succour', etc. That Marxism is

---

[17]F. Engels, Paul and Laura Lafargue, *Correspondence,* 3 Volumes, Moscow, 1959, 1960.

precisely the scientific study of society, that it is the philosophy of the working class not because it is pro-working class but because the working class interests and world view today correspond to the scientific view of society is forgotten. Marxists study real society to change it; they do not like practitioners of magic change it by portraying it in sympathetic colours. One sometimes wonders whether the historical account of the rise and role of Capitalism in *Das Capital* and Lenin's *The Development of Capitalism in Russia* could have been written in India without inviting the charge of being a 'glorification' of the ruling class and the capitalist system.

4. The fourth, and perhaps the most important, factor in the lack of free discussion is what may be described as 'the theory of confusion', which has, moreover, certain other roots and dimensions. The Indian Marxists are terribly afraid of one thing-that other Marxists, particularly those coming from the poorer and illiterate sections or those constituting the rank and file, even when coming from the educated strata, would get *confused.* This fear, this spectre, has haunted them for the last 30 years or more. Any open and free discussion has the possibility of spreading confusion. And since confused men, it is said, cannot act, men must not be confused. The best way to avoid confusion, many come to believe, lies not in making the people and the politically involved understand the social reality or the programme through clash of ideas and their own political experience and practice, but in keeping 'wrong' and 'confusing' ideas out of their reach.

This 'fear of confusion' is produced by, and produces in turn, several other phenomena. It is the result of the middle and upper class roots of many of the Marxists and the consequent feudal and bourgeois ideological remanents in their minds. Feudal and bourgeois ideologies inculcate *contempt* for the masses and *fear* of them. Their influence leads a person, even a Marxist, to believe that the masses, even the petty bourgeois literate masses, are dumb and would get confused if any but clear-cut and predetermined ideas are put before them. This also explains the refusal to take Marxism, as distinct from a party programme, to the people, lest they get confused.[18] As a Marxist. leader of Delhi once put it to workers clamouring for education in

[18]The whole thing becomes a vicious circle. Once the intellectual, theoretical, and cultural level of the workers and cadre remains low, the theory of confusion does start acquiring certain objective validity. This very low level in turn becomes an obstacle in the path of the struggle for free debate and spread of Marxist ideas.

Marxism in the early 1950s, "half-baked Marxism is bad for workers". The reasoning was very clear: since workers had no 'brains' and could therefore acquire only 'half-baked' and not 'subtle' Marxism, they were better off without any Marxism at all.

Consequently, the Indian Marxists have made few serious attempts to spread adult education among workers, peasants, and women and subsequently to bring to them the best of the cultural and intellectual heritage of humanity. And since a party programme and trade union activity *alone* cannot produce a working class intelligentsia, the Indian proletariat has failed to produce intellectuals and leaders from within its own class ranks. Instead of playing its historical role as the carrier of Marxism to the working class and thus initiating the socialist movement, the middle class Marxist intelligentsia has become its perpetual leader, whatever might have been its subjective intentions.

Once the 'theory of confusion' prevails, it is also applied to the petty bourgeois intelligentsia and even the Marxists, who are sought to be protected from 'confusion' by discouraging real discussion or even exposure to clashing opinions or views of reality. Increasingly, the closed mind is seen as the best guarantee against confusion. The 'thinking function' is then transferred to a few persons, who are given this 'right' either because of a long record of leadership or because of some 'mysterious' or 'immanent' process, usually linked to their nearness to some leader.[19] They are 'safe' and are sure not to spread 'confusion'.

Secondly, the Indian Marxists, including the intellectuals, have acquired, and produced, a deep anti-intellectual bias and tradition. An intellectual, even the Marxist one, is often seen as the potential carrier of germs of confusion. Thus, instead of all communists being seen as intellectuals, as Gramsci suggested, the intellectual is seen as a potential subversive, as a threat, especially if he insists on thinking, *and expressing* his thought, for thought without expression is

[19]There is a certain resemblance to similar phenomena in the pest, For centuries the Brahmins alone could read or interpret the Vedas. Even the most ignorant Brahmin could do so. The Shudras and women were forbidden the study of Vedas. Even the most learned of them was not competent to interpret them precisely because of his or her not being a male Brahmin. Similarly, in the colonial period, only those belonging to the charmed circle of western-educated intelligentsia—and preferably those educated in the west—could provide thought on modern questions.

no thought; such unexpressed thought—'thought for thought's sake'—even the most authoritarian structures permit. This is not to say that the intellectual is not shown 'respect'. He is shown plenty of respect, so long as he is a mere 'flag'—a non-intellectual in practice. I must of course make it clear that I am not discussing the question of the 'importance' of the intellectual, for no Marxist worth his salt can for a moment believe in exalting the intellectual function over other social and political functions or in separating the former from the latter.

Thirdly, the fear of 'confusion' also partially explains the attitude of neglect of and arrogance towards non-Marxian thought in the social sciences as also the neglect and fear of Marxist theory. And thus resulted a recent slogan that the more a person reads—even if these be the writings of Marx, Lenin, or Mao-the more of a fool he becomes. The young men who put forward this slogan so frankly and so honestly were merely laying bare a deep-seated anti-theory and anti-intellectual attitude that has been the bane of Indian Marxism from its very inception, only normally it finds more disguised expression.

Two further points may be made in this respect. There have been short periods in the history of Marxism when free debate has taken place to a limited extent. This was the case from 1933-1939 when it was choked off on the assumption that since the prevailing confusion had been cleared and a rapidly growing Marxist-Leninist party with a correct political line founded, there was no further need for free discussion. Similarly, basic issues were raised and discussed in the 1950s as a result of the disaster that overtook Indian Marxists from 1948-1950. But then it was once again choked off in the 1960s in the name of fighting against revisionism or left-wing deviations and organizational looseness. The latter, interestingly enough, has continued to prevail and even grow; only free debate has been brought to an end. That the Indian Marxists are no nearer to making 'an exact appraisal of the specific historical situation, and primarily of economic conditions' of India and of 'the specific features' distinguishing it from others within our epoch, shows where real failure has lain.

To sum up: the specific task before Indian Marxists was and still remains to understand the specific historical situation and conditions of India and on that basis to organize the people for the overthrow of the existing social system; in other words, to make the Indian revolution. And for that it is necessary to overcome the basic weaknesses discussed above: (a) the neglect of political work among the basic working classes: the industrial workers, the agricultural labourers, and the poor peasants; (b) the near absence of ideological work and political education and agitation; (c) the failure to spread Marxism as a world view; (d) the failure to study the concrete Indian reality fearlessly and objectively; and (e) the virtual absence of free and open debate among the Marxists.

9

Changes in Agrarian Structure and the Communist Party, 1955-56

The Congress leadership was committed at the moment of freedom to changes in the semi-feudal agrarian structure. Its long-term strategy for the evolution of a new agrarian structure was based on the acceptance of three constraints: (1) Rapid increase in agricultural surplus to the cities could be brought about not by petty proprietors but capitalist farmers and rich peasants; (2) rapid industrialisation would not be able to absorb the vast rural masses who must therefore remain in the villages; capitalist farming would also not be able to absorb them, rather the opposite; and (3) capitalist farmers and rich peasants could, therefore, not be permitted to dispossess peasant proprietors on a large scale since this would pose serious social and political danger. Hence the need for a new agrarian structure which would be neither feudal or semi-feudal nor wholly or predominantly capitalist, which would gradually generate a layer of capitalist farmers and rich peasants, on the one hand, and preserve the small and petty peasants on land for a long period, on the other. In other words, the agrarian structure would have at its base a large number of small and dwarf peasant proprietors and at its top rich peasant-cum-capitalist farmers. This policy had been suggested in late 19th century by Justice Ranade; it had gradually percolated among nationalist leaders and intellectuals daring the 20th century.[1]

---

[1]See M.G. Ranade, *Ranade's Economic Writings,* edited by Bipan Chandra, New Delhi, 1990, chapters, 1,4,11,13,14, 15.Also see Bipan Channdra, *The Rise and Growth of Economic. Nationalism in India,* New Delhi, 1966, pp. 486 ff. Another school arose at the same time, represented by G. V. Joshi, which pleaded for small peasant-based agriculture, to be bolstered by tenancy legislation, low land tax, and cheap credit. See *ibid.,* pp. 441-2.

Arguing against the zamindari system, which he described as semi-feudalism, Ranade pleaded for a policy of land to the tiller, leading to the majority of cultivators becoming small peasant proprietors, accompanied by the transformation of the old zamindars into capitalist farmers, and the raising of the upper strata of the peasantry to this status, These last two social groups would constitute the small dynamic sector at the top. Thus he wrote:[2]

> A complete divorce from land of those who cultivate it is a national evil, and no less an evil is it to find one dead level of small farmers allover the land. High and petty farming".... this mixed constitution of rural society is necessary to secure the stability and progress of the country.

This policy of gradually replacing semi-feudal landlordism by rich and middle peasants while keeping the small, subsistence farmers-cum-commodity producers intact so that there was no large-scale proletarianisation and disintegration of the peasantry was accepted by the Congress Party and the Government of India after 1947.[3]

I

Land reform was one of the major promises of the national movement that the Government was expected to keep after independence. In 1948, the Congress Agrarian Reforms Committee submitted its report which was quite radical. It recommended full implementation of the policy of land belonging to the tiller and full protection to all categories of tenants against rack-renting and evictions. The different state governments framed laws in early 1950s abolishing the zamindars and other intermediaries in the zarnindari areas and making the existing tenants the owners of land. The zamindars were paid compensation amounting to nearly Rs.600 crores. The zarnindars went to the courts and appealed to the Fundamental Rights provisions of the Constitution. The courts tended to pay heed. Consequently, the Constitution was amended in 1951 to put abolition of the zamindari system and acquisition of the zamindars'

---

[2]Ranade, *op. cit.;* p. 233.

[3]Bhowani Sen, *Evolution of Agrarian Relations in India,* New Delhi, 1969, chapter VIII; Tarlok Singh, "India's Rural Economy and its Institutional Framework; A Re-examination", in *Studies in Indian Agricultural Economics,* edited by J.P. Bhattacharjee, Bombay, 1958, pp. 300ff.

estates beyond such consideration. The Constitution was amended once again in 1955 to make the adequacy of compensation non-justiciable.

While making a basic departure in the field of agrarian relations, the land reform legislation suffered from several weaknesses which have been very well documented in the existing literature. The payment of such a large sum as Rs. 600 crores was itself a major defect. Furthermore, erstwhile zamindars were permitted to resume large chunks of land for self-cultivation. This led to large-scale evictions, open or disguised, as 'voluntary' surrender of land, of small tenants. In many parts of India, tenancy legislation was also successfully evaded and old landlordism continued in disguised forms. The legislation was enforced through an inefficient and corrupt administrative machinery which often colluded with zamindars and big tenants. The mass of peasants were not involved in any manner with the implementation of the legislation.

Moreover, there was hardly much distribution of land among the landless or small cultivators. Agrarian legislation of the late 1940s and early 1950s did not touch landlordism in the ryotwari areas where it was quite prevalent.[4] It also did not try to guarantee security of tenure and fixity of reasonable rent to sharecroppers and other tenants-at-will.

However, while post-independence agrarian legislation hardly benefitted the mass of poor peasants and agricultural labourers, it did not amount to preserving semi-feudalism; it *did* mark the beginnings of a structural change in Indian agriculture. Zamindari abolition put large chunks of land in the hands of old occupancy tenants many of whom became substantial owners of land, who gradually took to capitalist agriculture as rich peasants or large-scale capitalist farmers. Their ranks were also strengthened when many of the erstwhile zamindars and landlords took to capitalist agriculture on the lands they had resumed for self-cultivation.[5] Tenancy legislation also created large strata of small and middle-level owner cultivators.

---

[4]When such legislation was passed in the latter half of the 1950s, it reproduced most of the negative features of the earlier agrarian legislation.

[5]Later, when land ceiling was imposed, the large owners evaded it by dividing land among relations and children. Land ceiling did not generate land for distribution but it did generate a large number of rich peasant and capitalist farmer holdings.

While semi-feudal landlordism survived in *large parts of the country during the 1950s, the emerging reality was represented by this new breed of capitalist farmers and rich peasants sitting atop a structure at whose middle level lay a large number of middle peasants and at bottom the mass of small peasant-proprietors and agricultural labourers.*

Increasingly, political and social power also began to veer towards these new strata of rural bourgeoisie and petty bourgeoisie. They were the initial beneficiaries of the democratic electoral process, evolution of administrative power to the village and district levels, community development and other efforts of the Government to develop agriculture, growth of cooperatives, and the gradual extension of cheaper credit to the rural sector. The new politics of legislatures and political parties, caste and linguistic movements, and even of popular political mobilisation could not be understood without taking into account the role of these new rural upper strata.[6] The basic thrust of government policies was towards bolstering of these strata and not the preservation of the old-fashioned semi-feudal landlords, who did, of course, remain influential because of their social hold over village life and their consequent capacity to influence elections, administration and bureaucracy.

Here an important distinction had to be drawn. While compensation and resumption of land enabled the old semi-feudal landlords to survive as persons and to remain rich and powerful, they *increasingly,* though gradually, *disappeared as a social class.* Those who took to capitalist agriculture might carry old, feudal values and attitudes into social, cultural and political life, but they no longer constituted feudal or semi-feudal strata, they were no longer semi-feudal landlords. Their class status had changed. They no longer 'practised' feudalism or carried on feudal relations. They were part of a new social configuration in the village; they were part of a new agrarian structure that was gradually coming into being. The feudal aspects of their social and cultural values and attitudes and even economic activity were increasingly articulated with this new agrarian structure.

---

[6]These strata, and not only semi-feudal landlords or perhaps not even in the main landlords, were to playa crucial role later in frustrating the efforts at imposing land ceilings, which alone could have made a significant amount of land available for redistribution among the landless.

Land reform laws were not pro-poor peasant but they did transform the agrarian structure, though from above, and in a reformist and not revolutionary manner. Compensation and resumption provisions represented a compromise with feudal elements but not a compromise with feudal land relations. While it could be said that land reforms were 'pro-landlord', it would not be correct to maintain that their basic thrust was the protection and maintenance of feudalism and that, therefore, the Congress Party and Government represented, in the main, the forces of feudalism. In this respect, the path followed in India was similar to that followed in Britain, Germany, Italy and Japan-in fact India was in the mainstream of the capitalist mode of transforming agriculture, France providing the exception, though perhaps a partial one.

This also meant that class relations in rural India were undergoing a basic change. The class alliances as also the nature of class struggle and the principal contradiction in agriculture were bound to follow suit.

II

The basic framework laying down the party's basic understanding of Indian social structure, its basic line of development, and the stage and strategy of Indian revolution on this basis was adopted by the Communist Party of India (CPI) in 1951 in two documents, *the Programme* and *the Statement of Policy.* The latter was the legal version of the document, the *Tactical Line,* drafted in consultation with J.V. Stalin and other leaders of the CPSU.[7] The latter also helped amend an earlier version of the *Programme.* In 1951. the understanding embodied in the two documents was put in a popular form in the *Election Manifesto* and the pamphlet, *On Our Programme, by* Ajoy Ghosh (pseudonym Prakash), the new General Secretary of the party.

The 1951 party documents declared India to be still, a "dependent semi-colonial country" or "essentially a colonial country" with a "backward and basically colonial economy".[8] Indian society and social order were also declared to be feudal with the Indian state committed to

---

[7]These documents are to be found in *Documents of the History of the Communist Party of India,* Volume VIII. 1950-56. edited by Mohit Sen. New Delhi. 1977. Hereafter referred to as *Documents.*

[8]*Documents.* pp. 7. 18-22.45.

defending landlords and princes.[9] Landlords and imperialism were, moreover, declared to be structurally linked, for the landlords were the main props of imperialism and the latter was the feudals' master.[10] The *Programme* characterised the Nehru Government as "this government of landlords and princes and the reactionary big bourgeoisie, collaborating with the British imperialists."[11] According to *the Statement of Policy,* the Indian Government was mainly serving "the interests of feudal landlords and big monopoly financiers and the hidden power behind them all, the vested interests of British imperialism".[12] Feudal landlords were thus seen by the 1951 documents as a basic constituent of the ruling classes, the Government being pledged to preserve their class existence and interests. The Government was, in fact, "run by the landlords and profiteers."[13]

Consequently, the party *Programme* and other documents asserted that the first stage of revolution in India was not over and the task of the revolutionary forces was to complete the incomplete tasks of the bourgeois democratic revolution, that is, "the achievement of full national independence and freedom" and "the complete liquidation of feudalism."[14] Thus Indian Revolution was to be anti-imperialist and anti-feudal.

According to the *Programme,* the agrarian reform efforts of the Government were wholly hypocritical; its schemes for abolition of landlordism were really ways pf enabling the landlords "to indirectly realise their rent through the state from the toil of the peasant."[15]

It seems that Stalin, who had helped unify the leadership of the CPI, was aware that the Indian reality was more complex than its portrayal in the *Programme* and the *Tactical* Line and that these two documents were also not specific enough to the Indian situation. In a

---

[9]*Ibid.,* pp. 7, 20, 45, 66.

[10]*Ibid.,* pp. 45-6, 66.

[11]*Ibid.,* pp. 4-5. Ghosh repeated all this in *On. Our Programme,* pp. 10, 12.

[12]*Documents,* p. 42.

[13]*Ibid.,* pp. 1-2.

[14]*Ibid.,* pp. IQ, 5 and 8, and 45 and 47.

[15]*Ibid.,* p. 2. Similarly, the *Election Manifesto* asserted that the Nehru Government had preserved "the system of feudal exploitation" and that its schemes of zamindari abolition were really designed to pay hundreds of crores of compensation to the *zamindars. Ibid.,* pp. 65-6. How could one both pay compensation and preserve zamindaris was a question that was never asked.

question-answer session with the Indian Communist leaders, he tried, though in a rather simplistic fashion and within the confines of P51,[16] to caution them against theoretical rigidity and one-sidedness.[17] Stalin's clarification covered several areas. Regarding the agrarian structure, Stalin was perhaps worried that the description of the agrarian structure in India as feudal might lead the party to ignore its specificity as well as changes in it. He therefore tried to introduce caution in three respects. Firstly, the agrarian programme must take into account the complexity and wide differences in different regions. The Indian Communists should therefore not rely overmuch on other models and must "prepare a special agrarian programme of your own".[18] Secondly, a distinction must be made between feudal landlords and capitalist landlords. While the former were to be expropriated, in the case of the latter only a limit was to be placed on their total land holdings.[19] Thirdly, Stalin took note of the existence of the kulak or the rich peasant in the countryside and of his social importance. While pointing out that the kulak could be won over or neutralised in the course of the anti-feudal struggle, he recognized that the kulak benefitted from the Government's policies and therefore sympathised with it. "When the Government cry 'buy land'," he pointed out, "it addresses itself to the kulak and the kulak appreciates". Stalin was thus, though very tangentially, warning against looking upon the policy of zamindari abolition with compensation as a *simple* pro-feudal measure which changed very little in the

[16]The CPI went through a great deal of inner turmoil and division during 1947 and then again during 1948-51. In the end a strategic paradigm, based on the integration of several components of previous communist paradigms in India and abroad, was structured in 1951 which succeeded in unifying the party at that time. We have referred to this paradigm as P51.

[17]*Ibid.*, pp. 35 ff. Because Stalin's comments were attached to the highly secret document, the *Tactical Line*, and were therefore not available to the ordinary party members, cadre and middle-level leaders, the party leadership decided to make them available to the membership in an elaborated' form and fully integrated with the overall framework of 1951 through Ajoy Ghosh's pamphlet, *On Our Programme.*

[18]*Documents*, p. 37.

[19]*Ibid.* Also see Ajoy Ghosh, *On Our Programme*, p. 4. In 1951, the party recommended 100 acres ceiling, thus protecting the personal holdings of rich peasants, capitalist farmers and small and medium landlords.

agrarian structure. Though this policy did not benefit the mass of peasantry, it did, he hinted, benefit the upper strata of the peasantry and thus change social stratification in the countryside.[20]

Stalin also tried to warn the Indian Communists against the easy and hoary assumption that the Indian bourgeoisie especially the big bourgeoisie, was organically linked to feudalism and would therefore oppose land reforms and was at least in this respect reactionary. This was not so, said Stalin: "Not only small but many of the (big, B.C.) bourgeoisie feel that the inner market is too narrow and will not prevent land being handed over to the peasants."[21] Furthermore, one reason why the big bourgeoisie or one section of it opposed the Government was because it "plunders the peasants and restricts the home market. It may not shout from the house-tops about it, but it is opposed to this all the same."[22]

Similarly, to the question, "what is the class character of the Nehru Government? We think this is big burgeois-landlord government collaborating with imperialism", Stalin replied: "Not quite. Nehru bases himself not only on these classes but also on the kulaks.... So the basis is not as narrow as you think." "'Therefore", he added, "it is not a puppet government"; it would not be easy to overthrow it. To do so, "One has to work hard."[23] Unfortunately, the party was not able to fully absorb the Stalin clarification, perhaps because it was made from within the framework of the 1951 *Programme* and that too in a rather hesitant manner.

III

The unification of the party did not last long. During 1952-55 serious differences arose within the party. The reality. or social development increasingly diverged from the promises of the *Programme* and other 1951 documents. The effort to adhere to the 1951 framework and to reconcile it with the reality produced sharp political differences leading to a crisis within the party. Gradually, even unity on the tactical line broke down. In the end, the party was split

---

[20] *Documents,* pp.39-40. Ajoy Ghosh recognized this aspect explicitly. See *On Our Programme,* p. 12. Contrast with the formulation in the *Programme. Documents,* p. 2.

[21] *Documents,* p. 39.

[22] *Ibid.*

[23] *Ibid.*

in 1964 and one of the successor parties was again split in 1967.

A very important moment in this prolonged crisis was the intense inner-party debate during 1955-56. Even though differences on the agrarian question did not lie at the heart of this debate—the main issues in it being those of India's status as a free country, role of the bourgeoisie, and the party's tactical line-they did surface during it. The remainder of this paper deals with the different approaches on the question adopted by the three broadly distinguishable lines represented in this debate, the Right, Left and Centre. At the outset we want to make it clear that we use these terms not in the traditional, value-loaded sense but as convenient short-hand labels. The positions of the Right, Left and Centre are defined by their approaches and not by these terms themselves. In other words, for us the term Right was not equal to 'reformism', the Left to 'sectarianism' or 'revolutionariness', and the Centre to 'Centrism' or a mechanical and opportunistic effort to find a middle path. In fact all the three were Communist positions; all the three were committed to the spirit of struggle and to revolution. We may also note that the three were agreed that the stage of Indian revolution was anti-imperialist and anti-feudal.

IV

Though the Right accepted that one of the two basic tasks of the Indian revolution was the struggle against feudalism, it believed that the government policy was turning towards making changes in a positive direction in agriculture. Thus Bhowani Sen argued that the Second Plan aimed at fulfilling "to a great extent the requirements of India's independent capitalist development even in agriculture." He referred to the Plan's emphasis on land reforms, ceiling on land-holding, transfer of property rights to the actual tillers, provision of credit, marketing and other such facilities in the rural areas, and prevention of a sustained fall in agricultural prices.[24] P.C. Joshi and others endorsed this view and felt that a new policy to "curb feudalism" was being adopted.[25] Though critical of the Government for certainly not having done all it should and could so far as abolition of feudalism was concerned, Ravi Narayan Reddy said that despite lacunae in agrarian legislation, failure to prevent large scale evictions,

---

[24]Fourth Party Congress Document, *Forum,* No. 1, p. 7.

[25]*Ibid.,* pp. 34-5. Also see Somnath Lahiri in *Forum,* No.6, p. 30.

etc., it was. wrong to suggest that the Government strengthened or consolidated feudalism. "On The contrary", he wrote, "definite curbing of feudalism has taken place." He referred in this context to the curtailment of the powers of the princes, the abolition of jagirs and tenancy legislation in Hyderabad, the announcement of the policy of ceiling on land-holdings and the amendment. of the Constitution with respect to compensation.[26]

V

The Left section of the leadership was represented in the 1955-56 controversy primarily by P. Sundarayya, M. Basavapunniah, Harkishan Singh Surjeet, M. Hanumantha Rao and N, Prasad Rao. The Left leaders held that the Government was defending and protecting feudalism[27] but not maintaining it "intact". The Congress agrarian legislation was intended "to develop capitalist mode of production of agriculture." It was aimed at compelling the feudal landlords to sell their lands and serve as an appeal to the rich peasants to buy their lands.[28] They said that this legislation and the development schemes, of the Government had given certain concessions to the rich peasants and enabled a small section of them to prosper. This had also enabled the bourgeoisie and the Congress to extend their mass base in the countryside. But this did not mean that the Government was abolishing feudalism or opening the path to its elimination. In fact it was pledged to defend it. 70% of the peasants, consisting of agricultural labourers and poor peasants, had not secured any land. There were large-scale evictions, increase in the debt-burden of the peasantry, fall in the prices of agricultural products, increase in tax-burden, etc.[29] The party should, of course, they said, utilise the limited agrarian reform, but it should not "nourish any illusion that the present Government would itself bring about far-reaching agrarian reforms to the extent of abolishing landlordism."[30] Such an understanding would "in practice weaken the efforts to build a powerful and broad-based revolutionary agrarian movement."[31]

---

[26]*Forum,* No.1, pp. 57-8.

[27]*Forum,* No. 5,pp. 19,31-2; *Forum,* No.4, pp. 26, 31; *Forum,* No.1, p.86.

[28]*Forum,* No.1, p. 77; *Forum,* No.4, pp. 11-2, 16.

[29]*Forum,* No. 4-, pp. 11, 30; *Forum,* No.5, p. 53; *Forum,* No.1, p. 85; Basavapunniah, *Minutes of the* CC *Meeting,* 21 June 1955.

[30]*Forum,* No.1, pp. 84-5. In fact, the Government was pledged to "defened imperialism and feudalism in their essential aspects." *Forum,* No.5, p. 19.

[31]*Ibid.,* p. 85.

A strong element in the Left's analysis of the Indian reality was the belief that revolution in India could only be made on an anti-imperialist, anti-feudal basis. Any other reading of the reality was seen as an effort to dilute the revolutionary zeal of the people. Thus, to suggest that the Government could break "the feudal and imperialist fetters on production" was wrong as it "would only confuse the masses and create illusions about the bourgeoisie." It was "a line of disarming the masses before the ideological onslaught of the bourgeoisie."[32] The Left opposed the notion that the Indian bourgeoisie was the decisive force in the ruling class combine because this would mean that the bourgeoisie was in a position to decide issues in its favour in its conflicts with the imperialists and landlords. This would in turn mean that the bourgeoisie was capable of fulfilling the major part of the democratic tasks even if it could "paralyse the struggle of the proletariat for its hegemony over the democratic revolutionary movement."[33] Similarly, why would it be an illusion and absolutely wrong to believe that the Congress Government was capable of bringing about agrarian reforms to the extent of abolishing feudalism? Because, said the Left leaders, it would "in practice weaken the efforts to build a powerful and broad-based revolutionary agrarian movement."[34] This entire line of reasoning was circular and predicated upon the 'truth' of the framework of 1951. The reality was to be viewed through the prism of this framework. In this case, for example, since it was axiomatic that the Indian revolution was to be a revolutionary struggle against feudalism, to say that the agrarian structure was being changed was tantamount to denying the revolution. Hence the reality could not be so. It had to be perceived differently. In other words, the revolution was not to be based on the reality but the reality was to be seen in terms of the coming revolution as defined in the 1951 documents.

VI

Even though there was not much controversy in the party regarding the feudal character of Indian agriculture, and the Centre supported this view, it at the same time made an attempt to make certain innovations. We have taken Ajoy Ghosh's speeches and other interventions at th Central Committee meeting of June 1955 and his later

---

[32] *Forum,* No.4, p.14.

[33] *Forum,* No. 1, p. 84.

[34] *Ibid.,* p. 85.

speeches and writings during 1955-56 as representative of the Centre's approach on the subject.

So far as the direction of change. in agrarian relations was concerned, Ghosh adopted a very genera! approach close to that of the Programme during the June discussions. The half-hearted official schemes of agrarian reform, he said, had tried to curtail only "some of the existing rights and privileges of the feudal elements" while permitting them to retain lakhs of acres of land and to eject tenants on a large scale. In the process, "in the main, only a small section of the peasantry" had benefitted and the agrarian crisis had deepened.[35] He did not, however, ask what were they doing with these lakhs of acres.

However, when it came to the questions of the agrarian policy of the Government and the party's attitude towards the peasantry, Ghosh took a detailed position and revealed deep insights into the reality.

According to Ghosh, the agrarian policy of the Government, as embodied in the land reforms carried out by it, was geared to two objectives: "(1) A certain amount of 'curbing', of feudal landlordism and encouraging of big landowners to develop as capitalist landlords... ; and (2) creation of a narrow stratum of rich peasants who can act as the social base of the ruling bourgeoisie in the countryside." But, at the same time, these reforms had "also given relief to the mass of peasants from feudal exactions of various kinds." This relief was, however, totally inadequate.[36] Ajoy Ghosh widened this understanding to a certain extent in the context of the tactics to be adopted by the party towards the peasantry. Acknowledging the social and economic, and even numerical, weight of the middle and rich peasants in the countryside, he ascribed the Congress success in Andhra elections to the support it gained from rich peasants and "a good chunk of middle peasants." And then concluded that all over India the government policy of land reform, rural development, provision of credit and other facilities, etc., was geared to the winning over of *these two* peasant strata. In a very perceptive analysis, of the real agrarian situation and going beyond the simple anti-feudal formula and the general position that the Government was pro-feudal and coming

[35]*Documents of the Central Committee Meeting of June* 1955, No.3, p. 18. (Hereafter referred to as CCD).

[36]*Ibid.*, p. 27.

closer to the real class relations and politics in the countryside, he pointed to the real class struggles that prevailed in the countryside and which were used by the Congress to weaken peasant unity and keep its hold in the villages: conflict between small peasant leasers out and their tenants, between rich peasants and the large mass of the rural poor, and between peasants of all sizes, who used wage labour, and wage labourers. These conflicts, he said, created a complex situation that admitted of no easy solution; they could not be solved or dealt with by the simple formula of anti-feudalism. "It should be recognised that each of these conflicts is so serious in its intensity and so complicated in its character that it would be foolish to attempt to work out any simple solution to it." For example, the questions of "the right of the tenant to continue to hold the land he cultivates and the right of the small holders" (especially those who had migrated to the city as workers and middle class employees, he added) "to resume his land for self-cultivation are so mutually contradictory that there is no simple solution for it." The same was the case with the problems of land ceilings, fair wages, etc. Any "mechanical solution" adopted by the party would only enable the Congress to rally one rural group or the other to its side. In fact, said Ghosh, "A paradoxical but true situation had already arisen in which the party and kisan movement are being attacked from both ends by th same social forces as seen in relation to Andhra elections."[37]

Faced with such a difficult situation, Ghosh too tended to fall back on the old stand-by-struggle against landlordism. Since peasant unity was a political necessity and the *Programme* had laid down that the rich peasant would be a part of the four-class alliance which would fight for the people's democratic revolution, it was necessary to take up issues in which all sections of the peasantry were on the same side. "The entire peasantry is one in its struggle against landlords, moneylenders, bureaucratic officials and the Indian and foreign monopolists who manipulate the internal and foreign market". Furthermore, the party should take up simultaneously the demands of all sections of the peasantry including the demands of the agricultural labourers for higher wages, the landless for land ceiling, and the middle and rich peasants for fair prices for agricultural products, supply of cheap and timely credit, reduction of taxation, fixing of land ceilings so that only landlords and not rich peasants were affected, and so on.[38]

---

[37] *Ibid.*, pp. 66-7.

[38] *Ibid.*, pp. 67-8. Earlier Ghosh had warned against two 'deviations': (i)

But, once again, Ghosh would not ignore the reality. Even this strategy of fighting for the economic demands of the rich and middle peasants would be "insufficient to unite them in one solid force with poor peasants and agricultural labourers." Hence, he argued, the party must supplement its economic appeal and capacity to organise struggles on, economic demands, its "narrow, economic sectional approach", with a political and social vision of national and societal development. The longer passage on this aspect in his June speech deserves fuller reproduction.[39]

> Such (peasant) unity would be possible only if the party and the Kisan Sabha combine the struggle for partial economic demands of the rich and middle peasants with the national- political campaign on the basis of a plan for national reconstruction .... (like the national bourgeoisie and the petty bourgeeoisie) the rich peasant and middle peasant are politically conscious and have a great deal of national pride and national aspiration. It is as much (by) utilising these characteristics of the rich and middle peasants, as by giving concessions to their economic demands, that the Congress is today rallying them around itself. The Communist Party and the Kisan Sabha can win them over for democracy and socialism only if they are made to see that the Party and the Sabha are the only forces of genuine nationalism and democratic national reconstruction. It is the lack of such a national approach that makes all our campaigns for the demands of the peasantry appear to be sectional demands not even of peasants as a whole but of this or that section of the peasantry.

Later, under the pressure of the Left, Ghosh tended to shy away from innovation and interpreted the phrase 'curbing feudalism' to mean an effort not to weaken and destroy feudalism but in some way to preserve it. Its aim, he said, was to strengthen the alliance between the big bourgeoisie and the landlords and to place it on a more durable

there should be no vacillation in defending the interests of agricultural labourers and poor peasants even if that adversely affected rich peasants; for example, separate organizations of agricultural labourers should be set up and ceilings on land holdings supported; (ii) at the same time, the tendency to base the party on agricultural labourers and poor peasants and to fight only for their demands should also be avoided for it led to slogans and tactics which alienated the rich peasants and a large section of the middle peasants. *Ibid.*, pp. 65-6, 69.

[39] *Ibid.*, pp. 68-9.

long-term basis by transforming feudal landlords into capitalist landlords. At the same time, he asserted that contradiction between feudal and bourgeois interests was growing.[40]

Ajoy Ghosh frankly recognised that the peasantry and peasant movements had remained relatively passive politically. In his June speeches, he noted that even when popular movements of the other sections of society were growing, the peasant struggles had not assumed "such big proportions for some time."[41] In November, he suggested that a major reason for the fact that "the mass democratic movement as a whole remains weak" was "the weak state of the peasant movement taking the country as whole." This was in particular important because "our revolution in the present stage is predominantly an agrarian revolution."[42] But why was this so? Ghosh gave two answers: "The Government tactics of splitting the peasantry" and the lack of attention by the party to the peasant problem and the problem of defeating the government tactics.[43] He also referred to the prevalence in the party of divergent views on the question of peasant unity. But why was the Government successful in dividing the peasantry? Was it the result of social development and changes in the agrarian structure or of a better organised conspiracy' by the ruling classes? And why did the party leadership persistently neglect a problem on which hinged the present stage of revolution? Ghosh gave no answer. Earlier in his June speeches he had noted the complexity of the problem, but had failed even then to look critically at the party's understanding of the developing agrarian structure and the role of government policy in it. though he had suggested that the main direction of government policy was towards an attempt to develop India "along capitalist lines in industry as well as in agriculture." But he did not develop this line of thought further, perhaps because that would mean questioning the framework of 1951 in one of its basic aspects. The consequence was a seriously wrong reading by the party of the direction of government policy as also of the developing agrarian structure in India.

One theoretical assumption that the Communist movement as a whole made was that there was only one path of agrarian change or

[40] *New Age* (Weekly), 10 July 1955, p. 13.

[41] *CCD,* No.3: p. 22.

[42] *On the Slogan of a 'New Path',* Fourth Party Congress Documents, p. 13.

[43] *Ibid.,* pp. 13-4.

transformation, that of the radical seizure of the landlords' land and its distribution gratis among the small peasantry and the landless, that is, the path of the French Revolution. But, in fact, in most parts of the world, except the Communist countries, agrarian relations have been changed from above by a rather prolonged process, spread over an entire historical period, transforming feudal landlords into capitalist landlords and capitalist farmers and raising a part of the peasantry to the status of rich and middle peasants. This was the path followed in 19th century Germany, Italy and Japan and even in Britain during the 17th and 18th centuries. And this was also the process initiated by the Congress Government in India in the early 1950s. In fact, because of the man-land ratio, the political imperatives of a political democracy based on adult franchise, and the existence of viable communist and pasant movements, the proportion of small and middle peasants in India was far larger and of capitalist farmers far less than in Britain, Germany and Italy or even France. Moreover, this process was to be seen in its main thrust and direction and not evaluated at a specific period or at its very beginning.[44] In private discussions, Ajoy Ghosh would himself repeatedly point out that there were two ways of transforming agrarian structure: one from below based on agrarian revolution by the peasantry which was pro-peasant, and the other from above, based on executive or legislative action by the ruling classes, which made the mass of peasants suffer. But both led to the transformation of the feudal or semi-feudal agrarian structure. It was the second path, Ghosh would say, that was being followed in India.

Another leader of the Centre said all this in print. The Indian bourgeoisie, said S.A. Dange, could no longer "lead an agrarian revolution *from* below." But it certainly wanted to use the state power. "now in its hands" "to change the situation *from above* in its favour, without rousing the forces of agrarian revolution from below". Answering the question "Is this possible theoretically", Dange said: "it is possible and can be done". He cited the examples of Bismarckian Germany and the Kemalist Turkey. The Nehru Government was also showing this tendency, he said, though it was not possible to say whether it would succeed or fail. It depended on "certain conditions". But neither possibility could be foreclosed. Very perceptively, Dange pointed out that the peasant movement would have an important role in

[44]Bipan Chandra, *Nationalism and Colonialism in Modern India*. New Delhi. 1979, pp. 340-1. 361-2.

the outcome. Even transformation from above would occur "only if the peasant struggles from below-not otherwise." And here he cited the example of the role of Telengana struggle in the passing of the Hyderabad Land Reform Act. Hence the role of the peasant movements was not eliminated by recognition of the second possibility.[45]

The 1955-56 debate threw up a heretical view in the form of notes by Jagannath Sarkar of Bihar and Balachandra Menon of Kerala. Between the two of them, they questioned the 1951 framework in all its basics including the conception of the Indian revolution as being primarily anti-imperialist and anti-feudal.

Both of them asserted that the Government was taking anti-feudal measures and trying to transform agrarian relations in a capitalist direction.[46] Government measures, said Menon, had, in the main, "broken the back of feudal structure in our country." The basic, emerging feature in agriculture was "the capitalist land relationship" though "relics of the feudal system" still remained.[47] Both Sarkar and Menon also said that agrarian relations were being transformed not in a revolutionary manner but from above and therefore without benefitting the mass of rural poor consisting of petty tenants and agricultural labourers.[48] Certain other sections were, however, said Sarkar, being spared, while a section of rich peasants was being helped through technical facilities, etc., to develop into capitalist farmers.[49] Menon was even more perceptive. Government, he said, favoured rich-peasant farming along with capitalist farming.[50] What is more important, on the one hand a large mass of petty peasants were disintegrating and becoming landless, on the other *the system of small holdings was being encouraged and consolidated.* Menon thus brilliantly foresaw that the policy being followed was not that of perpetuating landlordism or full-scale capitalist farming but of

---

[45]*Forum,* No.7, pp. 8-10. He could have added the example of agrarian legislation in the PEPSU in 1953. In another manner, this was how later the bourgeois government at the centre permitted the Communist governments in Kerala and West Bengal to introduce radical agrarian reform.

[46]*Forum,* No.3, p. 17; *Forum,* No.6, p. 17.

[47]*Forum,* No.6, p. 14.

[48]*Ibid.; Forum,* No.3, pp. 18-9.

[49]*Forum,* No.3, p. 19.

[50]*Forum,* No.6, p. 17.

maintaining a system of small commodity producers, or small peasant producers, topped by rich peasants and capitalist farmers, though after an initial period of ejection of tenants-at-will and sub-tenants.[51]

Sarkar and Menon frankly accepted that Indian bourgeoisie has come to power in 1947 and that it was the leading force in the state and government.[52] Sarkar said that government policies, opposed to imperialism and feudalism, were being determined in the interests of the capitalist class in general and monopoly capitalists in particular. So far as the common people were concerned there was intensification of oppression at the hands of the bourgeoisie.[53]

---

[51] *Ibid.*, pp. 14-5.

[52] *Forum*, No.3, p. 19; *Forum*, No.6, p. 14. Menon added: "The transfer of power to Indian hands meant a real change in the class relations in the country." *Forum*, No.6, p. 14.

[53] *Forum*, No, 3, pp. 18-9. Also see *Forum*, No.6, p. 17.

10

Agrarian Structure and Peasant Movement in Punjab

The study of peasant societies, agrarian structures and peasant movements has drawn increasing attention of historians and other social scientists in recent years. The agrarian society and peasant protest in Punjab have been no exception. Their study has been taken up by a large number of young and old scholars. It is perhaps high time that on the basis of existing research some tentative generalizations are put forward with a view to their further testing, revision, or overthrow so that new lines of research are opened up.

As in rest of India, in Punjab too, colonialism brought into being a new agrarian structure which was neither 'traditional' nor a perpetuation of the past nor modern capitalist in character. The study of colonial Punjab's agrarian structure is no virgin field and one would tend to assume that the basic spade-work for the study of peasant movements has already been done at least in this respect. Unfortunately, this is not largely so. Despite some excellent work by writers like Darling, Calvert, and Briji Narian, some basic questions were not raised. What is even more unfortunate, there has developed a stereotyped study of Punjab agrarian structure as basically consisting of people, who were sturdy, undifferentiated peasant proprietors and. who developed agriculture on progressive lines, taking full advantage of irrigation, commercialisation, export, *etc.* The only fly in the ointment was the wily money-lender. This stereotype has prevailed despite several

*I have drawn heavily on the research of my student and colleague, Mridula Mukherjee, whose recent work has filled in many of the lacunae in this field.

studies which have pointed out that nearly half of pre-1947 Punjab's land was under tenancy and that the tenants constituted the largest segment of Punjabi rural society. The other day a well-known sociologist-historian desiring to work on Punjab was surprised to discover that Western Punjab was an area of landlords and the Unionist Party represented there not the Muslim Jats but the big Muslim landlords.

All sorts of myths have also been built around the peasant movement in Punjab. Their being hardly any serious scholarly study on the subject, the myths have a more popular origin as well as currency. Even such simple aspects of the movement as its quantitative and qualitative levels have yet to be documented in a serious and scientific manner. For example, how far is it true that, from the 1920s onward, Punjab was the centre of a wide-spread, well-organized movement in which all sections of the peasantry from the rich peasants to the landless labourers actively participated. We would like to have answers to such questions as the types of peasant organizations, a detailed history of the different minor or major agitations and struggles, their socio-economic base or the involvement of different sections of the peasantry, the social-class character of the movement's leadership, the goals and demands of the movement, the role of casteism and communalism, its ideological aspects as also the level of awareness of the ideological elements among the participants, its strategic perspective and the forms of struggle, the methods and forms of mass mobilization, its strength and weaknesses, and, of course, its relative successes and failures.

Since the study of Punjab's peasant movement is just beginning, we can at best raise some significant questions and perhaps suggest tentatively some of the lines along which answers may be found.

To start with, the agrarian structure of colonial Punjab has to be studied afresh in this context. This will help us bring out the socio-economic stratification of Punjabi society and the nature of the resultant major contradictions which gave birth to the peasant movement. We have, of course, to keep in view that the agrarian structure varied widely, region-wise as well as from time to time.

I

A basic feature of Punjab's economy was its rapid colonialisation after 1850, leading to its integration with the rest of Indian colonial economy and also with the world capitalist economy in a subordinate position. Even though for various reasons, including a more favourable land-man ratio, larger provision of irrigation, large remittances from the army and overseas, and, for political reasons, a more responsive administration, Punjab's agriculture underwent a certain growth and Punjab peasant had a higher per capita income than the peasant in other parts of India. Punjab's economy was no less underdeveloped and colonial in its basic structure than the economy of India as a whole. This became evident when the general crisis of the colonial economy set in after the First World War. Punjab's economy and agriculture also entered a period of stagnation thus showing that the social basis of Punjab's agricultural development was in no way different from the development of the rest of the country. Having said this, we may also point out that an analysis of the complex manner in which the colonial economy functioned in Punjab and-affected its agriculture is waiting the attention of a concerned scholar.

At a more mundane level, the growth and structure of landlordism as also changes in the techniques of agricultural production have still to be properly studied. The heavy indebtedness of the Punjab peasant is widely known, but its significance for production relations is much less so. Similarly, it is known that modern industry did not make much headway in Punjab—the number of workers covered by the Factory Act in Punjab was, in 1930, less than 45,000. But the ruin of Punjab's flourishing handicraft industry has yet to be properly traced. The result was that, after 1918, Punjab too felt the pressure of population on land and its agriculture was a victim of all the consequent evils. We may also point out that, at the level of the widest generalization, the mode of production in Punjab agriculture has yet to be theoretically explained with the backing of adequate empirical data.

II

For the study of the nature and character of the peasant movement, the basic question is: What is peasantry or who constitute the peasantry in a specific historical situation? Is the peasantry more or less a single homogeneous mass or does it consist of diverging and perhaps even mutually antagonistic rural strata? The question is in turn linked to the process of the internal differentiation within the peasantry under the differential impact of colonialism.

Scholars and peasant activists may not agree on the degree of internal differentiation and stratification within the Punjab peasantry or on the manner in which the differentiated peasant strata should be defined. But that differentiation marked Punjab's agrarian class structure and that this differentiation had reached an advanced stage is perhaps not in doubt. The pattern of land holdings as also of land ownership was already highly skewed and differentiated. For example, in 1939,48.8 per cent of the total holdings were in the size of three acres or less constituting only 6 per cent of the entire agricultural area, while 6.3 per cent of all holdings with 25 acres or more of land constituted 52.8 per cent of the area. Thus already Punjab was not a land of undifferentiated peasant proprietors but of landlords, rich peasants, middle and small peasants, occupancy tenants, tenants-at-will, share-croppers, and agricultural servants and labourers. In fact, several Punjab scholars have in the past made an attempt to study this aspect, especially relating to the systems of tenancy and share-cropping. In this, as in many other respects, this is perhaps a fit occasion to acknowledge our debt to one of Punjab's great scholars, Prof. Brij Narain.

At the top of Punjab's agrarian structure came landlords. It has been estimated that between 40 to 50 per cent of all land was under the control of landlords. There also prevailed considerable differentiation among landlords. Rich peasants constituted another important upper segment of the countryside. Theirs was a very complex, mixed up social situation which has yet not been properly studied or analysed. As landowners, they were also subjected to colonial exploitation through land revenue and water rates or *abiana,* or as sellers of agricultural surpluses. They were also the victims of the price fluctuations of a colonial economy and also of colonial under-development in other ways—for example, in the absence of employment and other economic opportunities for their children, normal increase in their population tended to reduce the size of their holdings. They also suffered to a certain extent from the money-lender's greed. On the other hand, they were the major beneficiaries of the gains from irrigation, commercialisation, cooperative credit, price rise, etc. Taking advantage of anti-money-lender legislation they were increasingly taking to lending money to other rural strata, especially to the petty peasant proprietors whose lands they could now control under mortgage or later through outright possession. Those among the rich peasants who managed to acquire more land rapidly took to land-lordism through the system of tenancy-at-will or *batai* (share-cropping). In fact, the emergence of rich peasant money-lenders and landlords was an important aspect of rural differentiation. It also made the task of defining rich peasants quite difficult. Since few rich peasants took to capitalist or semi-capitalist farming, most of them tended to become, as soon as they could, semi-feudal landlords. In fact, in many parts of Punjab, there was little difference between rich peasants and small landlords except that the former cultivated part of their land through family labour and hired labourers while leasing out the remainder to tenants-at-will.

The category of middle peasants, who owned between five and fifteen acres of land or who held land as occupancy tenants, would not form more than 30 per cent of rural population.

The vast mass of peasant proprietors-nearly 65 per cent of all owners-were petty or dwarf holders. They owned less than five acres of land and therefore clearly constituted, along with the tenants-at-will, the category of poor peasants. At the same time their social position and relations with the colonial state, rich peasants and landlords differed from those of tenants-at-will. As pointed out earlier, the tenants-at-will held 48.2 per cent of all land. Most of the tenants-at-will held land under the system of *batai* and they did not enjoy any security. They were often subjected to illegal exactions and rack-rent. They were also compelled to borrow at most unfavourable terms. We should, of course, keep in view that the entire area of tenancy in Punjab is full of haziness. The official definition of tenants was rather confusing. Moreover, a large number of tenants in Central Punjab were simultaneously petty peasant proprietors. In fact, pure tenants were to be found mainly in Western Punjab and parts of South Eastern Punjab.

Though the subject is largely unresearched, it is believed that agricultural labourers and servants were not yet a major rural stratum. They were, of course, not insignificant either. According to Surendra J. Patel they constituted nearly 14.4% of the total rural work force in Punjab. Moreover, their number was already beginning to increase steeply after 1921 due to the unabsorbed growth in population. Their social condition was of extreme poverty. At the slightest touch of adversity, they tended to starve.

Some of the rich peasants and perhaps a few of the landlords strove to become capitalist or semi-capitalist farmers. But their extent is, for the time being, not known. The tendency for most of them was to take to landlordism and usury.

It is thus obvious that while the study of differentiation in the peasantry is as yet in an early stage and could easily absorb the services of a large number of scholars, the Punjab peasantry was already differentiated to a significant extent.

The question here is to what extent did the peasant movement take cognisance of or reflect this differentiation? Or rather, the task before the peasant movement was to organize the peasantry while keeping in view the different external and internal contradictions that it faced. Clearly, the nature and character of the peasant movement would be largely determined by the nature of contradictions and alignments between different agrarian classes and strata, between agrarian classes and urban social groups, and above all between the people of Punjab and India and colonialism and the colonial state. On the other hand, it would be the task of the peasant movement to identify on the basis of the study of the concrete social reality areas of potential or actual class conflict and class harmony and to consciously accentuate or mute them in accordance with the broader view and the overall strategy. All these questions merit a detailed study.

There were several contradictions between the Indian people and colonialism which blocked their social development and under-developed their economy. Those who study peasant movement would have to keep this fact in view. Moreover, the peasantry's own principal or primary contradiction lay at the time with colonialism. The landowners and the tenants-at-will, who paid in Punjab half of the land revenue and water rates, had a more specific and directly perceived contradiction with the colonial state on the question of land revenue and water rates which siphoned off a large part of the agricultural surplus. Their burden on the peasantry was increased steeply during the depression years when there was a sharp fall in agricultural prices. This put a large section of the revenue payers in a radical mood. The impact of the depression was of course a varied one and tended to further accentuate the differentiation in the countryside.

A major internal contradiction within Punjab's rural society related to the relations between tenants-at-wiil and landlords. The agricultural labourers clashed with their landlord and rich peasant employers. There also existed a sharp contradiction between all kinds of rural debtors from landlords to agricultural labourers and the money-lenders. This contradiction was further accentuated because the peasants as sellers of agricultural produce often faced the same social stratum this time in its incarnation as merchants. This enabled the small as well as big landlords to rally the different strata of the peasantry around their own class politics.

III

One of the basic tasks in studying a peasant movement is to make a detailed and in-depth analysis of its demands, the grounds on which appeal was made at the grass-roots level. These demands would help us determine the social content of the movement.

It seems on the basis of our existing knowledge that the basic and the most persistent demands of the peasant movement related to the burdens imposed on the rural sector by the colonial state. Several agitations were launched, especially during the depression years, for the reduction of land revenue and water rate (or *abiana)*. Several struggles were also launched to prevent the raising of land revenue demand as a result of resettlement operations. Another popular demand was for the better supply of water. During popular agitations and conferences, the demand of the small peasant proprietors for exemption of uneconomic holdings from land revenue was also put forward. An allied demand was for the levy of land revenue on agricultural income on the same basis as income tax and not as a flat rate per acre. This amounted to demanding the exemption of most of the land holdings from land revenue. But while including these two demands in their charters of demands, no popular agitations or struggles were organized around them. Mass mobilizations and agitations were I confined to the demand for the reduction of land revenue and asking for more irrigation and marketing facilities.

The peasant movement in British Punjab seems, on present evidence, to have paid little or no attention to the tenants' and share-croppers' demand for land. Their demands for security of tenure or reduction of rent were also not taken up. No struggle or even agitation was Organized around their demands against eviction, rack-rent, forced labour, illegal exactions, and the debt burden. This was all the more inexplicable because in theory the peasant movement and its left-wing leadership constantly reiterated its anti-feudal objectives and even put forward the radical demand of land to the tiller. In practice, not even the mild versions of the latter were taken up for agitation, though it was sometimes put forward in an abstract manner in theoretical and propagandistic documents. In fact, the peasant movement in British Punjab took up hardly any demand which would go against the interests of the semi-feudal landlords.

The Nilibar, Montgomery and Multan agitations of 1938-39 were the only major agitations which took up some of the tenants' demands. They protested against illegal enchancement of rent, *begar* or forced labour and ejectment and demanded reduction of rent and increase in the share of the sharecroppers. The reach of these agitations was not large; nor were these agitations sustained over long enough period. Moreover, their main target was foreign companies which had taken up land on lease.

Similarly, the demands of the agricultural labourers for better conditions of work and higher wages were not taken up by the peasant movement. Not even simple ameliorative measures for them were fought for. This neglect was in a way in line with the approach of the main segment of the nationalist leadership even though in Punjab the peasant movement was headed by the Communists, Congress Socialists, and other left-wing groups.

One line of explanation can be that the peasant movement was acting on the strategic concept of uniting the entire peasantry in its confrontation with the colonial state. For the same reason, it did not sharpen class struggle in the countryside or promote class war. In the circumstances of the time, that is, in view of the primacy of the Indian people's contradiction with colonialism, this was perhaps a justifiable strategic approach. But it could have been achieved in a different manner by consciously adjusting, through mutual concessions, the interests of the different peasant strata. It was not necessary to unilaterally sacrifice or bypass the demands or interests of the most exploited sections of the rural masses. One consequence of the actual policy followed by the leadership of the peasant movement was the establishment of the strong hegemony of the middle and rich peasants over the movement.

The peasant movement also did not take up with vigour the problem of indebtedness, though for a short period between 1935-1937 agitations were organized around the demands for a moratorium on debts and even for their cancellation. The peasant movement also supported the Punjab Government's debt legislation during 1937-38, though at the same time it pointed out its limited scope in operation so far as debtors were concerned.

Most of these remarks do not, of course, apply to the peasant movement in Punjab states, especially Patiala.

What was the social base of the peasant movement in Punjab? That is, what was the involvement of the different strata of the peasantry in the movement? On the whole, the real social base of the movement was rather limited. Firstly, it was limited to the small peasant proprietors who were, it seems, able to get the social, financial and moral support of their more well-off neighbours. On the other hand, the tenants-at-will and agricultural labourers were virtually outside the ambit of the peasant movement. Secondly, the movement was concentrated in the districts of Central Punjab. It had a very weak, almost negligible, base in Western Punjab, now part of Pakistan, and in South Eastern Punjab, now forming Haryana. Thirdly, it was largely confined to the Sikh peasantry the participation of the Hindu and Muslim peasants being marginal. In other words, the peasant movement was limited to the ranks of the small Sikh Jat peasant proprietors of Central Punjab.

Why did the movement succeed in securing a solid base among the small Sikh Jat peasant proprietors of Central Punjab? Why did it fail to find roots in other regions, and why did its roots not go down to the lowest sections of the peasantry, are questions which require detailed investigation. The existence of a militant religious reform movement and powerful anti-imperialist traditions among the Sikh Jat peasants of Central Punjab may provide part of the answer. The firm hegemony of the middle and rich peasants over the agricultural labourers and small tenants may be another part of the explanation.

We must also remember that once initiated the process would have a tendency to perpetuate itself unless consciously reversed. The social composition of the peasant movement and its leadership limited the range of demands that the movement would take up. The rich peasant, who was in the colonial context an actual or potential landlord as well as an actual or potential employer of labour, was hardly likely to favour the taking up of the demands of tenants, share-croppers and agricultural labourers. This in turn limited the appeal of the movement and therefore its capacity to expand its social base. The caste factor also may have a certain explanatory value. In Central Punjab the agricultural labourers invariably belonged to the lower castes; this also to a certain extent prevented their coming together in a common movement with the Jat peasantry. On the other hand, a common social-caste position not only enabled the coming together of the middle and rich peasants but also enabled the latter to exercise a certain pull over the small peasant proprietors.

The failure of the politically radical leadership of the peasant movement to take note of, analyse or conceptualise the differentiated character of the peasantry also contributed to the limited social base of the movement. Once the peasantry was conceived or viewed in an undifferentiated manner, it was easy for the leadership to start identifying the peasant movement with the interests, urges and demands of the peasant proprietors, especially of the more well-off and articulate among them.

IV

Several questions regarding a peasant movement in the colonial context are just opening up. One set of questions relates to the movement's underlying strategy and forms of struggle.

Despite a great deal of radical rhetoric, the forms of struggle adopted by the peasant movement in British Punjab were basically agitational and not different from those adopted by the national movement. They consisted of meetings and conferences of peasants, demonstrations, *jatha* marches, and ultimately the courting of arrest by the peasant *jathas* or groups of volunteers. The strategic perspective, guiding the forms of struggle, at no stage was that of making an agrarian revolution, peacefully or otherwise, that is, of bringing about changes in agrarian structure through direct peasant action. The perspective was more in the nature of putting pressure on the government through varying degrees of mass mobilization in order to persuade or pressurise it to accept the peasant demands wholly or in part. The demands were, moreover, never non-negotiable or fundamentalist in character. Unlike the basic demand and ideological structure of the anti-imperialist movement, the demands of the peasant movement did not question the basic elements of the agrarian structure or its legitimacy; they were invariably designed to remove the illegal or socially undesirable exactions added on to the system; or they opposed the excesses of an unrepresentative, inefficient and high-handed administration. Consequently, they could be dealt with through a counter process of denial, suppression and negotiation by the ruling authorities. The real character of agitations is clear from the structure of demands: the more radical of its demands, such as the abolition of land revenue on the small, uneconomic holdings, were put forward only in resolutions and speeches, *i.e.*, they were not made the object of active struggle or agitation.

What do the mildness of targets and the absence of militant methods of struggle signify? Our intension is not to suggest that this flawed the movement in a basic manner. It can be logically argued that they represented the right strategic and tactical approach in the context of the semi-authoritarian, semi-hegemonic character of the British colonial state. They also reflected the symbiotic relationship of the peasant movement with the strategic and tactical approaches of the contemporaneous national movement. It may be suggested that the basic flaw in the Punjab peasant movement pertained not to this realm but to the earlier discussed realm of its demand structure, its narrow social and regional base, and its failure to acquire a broad sweep within the context of its own strategic and tactical perspective. That is, even the mild or non-militant forms of struggle and the strategic perspective of winning concessions through the pressure of a mass peasant movement did not in practice encompass mass activity by the bulk of peasantry. To repeat, this was perhaps its basic flaw.

The peasant movement in Punjab promoted the ideological notion of the peasantry or *kisans* constituting a single cohesive social group or class. This notion could have served a very useful purpose in helping to overcome the peasantry's division on caste, communal or regional basis. Unfortunately, this did not happen and the British rulers with the help of vested interests and semi-feudal classes could successfully deal with the agitation. Peasant 'class' consciousness existed to a certain extent, but in practice the edge of this consciousness was not turned against the semi-feudal landlords or fully against the colonial state. Instead, because it helped to paper over the emerging differentiation within the peasantry, it became an instrument for the structuring of rich peasant-middle peasant hegemony over the peasant movement. Moreover, it was in part responsible for the failure of the peasant movement to counter the landlord-rich-peasant-colonial administration sponsored ideology of zamindarism or agricultural caste interests.

The peasant movement also failed to transcend the limits of economism—that is, it operated almost wholly at the level of economic demands and failed to give any significant political dimension to the movement or the role of the peasantry or to impart higher-level political consciousness to the peasantry.

The relationship between the peasant movement and the national movement in Punjab has yet to be investigated empirically within an adequate theoretical perspective. We only know that from both sides there was inadequate integration of the two. The Punjab Congress with its strong bias in favour of the merchants and other urban groups failed to mobilize the peasantry in the anti-imperialist movement which consequently remained quite weak. The peasant movement, in turn, while stressing the importance of the anti-imperialist struggle and the role of the peasantry in it, failed in practice to link the two movements.

The weakness of the two movements in Punjab had another significant dimension. They had succeeded in creating a strong anti-imperialist tradition and an atmosphere of opposition to political authority and of struggle against oppression. Similarly, in the Punjab states peasant struggles were linked to and occurred in the broad context of the struggle for democracy against the pro-colonial feudal rulers. But neither of the two movements could spread to Western and South Eastern Punjab. The general weakness of the national movement in the latter regions kept the peasant movement also very weak there, for the healthy stimulant provided by the former was missing. On the other hand, the near absence of the peasant movement in these regions prevented the growth of nationalist forces there.

Communalism also played an important role in keeping the peasant movement weak, especially in Western Punjab. Muslim landlords .and the colonial state cleverly utilised the social fact that the landlords and tenants of Western Punjab were Muslim while the money-lenders were Hindu to turn the politics of the tenants into communal channels and to line up the tenants behind landlords on religious and communal grounds against the Hindu money-lenders. The latter too were opposed to agrarian radicalism and promoted their economic interests through Hindu communalism. In fact, even the broadly nationalist and left-led peasants of Central Punjab were not able to divest themselves of elements of Sikh religious and communal consciousness with the result that till this day Sikh communalism remains a strong force in Punjab along with Hindu communalism. In reality, in the communal and caste situation as prevailing in Punjab, a broad peasant movement against landlords, money-lenders and the colonial state could help vastly in forging national unity for furtherance of national struggle for independence. One result of the failure to do so was the establishment of political hegemony of the Unionist Party in Western and South Eastern Punjab and the strong position of Muslim communalism in Western Punjab. The colonial state and the landlords succeeded in these two regions in making politics centre around the contradiction between the traditional merchants-money-lenders on one side and the peasant debtors, landlords and the emerging agriculturist money-lenders on the other.

Thus, inadequate development and integration of the two movements was to weaken both in a serious manner. We might make a wider point in this connection. Since the peasants were the main component of the Indian people, the national movement as a people's movement should have been above all their movement. Their active participation in it and the reflection of their interests in its programmes, policies and organizational structure should have been ensured so that after the ending of colonial rule a society and a state would be created which would promote their interests. At the same time the peasantry could have been constituted as a major social force or an ensemble of social groups on a national or provincial scale only through the anti-imperialist struggle which would bring together the divergent peasant interests and unite it with the other anti-imperialist classes and social strata.

V

In the end I would like to make a plea to the Governments of Punjab, Haryana, and Himachal Pradesh on behalf of the students of Punjab's history. The study of rural people and their agrarian structure and peasant movements is seriously hampered by the absence of Punjab Government's records which are situated in Lahore. Moreover, Punjab is perhaps the only state which suffers from this. Whatever the changing political relations between India and Pakistan, it is high time that long-term arrangements were made for exchange of scholars and archival facilities between the two countries. Also an effort should be made to xerox and microfilm the basic Punjab records at Lahore on the needed scale. The Punjabi people, I am sure, are farsighted enough to realise that the costs involved would be meagre compared to the returns. In any case, the cost would be well within the capacity of the Punjab exchequer. Joint financing with the Governments of Haryana and Himachal Pradesh can also be organized, if found necessary.

A second major source for the study of the peasant movement could have been the records of different peasant organizations. Unfortunately, they do not exist. Luckily, many of the participants in the peasant movement are still alive. A massive effort needs to be made to record their impressions on tapes. And for this purpose the net should be spread very wide. Not only the big leaders but all activists need to be covered.* In the very nature of things—it is 34 years since 1947-the matter should receive urgent attention.

*Luckily, Mridula Mukherjee has been since then able to do so on a significant scale and her work to be published soon uses interviews with the peasant activists to great advantage. Still, more institutional and personal efforts are needed.

PART II

1

Bhagat Singh and Atheism

Bhagat Singh was not only one of India's greatest freedom fighters and revolutionary socialists, but also one of its early Marxist thinkers and ideologues. Unfortunately, this last aspect is relatively unknown with the result that all sorts of reactionaries, obscurantists and communalists have been wrongly and dishonestly trying to utilize for their own politics and ideologies the name of Bhagat Singh and his comrades such as Chandra Shekhar Azad.

Bhagat Singh died young at the age of 23. His political thought and practice started evolving very early when he made a quick transition from Gandhian nationalism to revolutionary terrorism. But already by 1927-28 he began to move from revolutionary terrorism to Marxism. During the years 1925 to 1928, Bhagat Singh read voraciously, devouring in particular books on the Russian Revolution and the Soviet Union, even though getting hold of such books was in itself at the time a revolutionary and difficult task. In the 1920s, Bhagat Singh was one of the most well-read persons in India on revolutionary movements, anarchism and Marxism. He also tried to inculcate the reading and thinking habit among his fellow revolutionaries and younger comrades. He asserted during his trial before the Lahore High Court that "the sword of revolution is sharpened at the whetstone of thought". Already by the end of 1928, he and his comrades had accepted socialism as the final object of their activities' and changed the name of their organization from the Hindustan Republican Association to Hindustan Socialist Republican Association.

From now on, before his arrest in June 1929 and after, Bhagat Singh's furious march towards the acquisition and mastery of Marxism continued unabated. In the process, he brought under critical scrutiny all contemporary views, including his own, regarding the nationalist movement, the character of the contemporary world-wide revolutionary process, anarchism, socialism, violence and non-violence, revolutionary terrorism, religion, communalism, older revolutionaries and contemporary nationalists, etc.

It is one of the greatest tragedies of our people that this giant of a brain was brought to a stop so early by the colonial authorities.

In this small pamphlet* are brought before the reader two relatively unknown articles written by Bhagat Singh in jail during 1930-31, while he was awaiting the action of the gallows. In these articles, as in numerous other letters, statements and articles, he clearly emerges as a revolutionary fully committed to Marxism and capable of applying it with the full complexity of its method.

I

In the first article, Bhagat Singh deals with religion and atheism. He traces his own path to atheism though influenced in early childhood by religion and later by the early revolutionary terrorists such as Sachindra Nath Sanyal, whose book *Bandi Jivan* was a basic textbook for all revolutionaries during the 1920s. These early revolutionaries relied upon religion and mysticism to acquire the spiritual strength they revealed in their immensely courageous activities. In this article, as also in the second, Bhagat Singh shows full understanding of the approach and viewpoint of the early revolutionaries and traces the source of their religiosity. He points out that in the absence of a scientific understanding of their own political activity, they needed irrational religious beliefs and mysticism to sustain themselves spiritually, to struggle against personal temptation, to overcome depression, to be able to sacrifice their physical comforts, families and even life. When one is constantly willing to risk one's life and make all other sacrifices, a person requires deep sources of inspiration. This necessary need was, in the case of early revolutionary terrorists, met by mysticism and religion.[1] But these were no longer necessary as

---

*Bhagat Singh, *Why I am an Atheist and An Introduction to the Dreamland,* Delhi, 1979.

[1]Though not directly brought out by Bhagat Singh in these essays, they help clarify one. other important aspect-that of the difference between religion as a source of nationalist inspiration and communalism. The early revolutionaries took to religion and mysticism for inspiration and ideology, but they were not communalists. To them,

sources of inspiration for those who understood the nature of their activity, who had advanced to a revolutionary ideology, who could struggle against oppression without artificial spiritual crutches, who could confidently and without fear mount the gallows without requiring the consolation and comfort of 'eternal' salvation, who fought for freedom and emancipation of the oppressed because they "could not do otherwise".

Bhagat Singh was himself at the time waiting for the noose to fall around his neck. He knew that at such a moment it was easy to take recourse to God. "In God man can find very strong consolation and support". On the other hand, to depend on one's own inner strength was not easy. As he put it: "To stand upon one's own legs amid storms and hurricanes is not a child's play". He also knew that the task required immense moral strength and that the modem revolutionaries were following a moral path of a unique nature. This path led one to devote oneself to "the service of mankind and emancipation of the suffering humanity". This was the path followed by men and women who dared "to challenge the oppressors, exploiters, and tyrants" and who, opposing "mental stagnation", insisted on thinking for themselves. As Bhagat Singh further put it: "Criticism and independent thinking are the two indispensable qualities of a revolutionary".

Bhagat Singh points out that it is not easy to live the life of a reasoning person. It is easy to take consolation or relief from blind faith. But it is our duty to try ceaselessly to live the life of reason. And that is why Bhagat Singh asserts at the end of the essay that by proclaiming himself an atheist and a realist (materialist) he was "trying to stand like a man with an erect head to the last; even on the gallows".

---

religion was a source of inner strength and not the basis of their politics. It inspired them to become fighters for national liberation of all Indian people and not organisers of communal politics spouting hate against other sections of Indian people. While their religious and mystical beliefs led them to fight against imperialism, the communalists were often pro-imperialism subjectively and invariably served imperialism objectively by dividing the united Indian people and turning the edge of their politics against other Indians and not against imperialism.

II

In Bhagat Singh's analysis of religion and its basic causation, we get a glimpse of his powerful intellect, his revolutionary commitment and his capacity to think in a historical, materialist and scientific manner.

Religion, he notes, is not merely created by the ruling and exploiting classes to decieve the people, to legitimize their class privileges and power, and to keep the people socially quiet, though it also serves that purpose in real life and therefore it becomes an ally and instrument of these classes. But religion is much more the consequence of the inability of the primitive man to fully understand his natural environment, to understand his own social activity and social organization, and to control his own life and overcome its limitations. God then becomes a useful myth. This myth was "useful to the society in the primitive age."

Moreover, "the idea of God is helpful to man in distress". God and religion enabled the helpless individual to face life with courage. "God was brought into imaginary existence to encourage man to face boldly all the trying circumstances, to meet all dangers manfully and to check and restrain his outbursts in prosperity and affluence". "Belief softens the hardships, even can make them pleasant. In God man can find very strong consolation and support". Thus, to the distressed, the betrayed and the helpless, God serves as "a father, mother, sister and brother, friend and helper".[2]

---

[2]How close is young Bhagat Singh to the thinking of young Marx. This is what Marx wrote in 1844: "Religion is the general theory of that world, its encyclopedic compendium, its logic in a popular form, its spiriualistic *point d'honneur,* its enthusiasm, its moral sanctions, its solemn complement, its universal source of consolation and justification.... Religious distress is at the same time the *expression* of real distress and also the protest against real distress. Religion is the sigh of the oppressed creature, the heart of a heartless world, just as it is the spirit of spiritless conditions. It is the *opium* of the people. To abolish religion as the illusory happiness of the people is to demand their *real* happiness". *Collected Works,* Vol. III, 1975, pp. 175-6. Even though Bhagat Singh could not have read this passage, he understood better than most others what Marx meant when he described religion as "the opium of the people".

But, says Bhagat Singh, when science has grown and when the oppressed begin to struggle for their self-emancipation, when "man tries to stand on his own legs and become a realist (Bhagat Singh uses this word in place of rationalist and materialist)", the need for God, this artificial crutch, this imaginary saviour comes to an end. In this struggle for self-emancipation, it becomes necessary to fight against "the narrow conception of religion" as also against the belief in God. "Any man who stands for progress", says Bhagat Singh, "has to criticise, disbelieve and challenge every item of the old faith. Item by item he has to reason out every nook and comer of the prevailing faith.... A man who claims to be a realist has to challenge the whole of the ancient faith .... the first thing for him is to shatter the whole down and clear a space for the erection of a new philosophy".

III

Bhagat Singh's sympathetic though critical understanding of his predecessors, his capacity to place philosophic and political approaches and ideas in a historical setting, and his basic Marxist reasoning also emerge clearly in his discussion of several other issues.

In the second essay, *An Introduction to The Dreamland,* the poetical work of the old revolutionary Lala Ram Saran Das, sentenced to transportation for life in 1915, Bhagat Singh indirectly traces the change from the earlier 'pure' nationalism, based on the single idea of overthrowing foreign domination, to a nationalism that was simultaneously committed to the total reconstitution of the existing social order. Writing more like a poet than a political-philosophical commentator, Bhagat Singh first establishes his own generation's continuity with the old revolutionaries from whom it imbibed the spirit of nationalism, love of the people and the capacity to sacrifice. He then brings out his philosophical, political and ideological differences with them.

In the very beginning of the essay, he brings out, as already discussed in an earlier section of this introduction, the difference between their reliance on mysticism and religiosity for inspiration and his own firm commitment to materialism, reason and science.

He also deals with the contemporary and complex and vexed question of violence and non-violence. Going to the heart of the matter, he describes how the revolutionaries want to build a social order from which violence in all its forms will be eliminated, in which reason and justice will prevail and all questions will be settled by argument and education. But this is precisely what imperialists, capitalists and other exploiters will not permit. Instead, they mercilessly suppress any effort to evolve socialism through education of the people and by peaceful methods. Hence, revolutionaries have to adopt violence as "a necessary item of their programme". The entire question is brilliantly summed up when Bhagat Singh says that the revolutionaries "have to resort to violent means as a terrible necessity". Once socialist power is established, methods of education and persuasion would be employed to develop society; force would be used only to remove the obstacles.

In his essay on Atheism also he had put the issue in the same way. The new generation of revolutionaries had replaced "the Romance of the violent methods alone which was so prominent amongst our predecessors", and had come to believe that the "use of force (was) justifiable when resorted to as a matter of terrible necessity", while "non-violence as policy (was) indispensable for all mass movements". Thus the revolutionaries do not glorify violence; revolution is not based on the cult of violence. At the same time, revolutionaries do not shun the necessary violence. Where history and the ruling classes force upon them, they take recourse to it as a "terrible necessity" in order to overthrow the existing social order.

IV

Bhagat Singh simultaneously sees the utopian character of much of early revolutionary thinking, the positive historic role that utopians play in certain stages of social movements and social development, and the inevitable decline of utopias once the revolutionary movement starts acquiring a scientific outlook and philosophy on the basis of "scientific Marxian Socialism".

Bhagat Singh deals at length with one aspect of utopian thought: How to combine mental and physical labour? He accepts that elimination of the gap between the two is basic to the building of a socialist society. But this elimination, he feels, cannot be brought about by mechanical and utopian means suggested by Ram Saran Das such as making all mental workers do physical and mental labour for 4 hours a day. The nature of physical and mental labour is different. The root of the problem lies in the existing inequality between the two. The answer lies in treating both as productive labour and opposing the notion that mental workers are superior to manual workers.

V

Lastly, Bhagat Singh was a critical revolutionary in the best traditions of Marx, Engels and Lenin. Asking young men to read *The Dreamland,* he warns: "Do not read it to follow blindly and take for granted what is written in it. Read it, criticise it, think over it, and try to formulate your own ideas with its help".

2

Congress Socialist Party, 1934-48

Emerging as a political force in the early 1930s, the Congress Socialist Party (CSP) came to play a significant role in the Indian national movement. In particular, it contributed to the movement's socio-economic radicalism and political militancy. Along with other left-wing individuals, groups and parties, it succeeded in making socialism the accepted creed of the youth of India during the 1930s and 1940s. Within the National Congress the left was able to command influence over one-third votes on important issues. Yet, there is no well-researched history of the CSP. Dr Girja Shankar's study*, based on extensive use of published and unpublished sources, fills in this lacuna.

Dr Girja Shankar has traced at length the formation and growth of the CSP. In the early 1930s, the move towards the formation of a socialist party was made in the jails during 1930-31 and 1932-34 by those who were dissatisfied with the Gandhian strategy, tactics and leadership. Many of the founders of the CSP were active in the youth movements of the 1920s. Almost all of them had joined the Civil Disobedience Movement during 1930-31 and 1932-33. They were disillusioned by the Gandhi-Irwin Pact in 1931—many of them opposed the Pact at the Karachi session of the Congress—and felt frustrated by the successful suppression by the Government of the second phase of the movement. In jail they got the time to study and discuss Marxian and other socialist ideas. They looked for an alternative to Gandhism and liberal nationalism. Revolutionary terrorism had already declined. Attracted by Marxism, Soviet Union and Communism, they did not find themselves

---

*Girja Shankar, *Socialist Trends* in *Indian National Movement,* Meerut, 1987.

in agreement with the current political line of the Communist Party of India. Many individuals and groups were groping towards an alternative. Ultimately they came together and formed the Congress Socialist Party at Bombay on 22 October 1934.

From the beginning, all Congress Socialists were agreed upon four basic propositions—and perhaps on nothing else—that the primary struggle in India was the national struggle for freedom; that they must work inside the National Congress because it was the premier body leading the national struggle and, as Acharya Narendra Dev put it in 1934, "it would be a suicidal policy for us to cut ourselves off from the national movement that the Congress undoubtedly represents"; that they must give the Congress and the national movement a socialist direction; and that to achieve this objective they must organize the workers and peasants in their class organizations and make them the social base of the anti-imperialist struggle.

There were differences among the founders of the CSP on the character of the Congress. Some saw it as a bourgeois organization; others as a broad mass organization whose leadership was "predominantly bourgeois"; a few described the leadership as "petty bourgeois". But all of them agreed that the Congress as constituted had failed to evolve a radical economic programme and was incapable of leading the masses to higher forms and stages of anti-imperialist struggle. The CSP, therefore, from the beginning assigned itself the task of transformation of the Congress and strengthening it. The task of transformation of the Congress was understood in two senses. One was the ideological sense. Congressmen were to be gradually persuaded to adopt a socialist vision of independent India and a more radical pro-labour and pro-peasant stand on current social and economic issues. Moreover, this ideological and programmatic transformation was to be seen as a process and not as an event. As Jayaprakash Narayan repeatedly told his followers in 1934: "We are placing before the Congress a programme and we want the Congress to accept it. If the Congress does not accept it, we do not say we are going out of the Congress. If today we fail, tomorrow we will try and if tomorrow we fail, we will try again."

The transformation of the Congress was also seen in terms of changes in its leadership at the top. Initially, the task was seen in terms of the displacement of the existing leadership, which it was believed was incapable of developing "within the framework of its conception and interests the struggle of the masses to a higher level". The CSP was to develop as the nucleus of the alternative socialist leadership. As the

Meerut Thesis of the CSP put it, the task was to "wean the anti-imperialist elements in the Congress away from its present bourgeois leadership and to bring them under the leadership of revolutionary socialism". But, as Dr. Girja Shankar shows, this perspective was soon found to be unrealistic and was abandoned in favour of a 'composite' leadership in which Socialists would be taken into the leadership at all levels. The notion of alternate left leadership twice came up for realisation in Tripuri in 1939 and at Ramgarh in 1940. But having supported Subhas Bose in the election to the Congress presidency, when it came to splitting the Congress leadership on a left-right basis and giving the Congress a left-wing leadership, the CSP shied away. Its leadership realized that such an effort would not only weaken the national movement but isolate the left from the mainstream, that the Indian people could be mobilised into a movement only under Gandhiji's leadership, and that, in fact, there was at the time no alternative to Gandhiji's leadership—a fact which the right wing in India did fully realize. The CSP leadership, as also the leadership of other left parties and groups, were not able to fully theorize this understanding and so they went back again and again to the notion of alternative leadership. The CSP was better grounded in the reality of Indian situation. 'Therefore, whenever it came to the crunch, it gave up its theoretical position and adopted a realistic approach close to that of Jawaharlal Nehru's. This earned it condemnation of the other left-wing groups and parties-for example, in 1939 for their 'betrayal' of Subhas Bose. At such moments, the Socialists defended themselves and revealed flashes of an empircist understanding of Indian reality. Jayaprakash Narayan, for example, said in 1939 after Tripuri:

"We Socialists do not want to create factions in the Congress and to establish rival leadership. We are only concerned with the policy and programme of the Congress. We only want to influence the Congress decisions. Whatever our differences with the old leaders, we do not want to quarrel with them. We all want to march shoulder to shoulder in our common fight against imperialism."

The right wing of the Congress carried on a multi-sided struggle against the left, including the CSP. Dr. Girja Shankar deals at length with the mutual struggle between the CSP and the right-wing Congress leaders. It becomes apparent that the right wing had a big advantage over the CSP leadership—it showed both ideological and tactical flexibility. It readily accommodated the left at organizational as well as programmatic levels opposing it only at the ideological plane. It was willing to accept Socialists and other left-wing leaders at all leadership levels from the Working Committee downwards. It gradually accepted large parts of the left stand on concrete issues from land reforms to foreign policy. The left could have met its challenge only by following an equally complex and subtle approach towards the right wing. But it tried to oppose the right with simplistic formulae and radical rhetoric. It was invariably worsted in any serious confrontation. For example, its most serious charge against the Congress right wing was that it wanted to "compromise" with imperialism, that it was frightened of mass struggle, that its anti-imperialism was not wholehearted because of bourgeios influence over it. The right wing had little difficulty in disposing off such charges. The maturity of the right wing and the immaturity of the CSP leadership is very lucidly brought out by Dr Girja Shankar in the last phase after 1945 when the CSP was gradually manoeuvred into leaving the Congress. At this time, the CSP had the advantage of having Gandhiji's full support. But the CSP leaders once again developed a simple formula: the Congress was developing from a movement into a party; a party can have only one class content or character—either bourgeois or socialist—and since the Congress was not socialist it had become a full-blooded bourgeois party; and hence the Socialists must leave it. They were of course right in seeing the transformation of the Congress into a party as also its increasing domination by bourgeois elements. But what the Socialists failed to see was that this reverse transformation of the Congress was also bound to be a process and not an event. Gandhiji backed the Socialists at this stage, but he constantly advised and urged them to remain and function within the Congress and to increase their influence within it by hard grass-roots level work and not look at the problem from the organizational angle. The CSP leadership failed to heed the advice and fought on the question whether the Congress would permit them to function within it as a separate party with its separate organization and discipline. They failed to see that the right wing was on solid ground on this question—the Socialists own experience in the 1930s to let a party function within a party should have made them see the good sense in the right wing stand. It is debatable whether the socialist movement in India would have gained if the Socialists had stayed in the Congress after independence. But the grounds for staying or leaving should have been debated on a different terrain.

Socialists and Gandhiji developed in time a close and complex relationship. Starting with the project of declaring "war on Gandhian ideas" and exposure of the theory of non-violent struggle for social and political transformation and of Gandhiji' s role as the spokesperson of the bourgeoisie, most of the Socialists ended up as admirers of Gandhian methods and of Gandhiji's "basic and increasing radical commitment." Gandhiji too over the years found himself more and more in agreement with the Socialists on socio-economic issues. In fact, it was only on the issue of non-violence and their 'unreal' and 'bombastic' style that he disagreed with them. Dr. Girja Shankar has made a thorough study of this fascinating relationship between Gandhiji and Socialists throughout this work.

The CSP was started with a basic commitment to unite all left-wing groups and parties into a single united party or at least a united front of all left-wing elements. In pursuit of this objective the CSP opened its doors to the Communists and Royists and tried to develop close working relationship with Jawaharlal Nehru and Subhas Bose. In no other field or endeavour did the CSP suffer greater frustration. Royists could not remain within it; the Communists and Socialists soon became sworn enemies; Nehru could not be incorporated into the CSP, nor would Nehru even coordinate his politics with those of the CSP; Bose and the Socialists could no longer work together after 1939-40.

The relationship of the CSP with other left groups and individuals, and especially with the Communists, is a virtually unresearched subject, though it has, of course, aroused a great deal of heat and passion and polemics among the participants, with each side blaming the other. Dr. Girja Shankar has made a beginning in this direction and provided material for a scientific discussion of the subject. The basic weakness, it seems to me, was the dual conception of the CSP as a party within the Congress and as a broad-front within which other organized parties and groups could function. The Congress could function as such a party because of its character as a popular mass movement which was organizationally loosely structured. It was not possible for the CSP to so function unless its leadership abandoned the role of a party or group with its own structure, leadership and discipline, that is, unless it agreed to be just an ideological current which would provide cover to the underground activities of other left parties and groups and act as a recruiting ground for them. The CSP leadership saw the party in its first role, as the nucleus of a cadre-based socialist party; Royists, Communists and others saw it as performing the second role. It was therefore inevitable that they felt that. it was legitimate to do 'fraction work' inside it, and, to quote M.N. Roy, to absorb its "real proletarian elements in his own party". The CSP leadership, on the other hl\9d, declared such 'fraction work' to be a betrayal of its trust in the others. The flaw was in the very conception that a Marxist-Leninist party could act as a box within another larger box which was another Marxist-Leninist party! The inevitable result of such an absurd experiment was the disastrous long-term schism between a Socialist Party which suffered from an anti-Communist phobia and a Communist Party which saw every Socialist leader as a potential bourgeios or even American agent.

Dr Girja Shankar has traced and analysed the evolution of the CSP's ideology at great length and with deep insights. He has shown how from the beginning the party's leadership was ideologically divided into three ideological currents: the Marxian, the Fabian and the current influenced by Gandhiji. This would not have been a major weakness for a broad socialist party which was a movement. But the CSP was already a party within a movement. Moreover, the Marxism of the 1930s was incapable of accepting as legitimate such diversity of political currents on the left. The result was a confusion which plagued the party till the very end. The differences were papered over for a long time because of the personal bonds among most of the founding leaders of the party, the acceptance of Acharya Narendra Dev and Jayaprakass Narayan as its senior leaders, and the existence of "a strong undercurrent of nationalist feeling" in the party.

Despite the ideological diversity among the leaders, the party as a whole accepted Marxism as its basic ideological lodestar. Though with all sorts of added qualifications, Marxism was to remain the guiding creed of the CSP till 1948. Gradually, however, large doses of Gandhian and liberal democratic thought were to become basic elements of the CSP leardership's thinking. This was, however, not to prevent the CSP from throughout having a strong dogmatic strain, or, in the words of Dr. Girja Shankar, "doctrinal approach to politics". For one, the Socialists were at one with other leftists in failing to make a deep study of Indian reality. They continued to see the dominant Congress leadership as bourgeois, its policy of negotiations as working towards a 'compromise' with imperialism, and any resort to constitutional work as a step towards the "abandonment of the struggle for independence". They took recourse to a simplistic model of analysing Indian social classes and their political behaviour. Their approach towards communalism. was principled but economistic. They chose to fight the right wing not on questions of ideology but on methods of struggle and such issues as office acceptance, collective affiliation of the trade unions and kisan sabhas to the Congress, and the record of the Congress

Ministries. They saw all efforts to guide the national movement in a disciplined manner as imposing restraints on the movement. They constantly counterpoised armed struggle to non-violence as a superior form and method of struggle even while accepting non-violence in practice. They were convinced that the masses were ever ready for struggle, if only the leaders were willing to give a call. Above all they failed to grasp the Gandhian strategy of struggle. Consequently, they invariably fought the dominant Congress leadership on wrong issues and when it came to a crunch were forced to trail behind that leadership lest they were isolated from the mass of Indian people.

This became clear thrice: in 1936-37 on the issue of elections and office acceptance under the 1935 Act, which was seen in terms of a compromise with imperialism; in 1939-42 on the issue of initiation of a mass movement, when Gandhiji' s reluctance was seen as the missing of a golden opportunity; and in 1945-47 on the question of negotiations for the transfer of power, which were seen as British imperialism's last ditch effort to prolong their domination. Moreover, they saw the first post-1947 Congress Government as an already fully structured bourgeios government and the Congress Party as an integrated bourgeois party. The only comfort that a CSP leader can now derive from these instances of a totally wrong reading of the situations is that the other party of the left in India, the Communist Party, was one with them and even ahead of them in all these instances.

The Socialists paid a heavy price for their dogmatic understanding of reality. They had emerged as shiny heroes from the Quit India Movement. They had the blessings of Gandhiji. They had adopted a more or less correct approach towards the partition issue. And yet, in a few years time, the party had been split, many of its leaders had retired from politics, and the party had become an institution of the past-today even the name of the Socialist Party does not exist.

It is one of the major enigmas of modem India as to why did a party with such great promise come to nought. The party had everything 'going' for it. It had prestigious leaders. It was able to establish a strong and integral relationship with contemporary nationalism and the national movement. Despite zig-zags, it did arrive, at least pragmatically, at a correct grasp of most issues. It functioned in an open manner and freely debated issues. A perusal of Dr. Girja Shankar's work would enable a student of history to find some of the answers. Perhaps the one single answer lies in the immaturity anti ineptness of the leadership. It seems that the calibre of a leadership is a crucial determinant of the fate of a movement or a party. It seems from Dr. Girja Shankar's work that it was perhaps a great tragedy for the CSP that one mature leader that it had—namely, Acharya Narendra Dev—could not play an active guiding role in the party because of his personality, termperament and health.

Dr. Girja Shankar's pioneering work has many merits. But none is weightier than its objectivity. It is usual for a writer to unduly favour or castigate the person or party whose biographer he or she is. Dr. Girja Shankar has avoided this pitfall and presented us with a work which can be used by others to build alternative hypotheses if they so desire. I have great pleasure in recommending to the reader this work which will be indispensable to any student of the history of the left and of the national movement in the 1930s and 1940s.

3

Some Reflections on Maoism in India

Dr. Shantha Sinha's brilliant work* is the first detailed study of the concrete Maoist movement-also popularly known as the Naxalite movement-in a major region and based on detailed documentation, a firm grasp of the ideological, strategic and tactical issues involved, and a sympathetic though not uncritical approach.

Maoist movement, initiated in Naxalbari in West Bengal in 1967, represented a dramatic development which held centre of the stage for nearly a decade for thousands of left-wing youth and a section of the intelligentsia. The movement caught the imagination of and inspired immense devotion and a sense of sacrifice among lakhs of rural and urban youth in large parts of the country. It carries on in old as well as new forms till this day in Bihar and Andhra Pradesh and in small pockets in all parts of India. It is important from the point of view both of contemporary history and of present day politics to understand it and to critically assimilate its meaning. Dr. Sinha's work is bound to be an important input into this effort.

I

Dr. Sinha relates at length the events which constituted the Maoist movement in different parts of Andhra during its different phases and under the leadership of different individuals and groups. She describes the advances and retreats of the movement, its different programmes and policies, the social groups on which it was based, the issues that it took up, the forms of mobilization and struggle it used and the. strategy and tactics it employed, the changing government

*Shantha Sinha, *Maoisls in Andhra Pradesh,* New Delhi, 1989.

policy towards it and the theoretical and ideological debates which tended to unite or divide different Maoist groups. In the process, Dr. Sinha makes us familiar with the leaders of the movement at different levels, especially the little known squad leaders who became the local heroes.

In the initial chapter, Dr. Sinha deals with the development of the Maoist trend in Bengal and the rest of India within the ranks of the CPI(M). The breaking point came when in 1967 the Naxalbari peasant uprising broke out under the two CPI(M) leaders, Charu Majumdar and Kanu Sanyal, who declared that they were implementing Mao Ze Dong's ideas (Maoism) in Indian conditions and who visualized the rapid spread of agrarian revolution based on peasant guerilla struggle leading to the formation of a People's Liberation Army and the overthrow of the Indian State. On the international plane, they declared that the Soviet Union was undergoing capitalitst restoration, collaborating with US imperialism, serving as its agent and intriguing with the USA against revolutionary China. Unwilling to let any local constituent overstep the party's overall strategy, however strong the local feelings and justified its actions, the CPI(M) leadership expelled the Naxalbari leaders from the party and, being incharge of the Home portfolio, ordered full scale police action against Naxalbari rebels for having taken to violent forms of political action. Charu Majumdar and many other dissident leaders, in turn, declared that the CPI(M) leadership was curbing the revolutionary energies of the masses and the rising crescendo of revolutionary upsurge in the *country.* They accused it of having become class collaborationist and revisionist and having fallen prey to parliamentarianism. Many of the CPI(M) middle-level leaders and cadres now separated from the party, formed a coordination committee and then founded the CPI(Maoist-Leninist) (ML).

Dr. Sinha goes on to discuss the emergence of the Maoist trend in Andhra, leading to nearly 50 per cent of the leaders and cadres leaving the CPI(M) and forming the Andhra Pradesh Revolutionary Communist Committee (APRCC) in 1968.

In the next chapter, Dr. Sinha examines the important political, ideological and tactical differences between the CPI(ML) and the Bengal Maoists and the APRCC of Andhra Maoists. According to the Bengal Maoists the situation in the country was "ripe for a revolution, a revolutionary mass upsurge existed and the people were fully politically conscious and even prepared to take part in revolution immediately". What was needed was "courageous and determined leadership".

Furthermore, "militant struggle must be carrried on not for land, crops, etc., but for seizure of state power." The seizure of state power through armed struggle was on the immediate agenda.

The Andhra Maoists agreed with much of the basic thrust of Bengal Maoists' analysis and programme. Russia had gone revisionist and was going over to capitalism; Indian independence was formal-India was in reality a nee-colony: the Indian bourgeoisie was comprador and was allied to feudalism; India was in the midst of a deep economic and political crisis; Indian revolution was on the agenda and was to be achieved through armed struggle or people's war to be based on guerilla struggle by the peasantry. The Andhra Maoists, however, had also a basic difference with the Bengal Maoists; despite the economic and political crisis of the ruling classes and the complete disillusionment of the masses, conditions were not yet ready for immediate armed revolt all over the country. In a vast country like India, because of uneven development, different tactics would have to be followed in different parts of the country, and people would have to be carefully prepared for a protracted people's war. Consequently, an immediate call for armed struggle could not be given. "Armed struggle for liberation could only be an end-product of a series of struggles by the peasantry against feudal oppression." There were also, as Dr. Sinha brings out, differences among the Andhra and Bengal Maoists over party organization, forms and issues of popular mobilization, and nature of the united front of various classes to be mobilized. One result was that APRCC was after some time denounced by the CPI(ML) as "enemies of liberation" and "last reserves of reaction". This led to some sections leaving the APRCC and accepting the leadership of the CPI(ML) and Charu Majumdar.

In the fourth chapter Dr. Sinha traces with master strokes and telling narrative the progress of the communist-led mass movement in the Srikakularn district of Andhra Pradesh during the years from 1957 to 1967. The tribal people of the district were suffering from a constantly deteriorating economic and social position and subjected to increasing exploitation and oppression by moneylenders and traders. The communist workers organised *sanghams* (unions or associations). and over the years led series of agitations and movements against *vetti* (forced labour), for higher wages against forest contractors, against the corruption and high-handedness of revenue, excise and forest officials and finally against landlords for fair rents. They also worked for social reforms and participated in panchayati and assembly elections. They succeeded in a large measure in installing a sense of self-respect, dignity and self-confidence among the tribal people.

In time, however, the movement in Srikakulam entered a stage of stagnation. It faced intense repression by the police; one evidence of this was the involvement of over 600 *sang ham* members in police cases in 1964 and the killing of some 70 activists from 1952 to 1968 in Srikakulam and Telengana areas. How was the movement to overcome this impasse? The dominant tendency was to opt for greater militancy. Most of the Srikakulam communist leaders ended up in 1968 in the CPI(ML) and with Charu Majumdar around the line of raising the movement to the higher stage of armed guerilla struggle. Starting out with armed squads, the leaders hoped to create a people's army and a liberated zone. They ended up along with the CPI(ML) leadership with the tactic of individual annihilation of class enemies, i.e., landlords, moneylenders, police informers and policemen. Initially *Ryutu sanghams,* youth associations, etc., were organised on a significant scale. In many of the initial acts of armed resistance or seizure of crops of the landlords and occupation of temple lands, etc., large mass of villagers were involved; but later a shift to pure squad actions was made. The movement also remained confined to the tribal people of the Agency areas who constituted slightly more than 8 per cent of the district's population. Finally, during 1969-70 the Government was able to suppress the movement, killing most of its leaders. The movement was, however, able to make major economic and social gains.

Dr. Sinha discusses in great detail the organizational structure and the working of Maoist armed squads. Her conclusions in this respect relate to the failure of the leaders of the Srikakulam movement to face up to the reality of the movement on the ground, to mobilize the masses in their armed actions, to guage correctly the lack of people's preparedness for armed struggle, and to assess correctly the capacity of the Indian state to suppress violent protest or struggle. Whenever the movement was curbed by state repression, instead of making a reassessment of their basic assumptions, the leaders responded only by modifying their tactics or took recourse to such simple formulations as "the more there is repression on the people, the greater is their strength", or that vis-a-vis the police "the guerilla having people's support and sympathy and capable of conducting mobile warfare had an upper hand" or that repression would "isolate the Government from the people and also enable us first to identify our real friends since at this moment one is forced to choose one's sides". The consequence was that, as Dr. Sinha points out, they were inexorably drawn towards adopting a more and more extreme stance,leading to "alienation from the masses".

In chapters six and seven, Dr. Sinha takes up the Maoist movement in Telengana area of Andhra Pradesh where the Maoists followed different policy, tactics and programme based on a different assessment of the situation. She traces the growth of the Maoist ideas in Andra CPI(M) partially to the party's failure on the electoral front. The APRCC grew rapidly but then gradually split into several groups especially under the pressure of the popularity and glamour of the Srikakulam movement, the CPI(ML) and Charu Majumdar.

The Andhra Maoists under the APRCC leadership followed in the initial years the line of partial struggles leading to a graduated and protracted struggle. For historical reasons the movement was not able to take off in Coastal and Rayalseema districts of Andhra Pradesh but it grew in the forest areas of Telengana where tribal population was concentrated. Here popular mass movements were built around such issues as occupation of *banjar* (fallow) land and land seized by landlords in recent years, struggle against *vetti* (forced labour), wage struggles of agricultural labourers and corruption of and oppression by forest and other officials.

The perspective was that of raising the political and revolutionary consciousness of the masses through "a process of economic and political struggles" leading to the exposure of the true character of the state and development of political armed struggle for the overthrow of the rulers. Nor was guerilla struggle the only form of struggle, though it remained the main form of struggle. The objective, of course, remained the development of guerilla zones and then a liberated area.

The movement led by the APRCC faced two major pressures: one was the popularity of the Srikakulam movement and the other the increasing oppression by the police. How was the mass movement to develop further or even maintain itself? The only answer, it appeared to the leadership, was for the party to form into armed squads to defend themselves and the people from the landlords and the police. The cadres too were pressing for arms and armed defence. The leadership was forced to adopt a more and more militant line though initially for defensive purposes. At the same time there were several splits in the party. The armed struggle programme soon collapsed in all areas except the forest areas inhabited by the tribal people. Moreover, under police pressure the revolutionaries were soon isolated from the masses. The APRCC reorganized its activities after July 1970 around a programme of popular agitations, political education and land occupation though the programme of creating armed squads and liberated zones remained the long term objective.

The APRCC began to split up around 1971, the lead being now taken by Chandra Pulla Reddy (CP) who advocated the more militant line of the simultaneous launching of militant mass movements for land distribution and armed struggle. CP was able to carry most of the Maoists with him. Since then the Maoist movement has continued in Andhra Pradesh till this day, though in an attenuated form. The main reason for this, according to Dr. Sinha, was the failure of the Maoists to broaden the mass base of their movement. On the other hand, often their tactical line led to the narrowing down of their base. Question, of course, still remains: could mass work and reliance on the masses have been combined with armed squad action in Indian conditions?

In the last two chapters, Dr. Sinha discusses the break-up of the CPI(ML) after the death of Charu Majumdar in 1972 and the state of the Maoist movement during the Emergency and the post-Emergency years. In particular she deals with the strategy and policies of the CP group and the CPI(ML), People's War Group led by Kondapalli Seetaramiah (KS) and the activities of the cultural groups, student unions and civil liberty organizations aligned with the Maoist groups.

II

There were major areas of 'darkness' in the fierce debates among the Maoist groups. None of them took note of or examined the development of capitalism in India. The assumption remained that capitalism could not develop in the period of the general crisis of capitalism especially if the class which could develop it was comprador. The comprador character of Indian capitalism, that is, its subordination to imperialist capital, was treated as a self-evident maxim. The entire trend towards the development of independent capitalism both before and after independence was ignored or denied. The only option before Indian capitalism, it was suggested, was to be dominated by British or US capital or by 'Soviet Imperialism'—unless, that is, it joined the people's democratic front led by the working class.

Similarly, the changes in agrarain structure being introduced from above were ignored as was also the existing as well as the growing class differentiation in the countryside. In practice, of course, it became impossible for political workers working deep among the people to do so. Consequently, as has been well brought out by Dr. Sinha, in several areas and phases of the movement the interests of the agricultural labourers and poor peasants were defended and promoted against rich peasants, and not only against landlords and moneylenders. But all this found no reflection in theory where the struggle was still seen to be between peasantry and feudal classes.

The Maoists also ignored any detailed discussion of the character of the Indian state, critical differences between the Indian state and society and the state and society in pre-liberation China or Vietnam (something which the 1951 CPI policy documents had recognized), the role of democracy and reforms in the functioning of the Indian state, its basic strength, etc. The state as well as the political and economic structure in India were assumed to be in a perpetual crisis—'tottering' as the pharse went. Similarly, the only reaction to state suppression of their efforts at revolution through squad activity or individual annihilations was to condemn the suppression of civil liberties or the 'fascist' character of the state rather than examination of their basic paradigm of taking to violence in a basically civil libertarian society marked by class domination and class violence.

Also left severely alone were such questions as the role of hegemony in the political system and forms of its legitimization, role of violence in a democratic society, relative autonomy of the state, relation between a party and a class, nature of the ruling classes and the relation of the different social classes and strata to the state, the possibility of a small minority making a revolution under modern conditions and in a modern democratic country though a bourgeois one, and so on. Nor did the Maoists ask why were their movements successful only among the tribal people who were not yet fully hegemonised and integrated into the system as was the rest of the population. They did not discuss in any serious manner even the setbacks to their movements or even raise the question: why could the police succeed in suppressing them? It is interesting and important that none of the successive Maoist groups questioned the basic CPI (MI.) characterization of the state, economy and society in India.

It was particularly important to reexamine the entire Bolshevik and Chinese Maoist paradigms as applied to democratic and civil libertarian politics. After all the failure to make or even initiate revolutions had occurred not only in India. In nearly 50 years of its existence (till 1967) Bolshevism had not succeeded in even attempting a revolution in any democratic polity. A critical reading and application of the writings of Marx, Lenin, Mao Ze Dong and Gramsci would have proved extremely fruitful. This would have of course led to a total rethinking of the role of violence and non-violence and of the past strategies of revolution in democratic, semi-democratic or even non-democratic societies. In particular there was the need to rethink the equation of violence with the working class, the peasantry and revolution and of non-violence with the bourgeoisie, landlords and the maintenance of the status quo. The Grarnscian proposition of war of position or trench-warfare had also to be examined in this context.

There were of course no simple answers. As soon as radical political workers committed to organizing the masses to defend and enforce and extend their legal rights enabled or led the masses to do so, the exploiting classes in the countryside hit back, often through violent means. The police and bureaucracy sided with the latter. Often the judiciary too did so. But even when a case was won in the court, the verdict could not be enforced in the field. The militant among the rural poor were beaten up (or even killed in rare cases) by the rural rich often with the connivance of the police. The normal reaction was to hit back at the rural rich and their defenders, the police. What other way was there? This is where a real innovation or theoretical and practical-political-organizational breakthrough was needed. The choice was either to go on to some form of counter-violence through squads, annihilations, etc., leading to armed struggle and revolution, or to mobilize the people in non-violent struggles, learn to take a beating in order to advance in the long run by compelling the ruling classes to pay a heavy price for violent acts in the form of loss of their hegemony (after all armed struggle also makes one learn to take in one's stride losses in life and property and even defeats), build wide movements in defence of popular rights, form civil liberties unions, organize newspaper campaigns, *bandhs, hartals,* morchas and demonstrations and to agitate in the assemblies and the Parliament. Both paths were exclusive of each other. It was not possible to combine the two in the name of combining the legal and the illegal. Both required major theoretical and organizational efforts.

All the questions raised above indicate the need not so much to apply Marxism or Leninism or Mao Ze Dong Thought to Indian conditions as to develop Marxism in the context of the new Indian and world conditions. It is a tragedy that the Maoists as also other Indian communists were not even aware of the task.

One way of opening up the possibilities of such basic thinking would have been to make a critical analysis of the past of the Indian communist movement. But none of the Indian communist parties and groups have so far made any effort in that direction, The Maoists also did not undertake the task. In view of their commitment to armed struggle, it was necessary to examine why did the CPI, starting with analysis similar to theirs in 1948-49 and then 1951, end up with the Amritsar Thesis of the possibility of peaceful transition to socialism, or why have the united CPI and its offshoots, the CPI and the CPI(M), not taken even once to any form of armed struggle since 1951 even though they, particularly the CPI(M), are committed to armed struggle in the final phase for the capture of state power. The only reason assigned for this by the Maoists was reformism of the leaders of the CPI and their betrayal. It Was assumed that the communist leaders of the 1950s-A.K. Ghosh, P. Sundarayya, E.M.S.Namboodiripad, S.A. Dange, C. Rajeshwara Rao, Harkishan Singh Surjeet, Basavapunniah and others were made of inferior stuff than Charu Majumdar, Kanu Sanyal, D.V. Rao, T. Nagi Reddy, Chandra Pulla Reddy, and others. Except juvenile romanticism there was no historical or theoretical 'truth' or usefulness in this ascription. This need to analyse the past and the road leading from armed struggle in 1948 to Amritsar in 1957 was not realized even by those who were giving up immediate and permanent armed struggle in favour of mass organizations, mass movements, partial struggle, raising of the revolutionary consciousness of the masses and making preparations for future armed struggle. After all, they were doing exactly what the CPI leaders had done in 1951 and after. Some leaders like the CPI(ML) People's War Group, led by Kondapalli Seetharamiah (KS) did see the similarity; but not wanting to travel down the old road, they stuck to modified armed struggle strategy. Similarly, those who have criticized the Maoists have not asked whether the rise and growth of Maoism was not the result of the type of Marxism and political militancy which they themselves—and the communist movement-have practised and represented as the quintessence of revolutionariness.

In fact, the rich experience of the Maoist movement should enable the forces of socialism to draw important theoretical and strategic conclusions; otherwise I have a bitter feeling that the adage that those who refuse to analyse the past are condemned to reliving it would continue to apply to them. All those who want to make a basic analysis of the past of the communist movement in India or who want to learn from the past will find in Dr. Sinha's work an indispensable tool.

4

Lakshman Naik—A Legendary Nationalist from Orissa

I have great pleasure in introducing Dr. Nihar Ranjan Patnaik's fascinating study of Lakshman Naik*. Over the last 30 years or so, several major studies of the all-India leaders of the Indian National Movement have been published. But the study of local-level leaders has been relatively neglected. Yet the movement acquired its striking power primarily from its grass-roots components led and organised by local leaders.

The Indian national movement was a many splendoured movement encompassing the political activity of the diverse Indian people. The tribal people in different regions of India played a significant role in its mass phase after 1918. Lakshman Naik's role was to make him a legendary figure in Orissa, and he deserves to be known in the rest of our country. Dr. Patnaik's study fulfills the need.

Dr. Patnaik fully brings out the social and physical setting of Lakshman Naik's endeavours in the Koraput area in general ana the more specific taluk of Malkanagiri. Malkanagiri was a part of the Jeypore estate, which administered the tribal and non-tribal population through the village heads known as Mustadars or Naiks who helped the Raja's officials collect the land revenue.

Apart from the revenue demand of the Raja and exploitation by the Mustadars, the tribal and non-tribal peasants were crushed under the triple burden of *goti, bethi* and *gudam-terms* properly defined in Dr.Patnaik's study. Furthermore the traditional rights of the peasants over forest produce and forest use were gradually eroded.

---

*Nihar Ranjan Patnaik, *Lakshman Naik-A Study in Tribal Patriotism*, Bhubaneswar, 1992.

Lakshman Naik was born on 22 November 1899 in the family of a tribal Mustadar in the village Tentuligumma. What is more important, he was heir to a prolonged tradition of rebellion both against the colonial authorities and the local rajas and chieftains. The Koya revolt of 1879 became a part of the recent historical memory of the people of Malkanagiri while the Bastar uprising of 1910-1911 inspired the young Lakshman. The Rampa rebellion led by Alluri Sitaram Raju during the 1920s had a direct bearing on the political formation of the youthful Lakshman. One of the participants in the Rampa rebellion, Chandra Kutia, became a friend of his. Perhaps the idea of acquiring the *Desari* traits of acting as a priest, medicineman and astrologer to his people to acquire roots among them was adopted from Sitaram Raju's practice. He also gradually acquired a competent knowledge of Oriya.

Lakshman Naik succeeded his father as a Mustadar in 1930, but he was not happy with the position. He continued to work on his land along with his relatives. Moreover, he worked even more actively for the welfare of the tribal peasants under his jurisdiction, undertaking measures such as the widening of roads and digging of drains and helping them avoid the clutches of the moneylenders. But he was apalled at the treatment meted out to the rural people by revenue inspectors and forest guards, and he had to tolerate it all as a silent bystander.

And, then, a new turn in his life came in the 1930s when, as Dr. Patnaik brings out so well, the overall framework and climate of his activities came to be provided by the national movement and the Indian National Congress. The Congress came to Koraput in the heady days of the Anti-Simon Commission Movement. Led by Radhakrishna Biswasray, who resigned his job in the Government, the movement took off in Koraput and struck deep roots. Many from the area participated in the Civil Disobedience campaign.

Lakshman Naik came into contact With Congressmen when in 1930 he attended a meeting of Congress workers in Malkanagiri and decided to join the Congress as a regular four-anna member. The Congress became highly popular in the region especially among the tribal and non-tribal poor, and Lakshman played an active role in this. This led to his becoming the President of the Primary Congress Committee of Tentuligumma and a member of the Koraput District Congress Committee.

Lakshman was determined to playa full and all-sided role in the national movement. He was also inspired by Gandhiji and his ideas of constructive work. In December 1937 he joined the 3 month-long Naupat training camp for constructive workers. The camp put special emphasis on the propagation of Khadi..

The Naupat Camp left an abiding impact on Lakshman Naik. Inspired by non-violence, he now gave up hunting and meat-eating. He also became more active in doing political work among the people wandering from village to village, walking "through dense forests and mountains" and swimming "across rivers." This phase of his grass-roots political work has been discussed at length by Dr. Patnaik, who also brings out the nature and content of political agitation at the popular plane among the tribal people.

Lakshman Naik also led numerous local struggles around people's day-to-day demands and problems such as the practice of illegal tax collection at market places, petty oppression by the Raja's employees and large-scale sale of liquor, opium and other narcotic drugs. He also led a major no-tax campaign in his area. This lei to his being deprived of his position as a Mustadar and the land assignment that went with the position. The people rewarded him by calling him "the Gandhi of Malkanagiri".

Lakshman was an active participant in the Individual Satyagraha Movement of 1940-41. He courted imprisonment twice. It was, however, in the Quit India Movement of 1942 that he achieved his height as a patriot and a leader.

The failure of the Cripps Mission in April 1942 led to frustration . and anger among the Indian people. Inspired by Gandhiji, they now began to move towards the final assault on the alien regime. Active political and ideological preparations began all over the country. Orissa and Koraput were in the forefront of these preparations. On 31 July, the Congress workers of Koraput including Lakshman Naik met at Jeypore and discussed the preparations for the corning struggle.

As soon as the news of the arrest of Gandhiji and other Congress leaders on 9th August reached Orissa, the people of Orissa erupted. In the Malkanagiri area the popular outburst was led by Lakshman Naik who organised several massive protests. As a result of one of his mass actions—the massive attack on the police station at Matili—the police arrested Lakshman and framed him for murder. Lakshman was to die a martyr's death at the hands of the colonial administration and pass into a legend. His was a life fulfilled. Dr. Patnaik has narrated this last heroic episode in the life of Lakshman Naik in graphic details. He has also reproduced at length the poems composed at the time of Lakshman's martyrdom as also later.

One of the determinants of a people's calibre is the treatment that the later generations accord to their great daughters and sons who have spent their lives in the service of the people. Dr. Patnaik's is a highly praiseworthy effort to bring alive before the people of India the life of one of its most outstanding sons.

5

Ravi Narayan Reddy

Most of us, along with the rest of the country, came to know Ravi Narayan Reddy when he got elected as a member of the Parliament in 1952 with the. largest majority in the country, polling over 3 lakh votes. Along with my colleagues, I had the privilege of interviewing him at length during July 1984. I had, of course, earlier read several of his party notes and his illuminating work on the Telengana struggle. I and my colleagues were greatly impressed by his frankness, thorough grasp and unblinkered view of the movements and organizations he had formed, led or participated in. Comrade Ravi Narayan's laughter was infectious. Having sacrificed so much since the age of 20, he gave no sign of the consciousness of his sacrifice. Clearly, he had enjoyed serving the people and fighting for their causes.

I

Coming from a big landlord family, sheer intellect, social consciousness and social commitment, or, as he put it, "spirit of service", led him in the end to communism.

Even as a young college student, he became active in political and social causes. During 1927-28, he spoke in public meetings in various villages in Telengana organized to protest against *begar* being forcibly exacted from the people by touring officials.

He entered politics as a Gandhian. As a student of intermediate, he read Gandhiji's *Autobiography* and became his follower. He was not impressed much by Gandhiji as a thinker. It was Gandhiji's staunch anti-imperialism and the capacity to mobilize the millions into the anti-imperialist struggle that he found most attractive.

His political life was initiated when he joined the Salt Satyagraha in 1930. Since no political movement existed in Hyderabad, Ravi Narayan

Reddy went along with a few friends to Kakinada to participate in the Civil Disobedience Movement. After spending a month or two there, he returned home under strong family pressure, but then he laid down a condition: he would be given the financial resources to start a khadi centre in his village. After the Gandhi-Irwin Pact in 1931, he launched the Harijan Sevak Sangh, becoming its general secretary for the entire Hyderabad state. He continued to work in the Sangh till 1938. The Sangh succeeded in starting 100 schools and 2 hostels for Harijans in different districts.

In the meanwhile, Hyderabad was engulfed by its first major political movement, the State Congress Satyagraha waged mainly on the question of civil liberties in general and the right to form a political association, i.e., the State Congress, in particular. Ravi Narayan' Reddy represented Telengana in the leadership of the Satyagraha and was the first Congressman from Telengana to go to jail in its course.

Continuing his reading throughout, he soon, in early 1930s, came across Jawaharlal Nehru's writings and was powerfully influenced by Nehru's socialist ideas. From Nehru to the study of books on the Soviet Union and then on Marxism through indirect contact with P. Sundarayya was the inevitable step, leading to his joining the Communist Party in 1939.

In fact, this Gandhian and Nehruvian influence was a major strand he brought to the Communist Party. Along with many of the other prominent State Congress Satyagrahis of 1938, he later joined others to form the Communist Party in the Hyderabad state. As he remarked in 1984, "the Communist Party is strong only in those places where comrades who have come from the national movement have organized it". And this, he said, was because these comrades were "able to see the entire forest" and not merely the trees. In Telengana too, one reason why the Communists were so successful was because they worked through the Andhra Mahasabha, amass anti-Nizam, anti-feudal, anti-imperialist organization.

II

In time, Ravi Narayan Reddy also became the driving force behind the Andhra Mahasabha. The first session of the Sabha was held at Jogipet in 1930. It was, at the outset, a liberal social reform organization and dealt with problems like child marriage, widow remarriage, untouchability and the social problems of women's uplift. Later,quite early, it also took up the economic problems of the peasantry, though mostly of its richer sections.

In 1936, when constitutional reforms were on the agenda all over India, the Nizam too proposed reforms which were totally reactionary and which gave little voice to the overwhelming majority of the people in a powerless legislature. The Andhra Mahasabha for the first time took up a political question at its seventh session in 1939 and opposed the official reforms. Led by Comrade Ravi Narayan, the younger leaders overwhelmingly defeated the conservative leaders who wanted to accept the official reforms. Instead, the Mahasabha asked for a responsible government to be elected democratically, though under the aegis of the Nizam.

Even earlier, Ravi Narayan Reddy fought his first major ideological battle in the Mahasabha. In 1935, the language fanatics ordained that nobody would be permitted to speak in the Andhra Mahasabha session except in Telegu, thus preventing the Marathi aand Kannada speaking leaders from addressing the 4th and 5th conferences of the Mahasabha.

At the head of a group of young people, Comrade Ravi Narayan decided to fight this language fanaticism and, at the Nizamabad session of the Mahasabha in 1937, he inflicted crushing defeat on the fanatics. Leading the battle, he put forward an ingenious argument before the audience. Suppose, he said, Gandhiji came and wanted to address the conference, would he be permitted to do so or would he be told that since he could not speak in Telegu he should go back.

Ravi Narayan Reddy became the President for the 8th session of the Mahasabha at Chilkapur in 1941. Naturally, his address marked a sharp departure from previous presidential addresses and initiated a new turn in the political and ideological character of the activities of the Mahasabha; for example, he dealt at length with anti-imperialism, the character of the war, socialism, and women's liberation.

Comrade Ravi Narayan presided once again over the Mahasabha at its 11th session in 1944. From now on, the Mahasabha came under the leadership of the Communist Party and also entered its radical, mass phase.

III

In 1939, Ravi Narayan Reddy became a founder-member of the Communist Party in Hyderabad state. From that year onwards, along with B. Yell a Reddy and D. V. Rao he played a leading role in building the party at the grass-roots level through study circles and later the organization of the peasantry.

All his life, Comrade Ravi Narayan was proud of the great sacrifices and achievements of the Communist Party. After all, as he was fond of pointing out, no other segment of the Congress or the national movement contributed as many martyrs in the freedom struggle. At the same time, he was very keen that for the sake of the younger comrades and of the future of the Communist movement in India, a critical assessment of the entire history of the party should be made, a task which the party had, he felt, sadly neglected so far. Even though the party had grown and made an immense contribution to the national movement and other causes of the people, why had it not acquired a far greater influence among the people, he asked?

His own analysis was in this respect quite profound. One major regret, as he put it, was: "We were experts in isolating ourselves from the national current". For example, the 1930-33 period was the basic formative phase of the national movement but "the party was nowhere in the picture." On the other hand, once the party joined the Congress in 1935-36, it entered the period of its real growth. In particular, he felt that the party was not able to fully understand the role of Gandhiji. As he put it, "we were born abusing Gandhi. Immediately after we were born, we were abusing Gandhi." The Communists were, he felt, right in differing from Gandhiji on many basic issues such as the emphasis on non-violence, but Gandhiji was "a great anti-imperialist leader who had moved lakhs and lakhs of people against imperialism in India."

Comrade Ravi Narayan also held very specific and illuminating views regarding the Communist role in the 1942 movement, the party policies adopted in February 1948 and the decision to continue the armed struggle in Telengana after the entry of Indian troops in 1948-views which bring out his political acumen as also deep understanding of contemporary developments.

Regarding 1942, he felt that the Communist Party's policy of People's War was strategically correct, for fascism was the enemy of the entire world people and democracy. But the policy was tactically wrong. The party ought to have taken more careful note of developments in the European and Asian theaters of war as also in Indian politics. In particular, the party should have changed its tactical line, joined the movement, supported Satyagraha, etc., after the Battle of Stalingrad.

At the same time, Comrade Ravi Narayan strongly felt that the party had nothing to be ashamed of; and, in particular, the party members and the people should not forget the massive and "wonderful" role played by the party in the post-war upsurge, leading to freedom.

He was very critical of the programme and decisions adopted in the Party Congress in February 1948. Basically there was the failure to understand the nature and strength of the national movement and the achievement of independence in 1947. Instead, totally wrong formulations regarding the latter underpinned the party decisions: that there was no independence, that the national leaders had become "stooges of imperialism", and that the Indian people were "ready for a revolution". The result was that the Communists were "almost discredited before the nation." Referring to the B.T. Ranadive line, the P. Sundarayya-C. Rajeshwara Rao line, the 3 P's document by Ajoy Ghosh, S.A. Dange and S.V. Ghate, and the document framed in consultation with Stalin, Comrade Ravi Narayan held that the first two were strategically as well as tactically wrong, while the last two were tactically right but strategically wrong. In fact, all the four were based on a common strategic framework. One result was that it took nearly a decade for the party to accept that India was an independent nation. It is interesting to note in this respect that Comrade Ravi Narayan was one of the Communist leaders to argue in 1954-55 that India was a fully independent country. He was also one of the first to critique in 1954 the policy of anti-Congressism,

The task in India, he said in 1984, was to evolve an Indian way for revolution based on a hard study of Indian reality, Indian historical development and the psychology of the Indian people. For example, after independence, the Indian people above all wanted development. The party should have interacted positively with Nehru's development plans, evolved its own strategy of development and integrated and coordinated its grass-roots political work and mass struggles with a constructive though critical role in the development process. In this context, he would not say anything publicly about the politics of the CPI in the 1980s; but he was quite derisive about the politics of "the opposition conclaves", so popular at the time; and he made his position clear in his inner-party documents.

IV

Comrade, Ravi Narayan Reddy played a great role in the Telengana struggle as also made a profound analysis of it later.

First of all, Comrade Ravi Narayan Reddy was fully conscious of the all-India dimensions of the struggle. The Telengana struggle was, in general, a part of the India-wide anti-imperialist struggle as also of the India-wide post-war upsurge. It did not pertain only to Telengana or Hyderabad. At the same time, Telengana witnessed a big movement and a powerful armed struggle because of certain specific features. After all, he pointed out, feudal oppression existed in several other princely states. Similarly, armed struggle was not successful in coastal Andhra during 1948-50 or in Telengana after September 1948 when the Government of India sent in its troops against the Nizam. What were these specific features, according to Comrade Ravi Narayan?

(i) The national leaders of Telengana themselves became the founders and leaders of the Communist movement. They had taken up all the national causes from the State Congress to the Andhra Mahasabha and the Vande Mataram agitation.

(ii) Even though the Telengana leaders took up a firm secular approach, religious discrimination and communal oppression by Nizam's administration also helped the anti-Nizam movement become popular. Nizam was suppressing even religious civil liberties of the Hindus. Moreover, overwhelming majority of jobs were given to the Muslims.

(iii) Then there was the cultural suppression, including the suppression of Telegu, Kannada, and Marathi. For example, when in the 1930s the Andhra Mahasabha leader, Madapati Hanumantha Rao, started a High School with Telegu as the medium of instruction, the Osmania University refused to affiliate it.

(iv) Also crucial was the help given by the Andhra comrades in the form of ideological and political guidance as also monetary support. Moreover, the neighbouring Andhra areas provided the space where the Telengana comrades could freely function. Above all, the people of Andhra shared with the people of Telengana common love for 'Mabhoomi', their common land of Andhra.

(v) One reason why the Communists could capture the leadership of the Andhra Mahasabha was the weakness of its liberal leadership. "That could not have happened outside Telengana. The Congress leadership was very strong there." The liberal leadership being weak, the Communist Party picked up the banner of revolt.

(vi) The nature of the state in Hyderabad was also different from that in British India especially when the Razakars took over. British

Indian type of Satyagraha was no longer possible. The Razakars killed satyagrahis, raided villages, burnt houses, molested women and beat up and killed men. Arms had then to be taken, up. Guerilla warfare was the only answer. In fact, armed struggle had to be taken up because of pressure from below.

All these factors together, along with the resistance to feudal oppression and the desire for independence, made a wide mass movement possible. For example, because of these features, some of the smaller landlords took active part in the movement.

Ravi Narayan Reddy was one of the Telengana leaders who believed that the armed struggle should have been withdrawn after the entry of Indian troops in September 1948. Certainly, apart from bringing the Nizam to heel, the entry of the Indian army had a certain anti-Communist edge and it was necessary to defend the gains of the Telengana struggle, especially regarding the land distributed among the landless. But this required, recourse to other methods and other forms of struggle than offering armed resistance to the Indian armed forces.

Comrade Ravi Narayan's approach in this respect was based on his overall understanding of the nature of the Telengana struggle from 1944 to 1948. The struggle was, he believed, primarily an anti-imperialist struggle and a struggle against the Nizam who was a puppet of British imperialism. Secondly, the struggle was against feudal oppression and for agrarain reforms; the struggle was not for a social revolution; neither for socialism nor for an agrarian revolution. Under Indian conditions, the stage of anti-imperialism could not be mixed up with the stage of agrarian revolution. This became evident from the people's reaction to the Indian army. Everywhere the people welcomed the army. Another reflection of this aspect was the change in the strength of the armed squads. From consisting of nearly 100 persons, they got reduced to 10 persons or so. In fact. the armed squads were fast disintegrating. People felt that their struggle was over. Not that the people had turned pro-Congress. The election results of 1952 showed that they had not. They were still with the Communist Party. But they were not willing to fight· the Indian Government with guns in their hands.

The decision to continue the armed struggle after September 1948, this time against the Government of India, was wrong, believed Comrade Ravi Narayan, but he felt that it was the inevitable and logical consequence of the political line adopted by the party in

February 1948. A different line could have been followed in Telengana only if the February party line had been questioned simultaneously. But, unfortunately, nobody had the courage to do so at the time; and the perspective given in February was followed through in Telengana in September 1948. There was, said Comrade Ravi Narayan, one other major error involved. The Communist leadership of the time did not . fully understand that Telengana was not an isolated spot. It was a part of India as a whole. Politics had to be national politics. Failure to see this was perhaps a "tragedy of the Communist movement" in India.

Most of the deep political insights that Comrade Ravi Narayan put forward in his writings and in his inner-party notes, especially during 1955, have proved highly fruitful. His autobiographical fragments and these notes are part of the immense contribution he made to the struggle of the Indian people for a better life, a more just and democratic social order, and a socialist society.

6

Punjab Crisis

Punjab crisis: *Context and Trends** is a major effort to provide an analysis of the long-term historical, political, and socio-economic forces which have produced the current political crisis in Punjab. In other words, it provides a study of the specific conjuncture of the past one year or so in its wider setting.

This study defines communalism in a scientific manner and then identifies the three kinds of communalism—the conformist, the secessionist and the incremental-concessionist—that have surfaced in Punjab, sometimes separately and at other times in unison. While taking full note of the fact that communalism is the product of specific socio-economic and political circumstances and gives expression to actual, real social discontent which has failed to find a legitimate outlet in healthy protest movements, the authors point out that communalism fails to provide a correct understanding of, or socially relevant and viable remedies to, the social conditions which generate it. Instead, communalism undermines the real struggle for changing the social conditions. Consequently, communalism becomes a political and ideological instrument in the hands of vested interests to maintain their dominant position.

The authors point out that communalism is not a pre-capitalist but a modern ideology, which incorporates some of the elements of traditional ideologies. Its roots lie in the present-day social, economic and political structures. Communalism in Punjab today has grown because of the path of economic development followed after 1947. Its rapid growth in recent years is because "of relative stagnation in

---

*Pramod Kumar, *et.al.*, *Punjab Crisis: Context and Trends*, Chandigarh, 1984.

agriculture and lopsided industrial development which provides meagre scope for expansion of investment opportunities in industry and trade". In this context, communalism came in as "a handy tool to sectional interests to exploit and mobilise people for maintaining and enhancing their economic and political power".

The authors also maintain that while communalism utilises religious differences, it is not based on or caused by religion nor does it represent any genuine religious interests. At the same time, the communalists make efforts to increase religious intolerance so as to be able to utilise religion for their politics. Tracing the historical background of the communal problem in Punjab briefly, the authors then discuss the developments in the economy which have provided the economic base to the resurgence of communalism in recent years. They point out that the 1950s and 1960s witnessed rapid agricultural growth as well as a large number of agitations and movements which were economic in nature and often led by the secular communist parties. The growth of agriculture, however, created surpluses in the hands of the capitalist farmers and rich peasants which overflowed the confines of agriculture. The rural rich felt the need for fresh avenues of investment and they began to branch out into trade in agricultural products, trade in general, and small and medium industry. The lopsided character of economic development in general and industrial development in particular inhibited opportunities for investment in industry and trade, leading to intense competition among those already entrenched in these sectors and those wanting to enter into these. Both found it convenient to make an appeal to communalism in order to mobilise the people and thus throw political power in the scale.

Throughout the 1950s and 196Os, both Hindu and Sikh communalists also communalised the issues of the Punjabi language and reorganisation of the state on a linguistic basis. The more orthodox and fundamentalist tendencies among the Hindus and the Sikhs also perceived a threat to religious orthodoxy from modemising forces and hoped to utilise communal ideology and politics to neutralise the effect of such forces.

The base of communalism, especially Sikh communalism, has been undergoing a change over the years. A section of the Akali Dal began to fight its opponents within the party by making an appeal to caste and increasingly looking for support from the Jat Sikhs, especially the big and middle farmers, who were the major beneficiaries of the Green Revolution. By the early 1970s, this section had become dominant among the Sikh communalists. This section also began to project its political struggle for power as a clash between the peasantry and the "central" big bourgeoisie. The authors' discussion of this aspect is fascinating. In fact, they have touched upon a question which deserves a more detailed and separate treatment.

In the struggle for socio-economic and political hegemony between the agrarian interests of the rich peasants and the capitalist farmers and the capitalist interests of industrial bourgeoisie, which side is historically more progressive? Has any society progressed and remained democratic and independent where the so-called agrarian interests have been dominant? In view of the social tensions and social development in India today, these questions cannot be answered on the basis of the simple equation of who is small and who is big. The subject requires deep study. Perhaps a beginning can be made by studying the histories of Hungary, Poland, Romania, Bulgaria, Spain and Greece during the inter-war years (1918-1939).

That the communalists distort issues and often base their agitations on misinformation is well brought out by the authors in their discussion of the issues of water distribution and the enfranchisement of migrant labourers. A major theme in the present work is that of the political parties in Punjab and their changing social base and political fortunes. The communal parties, such as the RSS, the Jan Sangh (BJP) and the Akali Dal, are based on communal ideology and propagate and use this ideology in their politics. The authors have presented a detailed statistical study of the votes secured by the communal parties from 1952 to 1980. It then becomes clear that the highest percentage' of the votes secured by the Akali Dal was almost 31.43 in 1977. In other words, it has only once secured almost 50 per cent of the votes among Sikhs. More often, its vote has hovered between 30 to 45 per cent of the votes among Sikhs. This failure to win over the mass of Sikhs to communalism explains, in part, the desperation of the fascist-extremists among the Sikh communalists and the failure of the moderate (conformist and incremental) communalists to convince the more extreme sections that they can deliver the goods.

Similarly, the Jan Sangh vote in the Punjab-Haryana-Kangra belt could reach only the figure of 9.5 per cent in 1962 and in linguistically reorganised Punjab 9.85 per cent in 1967, which represents almost 25 per cent of the votes among Hindus. This percentage declined to 4.97 of the total votes in 1972.

Out of a desperate effort to get a share in political power and finding that it was impossible to do so on the basis of their own communal vote alone. the Hindu and Sikh communalists decided to share power once in 1967 and then again in 1969 when Akali-Jan Sangh coalitions were formed on the communal theoretical basis of the two "communities" sharing power. The coalitions failed because both communal groups found that their communal political base was discontented with the mutual communal adjustments. The authors point out that while these communal coalitions contained the demands of the extremist sections in the short run, they strengthened the penetration and spread of communal ideology as also the extreme communalists in the long run.

The secular parties, such as the Congress, have made their own contribution to the spread of communalism in Punjab. While these parties "do not have a communal content in their ideology and do not propagate such an ideology," they, in particular the Congress, have suffered from two major weaknesses. Firstly, they have taken an opportunistic stand towards communalism and have even used elements of communal ideology—often in a disguised manner—for electoral and political purposes, thus providing legitimacy to communal ideology and disarming themselves in the confrontation against communal political parties. Secondly, they have appeased the communalists and tried to accommodate them instead of confronting them politically and ideologically.

The authors trace "the politics of accommodation" followed by the Congress over the years. Twice, once in 1948 and then again in 1956, the Akalis were persuaded to dissolve the Akali Dal and merge with the Congress, with the Akali stalwarts joining the Congress. But the strategy failed. While those Akalis who joined the Congress seldom came out of it, very soon others, more extreme communalists, emerged and re-formed the Akali Dal, thus shifting the latter towards lesser moderate communalism. In the meantime the "merged" Akalis carried their communal politics and ideology into the Congress, making the latter into an arena of communal demands, mobilisation, etc. To counter this trend, the Congress followed the policy of simultaneously appeasing and accommodating Hindu communalists in its own ranks. Congress accommodation of the Akalis also strengthened Hindu communalism outside the Congress. Thus the politics of accommodation had the double effect of strengthening Hindu and Sikh communal isms in the state and communalising politics within the Congress. It also led the Congress to abandon all serious political-ideological struggle against communalism.

In very recent years, the politics of appeasement and accommodation was followed by Giani Zail Singh with disastrous consequences.

Sardar Darbara Singh, the Congress(I) Cheif Minister from 1980 to 1983 and a non-Akali from the beginning of his political career, made a serious effort to reverse this Congress policy and tried to confront both Hindu and Sikh communalisms. He was hamstrung by the Hindu and Sikh communalists within the ranks of his own party, opposed tooth and nail by the Hindu and Sikh communalists outside his party, given little support in his fight against communalism by the secular Left parties or his own party's high command, and in the end paid a heavy price for trying to remain secular in a viciously communal political atmosphere.

The authors also take the Left parties to task for their failure to understand the nature of communal politics, aligning themselves with communal parties for electoral gains or ease in political mobilisation, failing to provide a Left alternative to the social conditions, and refusal to frontally oppose communalism, communal ideology and communal groups and parties.

In conclusion, the authors point out that the social conditions which generate communalism have to be transformed. At the same time, they argue that communal ideology and politics-the subjective conditions—have to be dealt with firmly. Communal ideology and politics have to be confronted ideologically. They advocate a vigorous ideological political struggle against communalism. Besides, communal violence has to be handled firmly and decisively through the law and order machinery. Unfortunately, the short-sighted political leadership has failed to do either.

The authors do not rule out compromises and negotiations with moderate or conformist-incremental elements. But these should be treated as short-term solutions whose effectiveness would be lost and the opposite consequences result unless, simultaneously, a vigorous ideological struggle is launched against communlism. The time gained by short-term compromises has to be used properly, otherwise mutual understanding would only strengthen communalism and push it further towards extremism. A compromise should lead to the liquidation of communalism or else the acceptance of some communal demands would inevitably lead to the emergence of fresh, more extreme communal demands.

In this respect, the authors once again point out, in the end, that communalism cannot be treated as a pre-modern ideology. This concept inevitably led to the wrong notion that modernisation, especially modern economic development, would lead to the slow, automatic extinction of communalism. This has not happened. Instead, it is precisely the pattern of capitalist (modern) development followed in Punjab which has led to the present crisis. Hence, the authors argue for a different developmental strategy as well as active ideological struggle against communalism.

7

Hindu-Muslim Relations in the 1920s

Dr Thursby's* is in the main a study of the Hindu communal Press and publications and the Government policy towards them during 1923-28 in north India, especially in Punjab and V.P. Some aspects of Hindu communalism, its ideology and the means and techniques of its propagation have been studied Even within this narrow area, the focus is mainly on the activities of the Arya Samaj. Dr Thursby has consciously emphasized the Hindu side of the Hindu-Muslim relations or communalism. Though this makes his study a little one-sided, it does provide an important and welcome corrective, for in most of the recent studies of communalism, in modern India, "Hindu politics", that is, Hindu communalism, is neglected or is seen as a mere reaction to Muslim communalism or "Muslim politics".

The author has highlighted the role of religious controversies creating communal tension as also the role of the books and pamphlets—the newly created modem means of mass communication—in fanning such controversies. Indirectly, he has thus emphasized the need for the modernization of culture, or rather for a cultural revolution, if communalism was or is to be eliminated. He has also brought out clearly, and with a wealth of instances and quotations, the vicious and irrational character of Hindu communalism and its propaganda. In the process he has blown up the myths that Hindu communalism only or "merely" reacted to Muslim communalism and that it was less aggressive, if not also more meek and "cultured", than Muslim communalism. He has also brought out very well the ideologies

---

**C.R. Thursby Hindu-Muslim Relations in British India*: A *Study of Controversy, Conflict and Communal Movements in Northern India 1923-1928, Leiden, 1975.*

of "backwardness" and "dying race" with which the Muslim and Hindu communalisms operated. Several other features of Hindu communal ideology, its propagation and the utilization of history as a source of communal ideology formation and propagation have also been competently handled.

The main edge of Dr Thursby's study is on the Government policy towards communalism. The treatment is, however, narrower still. The author deals at length not with the official policy towards communal problem or politics but with the administrative policy towards communal tension with the objective of keeping public peace and order. The result is that he often misses the basic thrust and content of the official policy. This is a major weakness in a book or thesis whose main objective is to study the official policy towards the communal problem. The author does, however, take note of one important aspect of government policy, even though he fails to draw the resulting conclusion. He points out that the administration took much stronger notice of and action against sedition or anti-imperialist nationalist writing, propaganda and activity promoting hatred, contempt or disaffection towards the government than against communal hatred or violence. In fact, no legislation against communalism and its propagators was undertaken, while a series of laws were passed against the preaching of "sedition" from the end of the nineteeth century. Even at the administrative level, no effort was made to energetically suppress communal propaganda, however vicious. The author points out that this aspect was taken full note of by the contemporary Press. For example, an Urdu newspaper, the *Zamindar* of Lahore, noted on 26 October 1921 that "Anyone publishing a report that might be harmful to the Government is at once arrested, but section 153A has become paralysed against those who publish baseless and wild statements intended to sow feelings of enmity between the Hindus and Muhammadans". Similarly, in the field 01 history writing, both at the level of research and textbooks, the government discouraged and even suppressed any critique of colonialism, colonial policies and the very process of colonial conquest—even positive references to Tipu, Rani of Jhansi, Tantia Tope, Tilak, Bhagat Singh, Gandhiji, Nehru and peasant and tribal uprisings and movements. Communal writings glorifying "anti-Hindu" and "anti-Muslim" struggles and the heroes of the past were not only tolerated but often their authors were rewarded with promotions, titles, etc. The state and Government can always encourage a whole range of activities simply by failing to take adequate action against them. This is even more so if there is no administrative inefficiency or paralysis in other allied fields. In fact, this was a major aspect of British policy towards communalism; this was a major instrument through which communalism was encouraged. Dr Thursby does see this in a rather hazy manner when he says that the objective of government policy was not the eradication of communalism but the maintenance of public order. This last was, in fact, the only constraint on the policy of encouragement to, or at the most a *laissez faire* attitude towards, communal forces. On the other hand, Dr Thursby seems to accept the official view that no legislation against even the most provocative communal propaganda was passed because that would "restrict religious and civil liberties".

A few minor weaknesses of Dr Thursby's work may be pointed out before we take up its basic weakness or failure. The role of the nationalist and secular forces is not discussed at all. Yet communalism cannot be discussed without seeing it in the context of the major socio-political reality of the day, that is, nationalism, which also happened to be basically anti-communal whatever its deficiencies in this regard. This neglect inevitably leads the author to project communalism as the basic, all-pervading reality of Indian politics of the 1920s. In reality, communalism was a minor strand of Indian politics even "at the best of times" till 1930, and even after that it never overpowered or surpassed secular nationalism as a political trend. Dr Thursby's own book contains some evidence of this. For example, the communal movement for *shuddhi* and *sang than* never gathered sufficient popular support. As he notes, the annual income of the Bharatiya Hindu Shuddhi Sabha was Rs 99,237 in 1924, Rs 60,774 in 1925, Rs 21,764 in 1926 and Rs 52,020 in 1927.

Dr Thursby is also not able to "place" the leaders and newspapers he quotes in terms of their political weight. For him a quotation from Lal Chand, or somebody else like him, has a fixed meaning irrespective of the degree of political relevance or marginality of the writer or speaker. Similarly, he seldom asks the question as to what place the Hindu Mahasabha enjoyed in the politics of his period.

Dr Thursby's work on the whole fails in analysing the problem he has undertaken or even in presenting its basic contours. He is more or less unaware of the socio-economic or even the wider political dimensions of the problem of "Hindu-Muslim relations in British India". He has no proper framework for the analysis of colonialism and the national movement or even of colonial policy. And yet it is not possible to examine the communal problem without some such framework. Dr Thursby says that he has made an effort "to use a mixture of disinterested scholarship and human empathy". But, though valuable, these two qualities are not enough. Without an understanding of the basic socio-political elements of the situation, one is still likely to go seriously astray and fail to evolve any deep insights. One simple example may be given. Dr Thursby never asks the questions: in what sense were Gandhiji and other nationalist leaders "Hindu politicians"? Was politics in India divided between two strands—"Hindu politics" and "Muslim politics"—with colonial rulers as neutral arbiters? Or, should we talk of Hindu communalism, Muslim communalism and Indian nationalism?

Dr Thursby has concentrated as "his primary concern" on "the explicitly religious interests". Surely, the role of religion is important, but can it be studied adequately or even at all without providing it context and causation? Having noted the fact that religion and religion-based issues should not be viewed one-sidedly as being merely religious or merely reflections of the social situation, Dr Thursby opts in practice for the former. In fact, even the "explicitly religious interests" cannot be grasped merely by seeing the religious concerns of the people involved.

The fact is that such complex problems as communalism cannot, and should not, be handled by writers who are not familiar with the sociology of ideas and ideologies and social movements. Dealing with the communal problem particularly requires. a multi-sided "sociological" or "inter-disciplinary" grasp since it is a highly ideological sphere and requires a trained mind capable of penetrating deep layers of social reality and ideas and of establishing complex linkages. The communal problem cannot be scientifically studied by somebody who relies on surface religious controversies and official statements. In other words, the dangers facing research based on an empirical approach are even greater where empirical data consist of ideological statements. This is true not only of the openly ideological writings of the communalists; it is also true of statements contained in governmental records and private papers. They, too, have to be filtered through analysis before they are treated as statements of facts.

Dr Thursby is, however, not able to avoid the dangers facing a scholar who writes mainly on the basis of government sources. Thus all the bias of the contemporary officials embedded in the government sources creeps in. For example, because the contemporary officials were anti-Arya Samajists owing, as Thursby notes, to their fear that the Arya Samajists were dangerous 'seditionists' or nationalists, he also adopts a stridently anti-Arya Samajist approach. Similarly, because the officials were soft towards Muslim communalism seeing in it an ally, because officials launched fewer prosecutions against Muslim communalists and, we suspect, because there exist fewer quotations from Muslim communal propaganda in the official records and because fewer Muslim communal writings were proscribed, Dr Thursby assumes that Muslim communalists were less dangerous or vicious. Although this aspect has a positive angle—for it corrects much of today's communal or even secular writing which assumes the opposite—it is no less unscientific.

Most important of all, Dr Thursby does not question the basic colonial and communal assumptions or digits. To him the statements of colonial administrators and communal writers and politicians become given empirical data. For example, he accepts without questioning that communal interests-Hindu interests and Muslim interests—exist in real life or objectively because communalists and colonialists are constantly talking of them. He never asks the question whether the talk of these interests could be masking some other aspects of reality or some other interests than the so-called communal interests. He focuses rigidly and narrowly on controversies such as cow-slaughter and the playing of music before mosques without seeing the socio-psychological and political role that such controversies may be playing. Similarly, he accepts the Hindu and Muslim communalists at their face value as the leaders of Hindus and Muslims and as the defenders of their separate interests. This is the result of excessive reliance on official records and communal writings and speeches and the adoption of a non-historical and non-sociological approach, not to speak of the absence of "sociological imagination".

On the whole, Dr Thursby has not made any advance over such previous writers on communalism as W.C. Smith and K.B. Krishna in so far as an understanding and analysis of communalism are concerned. In fact, he hardly makes any contribution at the level of analysis. At the same time, there is a great deal of material in his monograph which can be utilized by others who would like to make such an effort.

8

The Cripps Mission

In his latest book, *R.J. Moore traces the complicated course of the war-time efforts of Stafford Cripps to bring the Indian leaders into the Government and thereby behind the war effort. He brings out ably the obstruction of these efforts by Churchill, the Prime Minister, Amery, the Secretary of State, and Linlithgow, the Viceroy, and shows how in view of their hostility towards the Congress, and their firm committment to the perpetuation of the empire after the war, the Cripps Mission had perhaps little chance of success from the beginning.

Cripps had built up a reputation in India as a supporter of India's cause during the late 1930s. In October 1939 he had advised Nehru not to accept anything short of "action which proves conclusively the faith behind words" and suggested that the Congress should "stand as firm as a rock upon its demands". His brief visit to India at the end of 1939 had further strengthened this reputation.

During the first two years of the war the British Government was not interested in arriving at a political settlement with the nationalist forces in India. The situation changed dramatically with Japanese invasion of South-East Asia, the entry of the USA in the war, and the-Japanese push towards Burma and eastern India. The Labour Party in Britain and the US Government began to pressurise for a settlement with the Indian leaders so that Indian resources in men and material could be fully utilised in the war. Churchill and other die-hards were not convinced but they found it difficult to withstand the dual pressure combined as it was with the resurgence of anti-imperialist sentiments in India. The

---

*R.J. Moore, *Churchill. Cripps. and India:* 1939-45, Oxford, 1979.

result was the Mission headed by the man who had behind him a reputation in India which was a major political asset and his undoubted political stature and ability to undertake the task successfully.

Moore traces the tangled web of political discussions and manoeuvrings through which the Declaration carried by Cripps to India was drafted. The Declaration, known as the *Cripps Offer,* promised Indians some sort of dominionhood whose constitution Indians would be able to draw after the war; it virtually accepted the Muslim League's demand for Pakistan by promising that any province that wanted to keep out of the dominion would be able to do so; it gave the Princes an important role in the constitution-making process, including the right to keep out of the new dominion. All these basic features went against the political approach of the National Congress, and its leaders were not willing to accept the Cripps proposals. But the actual success of the intricate negotiations between Cripps and the Congress leaders came to hinge on the question of Indians' entry into the Viceroy's Council during the war-period. The Congress leaders demanded and agreed to negotiate on the basis of the Viceroy's Council functioning as a quasi-cabinet with an Indian member being given charge of large areas of defence. Cripps seems to have accepted the Congress demand as the basis of an actual, functioning political system.

At this stage, Linlithgow, Amery and Churchill decided to call a halt. They had been forced to take an accommodating attitude because of the pressure from the Labour Party radicals and the American Government and public opinion. They now felt that the two had now become convinced of the British desire to settle with Indians. Time had therefore come to *scuttle* the Cripps Mission and to cut down Cripps to size. How this exercise was carried out has been brought out very well by Moore. In fact this is the best part of his work.

Cripps was now told to stick to the letter of the Declaration he had been given on his departure from Britian and that he had no warrant or authority to talk of a quasi-cabinet in India. In fact. the Viceroy's powers and prerogatives, laid own in the Act of 1935, were inviolable. Thus Cripps was left holding the bag while Linlithgow had the last laugh. Cripps was now faced with the choice of either bringing out all the facts and thus exposing his own war cabinet's game, or himself going under politically, indulging in a bit of political double-talk and sleight of hand and finding a scapegoat for his failure. He chose the patriotic course of not embarrassing his Government engaged in a global war of survival and decided to equivocate and even falsify so that the blame for failure could be laid at the door of the Congress leaders and above all Gandhiji. He did not even hesitate to take recourse in the end to the alibi that the British could not let down the minorities.

Moore brings out all this but fails to see the full implications of his own data. He is perhaps much too involved with his central character, and he tends to accept Cripps's contemporary political reading as a reflection of the actual political situation. The result however is that he fails to fully refute the tendentious account of the failure of the Mission carefully orchestrated at the time by British propaganda machinery and later put down in a book form by Coupland. Coupland's account, which has unfortunately come to be accepted widely, held that the Mission failed because of the Congress leadership missing a golden opportunity to advance to freedom because of the undue pressure of the doctrinaire Gandhiji. Moore does, of course, as pointed out earlier, bring out most of the details which go to refute Coupland's view. For example, he has shown how Coupland, Cripps's constitutional adviser, was kept ignorant of the fact that Linlithgow was opposed to the quasi-cabinet with the result that Coupland came to believe and assert that the Congress leaders had rejected a scheme which included the idea of a quasi-cabinet which Cripps offered with Linlithgow's support.

A major weakness of Moore's book is his inability to understand the broader framework of political forces within which the drama of the Cripps Mission Was played. After all, the basic reality of the period was the struggle between the forces of imperialism and nationalism, the latter being led by the National Congress. Consequently, the Congress was not, and cannot be seen to be, just a political party like the parties in Britain or France or USA or in India after 1947. Despite its many weaknesses and shortcomings, it was the organizer and leader of the anti-imperialist movement of the Indian people. Not that Moore lacks a basic sympathy for Indian nationalism. But despite good intentions, his understanding still operates within the older framework, still current, despite some linguistic modernisation and touch of sociology, in many of the British, American and Australian departments of Indian history. After all the basic political character of the two sides engaged in negotiations during the Cripps Mission should not be ignored. Gandhiji, Nehru. and Azad were the heads of a mass anti-imperialist movement while Cripps was, with all his good intentions and correct sympathies, the spokesman of a dying but not-yet-dead colonialism. One of the reasons for Cripps's failure was his inability to see this difference. But that is no reason why Moore should not see it and provide for it in his analysis. The result is that despite a sympathetic attitude, he is not able to analyse or understand the mainsprings of Congress policy and the thinking of its leaders.

This in fact points to an even more fundamental, hisoriographic weakness of Moore. He tends to limit his historical analysis by the uncritical acceptance of the internal bias of his sources. Not that he is a lone defaulter. The growing cult of private papers tends to spread the notion that private papers, because they are private, tend to reveal the 'truth'. An example of the negative influence of this historiographic error is Moore's tendency to equate Muslims with Muslim communalism, and thus his ready acceptance of Muslim communalists as the spokesmen of Muslim interests, and so on. Or his repetition of the view that Congress leaders should have formed coalition governments with the Muslim League. He does not even ask the question how a secular body could have joined hands with a communal body, especially as the latter insisted that the Congress should declare itself to be a Hindu communal body. Whether Indians would have avoided partition that way or not is an 'if' question, but what sort of independent India, partitioned or unpartitioned, would have been built by a party or movement which regarded itself as 'Hindu'?

Despite this bit of criticism, Moore's book is a valuable addition to the literature of the period; above all because of the light he throws on the sabotage of the Cripps Mission by the Linlithgow-Churchill axis and on the "reduction of Cripps."

9

The End of History?

Francis Fukuyama, who has served on the US State Department's Policy Planning Staff and is currently working at the Rand Corporation, a major U.S. think-tank, created quite a sensation in 1989 with his article entitled "the End of History?" He has now developed the theme further in the book under review. *

The book, a major work of synthesis, contains several arguments whose main merit lies in making us think of wider issues in this age of the 'micro' and the 'fragment'. Moreover, he states his argument with clarity and brevity, and in a scintillating manner. Let me, in the beginning, state my points of agreement with Fukuyama. First, there is both need for and the possibility of writing a universal history of mankind "that takes into account the experiences of all times and all peoples." Archaeologists, economic historians and historians of science and of philosophy have always made such an attempt. Certainly, the rise and spread of capitalism—a world system—made this mandatory. Whatever the social, cultural or civilizational differences in the past evolution of different societies, capitalism and the science and technology on which it is based are increasingly homogenising the world. Some may welcome this and others bemoan it, but the direction is very clear. This does not mean the inevitability of one single cultural pattern being extended to all. Rather it means entire humanity contributing over time to the evolution of a composite world civilization.

Fukuyama is also quite right in asserting that the notion of human progress is not outdated. Certainly in terms of science and

---

*Francis Fukuyama, *The End of History and the Last Man,* Penguin Books, 1992.

technology and acquisition of knowledge in general, styles of life, material and social culture and human freedom and development of human individuality, humanity has been making progress, despite setbacks on the way. The direction of human development is towards greater perfectability of man/woman, a goal towards which all great men and women of the past have worked and aspired. But this direction is not something imposed from outside of mankind itself or inherent in human genes; it is the result of the immense efforts made by mankind in its history; it is the result of the very dialectic of history.

The concept of rationality or the role of reason in the development of human society is under attack for the last 100 years or more. I agree with Fukuyama that basically this attack on rationality is flawed. It is, however, strange that Fukuyama divides rationality into Western rationality and non-Western rationality. But, as we shall see, this aspect is a part of his Euro-centrism and even imperialistic outlook.

Above all, I believe that Fukuyama is on solid ground in advocating liberal democracy as one of the highest achievements of humankind. Democracy, meaning representative government based on full acceptance and practice of civil liberties, is certainly today a fully accepted political system around which state and civil society are to be organized. There may be serious flaws in the practice of democracy but increasingly it is becoming the sole source of legitimacy of a political system. Fukuyama is also correct in rejecting the view that democracy, being a product initially of the political development of the West, was not a valid model for non-Western societies or that non-Western societies should work for some other political system.

My areas of disagreement with Fukuyama are many. But I will confine myself here to only four of them. First, his argument regarding the end of history is surprisingly trite. One meaning of this formulation is that capitalism and liberal democracy, symbiotically united, mark the end of the road for humanity. No other economic and political systems are possible: "We are now at a point where we cannot imagine a world substantially different from our own." Also, consequently, only one ideology is left to guide humanity—the ideology of capitalist democracy. This also means that no contradictions are left in society which might lead to systemic changes. Nor are such contradictions ever to arise in the future. I am afraid this view is one of the weakest points in Fukuyama's basic discourse. Perhaps, it has arisen from the victory of one side in the Cold War. I may point out that Fukuyama's approach is very similar to the left's euphoria in the 1930s that capitalism and 'bourgeois' democracy have entered their terminal phase and, therefore, the victory of Stalinist 'socialism' was inevitable.

In fact, I may point out parenthetically that the basic structure of representative· government, based on all-pervading civil liberties, having now come into its own, the struggle for the mass of people to have a real share in political and social power has just begun. That is what social movements of today, including the women's movement, are all about.

The second meaning of the phrase 'end of history', reflected here and there in Fukuyama's book, is that of a pre-set end—set by God, or the Hegelian Idea, or by History as such—which has now been achieved—the "Journey" has been completed, as he puts it. And, of course, it seems the end was pre-set wholly for the Europeans who were from the beginning destined to be liberal democracies .

Second, Fukuyama clearly defines liberal democracy as capitalist democracy or democracy based on capitalism. He cannot concieve of—nor does he argue why he does so—of socialist democracy that is democracy not based on private ownership of means of production. In fact, the case for incompatibility in the long-run of capitalism and liberal democracy has been argued at length and with a certain persuasiveness by many modem thinkers, especially the Marxists and radical liberals such as C. Wright Mills. Moreover, Fukuyama is not able to ignore the fact that capitalism has developed not only in Japan and Korea but also in Germany, France, Spain, Italy, Portugal, etc., under authoritarian and even fascist regimes. In fact even the USA and Britain had not much democracy or civil rights for the overwhelming majority of their people during the period of early capitalist development, i.e., during the take-off stage. Fukuyama's answer is that all this historical experience belonged to the non-mature stages of capitalism. But he makes not much of a case for the view that advanced capitalism would and could function only on the basis of liberal democracy.

I need not argue with Fukuyama's belief that capitalism is the only viable economic system possible hereafter—for he as well as I are not economists though it seems to me that his belief that market economy is equal to capitalism cannot be sustained. What I would argue is that collapse of capitalism need not and would not lead to the collapse of liberal democracy. Certainly, most of the 19th and 20th century socialists, including Marx, worked for a socialism that would incorporate representative government and civil liberties in its basic structure. On a narrower plane, capitalism is no longer based on the 19th century doctrine of *laissez faire* as Fukuyama seems to believe.

Active and massive state direction is quite compatible with not only market economy but also capitalism, as the experience of post-war Britain, France, Italy, and the USA indicates. Perhaps even Fukuyama would acknowledge this after Bill Clinton's election. In fact, it is increasingly evident that today liberal democracy can exist only when backed by strong state intervention in the social and economic life of the citizens.

Third, and this points to a major weakness of Fukuyama, claiming to write universal history or at least to bring out its essence, he ignores the real histories of most peoples and civilizations in the same manner as Hegal did. Lot of his generalizations are false because of Euro-centrism or inadequate study of world history. One example that combines both his weaknesses is his either complete ignoring of colonialism or its total misrepresentation. For example, why did Europeans take to colonial conquest? Answer: desire for recognition. What was the impact of colonialism? Answer: poverty was the alleged product of colonialism. When was the view that colonialism led to poverty and underdevelopment put forward? Answer: all this was misconceived 6y Lenin and the dependency theorists. (But in fact this view was fully developed by Dadabhai Naoroji, Justice Ranade, G.V. Joshi, G. Subramaniya Iyer and other Indians decades before Lenin. However, that would require some reading of Indian historical writing!) Fukuyama also does not ask the question, why no colony underwent—even when colonial rule lasted centuries—economic development or liberal democracy.

Fukuyama completely ignores a very basic feature of human liberation after 1945—the anti-colonial struggles and the resulting colonial liberation in country after country. He does not mention end of colonialism as a major achievement of the post-World War II period. Furthermore, in what way was the overthrow of colonialism less important than the disintegration of Communist regimes in Eastern Europe and Soviet Union? And were the anti-colonial struggles waged for "recognition" or against domination and exploitation? Fukuyama also ignores the fact that colonialism has to be overthrown before the path for social and economic development and liberal democratization opened before the colonial people. 'End of colonialism' might not have been a *sufficient* condition for such an opening, but it was a *necessary* condition.

What is more important for his own basic formulation, capitalism and liberal democracy in the advanced or core capitalist countries were and are quite compatible with, if not dependent upon, the peripheralization of the rest of the world. I need not, of course, comment on the absurd Hegelian notion that the world consists of Historical and Non-historical peoples, with only the former marching to complete the 'journey' and reach the pre-laid end.

Once it is accepted that 'non-historical' people like the Indians also have to contribute something to world history Fukuyama would have benefited from studying the developments in free India. For one, he, as also perhaps many recent Marxist converts to democracy, would have found that. years earlier, during the 1930s and 1940s and especially after 1947, Jawaharlal Nehru repeatedly asserted that socialism and democracy must go together and that, in the long run, one could not exist without the other. Nehru was as committed to liberal democracy as to independence, i.e., nationalism, and socialism, i.e., equality and fraternity. Moreover, India went in for large-scale planning and public sector not to promote authoritarianism but precisely to avoid it. India's is a unique historical effort to develop its economy on the basis of liberal democracy.

I could give many other similar examples. For example, what would happen to world civilization if and when India and China develop and begin to consume natural resources on USA's or Europe's scale? Would a new history then begin? Or are 'the non-historical' peoples destined to remain also permanently underdeveloped. But, of course, the basic point is that often world-wide generalizations can be easier made if they are based on a partial reading of world history!

Fourth, Fukuyama's treatment of nationalism is surprisingly shallow, misleading and unhistorical. For one, he fails to distinguish between aggressive and expansionist nationalism, which is so pervasive in the U.S.A. for example, and anti-colonial, development-oriented nationalism in the colonies and ex-colonies. He is also wrong in asserting that nationalism is receding in Europe and the U.S.A. To the contrary, Europe's partial unification is an effort to compete economically and politically with Japan and the U.S.A. Similarly, U.S.A.'s recent war against Iraq was for oil and clearly an aspect of nationalism, however wrong was Iraq's occupation of Kuwait. I wish he had also kept in view that while capital and technology move across .national frontiers: labour does not. It is not accidental that greater economic and political unification of Europe is accompanied by greater exclusion of non-Europeans,

The last part of Fukuyama's book deals with the basis of human development and progress. Here he takes recourse to trans-historical concepts like 'nature of man' or 'struggle for recognition'. I need not discuss this metaphysical part of his book except to remark that it goes against his own commitment to modernity and rationality and a historical approach.

The last sentence of Fukuyama's book is unexceptional but goes against his theory of 'the end of history'. Suddenly, he says: "Nor can we in the final analysis know, provided a majority of the wagons eventually reach the same town, whether their occupants, having looked around a bit at their new surroundings, will not find them inadequate and set their eyes on a new and more distant journey." I, of course, agree wholeheartedly. I would also say that despite some of its errors of omission and commission, Fukuyama's work is a necessary reading for those who want to understand our rapidly changing world.

Part I

1. "Jawaharlal Nehru in Historical Perspective", text of D.D. Kosambi Memorial Lectures, Department of History, University of Bombay, 1989.
2. "Nehru and Communalism", text of lectures at Khuda Baksh Library, Patna, 1989.
3. "Struggle for the Ideological Transformation of the National Congress in the 1930s", paper read at the Centinary Seminar on the Indian National Congress, Moscow, 1985, published in the *Social Scientist.*
4. "Historians of Modern India and Communalism", paper read in an abbreviated form at a seminar organized by the All India Radio in October 1968; and published in Romila Thapar, Harbans Mukhia and Bipan Chandra, *Communalism and the Writing of Indian History,* New Delhi, 1969.
5. "Communalism—The Way Out", text of a lecture delivered at Chandigarh in September 1984 under the auspices of the Centre for Research in Rural and Industrial Development, Chandigarh.
6. "Communalism and the State: Some Issues in India", text of a presentation made at a seminar organized by the *Social Scientist* in March 1990 at New Delhi.
7. "Communalism and Communal Violence in Modern India", from the volume, "Explaining Communalism in Contemporary India", edited by M. Bhattacharya, Burdwan, 1994.
8. "Marxism in India: Need for Total Rectification", published in the *Seminar,* New Delhi, No. 178, June 1974.
9. "Changes in Agraian Structure and the Communist Party, 1955-56", paper read at a seminar in Hyderabad in September 1982, organized by the Andhra Pradesh Ryotu Sangham.
10. "Agrarian Structure and Peasant Movement in Punjab", Presidential Address to the Punjab History Conference, Patiala, 1981.

Part II

11. "Bhagat Singh and Atheism", Introduction to Bhagat Singh, *Why I Am An Atheist and An Introduction to the Dreamland,* Delhi, 1979.
12. "Congress Socialist Party, 1934-48", Foreword to Girja Shankar, *Socialist Trends in Indian National Movement,* Meerut, 1987.
13. "Some Reflections on Maoism in India", Foreword to Shantha Sinha, *Maoists in Andhra Pradesh,* New Delhi, 1989.
14. "Lakshrnan Naik—A Legendary Nationalist From Orissa", Foreword to Nihar Ranjan Patnaik, *Lakshman Naik—A Study in Tribal Patriotism,* Bhubaneswar, 1992.
15. "Ravi Narayan Reddy", Introduction to Ravi Narayan Reddy, *Autobiography,* in Telugu, Hyderabad, 1992.
16. "Punjab Crisis", Preface to Pramod Kumar, et.al., *Punjab Crisis: Context and Trends,* Chandigarh, 1984.
17. "Hindu-Muslim Relations in the 1920s", Review of G.R. Thursby, *Hindu-Muslim Relations in British India: A Study of Controversy, Conflict and Communal Movements in Northern India,* 1923-1928, Leiden, 1975, in *Indian Historical Review,* Vol. IV, No.2, January 1978, New Delhi.
18. "The Cripps Mission", Review of R.J. Moore, *Churchill, Cripps, and India:* 1939-1945, Oxford, 1979, in *The Book Review,* September-October, 1980, Vol. V, No.2, New Delhi.
19. "The End of History?", Review of Francis Fukuyama, *The End of History and the Last Man,* Penguin Books, 1992, in *Bhashaposhin, Kottayam,* September, 1993.

Index

O

P

R